Plato, Prehistorian

Illustrations by
Ann Hatfield
Eliza McFadden
Elizabeth Wahle

PLATO PREHISTORIAN

10,000 to 5000 B.C.
Myth, Religion, Archaeology

Mary Settegast

Lindisfarne Press

Published by Lindisfarne Press
RR 4, Box 94 A-1
Hudson, New York 12534

Library of Congress Catalog Card Number: 86-61988

(*Plato, Prehistorian* was originally published
in a limited cloth edition by The Rotenberg Press,
Cambridge, Massachusetts)

ISBN 0-940262-34-7

Printed in the United States of America

Title page: Stylized bulls' heads from Halafian pottery designs
of late sixth and fifth millennia Iraq *(after Mallowan and Rose, 1935)*

To my parents

Lester Settegast
Sybil Carroll Settegast

Acknowledgments

A book that spans five thousand years of prehistory is obviously not the work of one person, and my thanks go first to the authors named in the bibliography, who provided the information on which this study is based. Some I have met, others I have corresponded with, and in almost every case I found the open-mindedness that traditionally has characterized the academic community to be very much alive. I am particularly grateful to Linda and Robert Braidwood, Gerald Brauer, John Finley, John Luce, C. C. Lamberg-Karlovsky, Ralph Solecki, Ian Todd, and Alex Wayman for reading sections of earlier versions of the manuscript and offering valuable comments; to Ofer Bar-Yosef, Richard Frye, Alexander Marshack, David Mitten, and E. O. Negahban for graciously answering my numerous questions; to Barbara Bender, Mary Boyce, and James Mellaart for their hospitality during an earlier trip to London, and again to Mr. Mellaart and the Braidwoods for continuing to share the results of their work in Turkey and Iraq. However differently we may look at the early world, I sincerely hope that upon reading the finished book, none of those named here will feel that their generosity was misplaced.

I am indebted to Harvard University for the use of its excellent research facilities, and especially to the people at Tozzer Library —Nancy Schmidt and Ed Evans, Gene DeVita, Maureen Mahoney, Jack Holt, and all of their colleagues who over the years have provided such exceptionally kind and energetic assistance. My gratitude also goes to Robyn Sweesy at the Peabody Museum for sharing her knowledge of how manuscripts become books, and to Dan Jones at the same institution for setting that process in motion. Those who worked directly with me in preparing the study for publication are to be praised as well as thanked: Dick Bartlett's contribution went well beyond the design of the book itself; Ann Hatfield, Eliza McFadden, and Elizabeth Wahle took part in the conception as well as the execution of the illustrative material; Duncan Todd's expert collaboration brought their work to printed form. The editorial skills of Morris Fry and Loftin Elvey have been invaluable at each stage of the book's development, and to the latter I owe the correction of several errors in the classical citations as well. Sandra Bennett's help in editing an earlier version is also gratefully acknowledged, as is the assistance of Deborah Davies with the mechanicals.

Without the interest and encouragement of several other friends, the project would have been neither undertaken nor completed. In one way or another Bill Thompson, Stevie Tucker, Jack Frishman, Bill Dougherty, and the late Glenn Isaac share in whatever merit the finished product may possess, and in the lasting gratitude of its author.

Finally, I am indebted to Penguin Books Ltd. for permission to reprint pages 33–40 and 129–45 from the 1977 edition of Desmond Lee's translation of Plato's *Timaeus* and *Critias* (Penguin Classics, 1971), copyright © H. D. P. Lee, 1965, 1971, 1977. It is the comparison of these passages with the archaeology of the early Mediterranean world that gives this essay its title and its theme.

M.S.

Cambridge, Massachusetts

Contents

III

The Neolithic Revolution, Phase I

IV

Çatal Hüyük: 6200–5300 B.C.

V

The Neolithic Revolution, Phase II

Plato, Prehistorian

Wer das Vergangene kennte, der wüsste das Künftige: beides
Schliesst an heute sich rein als ein Vollendetes an.

Goethe, *Prophecies of Bakis*

Introduction

The Collapse of the Old Model

The more we learn about early man, the more difficult it is to describe him as primitive. Even with the new and rightly placed appreciation of the so-called primitive peoples of today, it is becoming increasingly clear that at least some of the cultures of the Old Stone Age were both other and more than the gatherer-hunter societies of recent times, and their members very far indeed from the savage creatures that all Paleolithic men were once assumed to be.

As a result, the existing model of prehistory — the view that sees the development of human culture as a unilinear series of stages, rising from primitive Upper Paleolithic hunting and see figure 1a foraging, to Neolithic farming villages, to the high civilizations of the Bronze Age and ultimately the urban societies of today — is losing its fundamental premise.

For example:

(1) We have known for some time that as early as the fifteenth millennium, the Magdalenian peoples of southwest Europe were decorating the cave at Lascaux with paintings whose magnificence has yet to be surpassed, and which were not to be technically equaled until the Bronze Age frescoes of Egypt and Crete. It now seems that this same Magdalenian culture had already harnessed the horse by 12,000 B.C., some eight thousand years see figure 1b before the date assigned to the domestication of the horse in the conventional model.[9]

(2) Across the Mediterranean in Palestine, at a time when man was supposedly just emerging from Paleolithic primitivism, there appeared at the site of Jericho a massive stone wall and tower which the excavator felt would not have been out of place among the grander medieval castles.[209] Complete with an interior staircase of hammer-dressed stone steps and roof slabs, Jericho's tower was obviously not the first of its kind. Its recent assignment to the ninth millennium B.C.[181] requires the presumption

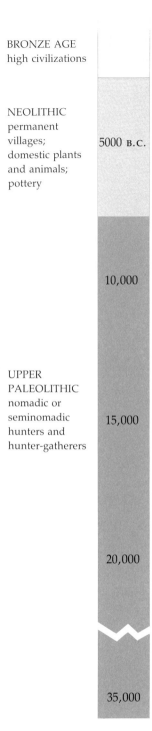

BRONZE AGE
high civilizations

NEOLITHIC
permanent
villages;
domestic plants
and animals;
pottery

5000 B.C.

10,000

UPPER
PALEOLITHIC
nomadic or
seminomadic
hunters and
hunter-gatherers

15,000

20,000

35,000

1a The old model of
cultural development

of a Paleolithic ancestor, although precedents to any part of this monumental defensive complex are unknown to the archaeological record.

(3) In seventh millennium Anatolia (modern Turkey), in what should have been the rustic-village stage of cultural development, excavations have recently unearthed what one archaeologist termed "an immensely rich and luxurious city,"[215] known today as Çatal Hüyük. Less than three percent of the site has been explored, but Çatal Hüyük has already yielded a wealth of religious art and symbolism that appears to be three to four thousand years ahead of its time. The mature complexity of traditions at this Neolithic site further presupposes, according to the excavator, an Upper Paleolithic ancestor of whom we have no trace.[275]

Each of these and the other anomalous events that will be discussed in this study bears the same message. Something is fundamentally wrong with the way we have pictured Upper Paleolithic man and, by extension, the course of human prehistory.

Archaeologists are aware of the inadequacy of the existing framework of thought.[339] For almost two decades prehistorians have been seeking a new paradigm, a wholly new way of looking at the early world that would accommodate the growing number of contradictions to the present point of view. Many archaeologists have turned from field work to model-making in an attempt to find a workable new perspective; but though they are warned by historians of science that a genuine paradigm shift is likely to be total, radical, and noncumulative,[226] their theories continue to reflect, however implicitly, the premises of the old unilinear sequence. And these theories continue to be inadequate. If an authentically new vision of man's past is to be achieved, our most basic assumptions about the way things were may have to be uprooted, at least temporarily, and the old model let go in its entirety.

Can it be done? According to one historian of science, the most difficult of all forms of intellectual activity is "the art of handling the same bundle of data as before, but placing them in a new system of relations with one another by giving them a different framework."[57] The way we look at the development of human culture is so familiar by now that many of us have forgotten that the whole scheme summarized at figure 1a was itself never more than a model and, like most models, tells us more about its own time than that which it claims to describe. Formulated in the nineteenth and early twentieth centuries, the view of prehistory as a progressive series of stages is indebted to Comte, to Darwin, and to what has been called the Whig Interpretation of History, the assumption that it was progress, upward development, which led to "that pinnacle of achievement, ourselves."[434] And since its most persuasive spokesman, V. Gordon Childe, was not only a gifted scholar but also a self-acknowledged Marxist, it is not surprising to find that the moving force on this ascending road to civilization was assumed to be economic, the struggle to obtain and improve the means of material subsistence.

It was also Childe who gave the name "Neolithic Revolution" to the transition from hunter-gatherer to farmer, considered by many scholars to have been the most important single event in human history. As Childe saw it, climatic changes at the end of the Pleistocene or Ice Age, which was also the approximate end of the Upper Paleolithic period, brought drought to the Near East, forcing men into restricted territories. They thereupon abandoned the hunting and gathering traditions of their forefathers and began domesticating the wild animals and grains which also inhabited these "oases."[71] It soon became apparent that this was not the way things happened (drought evidently did come to the Near East but long after the first farming villages were established), and although numerous modifications to the oasis theory have since been—and are still being—tried, the reason for the original switch from nomadism or seminomadism to settled agricultural life remains a mystery.

It is just at this point, in fact, that the pressures on the old model are most intense, again the result of our underestimation of the capacities of Upper Paleolithic men. For one thing, the control of animals and plants, once a definition of Neolithic culture itself, now seems certain to have been achieved in Paleolithic times. We have already mentioned the evident taming of the horse in Late Paleolithic southwest Europe. We shall later find suggestions of the management of Barbary sheep as early as 18,000 B.C. in North Africa,[357] and of the control of gazelle and goat in the Upper Paleolithic Near East.[234, 148] The recent and totally unexpected find of several grains of morphologically domestic emmer wheat at the Palestinian site of Nahal Oren also raises the possibility that grain was under cultivation as early as 14,000 B.C.[305] One is not surprised, therefore, to find archaeologists now tending to shy away from the term "Neolithic Revolution" in the belief that the changeover to plant and animal husbandry must have been a more gradual process than the word revolution implies.

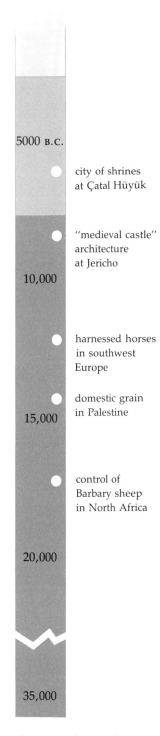

5000 B.C.

city of shrines
at Çatal Hüyük

"medieval castle"
architecture
at Jericho

10,000

harnessed horses
in southwest
Europe

domestic grain
in Palestine

15,000

control of
Barbary sheep
in North Africa

20,000

35,000

1b Anomalies to the old model

But from another point of view, the vanguard of Neolithic settlers that suddenly appeared in Anatolia, Syria, Palestine, and the Zagros mountains of Iran in the last half of the eighth millennium b.c. could not have been more revolutionary. They bore an astonishing diversity of traditions of settled life that were as well-established as they were unprecedented. As we shall see, virtually all of the skills that would form the basis of the civilizations of later times were suddenly present— advanced architectural and interior designs, fully domesticated animals and complex forms of grain, even a functional pottery tradition and the earliest signs of metal work. These were patently not nomads just turned farmer, but experienced settlers whose techniques had been perfected elsewhere, although direct ancestors are not to be found in the archaeological record of known earlier sites. Rather than ask why they settled, we might ask whence they came.

Almost two thousand years then passed without a significant innovation, and the "revolution" almost died, until a second great Neolithic impulse thrust permanent agricultural settlements into the far corners of Iran, out onto the plains of Mesopotamia, and as far west as the Balkan countries in the last half of the sixth millennium. This time we shall find that the changes do seem to have involved large numbers of formerly nomadic or seminomadic peoples, and the question of why they became farmers is now more appropriate, if again unresolved. For here the point has been made that these apparently local peoples had no economic advantage to gain by adopting the agricultural way of life. For example, one eminent prehistorian believes that the economic base of the pre-Neolithic forest dwellers of southeast Europe, who may well have controlled edible resources of their own (red deer, pig, fish, forest plants), was actually equal or superior in terms of both nutrition and reliability to the grain-sheep-goat-cattle complex that replaced it.[403] In her opinion, reasons *other than economic* must be sought for the Neolithizing of southeast Europe.

What we have then, in effect, is two Neolithic Revolutions, two major phases in the changeover to settled farming, neither of which conforms to the conventional framework of thought. The first, a late eighth millennium eruption of agricultural communities in the Near East, was generated by unexpectedly sophisticated peoples whose skills suggest a history of prior experience in sedentary living elsewhere. The second, a massive late sixth millennium adoption of settled agricultural life by local populations from Iran to southeast Europe, seems to have offered no economic advantage to its participants. The old model is on shaky ground indeed.

But if the conventional view of the early world is irreparably flawed, as even these brief observations would suggest, recent paleographic studies warn that a more accurate one will not be easily constructed. The magnitude of the loss of coastal lands to the rising seas during the transition from Pleistocene to Holocene conditions is now known to have been considerable. In the Greek Argolid, for example, sea level rose as much as three hundred feet between 13,000 and 7000 B.C., submerging vast areas of Greek coastal plains whose populations and subsistence patterns can only be imagined.[407] The very recent discovery of the presence of competent seafarers in the late Upper Paleolithic Aegean[322] further increases the probability that important settlements or seaports were lost along with the ancient coastline. But even before publication of these findings, archaeologists had begun to recognize the likelihood that a great many communities along Late Paleolithic coasts and rivers had been lost to either rising seas or alluvial deposition. (The Nile valley is believed to have been particularly vulnerable to the latter.) They are also aware of the probability that coastal and riverine sites, then as now, were the vital centers of culture. What this means, however, is that many if not most of the Late Paleolithic sites that do remain may actually have been peripheral settlements, and not truly representative of the level of cultural achievement at that time. Yet it is upon these surviving remains that our picture of the early world has consistently, inevitably, been based.

Considering the potential distortion already inherent in the practice of excavating no more than five percent of a site (and usually far less), and in the fact that except in unusual circumstances (flash fire, burial gifts) what gets left behind for the archaeologist to find is what was least important to the living occupants of a site, one wonders if the reality of man's past can ever be accurately known.

"The New Archaeology"

Many senior archaeologists feel, however, that the problem today is that we have too much rather than too little information. They fear that the current trend toward quantification and specialization within the profession, often identified with what is called "the New Archaeology," will result in an unmanageable overload of information, too great for any one theorist to gather into a meaningful picture of the past.

It is certainly true that archaeology, once the companion of art history in the humanities, is now wedded to the methods and technologies of the hard sciences. A passage from David Wilson's *The New Archaeology* is illustrative:

> The present day archaeologist may go into the field with a computer-terminal in his baggage or with a computer-programme guiding his plan of action. He may be going to a site which he cannot "see" when he starts digging; it had been located by aerial survey or by proton-magnetometer readings. If he is in a large party, the archaeologist may be accompanied by geologists, ecologists, plant-geneticists, botanists, and zoologists. In his digging he will have to bear in mind the demands of the radiocarbon daters or the thermoluminescence-daters. They will want chemical analyses or perhaps even samples of the earth and soil surrounding his finds. He may have to use the flotation process on almost every spadeful of soil he turns to find plant material for the paleobotanist. . . .[434]

Apart from some well-taken criticism that the fondness of New Archaeology for quantitative analysis leads to ignoring whatever cannot be measured (art, religion), most prehistorians grant that specialization has allowed great progress in many different directions. But some of the most respected scholars in the field fear that all this "centrifugal development" is creating a vacuum at the center.[98] With particular reference to the origins of agriculture, one authority expressed doubt that any single individual can now assess with equal competence the findings of all relevant fields of inquiry, and he adds:

> Highly specialized investigations into the minutiae of the problem are essential, but expertness in one science sometimes leads to myopia in other directions; it is often easier to examine the trees than to attempt to comprehend the wood.[171]

The tree-forest dilemma is certainly not confined to prehistoric studies in our time, nor is the accumulation of undigested data. But it is ironic that those same forces of specialization that are showing up the flaws in the old model should be threatening, by the excess of information they have generated, the chances of constructing a new one.

The reconstruction of the past is not, however, the primary concern of the New Archaeology. Born amid the cultural upheavals that followed two world wars, it has addressed itself to what are perceived as more critical and immediate needs of the times, namely, an understanding of the dynamics of cultural change. Its theoretical focus is on culture process rather than cultural history, on the discovery of universally applicable laws of change, valid for all periods, that would explain and thus help us to respond intelligently to the contemporary flux. And as it was the switch to sedentary life that seems to have put man on an irreversible track leading to today's over-urbanized world, the workings of this crucial process of change from hunter-gatherer to farmer have again received special attention. As a result, what is seen as a transitional period between Paleolithic and Neolithic ages, an *Epi-Paleolithic* or *Mesolithic* interim which in the Near East began around 10,000 B.C. and lasted until the eighth millennium, has taken on added importance, and a number of models have been devised to account systematically for the events of these times.

But this Epi-Paleolithic epoch was hardly a normal control situation from which one might derive universal laws of change. Of all the millennia prior to or following upon this two-thousand-year period of prehistory, no equal span of time was more unstable. The foundations of immensely old Upper Paleolithic cultures were disintegrating all around the Mediterranean, and while climatic irregularities undoubtedly played a part, it can only have been a secondary one. The drama of culture change was staged on all sides of the Mediterranean, including regions apparently unaffected by the reversals in climate. Over-population may also have been a factor in the decay of the Magdalenian culture of southwest Europe, but it cannot easily account for the changes in the Near East at this time.

We are therefore still without a satisfactory explanation for the extraordinary restlessness of these Epi-Paleolithic peoples, or for the Neolithic revolutions that followed in its wake. We now have neither laws of culture process nor a coherent picture of cultural history. And without some kind of intelligible past, what sense can be made of our confused and conflicted present?

The Value of Myth

Enter the myths. Whenever the ancient world lost its bearings (and we shall find that our present situation is not entirely without precedent), men presumably turned first to the myths for clarification. Modern man may feel that he lost that option when myth came to be defined in western culture as that which was untrue, that which was opposed to history. But for ancient man, some part of what we call mythology *was* history, the history of men as well as gods, of concrete as well as abstract events. And it was from the myths that his own place in time derived its meaning.

This is not euhemerism. Many myths undoubtedly describe events that are metaphysical, cosmological, or initiatory rather than, or as well as, historical. But others, which should perhaps be classed with legends or folklore, do seem intended to be read primarily as human history, and several archaeologists have already recognized the potential value of mythology as our "proto-historic" tradition.[259] The director of Athens' National Archaeological Museum also found myth to be an essential component of our understanding of the ancient world, and named mythology and archaeology "the two feet on which our knowledge of antiquity stands."[438] Furthermore, if it is possible to trace a continuum of certain traditions back through the Bronze Age to the Neolithic and even into the Upper Paleolithic period, as several prehistorians are currently demonstrating,[119, 162] some of our most ancient mythic themes may be as old as sapient man himself, encouraging a two-footed stance on the earliest ground of human prehistory.

One need not go that far back to find two myths in particular that could change our way of looking at the early world. Both are from the Greeks; both are connected in some way to Plato; together they offer room for virtually all of the anomalies in Upper Paleolithic and Neolithic archaeology. The first story begins, by its own dated claim, during the critical interim period of Epi-Paleolithic instability mentioned above. We have already noted the apparent inadequacy of either climatic change or overpopulation to account for the pan-Mediterranean cultural upheavals of this epoch. What is seldom recognized is that this same Epi-Paleolithic period was distinguished by the first recorded signs of violence in Old World archaeology. The earliest documented victims of violent death were interred in the Ukraine (including one collection in what the excavator described as a warriors' grave);[392] the massive fortifications mentioned earlier were raised at Jericho; the earliest battle scenes known to art history were painted on the rock faces of the Spanish Levant —all more or less contemporary with the appearance of unprecedented numbers of arrowheads at sites as far distant as northern Europe and the Negev desert. It seems more than fortuitous that the one mythological event that is specifically dated to this period should be an account in Plato's *Timaeus* and *Critias* dialogues of a tenth millennium war that involved all those living inside the Straits of Gibraltar.

Both major combatants in Plato's war, an ancient Athenian society and an Atlantic maritime empire, were overwhelmed at a later time by a combination of earthquake and deluge, "the greatest of all destructions by water" (*Timaeus* 23). As we shall see, catastrophic floods would not be inconsistent with the archaeology of Greece and Anatolia midway in the eighth millennium B.C. (which may be the middle of the ninth when carbon-14 dates are corrected to calendar time). If this was indeed the time of the *Timaeus* deluge, that earlier-mentioned first major phase of the Neolithic Revolution, the wave of inexplicably sophisticated settlers that appeared in the Near East in the last half of the eighth millennium B.C., may actually have been refugees from Plato's ruined cultures in the west. see page 4

The other potentially useful Greek myth could explain the second great surge of Neolithic settlement activity two thousand years later which, as noted above, effectively spread the agricultural way of life throughout Iran and Mesopotamia and ultimately into southeast Europe. When carbon-14 dates are corrected, the c. 5500 B.C. dawn of this wide-ranging impulse to settle and plant is expected to be approximately 65/6300 B.C.* It is again extraordinary that this date should almost precisely coincide with Aristotle's figure of around 6350 B.C. (6,000 years before the death of Plato) as the time of Zarathuštra, the legendary Iranian prophet for whose followers the establishment of agricultural settlements was a religious imperative, and whose missionary-borne message was said to have reached far beyond the borders of Iran. see page 4

Neither of these two events, the great war of the *Timaeus* or the seventh millennium birth of Zarathuštra, was considered mythic, in our sense, by its recorder. In the *Timaeus* (26) Socrates accepts the story of the war and the subsequent floods as "true history," as did Solon before him. Zarathuštra's early birth date was repeated by Eudoxus, by an annotator of the *Alcibiades I*, attributed to Plato, and, using a different standard of measurement, by Plutarch and Hermippus (Pliny, *Nat. Hist.* XXX.4; Plutarch, *De Isid.* 369). But as respectable as these sources would

---

* Radiocarbon dates earlier than the fifth millennium B.C. have not yet been officially corrected, but many archaeologists currently recommend the addition of 800 to 1,000 years to bring Epi-Paleolithic and early Neolithic carbon-14 dates into accord with calendar time.[280, 437]

seem to be, until recently there was not enough archaeological evidence in their favor to overcome the existing viewpoint, which holds that the level of culture implied by these events could not possibly have been achieved in the times to which they were dated. The situation is changing rapidly, however, and it now appears that the existing viewpoint is wrong. Did the Greeks have the right one after all?

Limits of the Investigation

This will necessarily be a story of the forest, not the trees. In order to get all the way around the Epi-Paleolithic and Early Neolithic Mediterranean, and attempt to see it as a whole, a great deal of detail has had to go. Those whose interest runs deeper may recover it from the bibliography. Atlantis-seekers may also be disappointed, as we shall be dealing here exclusively with peoples and events inside the Straits of Gibraltar. Plato's fabulous maritime empire will be our concern only when and where he claims it crossed the Straits.

The book is divided into five sections, spanning the period from 10,000 to 5000 B.C. Part I looks at the tenth through the eighth millennium from Plato's point of view, comparing the archaeological events of that epoch with the war described in the *Timaeus* and *Critias*. (The reader is encouraged to review these short dialogues; their relevant passages are presented here as Appendix A.) In the second section, other mythologies which might reinforce Plato's tale are introduced. Part III then takes up the archaeology of the aftermath, the "post-deluge" period from around 7500 to 5500 B.C. which came to a spectacular close at the Neolithic settlement of Çatal Hüyük. The possibility that among the swarm of cults at Çatal Hüyük were the decaying vestiges of Plato's vanished Greek cultures will be explored in Part IV. The last section, Part V, belongs to Zarathuštra. Here we compare what little is known of the prophet and his teachings with the spontaneous settlement of Iran and Mesopotamia in the middle of the sixth millennium B.C., along with unmistakable signs of reform in contemporary levels at Çatal Hüyük.

None of the material to be presented here is original. We are only going to look at the existing data from a different point of view (without forgetting the difficulty that was predicted for that process). The findings are those of prehistorians in a number of specialized fields, upon whose expertise I am entirely dependent. The perspective is provided by Plato. Both are open to interpretation, however, and the fault for misreading or mismatching the two will be mine. But this essay was written primarily as a stimulus to future research, and the validity of its premise—that certain myths can be used to compensate for what has been lost, apparently irretrievably, to early Mediterranean archaeology—should not be affected by the shortcomings of a single author. Prehistorians have been standing overlong on one foot. If the result of this imbalance is a collapsing model of man's past, it is surely time to shift some of the weight.

I

The War of 8500 B.C.

2 The "leaping cow" of Lascaux cave, fifteenth millennium B.C.; length, four and one-half feet. Wittily drawn, the animal appears to be jumping over something, with front legs thrust forward and hind legs kicking up high under the belly. The black and brown painting is part of the magnificent collection of cave art attributed to the Magdalenian culture of France and Spain (c. 17/15,000–9000 B.C.), the "Golden Age" of Paleolithic Europe. *(after Leroi-Gourhan, 1968)*

14   Plato, Prehistorian

The Priest's Tale

Oh Solon, Solon, you Greeks are all children. . . . you have no belief rooted in old tradition and no knowledge hoary with age. And the reason is this. There have been and will be many different calamities to destroy mankind, the greatest of them by fire and water, lesser ones by countless other means. . . . You remember only one deluge, though there have been many, and you do not know that the finest and best race of men that ever existed lived in your country. (*Timaeus* 22–23)[232]

The speaker of this passage from Plato's *Timaeus* was a very old priest of the city of Sais in the Egyptian Delta. The occasion was a visit by Solon, the famous Greek statesman, who was well-received by the Saites; they claimed a special kinship with the Greeks through the identity of their goddess Neith and the Greek Athena. But in the course of his conversations with the Saitic priests, Solon discovered that he and his countrymen were virtual "children" in matters concerning their own ancient history. Only in Egypt, claimed the priests, had records been preserved of all notable events around the Mediterranean from even the most ancient epochs—events whose memory had been erased elsewhere by time and circumstance, leaving the Greeks and the other peoples of Solon's day "in complete ignorance of what happened in our part of the world or in yours in early times" (*Timaeus* 23).

At Solon's insistence, the old priest went on to describe the actions and historical milieu of that superior race of men, who he claimed had occupied the site that is now Athens "9,000 years ago," or around 9600 B.C. if we add the early sixth century date given by Herodotus (I.30) for Solon's journey to Egypt:

Among all the wonderful achievements recorded here of your city, one great act of courage is outstanding. Our records tell how your city checked a great power which arrogantly advanced from its base in the Atlantic ocean to attack the cities of Europe and Asia. For in those days the Atlantic was navigable. There was an island opposite the strait which you call . . . the Pillars of Heracles, an island larger than Libya and Asia combined; from it travellers could in those days reach the other islands, and from them the whole opposite continent which surrounds what can truly be called the ocean. . . . On this island of Atlantis had arisen a powerful and remarkable dynasty of kings, who ruled the whole island, and many other islands as well, and parts of the continent. In addition it controlled, within the strait, Libya up to the borders of Egypt and Europe as far as Tyrrhenia. This dynasty, gathering its whole power together, attempted to enslave, at a single stroke, your country and ours and all the territory within the strait. It was then, Solon, that the power and courage and strength of your city became clear for all men to see. Her bravery and military skill were outstanding; she led an alliance of the Greeks, and then when they deserted her and she was forced to fight alone, after running into direst peril, she overcame the invaders and celebrated a victory; she rescued those not yet enslaved from the slavery threatening them, and she generously freed all others living within the Pillars of Heracles. At a later time there were earthquakes and floods of extraordinary violence, and in a single dreadful day and night all your fighting men were swallowed up by the earth, and the island of Atlantis was similarly swallowed up by the sea and vanished. (*Timaeus* 24 – 25)[232]

The *Timaeus* gives no further details of the war and its aftermath, but in Plato's unfinished *Critias* dialogue we are told that the postwar earthquakes and floods so devastated the Greek countryside that the few remaining survivors ("an unlettered mountain race") were forced to abandon the ancient traditions for many generations thereafter in order to provide the necessities of life for themselves and their children (*Critias* 109 – 110). The *Critias* also tells us more about the combatants in the great war. On one side: "all those who lived inside the Pillars of Heracles" (the Straits of Gibraltar), led by a modest Greek society comprised of priests, artisans, peasants (farmers and herdsmen as well as hunters), and an Athena-worshipping class of male and female warrior-guardians who were admired for their virtue throughout Europe and Asia. On the other: "those who lived outside" the Straits, a once great Atlantic maritime empire ruled by a federation of ten kings with an immense army of men, a taste for grand scale engineering projects and ornate temples, and a special fondness for horse racing (the horse being the animal emblem of Poseidon, ancestral god of the Atlantics).

When first read, the priest's tale seems preposterous. The archaeology of tenth millennium Greece consists of a handful of cave sites;[417] the floor of the Atlantic ocean has revealed no signs whatsoever of a sunken land mass the size of Atlantis;[177] and classical philologists, noting that the *Timaeus* and *Critias* contain the first certain literary references to Atlantis, assure us that the story was invented, "a creature of Plato's own imagination."[380] *

Then, too, there seems to be a chronological inconsistency in the two books. "9,000 years ago" is first given in the *Timaeus* (23) as the founding date of the ancient Athenian civilization, again in the *Critias* (108) as the date of the declaration of war. Several classicists have suggested, however, that the *Critias* may have been written considerably later than the *Timaeus*, and the confusion of dates thus caused by an "evident lapse of memory."[350] It is not impossible, of course, that both events took place within a few centuries of one another and could therefore be rounded off to the same 9,000 year figure. But if the duplication of dates is an error, Plato's known habit of polishing his finished works[380] suggests that the mistake would lie in the unfinished *Critias*. The founding of Ur-Athens in 9600 B.C., as stated in the *Timaeus*, may therefore be the more accurately dated event, with the outbreak of war perhaps as much as a millennium later.

Such, at least, is the present indication of early Mediterranean archaeology, although when radiocarbon dates of this period are corrected to calendar time, it may be we rather than Plato who are in error. As things stand now, it is c. 8500 B.C., in uncorrected carbon-14 years, that saw a coincidence of events which resembles nothing so much as a war involving all those who lived inside the Straits of Gibraltar. In reviewing the background and details of these events, we may find that the inconsistencies in Plato's account are less important than the story itself. For all its questionable exotica, this fragmented old tale may be our most reliable guide to the Epi-Paleolithic Old World.

---

* See also Cornford[86] and Taylor.[389] It has been thought that Plato's pupil Aristotle agreed with these modern scholars (Strabo II.102, XIII.598), although his contemporary, Crantor, the first to write a commentary on the dialogues, evidently accepted the story as "straight history" (Proclus, *Commentary on the Timaeus*). See Ramage[336] for an excellent summary of the early history of the controversy.

In some ways Plato's narrative is comparable to an important archaeological site that was excavated too early and, in the absence of the technologies that would have allowed its artifacts to be firmly dated and its stratigraphies properly defined, was of dubious value to modern archaeologists. The late nineteenth and early twentieth century enthusiasts who exhumed the *Timaeus* account under the leadership of Ignatius Donnelly[100] not only lacked scientific objectivity, but ultimately diminished the integrity of the story as a whole by consistently working only the Atlantic quarter. The war and the ancient Athenian civilization, Plato's main themes,[419] were seldom mentioned, due not only to the fascination of Atlantis, perhaps, but also to the scant evidence for either event in the Mediterranean archaeology of their day.

What Donnelly and other early Atlantis-seekers managed to accomplish was nevertheless remarkable for their time. Of the wealth of Old and New World correspondences in flora, fauna, and cultural forms which they claimed as proof of the former existence of some kind of a land-bridge across the Atlantic ocean, some are still provocative. But a great many others have since been shown to be equally attributable to continental drift, diffusion across the Bering Strait, or simply incorrect information.[137] Their claims were overdrawn (and not always faithful to Plato's original), and scientific advance left them, and by association the *Timaeus* account, on the fringe of respectable prehistory.

There remained, however, Plato's own expressed conviction that the tale was true. Socrates, present at the telling, agrees that it is "not a fiction but true history" (*Timaeus* 26). Critias, who is recounting to Socrates, Timaeus, and Hermocrates the story told to his grandfather by Solon, admits that the tale he tells is a strange one, "but Solon, the wisest of the seven wise men, once vouched its truth" (*Timaeus* 20). It seems highly unlikely that Plato would have jeopardized his own reputation, that of his Academy, the credibility of the remainder of the *Timaeus* (which contains his views on the origin of the universe and the nature of man), and the standing of the deceased Solon, one of the most respected of Greek statesmen, with an exercise in pure fancy. Nor, on the celebration of Athena's festival day, the setting of the two dialogues, would he have Critias offer to the goddess as "a just and truthful hymn of praise" (*Timaeus*

21) an intentional misrepresentation of Athena's own past history with the Greeks, for it is she who is said to have founded the Ur-Athenian society (*Timaeus* 23, *Critias* 109).

Respecting Plato's word, as well as the resources of Egyptian culture, several scholars recently attempted a reclamation of the discredited old story. These investigators[247, 146] presumed an historical matrix to the *Timaeus* tale but felt Plato's timing couldn't be right. Tenth millennium man was still living in caves, hunting and gathering his food. Not only was the horse-racing, seafaring, technologically adept Atlantic civilization quite out of the question in the Late Paleolithic period of prehistory, but even the more modest Athenians supposedly lived in a class-stratified society complete with farmers and herdsmen — more than three thousand years before the appearance of domestic plants and animals in the archaeological record of Greece.

Surmising, therefore, that one of the transmitters of the tale had got the chronology wrong, these authors updated the action to the second millennium B.C. and identified the sinking of Atlantis with the volcanic destruction of the Minoan civilization on the Aegean island of Thera, c. 1450 B.C. In so doing, however, as several of their colleagues have pointed out, the Thera proponents did not explain Plato as much as explain him away.[141] Thera is in the Mediterranean rather than the Atlantic, is a fraction of the size of the island continent, and was destroyed many thousands of years too late (and only partially at that, while Atlantis was completely submerged). Furthermore, Thera's candidacy as Atlantis rests largely on its cataclysmic destruction alone, while Plato's story had far more to do with a war between two antagonistic peoples than with the disaster that later overwhelmed them both.

Again the search for Atlantis has eclipsed the main themes of the narrative. And again the effort was too early. The Thera hypothesis was formed before seafarers were discovered in the Late Paleolithic Aegean, and before the magnitude of the loss of Greek lands to the postglacial seas was fully known. The extent of the mid-to-late ninth millennium spread of arrowheads was not yet recognized; the date of Jericho's fortifications had not been moved back to the last half of the ninth millennium; and the depth and complexity of Magdalenian culture, whose location in time and space closely parallels that of the European holdings of Plato's Atlantic empire, was still to be demonstrated.

These are but a few of the recent archaeological discoveries that suggest that the *Timaeus* and *Critias* account should be corrected only with caution. Given as well Plato's insistence that the story was true, it now seems wiser to take him at his word, at least for the moment, and treat all parts of his account with respect. This is not to say that the priest's tale should be read as literal history (the goings on in the Atlantic ocean are not only "outlandish" [*Critias* 116] but according to oceanographers, wholly impossible); rather that it might be foolish at this point to reject material that could become a good deal less farfetched as our knowledge of early man matures.

Furthermore, if outright invention on Plato's part seems unlikely, exaggeration somewhere along the way does not. Luce has suggested that Plato himself, rather than Solon, conversed with the Saitic priests and then elaborated on authentic Egyptian material in the "panegyric" fashion befitting Panathenaic festivals.[248] Plutarch, writing in the first century A.D. (*Life of Solon*), indicated that Plato may have embellished the story brought home from Egypt by Solon. Whoever did bring back the tale, if it was indeed embellished at some point (and theoretically Critias, the grandfather of Critias, or Solon himself would have also had the opportunity to do so), the question of which parts were overdrawn will be critical to the future usefulness of the account to prehistorians. Again I can see no more efficient means of separating fact from fiction than to start with the hypothesis that Plato's account of Mediterranean prehistory—prehistory inside the Straits—is basically accurate, and let the archaeological record show where the falsifying began.

The Mediterranean Before 9000 B.C.: Southwest Europe

Early in the *Critias* (109), we are told that details concerning the diverse peoples of the time will be forthcoming: "The course of our narrative as it unfolds will give particulars about the various barbarian and Greek nations of the day." Only the Athenian and Atlantic civilizations were described before the dialogue broke off, however, leaving that promise largely unfulfilled. To the archaeologist, therefore, falls the task of telling us just what the "particulars" of the cultures around the tenth millennium Mediterranean actually were, and thus providing a background against which the changes of the ninth can be more clearly perceived.

We do know from the *Timaeus* (25) that southwest Europe, "Europe as far as Tyrrhenia" (northern Italy), was allegedly under the control of the Atlantic empire. We are also told that the early Atlantic kings were divinely inspired, characterized for many generations by a "certain greatness of mind" (*Critias* 120). Theirs must hence have been a creative and benign governance before the race weakened, grew ambitious, and went to war. If Plato's tale does have an historical basis, we should therefore expect to find in the archaeology of southwest Europe not only signs of a qualitative degeneration just before or during the tenth millennium, but earlier, evidence of that inspired grandeur that distinguished the original colonizers.

The Magdalenian Cycle

Prior to around 20,000 B.C. all of Europe, from Russia to the Pyrenees, seems to have been loosely united under one great cultural banner to which the name *Gravettian* (after the French site of La Gravette) has been given. Best known for its fine mobiliary or portable art, the Gravettian collection includes representations of the human figure in the round (fig. 3), of which the most famous examples are the so-called Venus figurines

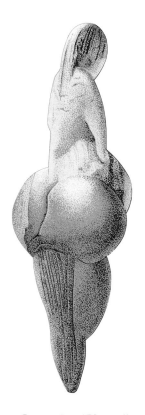

3 Gravettian "Venus" from Lespugue, France, 23/21,000 B.C.; mammoth ivory, five and one-half inches

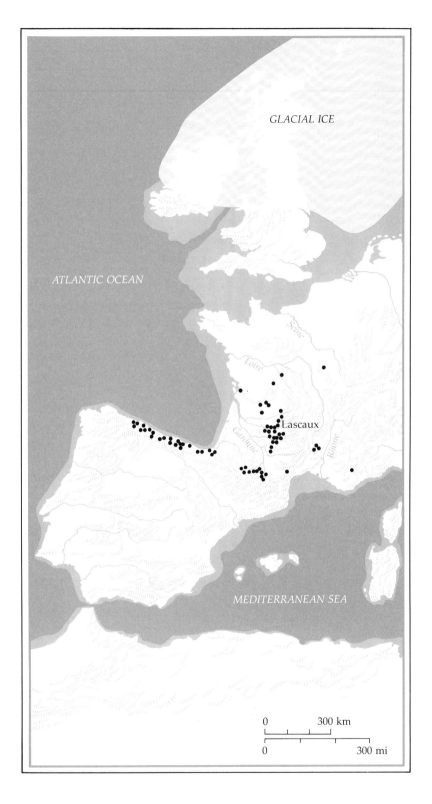

4 The distribution of decorated caves assigned to the Magdalenian era *(after Sieveking, 1979).* Lighter areas of color indicate the approximate extent of glaciation and of coastal plains during the maximum regression of sea level, c. 16,000 B.C.

GLACIAL ICE

ATLANTIC OCEAN

Lascaux

MEDITERRANEAN SEA

0   300 km

0   300 mi

found in both western and eastern European sites. East and west were to take separate courses after 20,000 B.C., however, when, as noted by Leroi-Gourhan, the links between them "appear to have been cut, or at least considerably weakened."[237] While eastern Europe remained in the Gravettian fold, western Europe ceased producing the Venus figurines and, following an interlude of fine projectile points, embarked on the greatest adventure in cave painting Europe would ever know—the art of the Magdalenians.

For six to eight thousand years, from approximately 17/15,000 to 9000 B.C., southwest Europe was dominated by Magdalenian culture and art. (The eponymous site is La Madeleine in the Dordogne valley.) Although Magdalenian influence was to spread across central Europe and into Russia during this period, the decorated caves for which these people are famed apparently were confined to a region bounded on the west by the Atlantic ocean, on the east by the Rhône (fig. 4). The majority of these caves are on or near large rivers, most of which empty into the Atlantic. At the beginning of the Magdalenian era, which approximately coincided with the maximum lowering of sea level, the Médoc littoral through which many of these waters ultimately flow (via the Garonne river) extended more than thirty miles into what is now Atlantic ocean.[396] What part of Magdalenian culture may since have been lost to the rising seas is incalculable; what remains cannot be described, in any meaningful sense, as primitive.

With the emergence of the Magdalenians, the painting and engraving that had been largely restricted to the daylight zone of the cave entrances began spreading deep into the interior chambers. Animals once represented primarily by forepart and dorsal line (fig. 5a) became superlative creatures of more than lifelike grace and proportion (fig. 5b; see also figs. 2 and 6). Increasingly conventionalized, they were still endowed in the thirteenth millennium with what Leroi-Gourhan called "a certain strangeness, a kind of aerial suspension."[237] But with the proliferation of detail, the animals grew more and more realistic until, at the end of the eleventh millennium, they are comparable to photographic images (fig. 5c). At around this time the deep interiors of the caves gradually began to be abandoned, with the art shifting to stone plaques. Less than a thousand years later, toward the end of the tenth millennium, a steep decline marked the end of Magdalenian art as a whole. The few remaining examples show a dissolution into "crudity and schematism."[237]

5 Representations of oxen from (a) Pair-non-Pair, (b) Lascaux, (c) Teyjat (*after Leroi-Gourhan, 1968*)

Was this the history of the Atlantic presence in Europe? Plato does not say when the divinely inspired sons of Poseidon assumed control of "Europe as far as Tyrrhenia," only that their corruption was evident by 9600 B.C. We are therefore limited to observing that, whatever the effects of calibration on the carbon-14 dates of this period, the timing of Magdalenian decay will be approximately as true to the chronology of the Atlantic decline as was the distribution of Magdalenian caves to the claimed Atlantic reach.

The Purposes of Magdalenian Art

The Magdalenian epoch has been described by one archaeologist as the Golden Age of the Paleolithic, "a peak of true culture in the history of humanity."[375] Indeed, as noted by another prehistorian, there would be no artistic achievement of comparable magnitude in western Europe until the outpouring of religious art in the cathedrals, basilicas, and crypts of the Middle Ages.[229] But for all its well-publicized magnificence, the art of the caves has yet to reveal its meaning and purpose. Frequently visible by torchlight or tallow lamp alone, the paintings were often executed in almost inaccessible spots: on rock projections reached only with risk, in hidden recesses, or, as at Lascaux, on the cave heights, leaving evidence of ropes and scaffolding.[240] To those critics who have wriggled down a dark tight tunnel on their bellies to view some of these works, "pleasuring the viewer" has seemed a particularly inadequate explanation of the motives of Magdalenian artists.

6 "Chinese horses" from Lascaux's axial gallery, fifteenth millennium B.C. Painted in bistre yellow and black, each is approximately four and one-half feet in length.

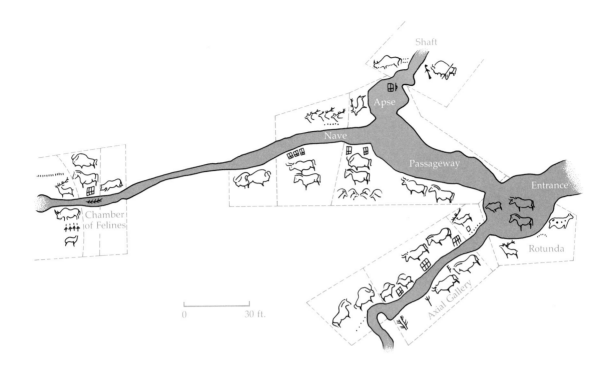

For the most part, to see the cave paintings as vehicles for sympathetic hunting magic, as earlier analysts believed, is equally unsatisfactory. Reindeer dominate Magdalenian faunal remains at many sites but appear infrequently in cave art (only one reindeer is represented on the walls of Lascaux, while faunal remains were almost exclusively those of this animal),[238] and the great majority of all animals are drawn in peaceful attitudes with no sign of a wound or deadly weapon. Moreover, there are many representations where the so-called arrow is about to miss, or has just missed, the animal at which it was supposedly aimed. As one team of investigators points out: "There is no conceivable reason why Paleolithic man should have wanted to shoot an arrow past a food or dangerous animal, or, as it would appear from many representations, wound such an animal just above the ankle."[405] Also difficult to interpret in terms of hunting magic are the apparently purposeful groupings, such as the fish painted along the back of a horse or the frequent juxtaposition of horse and bull at Lascaux. Several prehistorians now feel that not only the grouping of certain animals, but also the linking of animals to signs, the frequent superposition of the figures, and even the placement of animals on the walls of the caves (fig. 7) were all deliberate choices whose significance was clear to both the creators and the viewers of the art.[229]

7 Diagram of Lascaux cave showing the placement of animal species along the walls of various chambers (*after Leroi-Gourhan, 1968*)

The War of 8500 B.C.   25

Leroi-Gourhan has further suggested that the decorating of each of the great caves followed a predetermined plan and was governed by a symbolic formula of evident, if elusive, religious meaning—a formula which remained unchanged for at least 5,000 years.[238] The methodological restrictions under which this noted prehistorian has chosen to work allow only what he describes as the "utterly banal" statement that the religion of the caves was based on "the opposition and complementarity of male and female values, expressed symbolically by animal figures and by more or less abstract signs."[237] ("Banal" because as he points out, most of the great religions of antiquity were based on similar principles of duality, e.g., yin-yang.) Not all of his colleagues agree with Leroi-Gourhan's conclusions,[405] but few now dispute the premise that the more ornate of the Magdalenian caves were religious sanctuaries of one sort or another.

Several critics have suggested that the paintings were connected to rites of initiation, and that perhaps only the initiated were allowed access to the inner chambers of the caves.[260, 122] Youthful footprints on cave floors have been seen as possible indications of adolescent rites of passage; it may also be argued that the quality of many of the paintings suggests a higher level of initiatory experience. Indeed, if the finest of the Magdalenian works are to be compared to the much later painting and drawing of the Orient[175] (e.g., the "Chinese horses" at figure 6), the possibility that they sprang from similar principles, principles which in Asiatic art were intuitive, or initiatory in the mature sense, should also be considered. To do so in any detail would take us too far afield at this point, but as the patterns of initiation appear to be linked to the deepest structures of spiritual experience,[118] it would not be surprising to find an intuitive element in Paleolithic painting, particularly if a people "akin to the divine" (*Critias* 120) played a part in its execution.

Horses and Harpoons

If Magdalenian cave art was in any sense religious art, the horse, the animal most frequently represented in the caves, must have figured prominently in that religion. As the animal of Poseidon, the horse also enjoyed a special standing among Plato's Atlantics. According to the *Critias* (117), a course for horse racing had been laid out on the main island, with areas for exercise— "some for men and some for horses"—established throughout the empire. As popular Greek mythology also credits Poseidon

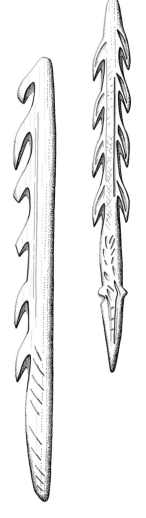

8 Magdalenian harpoons from Rochereil (left) and La Madeleine (right) *(after Jude, 1960; Julien, 1982)*

a

b

c

with being the first to tame the horse, one notes with interest the accumulating evidence of the presence of tamed horses in Magdalenian Europe.[9]

The idea that the horse was harnessed in Upper Paleolithic southwest Europe was first proposed eighty years ago,[331] based in part on the representations of what seemed to be bridles or cords attached to the heads of several horses in Magdalenian art (fig. 9a). Until recently, however, the prevailing opinion held that these must have been stylized anatomical features rather than external equipment. But in 1966 the team of Pales and St. Pereuse meticulously analysed the engraving of a horse's head from the Magdalenian site of La Marche (fig. 9c); and after considering bone structure and musculature, and using a relief imprint to determine the order in which the elements had been engraved, they concluded that the lines that seemed to form a harness were indeed secondary, and not a schematization of internal or superficial anatomy.[317] A more recent study of parietal art at the Grotte de Marsoulas included the engraving of a horse which, according to the analyst, had been supplied with a halter (fig. 9b).[333] In the opinion of a leading group of British paleoeconomists, the "onus of demonstration" has now definitely been shifted to those who continue to maintain that the horse was solely an object of the hunt in Paleolithic times,[202] but prehistorians have yet to find a means of incorporating this phenomenon into the conventional framework, which holds that the horse was not domesticated until the fourth or possibly the fifth millennium B.C.

Indications of human control over reindeer in Magdalenian times are less certain,[200, 201] but they will surely gain credibility with the confirmation of the taming of the horse. Considering as well the apparent scarcity of weapons in many Magdalenian sites (curious among a people who have long been described as the quintessential Paleolithic hunters), one begins to suspect that the economy of at least some of these early Europeans has been wrongly conceived. At Rochereil, for example, Jude found

9 Magdalenian engravings from (a) St. Michel d'Arudy, (b) Grotte de Marsoulas, (c) La Marche (*after Piette, 1906; Plenier, 1971; Pales and St. Pereuse, 1966*)

that the long, cleanly struck, Magdalenian blades reflected a "véritable souci d'élégance," but remarked that one searched in vain for any element that could serve as a weapon.[204] Even the carved antler implements believed to have been harpoon heads often had rounded tips at Rochereil (fig. 8), "hardly favorable for penetration." Common to many Middle to Late Magdalenian deposits, the harpoon heads are more lethal elsewhere,[206] but the most carefully carved and decorated of these pieces may well have served nonutilitarian purposes. It would be difficult in any case to imagine a more appropriate talisman for worshippers of Poseidon. As we shall see later, it is not inconceivable that the Magdalenian harpoon was ancestral to the emblematic trident or fish spear which was consistently identified with Poseidon in Greek myth and art.

The Paleolithic Signs

10 Examples of Upper Paleolithic signs (a), and characters in three of the early written languages which resemble the Paleolithic marks: (b) Indus valley signs, (c) Greek (western branch), (d) Runic *(after Forbes and Crowder, 1979)*

Another long-standing obstacle to the plausibility of Plato's tale as history has been the literacy with which the Atlantics were credited in the *Critias* (119). The laws of Poseidon were said to have been engraved on a pillar that was also inscribed with an oath invoking curses on any who disobeyed. But as unlikely as the notion of an Upper Paleolithic script once seemed (the Sumerians are supposed to have invented writing in the third millennium B.C.), a recent study of the abstract signs accompanying the cave art suggests that these enigmatic marks were just that. A pair of American scholars has found counterparts to the Paleolithic signs in many of the earliest written languages of Europe and Asia (fig. 10). Having eliminated the probabilities that these archaic signs were used as property marks, hunting scores, tally counts, or memory aids, Forbes and Crowder found that the "sole remaining possibility is writing, perhaps not writing as we know it today, but a precursor form not differing fundamentally from inscriptions in early written languages."[133] A successful interpretation of the Paleolithic signs could result, they feel, in a sweeping new understanding of both prehistory and history. For our purposes it is sufficient to record their belief that the Magdalenians, like Plato's Atlantics, were in some sense a literate people.

The Uniformity of Magdalenian Art

One final contradiction to conventional thought may be found in the remarkable unity of Magdalenian art, which unlike the tools (and the signs),[238] shows virtually no regional differentiation. Sieveking has noted that while primitive peoples in our own and recent times use art forms that are tribally (and thus in most cases territorially) distinct, a similar regional distinction seldom applies in the Paleolithic period—"and most particularly does it not apply in the Magdalenian." Throughout southwest Europe a uniform style is recognizable in the art, and whenever the style changed, it changed everywhere.[363, 364]

Using the analogy of a tree, Sieveking points out that one would normally expect the distribution of Magdalenian art to start from a common root and trunk, and then divide geographically into large and small branches. But Magdalenian art does not "branch." Major regional groups do not exist, and drawings from different and widely separated caves are often very much alike. Of the three possible explanations for this homogeneity —that the same artist painted both, that whoever painted the second cave had seen the first one or one like it that is now lost, or that both were copied from a portable prototype such as an engraved pebble—none has been found satisfactory. In Sieveking's opinion, "it is not possible to account for the uniformity of the figurative traditions and their widespread distribution without including something other and more than the vestiges that remain."[364]

Noting as well the maturity in execution of the samples of Magdalenian art that do remain, Sieveking estimates that as much as 95% of the original collection may be missing. She does not speculate on the whereabouts of the missing art. One suspects that the rising seas were partly responsible. But might it also be possible that the original source and conserver of the Magdalenian canon lay elsewhere, and that it is primarily this controlling center which is missing? Wherever it may have been located, this was, following Plato, the home base of the Atlantic governors, from whom the art of Europe as far as Tyrrhenia was receiving its uniform direction and style.

But when the divine element in them [the Atlantic race] became weakened by frequent admixture with mortal stock, and their human traits became predominant, they ceased to be able to carry their prosperity with moderation. To the perceptive eye the depth of their degeneration was clear enough, but to those whose judgement of true happiness is defective they seemed, in their pursuit of unbridled ambition and power, to be at the height of their fame and fortune.   (*Critias* 121)[232]

The archaeological sequence shows that by the thirteenth millennium, the Magdalenians had spread into Switzerland and southern Germany, creating what has been called a "Germanic type of Magdalenian" in regions that apparently had lain un-inhabited since pre-Upper Paleolithic times.[375] A Magdalenian flavor has also been detected in Levels 3 and 2 of the classic old eastern Gravettian site of Molodova V on the Russian river Dniester, dated to 11,700 and 9900 B.C. respectively,[35] and again at the (undated) Ukrainian settlement of Mezine. Possibly to be associated with this expanding influence was the decorating of a solitary cave in the Ural mountains (known as Kapovaia or Choulgan Tache) with horses, mammoth, rhinoceros, and schematic signs.[363]

Southwest Europe itself is said to have experienced some-thing of a population boom during this Middle to Late Magda-lenian epoch, with conservative figures for Late Magdalenian France ranging from 40,000 to 50,000,[35] and less conservative ones from 200,000 to 300,000.[375] As these population increases began before the start of the Alleröd warming phase (c. 9800–8800 B.C.), climatic change was apparently not a determining factor.[352] But the large Late Magdalenian population does seem to have been associated with several types of arrowheads (fig. 11). Laugerie-Basse points, slender "shouldered" points, stemmed or "tanged" Teyjat points, and curved-back Azilian points were all to be counted among various Late Magdalenian assemblages by 10,000 B.C.

Noting the new weapons, several analysts have suggested that it may have been the invention of the bow and its more efficient hunting power that brought on the last of the geo-graphical expansions and population increases (e.g., additional food for more people and the opening up of new ecological

11 Late Magdalenian flint points: (a) shouldered point, (b) Azilian point, (c) Laugerie-Basse point, (d) Teyjat point, *(after Bordes, 1968; Sonneville-Bordes, 1973)*

niches for settlement by more effective hunters).[176, 35] As one prehistorian pointed out, however, the bow actually has no mechanical advantage for hunters over the spear-thrower fabricated by some earlier Magdalenians, and he suggested that the apparent increase in the popularity of the bow might relate instead to "such factors as its suitability for warfare, it being lightweight and requiring less skill to operate."[207]

The arming of the Magdalenians also seems to have coincided with the gradual abandonment of the decorating of inner chambers of the caves. Although the execution of portable art would continue for a thousand years before it too vanished, the very rare cave paintings that can be dated to the tenth millennium are more often found at entrances than in the deep interiors of the caves.[237] In other words, while Late Magdalenians appeared to be at what might be seen, in terms of geographic and demographic expansion, as the "height of their fame and fortune" (as in the *Critias* passage above), their spiritual life—if these interior sanctuaries had indeed served religious purposes—was diminished.

Weapons continued to increase, art to decline, until in the ninth millennium the decay of Magdalenian culture was complete. Peoples who made curved-back points briefly held sway over western Europe; what has been termed the "Azilianizing" of Europe included various curved-back-point makers known in the literature as *Romanelli*, *Federmesser*, and *Creswellian*, as well as *Azilian*. (See map at figure 14.) Their origins are in each case ambiguous. The Azilians of southwest Europe did make a type of harpoon (fig. 12), and painted enigmatic designs on pebbles (fig. 13), but it is unclear whether Azilian culture represented an impoverished extension of Late Magdalenian or the intrusion of newcomers. At Rochereil, for example, Azilian followed Magdalenian (and the excavator expressed surprise at the high incidence of weapons in Azilian levels, as well as the "hurried and provisory character presented by a number of the pieces").[204] But carbon-14 dates show that the earliest Azilian sites actually coexisted with the final phase of Magdalenian culture, that is, from approximately the middle of the tenth millennium B.C.

From Plato's perspective, these curved-back-point peoples could have been either Greek-allied or Atlantic. In the *Critias* (121), after the description quoted above of the decadence concealed in the growing power of the Atlantics, the next passage reads:

12 Azilian harpoon from Rochereil *(after Jude, 1960)*

13 Painted pebbles from Mas d'Azil *(after Piette, 1896)*

14 The distribution of curved-back point groups in Epi-Paleolithic Europe. *(after S. K. Kozlowski, 1975)*. Lighter areas of color represent the early ninth millennium coastline.

> And the god of gods, Zeus, who reigns by law, and whose eye can see such things, when he perceived the wretched state of this admirable stock, decided to punish them and reduce them to order by discipline. He accordingly summoned all the gods to his own most glorious abode, which stands at the centre of the universe and looks out over the whole realm of change, and when they had assembled, addressed them as follows
>
> (*Critias* 121)[232]

It is here the *Critias* breaks off, and we are left not knowing the nature of the punishment chosen by Zeus. As classicists have pointed out, it was too soon for the sinking of Atlantis; the war itself had not yet taken place in the *Critias*, and, as other translations make even clearer, the intent of Zeus at this point was to chastise the errant Atlantics, not obliterate them. (Jowett's 1892 translation reads: "[Zeus,] perceiving that an honorable race was in a woeful plight, and wanting to inflict punishment on them that they might be chastened and improve. . . .") It has also been remarked that whatever means Zeus used, they were unsuccessful; the summary in the *Timaeus* assures us that war did indeed break out.

Several scholars have therefore suggested that this prewar attempt to discipline the Atlantics involved the dispatching of the goddess Athena to found the Athenian society and thus obstruct Atlantic designs on the free lands of the Mediterranean. This is one possibility, and it may not be accidental that the early tenth millennium saw not only the supposed founding of Ur-Athens but also (in uncorrected carbon-14 years) the advent of the Azilian culture in southwest Europe. At least one analyst has found the Italian or Romanelli member of the curved-back point family to be the most likely ancestor of the Azilians,[122] and as Romanelli elements were also known at Asprochaliko Cave in Late Paleolithic western Greece,[75] it is not inconceivable that curved-back points represent a Greek or Greek-allied influence moving from east to west to discourage Atlantic intentions.

On the other hand, if curved-back points were one of several Atlantic brands of weaponry, as their occasional presence in Magdalenian sites might suggest, their spread into Italy and Greece could have signaled an Atlantic intrusion into free Mediterranean territory. This may be the more likely alternative, for the Azilianizing of western Europe was immediately followed by, and in some cases overlapped, the ninth millennium emergence of the *Tanged Point Technocomplex*,[224] a superabundance of tanged or stemmed arrowheads in northwest Europe that was matched in the contemporary Near East. As we shall see later, the crystallization of this tanged-point complex around 8500 B.C. may have marked the official declaration of a war that had been incubating for a thousand years.

see figure 11b

We might note at this point that the sorting-out of the allegiances of the well-armed peoples of this Epi-Paleolithic epoch will be an enormously challenging task for any lithic analyst willing to take Plato at his word. Of the ten Atlantic rulerships, it was said in the *Critias* (119) that no two had precisely the same military dispositions. The diversity within the Greek alliance was evidently no less great, with some groups retaining their autonomy to the point of deserting the Athenians in wartime (*Timaeus* 25). Then, too, the loyalties of formerly colonized peoples in the west (e.g., the *Epi-Magdalenians*) are unknown and may in fact have been divided.

On the archaeological side, there are many varieties of both curved-back and tanged points, as well as quantities of geometric microliths, tiny flints shaped in the form of crescents ("lunates"), triangles, or trapezes, which were ubiquitous around the Mediterranean in this period and are believed to have been used as arrow tips or spear barbs (fig. 15). Moreover, some tool kits contained more than one of these major types of weaponry, others seem to have changed from one dominant type to another, and tanged points in particular are very often found without any associated remains that might identify their fabricators. In short, only a specialist in the tool types of this period is likely to be able to determine who was who, in Plato's terms, around the Epi-Paleolithic Mediterranean.

15 Microlithic flints inserted as tips or barbs in arrows and spears (after Tringham, 1971)

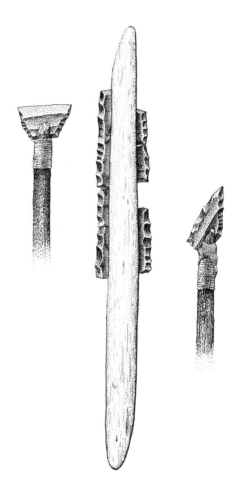

The Mediterranean Before 9000 B.C.: North Africa and Egypt

The Iberomaurusian Cycle

Not only southwest Europe but "Libya [North Africa to the Greeks] up to the borders of Egypt" was said to be under Atlantic control before the war (*Timaeus* 25). The archaeological record shows that a single culture, the *Iberomaurusian*, occupied the Maghreb region of North Africa from around 18/16,000 to 8000 B.C., during which time similar assemblages were to be found as far east as the Haua Fteah cave on the Cyrenaican coast (fig. 17).[60, 271] Not quite up to Egypt, but the proximity of Iberomaurusian deposits to the present coastline has suggested to investigators that many sites may have been drowned in the postglacial seas.[370]

The fragment of a barbed bone harpoon at Taforalt (fig. 16) indicates contact of some sort with the Magdalenians, and the "Mechta-Afalou" physical type associated with Iberomaurusian remains is of the same Cro-Magnon stock that seeded Upper Paleolithic Europe.[129] Moreover, the Iberomaurusians do not appear to have been descended from the earlier occupants of the Maghreb, and their origins are still a mystery. But this unspectacular and art-poor North African culture is so far removed from Magdalenian traditions that it is difficult to see how both could have been colonies of the same power. The Iberomaurusians not only lacked the Magdalenian artistic genius, at least in imperishable materials, but the two cultures fundamentally diverged in burial customs and initiation procedures. Hundreds of Iberomaurusian dead have been recovered from large cemeteries in North African caves, as opposed to the scarce and usually isolated Magdalenian burials, and all Iberomaurusian crania show evidence of tooth avulsion in puberty (in this case the removal of the two upper central incisors and occasionally the two lower ones as well),[60] presumably an adolescent initiation practice for which there are no parallels in Europe.

16 Harpoon fragment from the Iberomaurusian site of Taforalt (*after Camps, 1974*)

And yet the spatial and temporal boundaries of these North Africans do match up almost as well as the Magdalenians with the stated dimensions of Atlantic control. One wonders, therefore, if the marked cultural differences on either side of the Straits might indicate the presence of more than one Atlantic hand in Mediterranean affairs. In the *Critias* (114), the ten original kings and their descendants are said to have governed for many generations "their own territories and many other islands in the ocean and, as has already been said, also controlled the populations this side of the straits as far as Egypt and Tyrrhenia." If this passage is taken to mean that more than one of the Atlantic kings controlled populations inside the Straits, we would expect any differences between these rulers to have extended to their colonies.

That there were indeed differences, great or small, among the Atlantic kingdoms is further suggested in the *Critias* (113-14). The island continent is said to have been divided long ago into ten separate districts, which were distributed among the five sets of twin sons sired by Poseidon and a mortal woman. Of the first pair of twins, for example, the "biggest and best allocation" (the mother's home district and the land surrounding it) went to Atlas, the elder of the two, while Gadirus received the "furthest part of the island towards the Pillars of Heracles and facing the district now called Gadira" (Spanish Gades or Cadiz). Each lineage had then retained absolute power over its own territory for a presumably lengthy span of time and subsequent development; and as each is said to have developed differences in its military disposition (*Critias* 119), one suspects that these long-discrete and autonomous kingdoms would have acquired an individuality in social and economic spheres as well, an individuality which would have been reflected in the colonized territories of each.*

Alternatively, or perhaps in addition to this suggestion, the North Africans may have been serving a different colonial function. The excavator of the Iberomaurusian site at Tamar Hat has recently made a convincing case for the management of herds of Barbary sheep in North Africa as early as 18,000 B.C. As Saxon points out, not only do Barbary sheep constitute an abnormally high percentage of the faunal remains at Tamar Hat (94%), but

* The possibility that more than one Atlantic kingdom was represented in Africa will be raised again in Part II when we explore an exotic artistic tradition which apparently dates back to the Epi-Paleolithic period in the central Sahara, a far more hospitable region at that time and well within the "up to Egypt" bounds of Atlantic colonization.

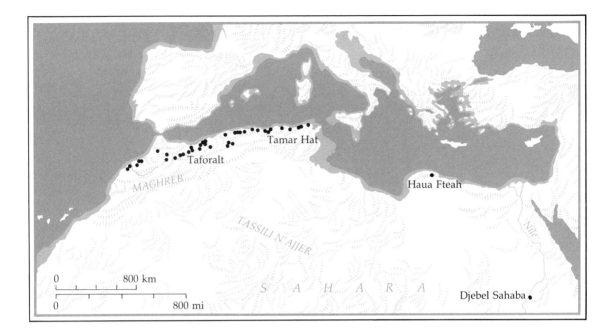

the culling pattern — young males and old females — is identical to that of a closely managed herd in a subsistence economy and would be termed domestication if encountered in more recent contexts. In his opinion, the Iberomaurusian tool kit (mostly small backed blades or bladelets) is also technologically unsuitable for hunting these wild sheep, the "ultimate challenge" even with rifles and binoculars. Saxon's conclusion: as early as 18,000 B.C., the men of Tamar Hat were managing the herds on the broad coastal plain that formerly existed in front of the cave — "the romance of Man the Hunter is no longer tenable for the Upper Paleolithic."[357] This is not to say that there were no hunters in Upper Paleolithic Africa, only that there were apparently shepherds, or herd managers, as well.

The peaceful image Saxon portrays, Iberomaurusian herdsmen with tools ill-designed for the hunting of Barbary sheep, fits well with Jude's observations on the Magdalenian tools at Rochereil, where one sought in vain for a weapon. Equally serene, evidently, were the social and political activities of each of these cultures. Dastugue and Lumley found the pathology of Upper Paleolithic European skeletons to be unmarked by trauma other than that caused by the accidents of everyday life.[93] Of some 273 Iberomaurusian burials recovered from North African cemeteries, Camps found no trace of an intentional violent act.[60] By way of comparison, however, he added that the peaceful life of the Iberomaurusians "contrasts vigorously" with the

17 The distribution of Iberomaurusian sites in North Africa, 16,000–8000 B.C., and other sites mentioned in the text *(after Camps, 1974)*

see pages 27–28

bellicose activities at the Nubian cemetery of Djebel Sahaba. As we shall see below, the first recorded Nilotic graveyard also contained the earliest known victims of violent death on the African continent.

The Late Paleolithic Nile

From the *Timaeus* (25) we know only that Egypt was one of the free lands within the Straits destined to be attacked by Atlantic military forces. The archaeology of Upper Paleolithic Egypt shows the traces of a number of differentiated cultural groups, without permanent art or architecture, following a shifting pattern of coexistence along the Nile from perhaps 25,000 to around 9000 B.C.[370] At some point in this period, possibly as early as 15,000 B.C., a complex of new features was introduced into the Nile valley. Numerous grinding stones and flints with "sickle sheen," the polish associated with the cutting of grass stems, are believed to indicate the beginnings of an intensive use of ground grain as a food source.[422] Whether the grain was cultivated or simply gathered from the wild is still a controversial question, but the presence of a few seeds of morphologically domestic wheat in fifteenth millennium deposits in Palestine,[305] if not intruding from later levels of the site, would strengthen the possibility that grain was grown in Late Paleolithic Egypt.

In any event, it is to one of the later "grindstone cultures," the *Qadan*, that the above-mentioned graveyard at Djebel Sahaba seems to belong. Of some 59 burials at this Nubian cemetery, Wendorf found that almost half of the deceased had died violently, the first collection of traumatic deaths known to Africa and perhaps to the Mediterranean world. The crude flints found with these skeletal remains were not, he assures us, grave offerings. Some were still embedded in the bones of the dead, others were found along the vertebral column, chest cavity, and lower abdomen. In Wendorf's opinion, "the ferocity in the deaths of many of these individuals indicates that the situation was more serious than that which leads to the occasional friction between neighboring groups."[420]

The date of the Djebel Sahaba burials is uncertain. Wendorf has suggested a time between 12,000 and 10,000 B.C. "or slightly later";[420] the Qadan culture itself is now believed to have disappeared around 9000 B.C.[370] We are in any case close enough in time to the *Timaeus* war to suspect some sort of connection between these signs of what Wendorf saw as political unrest

map at figure 17

along the Nile and the prewar Atlantic transgressions that angered Zeus at the end of the *Critias*. The presence of women see page 32 and children as well as men at Sahaba, and the apparently sporadic nature of the burials (which were sometimes small groups of up to four individuals) does suggest a population under extended pressure. Endemic raiding and ambush rather than all-out warfare was one prehistorian's conclusion,[187] but we have noted the conviction of the excavator that the situation at Sahaba was more serious than the predictable friction between neighbors. Might Atlantic interests have been represented among the diverse groups inhabiting the Late Paleolithic Nile?* And if so, are the burials at Djebel Sahaba more likely to have been the victims of their prewar expansion or the unwelcome trespassers themselves? (The Sahaba skeletal remains are said to show "striking morphological similarities" to the Mechta-Afalou physical type of Iberomaurusian North Africa.)[3] In any case, Wendorf concluded that "violence must have been a very common event in Nubia at this time, if we are to consider this graveyard as typical."[420]

Violence may have been equally common in the Ukraine during this period. Alone, Djebel Sahaba might remain a local phenomenon, questionable in its relationship to Plato's account. But when set beside the first cemeteries known to Russia, also undated by carbon-14 but estimated to an Epi-Paleolithic time frame by the Russians,[382, 392] their general contemporaneity and unmistakably similar contents suggest that the earliest collections of violent deaths in Africa and Europe may be related, both to one another and to Plato's tale. We shall therefore bypass the Near East temporarily on our way around the Mediterranean for a brief look at these Ukrainian burial grounds.

The Ukrainian Cemeteries

Of the three related graveyards on the Dnieper River above the Black Sea, Vasylivka III was the largest, containing 44 excavated burials and perhaps 20 more still in situ.[391, 392] Here as at Sahaba the bodies of men, women and children, occasionally buried in

---

* As we shall see later, the archaeological record of Egypt is almost blank from 8500 to 4500 B.C., but one of the last entries from Epi-Paleolithic times is a collection of arrowheads at Helwan in Lower Egypt. As these were among the several types of tanged points that dominated the eastern Mediterranean in the last half of the ninth millennium, Egypt may indeed have been involved in a larger war by that time.

small groups, were accompanied by flint points sometimes lodged in the bones of the dead. Neighboring graveyards at Voloske and Vasylivka I also revealed an abnormally high proportion of violent deaths. The Russians have sequenced these cemeteries in various ways, but most agree that a separate group of all-male burials at Vasylivka III seems to be slightly more recent than the others. (The weapons used to dispatch this group were somewhat more sophisticated, e.g., a bone spearhead with triangular flint barbs and microlithic triangular arrowheads.) In the opinion of the excavator, "this obviously is a collective grave of warriors who died in battle."[392]

map at figure 62

As we shall see later, these were not the only warriors known to the Epi-Paleolithic Old World, and it does seem curious that after some 20,000 years of apparently tranquil relations among Europe's *Homo sapiens sapiens* populations, the first known European collections of traumatic deaths should have occurred at a time that promises to intersect the chronology of Plato's war. A conflict involving all those who lived inside the Straits of Gibraltar may well have included Ukrainians, but at this point we are primarily interested in the earlier groups of mixed burials, and the possibility that these deaths by flint point were the result of prewar Atlantic encroachment.

In his own analysis of the Ukrainian hostilities, the excavator of Vasylivka III proposed that the violence revealed in all three cemeteries signified the forcing out of a native Proto-Mediterranean population by incoming Cro-Magnon groups from the north.[392] (The Proto-Mediterranean physical type is smaller, more lightly built, and considerably less well-differentiated sexually than Cro-Magnon man.) His idea of the expulsion of one people by another may in fact be applicable beyond the Ukraine, as "considerable cultural change" is said to have characterized much of central and eastern Europe in this Epi-Paleolithic era.[222] For example, Gravettian sites in the middle Danube basin and eastern Carpathian mountains apparently were abandoned at some point in the tenth millennium, followed by the appearance of both curved-back-point and tanged-point groups in ephemeral occupations.[301, 221]

The retreat of their favorite game animals to more northerly regions during the warmer Alleröd climate (9800–8800 B.C.) has been suggested as the reason for the uprooting of these native Gravettian peoples. But one notes that the east Gravettian settlement at Molodova V remained active throughout this period, taking on first Magdalenian and then Azilian coloration before finally being abandoned itself around 8500 B.C., after more than 20,000 years of almost continuous occupancy.[35] Moreover, as we shall see below, the major recipient of both Gravettian traditions and Proto-Mediterranean peoples in the tenth millennium seems to have been Palestine, clearly not the direction taken by the game.

The Mediterranean Before 9000 B.C.: Palestine and Greece

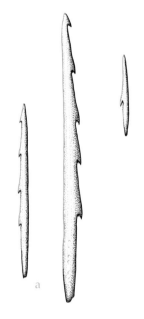

18 (a) Bone harpoons from the Mugharet el-Kebarah cave, Palestine; (b) recumbent gazelle (with missing head) from Umm ez-Zuweitina *(after Turville-Petre, 1932; Garrod, 1957)*

The Natufian Culture

A leading Near Eastern prehistorian has recently summarized the present state of our knowledge with regard to the sudden increase in the size of Palestinian settlements during the tenth millennium B.C.:

> The impetus for this change is unknown, and the possible hypotheses that relate it to climatic fluctuations, inherent social changes, technological innovations, different economic strategies, etc., still remain to be demonstrated effectively.[11]

The jump in settlement size was accompanied by a "virtual explosion"[374] of arts, crafts, and technologies that were heretofore unknown to the local peoples of Palestine. Some of these innovations were in fact new to the archaeological record of known sites anywhere in the world. Others were familiar, however, and connections to traditions both north and south of the Mediterranean can be detected among the extraordinarily rich diversity of these new Palestinian sites, to which the cultural label of *Natufian* (after the Wadi el-Natuf) has been fixed (fig. 19).

For example, contact with southwest Europe seems to be indicated by the presence of unilaterally-barbed bone harpoons at a few Early Natufian sites (fig. 18a). The animal art (fig. 18b) could point to either western or eastern Europe. Links to North Africa are suggested by the evidence of tooth avulsion at three Natufian sites, ties to Egypt through certain techniques of tool craft. The traditions of the native Upper Paleolithic Palestinians are also represented, although in the hands of the Natufians the crude stone mortars known to a few of these earlier *Kebaran* sites were transformed into works of art, and accompanied by marble plates and bowls, "decidedly elegant" footed vessels,[150] and containers with meander and curvilinear designs carved in relief on the surface: a display of expertise in the grinding, pecking, and polishing of stone that is without precedent in the archaeological record of known earlier sites (fig. 27).

It is to central and eastern Europe, however, to Gravettian Europe, that Natufian culture seems to owe its greatest debt. Burial customs among the more than two hundred Natufian dead that have been recovered (only two burials have been documented in the preceding 6,000-year-long Kebaran period) included the adornment of the dead with necklaces, bracelets, and most notably, dentalium shell headdresses which are near replicas of those found among central and eastern European Gravettian burials of Upper Paleolithic age (fig. 20).[76] One particular necklace from a Natufian burial at El Wad has been judged

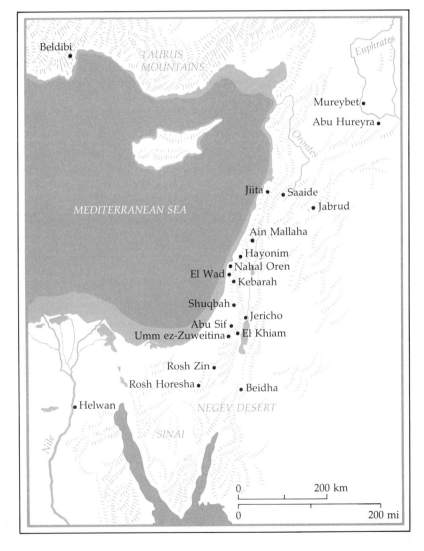

19 Principal Natufian and related sites in the Epi-Paleolithic Near East (after Cauvin, 1978)

20 Headdress of dentalium shells threaded on a network of cords, from the Natufian site of El Wad (after Garrod, 1937)

21 Necklace elements from (a) El Wad, Palestine, tenth millennium, and (b) Dolní Věstonice, Czechoslovakia, c. 20,000 B.C. (after Garrod, 1937; Marshack, 1972)

a

b

almost identical to one from Dolní Věstonice, a 23/20,000 B.C. Gravettian site in Czechoslovakia (fig. 21).[265] Natufian sickles or "reaping knives" (fig. 22) with multiple microflints inserted into horn hafts had Gravettian counterparts, inferior but based on the same principle, in the hafted knives of the Ukraine.[219] The semi-sunken round houses of the Natufian settlement at Ain Mallaha were also reminiscent of Gravettian structures in central and eastern Europe.[220] Rather primitive round huts have been discovered here and there among the earlier Kebaran campsites of Palestine,[378] but at Ain Mallaha some fifty substantial dwellings of Gravettian design formed what appears to be the earliest village yet recorded. Walled with boulders, paved with slabs of limestone, Mallaha's round houses measured up to twenty-eight feet in diameter.[326] Her anthropomorphic sculpture in the round (fig. 23) is also an art form generally associated with Gravettian Europe.

But if the traditions of Natufian sites such as Ain Mallaha seem particularly evocative of central and east European culture, they were far more advanced than those of any recorded site in Europe. One of Mallaha's earliest houses featured a plastered interior wall that had been stained with red ochre before being polished smooth, an integrated technique which, like the ground stone work described above, was without known precedents. This red-plaster-walled house was later converted into a "tomb" into which two apparently high status individuals were laid,[324] and the over-all variability of Mallahan burial customs adds to the impression of a socially stratified community. (Other individuals had also been carefully interred, while groups of secondary burials, excarnated remains, were informally placed in plaster-lined pits.)

The excavator of Ain Mallaha recognized the superiority of his site when comparing it to such ancient Gravettian establishments as twentieth millennium Dolní Věstonice, and he added, "with this difference: that here a greater cultural maturity has permitted spectacular progress."[324] But if his comparison of Mallaha to earlier sites in central and eastern Europe is obviously well-taken in light of the similarities noted above, it does leave unanswered the question of where such a spectacular improvement on other aspects of Gravettian culture could have taken place. Not in Palestine, it seems, as the traditions of Ain Mallaha appear to have been already established when the settlement was founded. Nor does Europe offer comparable progress in the Gravettian line; as mentioned above, no contemporary Gravettian culture could approach the Mallahans in terms of cultural achievement. That is to say, no *known* European culture could have directly fathered this Palestinian settlement whose ancestry seems so unmistakably European. We are left with the alternative of an unknown, advanced Gravettian society somewhere in Europe whose members, or some of them, saw fit to migrate to Palestine in the tenth millennium B.C. — by land or, as the discovery of Late Paleolithic seafarers may now make plausible, by sea.

This suggestion of a missing link at Ain Mallaha will become a necessary presumption a millennium later at Jericho, where the monumental wall and tower complex associated with a settlement of Mallaha-type round houses has most recently been estimated to c. 8300 B.C.[181] The occasional suggestions of plant and animal management among the Natufian sites of the preceding period are more explicit now; domestic emmer wheat and two-row barley have been recorded,[191] and some analysts believe that gazelle may have been rounded up and kept in captivity as they were in dynastic Egypt.[411] Moreover, the necessity of a hierarchical social structure to initiate and effect Jericho's architectural achievements seems unquestionable.[209] The great stone wall, some twenty feet high and nine feet thick, was joined by at least one apsidal tower which Kenyon felt would not have disgraced one of the more impressive medieval castles (fig. 39). Almost completely solid and more than thirty feet in diameter, the tower still stands to a height of thirty feet. An internal flight of stairs, whose treads had been formed of hammer-dressed stone slabs, led down to a horizontal passageway; both staircase and passage were roofed with even larger, similarly dressed stone slabs.

What part Jericho's wall and tower might have played in the war will be explored later. The point to be noted here is that her architects clearly did not come inexperienced to the job, and the existence elsewhere, before the mid-ninth millennium B.C.,

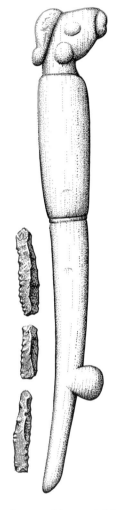

22 Grooved bone sickle haft from Mughâret el-Kebarah, with appropriate flints (*after Oates and Oates, 1976*)

23 Anthropomorphic stone sculpture from Ain Mallaha, tenth millennium B.C. Height of largest piece, three inches (*after Perrot, 1966*)

of a similarly walled community appears to be an unavoidable assumption. With Mallaha (or Gravettian) type round houses within her walls, we may also suspect that Jericho's ancestor belonged to the same, unknown, European-related tradition that founded Ain Mallaha in the tenth millennium. Recalling that the living quarters of Plato's warrior-guardians on the tenth millennium Athenian acropolis were surrounded by "a single wall like the garden of a single house" (*Critias* 112), we might want to delay the question of the origin of the Natufian culture of Palestine until we have looked at Greece.

Tenth Millennium Greece

Late Paleolithic Greece has generally, and with good reason, been considered an unlikely setting for Plato's ancient Athenian society. As summarized by one scholar:

> In the first place, although the evidence is sparse, archaeology has shown that the Athens which Plato describes could not have existed in 9500 B.C. or thereabouts. At that time Greece was in the late Paleolithic period and man was still living in caves or rock shelters and was hunting and gathering his food. Settlement was not to begin for another 3,000 years, and even then the process of civilization was a slow one. No amount of rationalizing can produce Plato's well-governed, well-structured and well-protected state in this early period.[336]

The logic here seems, or rather seemed, sound. But with the recent assignment of the walled town at Jericho to the middle of the ninth millennium B.C., and the necessity of presuming the existence of a similarly advanced ancestral community elsewhere, it now appears that a society approximately as "well-governed, well-structured and well-protected" as Plato's Athens did indeed exist in this early period, wherever it may have been sited. Furthermore, although the archaeology of Greece shows only cave sites in these times, the very recent excavations at one of those sites, Franchthi Cave in the Argolid, suggest that the Greeks of this epoch were far from backward, and that the scant archaeological remains may actually misrepresent the true level of Late Paleolithic Greek culture.

Of the several unexpected discoveries at Franchthi Cave,[196-199] foremost is evidence of an established tradition of seafaring in the Late Paleolithic Aegean. Small amounts of obsidian in deposits immediately above material dated to the eleventh

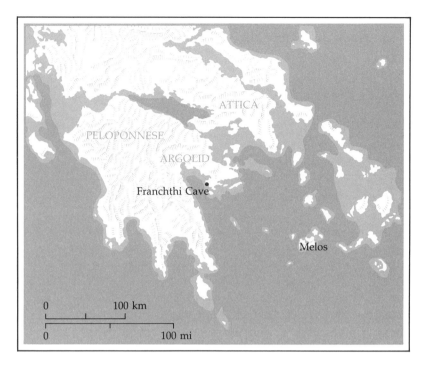

24 Map showing Franchthi Cave, the island of Melos, and the Late Paleolithic Aegean coastline *(after Perles, 1979)*

millennium have been identified as originating on the island of Melos, some 90 miles southeast of Franchthi over open seas (fig. 24). Melos remained an island throughout the maximum regression of sea level (which had already begun to rise by this time), and even island-hopping the long way round, a competent maritime technology apparently was required for the journey—and for the sea-borne explorations which must have preceded the discovery of this main Aegean source of obsidian. As Perles concluded: "There were indeed groups who braved the seas to provide the continent with obsidian . . . and not as a single or exceptional exploit, as obsidian continued to be present in all the following levels."[322]

The discovery of early seafarers in the Aegean should come as no surprise. We have known for some time that Australia was colonized at least 30,000 years ago by what studies show to have been purposeful and competent mariners.[397] And unless those unilaterally-barbed bone harpoons recorded in Epi-Paleolithic southwest Europe, North Africa, and Palestine were independently invented by three separate and contemporary populations, which seems extremely unlikely, their presence on three sides of the Mediterranean at roughly the same time suggests that Late Paleolithic seafaring may not have been limited to the Aegean.

The War of 8500 B.C.   47

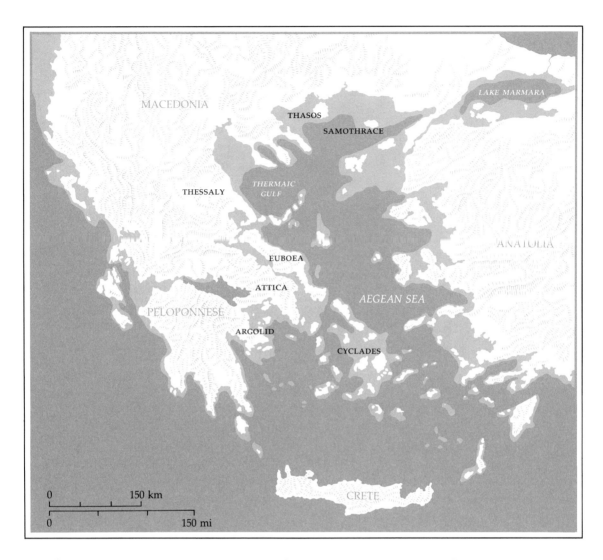

25 The Aegean coast during the maximum regression of sea level (c. 16,000 B.C.) compared to the present shoreline. The ancient coast of Crete is uncertain because of the island's tectonic instability. *(after Van Andel and Shackelton, 1982)*

In Greece the continuing presence of Melian obsidian at Franchthi Cave also presupposes the existence of at least one long-established coastal port that has since been drowned in the rising Holocene seas. Franchthi Cave itself, which today overlooks the Bay of Koilada, was four to five miles inland in Late Paleolithic times, and Koilada Bay a broad plain through which at least one major stream reportedly made its way to the sea.[199] Remains of any Late Paleolithic ports or settlements situated within four miles or so of the coast are therefore certain to have been submerged by the postglacial rise in sea level.

Elsewhere in Greece the loss of land to sea was even greater. The map at figure 25 shows the enormity of the changes wrought in Greek lands from 16,000 B.C. (the glacial maximum) to 7000

B.C., by which time the coastal geography of Greece was pretty much as it is today. As Van Andel and Shackelton have so well demonstrated in their recent study of this phenomenon, Late Paleolithic Greece was, to say the least, "a very different country."[407] Among its most striking features were extensive coastal plains, so rare in present-day Greece. Not only was Yugoslavia connected to Italy by a vast plain across the Adriatic, but on the northern end of the Aegean, coastal lowlands extended westward from northern Anatolia and the then "Lake" Marmara to the present Thermaic Gulf and Thessaly, incorporating what are now the islands of Thasos and Samothrace. A plain also existed between Attica and the southeastern Argolid, with isolated hills that today are islands. The straits between Euboea and the mainland were dry; the Peloponnese was connected to central Greece in both the northwest and northeast. In short, the Greek peninsula was both simpler in outline and much larger than it is today.

13,000 B.C. is believed to mark the approximate beginning of the rise in sea level. How erratic this rise might have been before 7000 B.C. is unknown; one might expect a period of stability, for example, during the return to colder conditions in Dryas III (8800–8000 B.C.), with an abrupt rise thereafter as the warming trend suddenly reasserted itself. In any event, Van Andel and Shackelton believe that the submergence of these vast areas of low-lying Greek lands between 13,000 and 7000 B.C. may have caused populations specializing in coastal plain resources to lose all or much of their economic base: "The distinct possibility exists that entire subsistence strategies based on coastal plains may have vanished as their territories became submerged."[407]

In the region around Franchthi Cave, for example, the principal resources would have been found in the rolling hill and valley-bottom country, on the coastal plain, and in near-shore waters. As it is in these now-submerged lowlands that the more important settlements of the day (including seaports) would have been located, Franchthi Cave seems very likely to have been a peripheral or marginal site, and less than exemplary of the true level of Late Paleolithic Greek culture as a whole.

But can the loss of coastal territories alone account for the striking and anomalous scarcity of archaeological remains throughout the Balkan peninsula and much of Anatolia? The emptiness of Epi-Paleolithic Greece was not limited to the coast; why should this part of the world in particular have experienced what has been termed "an extraordinary gap" in site activity between 9000 and 6000 B.C.?[434, 395] (See map at figure 26.) Is it

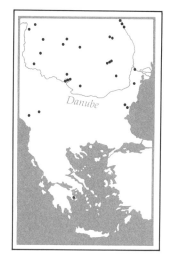

26 Recorded sites in southeast Europe, 9000 to 6000 B.C. (after Dolukhanov, 1979)

The War of 8500 B.C.   49

possible that this interval saw not only vast changes effected in the Greek coastline by the rising seas, but a dissolution of her interior landscape by waters from above? Like the paleogeographers at Franchthi Cave, Plato's Egyptian priest also saw the Greece of Solon's day as a "mere remnant" (*Critias* 111) of her former size—a remarkable coincidence in itself—but the priest blamed deluge, earthquake, and subsequent erosion:

> You are left, as with little islands, with something rather like the skeleton of a body wasted by disease; the rich, soft soil has all run away leaving the land nothing but skin and bone. But in those days the damage had not taken place; the hills had high crests, the rocky plain of Phelleus was covered with rich soil. . . .
>
> (*Critias* 111)[232]

The postwar deluge and earthquakes that destroyed Ur-Athens were the greatest offenders in this process, not only swallowing up the Athenians (*Timaeus* 25), but denuding the Acropolis and greatly diminishing its size (*Critias* 112). And as the only survivors of this "greatest of all destructions by water" (*Timaeus* 23) were said to be rude mountain folk, we must assume that all of those other Greek nations of the day which the *Critias* mentions but fails to describe were similarly overcome. If this disaster were of truly the magnitude claimed by the priest, the survival even of Franchthi Cave, the only active site known to Greek archaeology during that 9000 to 6000 B.C. "gap," would be somewhat miraculous.

We may never know the relationship, if there was one, between the catastrophe of the *Timaeus* and the postglacial rise in sea level. Evidence to be presented later, however, will suggest a period of heavy rains in the northeast Mediterranean midway through the eighth millennium, at which time the above-mentioned warming trend is likely to have further swollen the seas. It may be that Greece was indeed drowned from two directions.

Natufian Origins

Before returning to tenth millennium Palestine and the question of Natufian origins, we might note that any missing Late or Epi-Paleolithic Greek sites, whatever the agent of their destruction, are likely to have been of Gravettian ancestry. In spite of the individuality of Gravettian settlements and the often-considerable distances between them, this ancient tradition embraced virtually all of Upper Paleolithic central and eastern Europe, forming what has been termed an *oikoumene*,[127] a unified cultural region, which in this case included the Greek cave sites.[75] One therefore suspects that any vanished Greek settlements, however more advanced than the caves, were fundamentally based in the same tradition. It is from this perspective, perhaps, and recalling that the excavator of the major Natufian settlement at Ain Mallaha likened his site to a greatly improved Gravettian community, that one should approach the question of where at least some of the newcomers to tenth millennium Palestine originated.

see page 44

Late in her active career as an archaeologist, Dorothy Garrod confessed that she had waited twenty years for a connecting link to the Natufians to surface in the north.[150] She had found nothing convincing in the "rather uninteresting" indigenous Kebaran culture to recommend it as the Natufian ancestor, but when the missing link to northern sites failed to materialize, she felt there was no other recourse than to presume the Natufians native to Palestine. Garrod's reluctant conclusion has since been shared by the majority of her colleagues, who, while recognizing the changes in cultural remains that accompanied the Natufian advent (including the jump in size and sophistication of settlements, the new attentiveness to funeral arrangements and adornments, the extraordinary facility with ground stone, the uses of plaster, etc.) have still found no alternative to an autochthonous origin.

Yet they also admit that the Natufian artistic impulse was "already old" at the moment of its appearance in this land which formerly knew no art, or at least no imperishable art, of any kind.[2] Furthermore, carbon-14 dates show an apparent lacuna of perhaps 500 to 1,000 years between the last deposits of the *Geometric Kebaran A* culture (the presumed ancestor of the Natufians) and the earliest Natufian material,[418] and nowhere does the latter lie immediately over the former.

Something is surely wrong here, and if the indigenous nature of at least some of the Natufians seems doubtful, so too does the concept of the Natufians as a single people. Several factors argue against an original unity, among them the uncommon diversity of Natufian settlement patterns, which ranged from the open-air village at Ain Mallaha (with at least four stratified building levels of stone-based round houses), to large cave or cave-terrace sites without architectural remains and small ephemeral campsites similar to those occupied by the native Kebarans.[180] Moreover, the artistic impulse was not in evidence at all Natufian sites, nor were the elegant vases of Ain Mallaha (fig. 27). And when ground stone pieces do appear at such sites as Hayonim Cave, far from the nearest outcroppings of suitable stone, the absence of stone-flake residue has led one team of investigators to suggest that these items were actually part of a "commercial interchange" among Natufian communities.[15] The barbed bone harpoons were also known to only a few, early, Natufian sites (two of which had no immediate access to fishing, incidentally, while Ain Mallaha had fish but no harpoons).

27 Ground stone pieces from the Natufian site of Ain Mallaha, tenth millennium B.C. Height of large basalt mortar, twenty-four inches; other pieces not drawn to scale. *(after Perrot, 1966)*

A more fundamental difference among the Early Natufians is implied by the reported presence of tooth avulsion at only three sites (tooth-knocking was universally practiced in Ibero-maurusian North Africa) and most telling of all, perhaps, by the difference in physical types from one Natufian settlement to another. According to one physical anthropologist, all of the burials at Ain Mallaha were of the *Robust* or Eurafrican type of Proto-Mediterranean; all those at Nahal Oren were *Gracile* Proto-Mediterranean.[130] She believes that these two sub-races, which still dominate the Mediterranean populations of today, diverged from a common ancestor many thousands of years before meeting again in tenth millennium Palestine.

In short, the range and depth of the site-to-site differences suggests that the original Natufians were not only not all native to Palestine, but may in fact have come from several directions. The question then becomes why, as well as whence, they came. Plato's account is not much help at this point. All we are told of "Asia" is that her peoples were free, that they admired the Athenians, and that they were ultimately attacked by the same Atlantic forces that sought to enslave Greece, Egypt, and all other free lands within the Straits of Gibraltar (*Critias* 112, *Timaeus* 25). But we have seen evidence of population displacement and violent death in lands to the north and south (e.g., the Ukrainian cemeteries and Djebel Sahaba). If such incidents were indeed connected to prewar Atlantic transgression, one might see tenth millennium Palestine as a refuge, a haven for threatened or otherwise disaffected peoples from all around the Mediterranean. Not only southeast Europeans (Ain Mallaha?), but perhaps dissidents from Atlantic colonies in western Europe (harpoons) and North Africa (tooth-knocking) may have sought safety in the east. What has been termed "the Natufian culture" might then more realistically be defined as the result of the mutual encounter of these groups of immigrants with one another, and with the traditions of the native Kebaran population of Palestine.

It is also possible that the Palestinian land route between Europe and Africa, which saw much the greatest concentration of new sites in this period, was a strategic goal early on, with Atlantic-allied groups (harpoons, tooth-knocking) alongside those who looked to Greece. If this were the case, Ain Mallaha might have been a Greek-allied mission of sorts, founded to maintain the status quo in the free lands of the east. The apparently easy mixing and absence of violence does suggest a certain sympathy, however, if not an original unity, among the Palestinians of this epoch.

Whatever the circumstances of its beginning, the end of the Natufian occupation was apparently swift, its cause unknown. Radiocarbon dates are unfortunately scarce, but by 8500 B.C. at the latest, most if not all of the Natufian sites (including Ain

map at figure 19

Mallaha) had been abandoned. Present at the very few remaining or reoccupied sites were tanged, notched, or tanged-and-notched arrowheads. No change in faunal remains has been recorded which might explain the purpose of these new points. Similar weapons appeared at the new Epi-Natufian site of Mureybet on the Syrian Euphrates[68] and at the Natufian-related settlement of Helwan in Lower Egypt,[334] while a different type of tanged point emerged in the mid-ninth-millennium Negev desert.[264] Shortly thereafter the massive fortifications at Jericho were raised. Had the free East gone to war?

The War in the West

The Tanged Point Technocomplex

As noted earlier, the Magdalenian domination of western Europe gave way first to the makers of curved-back points and then, in the ninth millennium, to the Tanged Point Technocomplex, whose main varieties of stemmed arrowheads are shown at figure 28. Wolfgang Taute's thoroughgoing research counted some 372 tanged-point "find spots" in northern Europe alone;[387] their clustering around the present-day coastline suggests the loss of a good many more to the postglacial seas (fig. 29).

But in spite of their great numbers, the frequent absence of associated remains has left tanged-point origins obscure. Some analysts have suggested that the elder *Lyngby* tanged-point groups in Scandinavia moved down through Denmark and into northern Germany with the onset of colder conditions in Dryas III (which began c. 8800 B.C.), absorbing elements from the northern arm of the old curved-back-point complex and thus forming the younger *Ahrensburgian* tanged-point culture of 8500 B.C.[222] Others have seen tanged points as a more or less spontaneous adaptation for hunting the animals of the colder environment. Neither of these climate-centered views can accommodate the simultaneous spread of arrowheads in the Near East, however, where faunal remains (and presumably climate) were essentially unchanged. Moreover, tanged points of the *Lyngby* and *Swiderian* varieties had already begun to appear in Europe during the preceding Alleröd period of warmer temperatures (see chart at figure 151), and several investigators have therefore called into question the hypothetical relationship between these arrowheads and any change in fauna that might have resulted from the Dryas cold.[352]

Equally difficult to square with the climate-based hypotheses is the possibly eastern origin of the Swiderian member of the

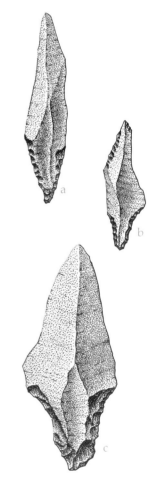

28 The principal types of European tanged points: (a) Swiderian point, (b) Ahrensburg point, (c) Lyngby point *(after Taute, 1968)*

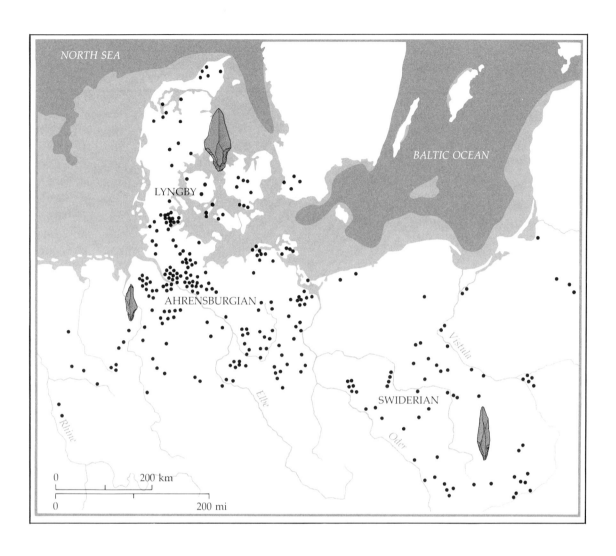

29 Tanged point find-
spots in northern Europe
(after Taute, 1968)

tanged point complex. Taute saw the predecessors of the willow-
leaf shaped Swidry point in the Gravettian leaf points of Upper
Paleolithic eastern Europe, and suggested that these eastern
points could have acquired a tang in the process of moving
westward, perhaps as a result of contact with Ahrensburgian
groups. Swiderian points have in fact been claimed for sites
as far south as Siuren II in the Crimea;[382] and in the Ceahlău
basin of Romania a "workshop" of Swiderian points has been
reported, accompanied by numerous deposits of haematite
(believed to have been used as body paint) and without the
faunal remains and hearths that had been characteristic of the
Late Gravettian sites in this region.[301, 221]

We might also note that while many analysts attribute the tanged point phenomenon to an "uncommon economic specialization" in reindeer hunting,[387] there are indications that the reindeer killed at the major tanged-point site of Ahrensburg may actually have been captive rather than hunted animals. (Jarman's team found suggestions of a high degree of human control in the frequency with which the shoulder blades of the reindeer at Ahrensburg were perforated at the ideal point for penetration of the heart.)[202] Elsewhere in northern Europe faunal remains of any sort were again a far less common tanged-point companion than considerable quantities of haematite.[387] Given as well the many scenes of bow-and-arrow warfare that we shall find recorded on the rocks of the postglacial Spanish Levant, the superabundance of ninth millennium European arrowheads seems quite likely to have been a political rather than an economic specialization.

But if these several types of tanged points were indeed the weapons of war—and specifically the weapons of Plato's war, as the concurrent appearance of arrowheads in the Near East further suggests—the question of who made them is still a puzzle. The occasional presence of tanged (Teyjat) points in Late see figure 11d Magdalenian deposits and of barbed bone harpoons in north European tanged-point contexts might suggest Atlantic craftsmen, while the possibly Gravettian origin of the Swiderian point could lead to the Greeks. Or did both sides find tanged points to be effective weapons in time of war? This question is again better left to the lithic analysts most familiar with these forms. Our aim is only to point out the likelihood that the ninth millennium Tanged Point Technocomplex was primarily a military institution.

The Battling Bowmen of Spain and Kobystan

Opinions are divided as to the age of the rock paintings in the Spanish Levant, but a Mesolithic time frame (post-Paleolithic and pre-Neolithic) is generally accepted. As shown at figure 30, the art is found in rock shelters from the Pyrenees to the Sierra Nevada. Of the unexpected emergence of this new style of painting, one critic remarked: "From the point of view of stylistic evolution, Levante art appears to have had no childhood. All of a sudden it's there."[413]

30 Distribution of Mesolithic art in the Spanish Levant (*after Bandi, 1961*)

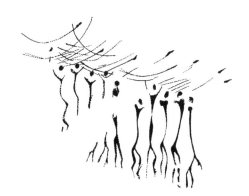

31 "Scene of execution" from Remigia cave; painted in red and black (after Sandars, 1968)

In contrast to Magdalenian art, Levantine painting is dominated by human rather than animal figures, and a narrative quality rarely found in the Magdalenian period. If the archetypal animals at Lascaux may be said to suggest nonhistorical concepts of time,[354] the new Spanish art is distinctly grounded in the incidental and the transitory. There are women clapping and dancing, men shooting deer and gathering honey, and above all, warriors armed with bows and arrows in every imaginable attitude of the fray.

Diversely drawn warriors hasten to battle, exchange arrows (figs. 32 and 33), participate in several scenes of execution—"the first pages of a penal code."[319] (Figure 31 is one of a number of portrayals of a group of archers waving their bows aloft, while a more distant figure lies pierced with arrows.) Both simple and composite bows are depicted in these battle scenes, and variations in arrow tips and feathering have been noted.[262] Most of

32 Detail of battle scene from "Les Dogues" rock shelter, Spain; painted in red (after Maringer and Bandi, 1953)

33 Detail of warriors painted in black from Civil, Valltorta Gorge *(after Sandars, 1968)*

the figures are quite small; those of larger size are believed to represent leaders in battle or other important personages. At Saltadora, for example, a large warrior is shown falling forward as his elaborate headpiece, evidently a symbol of authority, falls from his head (fig. 35). The headdress of others includes horns, animal masks, and feathered headbands; numerous body ornaments and suggestions of body painting have been detected as well.[354] Fringed waistbands are common (fig. 34); animal skins are occasionally shown around the waist with tails hanging down; and while some of the warriors appear to be wearing "knee-breeches" or loincloths, others wear nothing at all.[262]

Who these Spanish bowmen might have been, and to which culture these battle paintings belonged, remain a mystery. Their closest counterparts, surprisingly enough, are to be found a continent away in the rock shelters of Kobystan, just off the western shore of the Caspian Sea in the region known today as Transcaucasia. Again without known precedents, the first series of Kobystani engravings has been estimated by the excavator

34 Archer with chest ornaments and fringed waistband, Mas d'en Josep *(after Maringer and Bandi, 1953)*

35 Warrior stricken by arrows, Saltadora cave; painted in light red *(after Maringer and Bandi, 1953)*

The War of 8500 B.C.   59

map at figure 62

to "the early Mesolithic age at the latest,"[135] which should mean no later than the ninth millennium B.C. The earliest compositions portray groups of male figures up to five feet high, whose trunks and thick legs have been deeply hollowed out of the limestone surface (fig. 36). Some of the men carry curved objects believed to be bows; often one or more lines seem to cross the shoulders at an angle. They appear to be wearing the same sort of fringed waistband shown above on the Spanish warrior at figure 34, and again a long tail was reported attached to one of these Kobystani girdles. Deeply engraved figures of bulls are also present in this first series at Kobystan; their outlines have been stylistically compared to those of the bulls in Late Paleolithic western art.

36 Deeply engraved figures of men and bulls from the first series of rock art at Kobystan, west of the Caspian Sea (after Formozov, 1963)

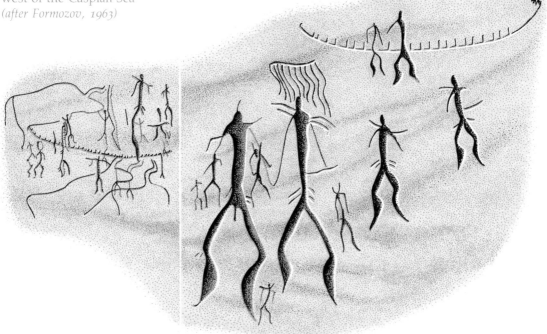

A second, presumably somewhat later phase at Kobystan included at least one composition that is believed to be a battle scene[280] (fig. 37). Here the bowmen are much smaller and the engravings only lightly incised, but the depiction of linked dancers in both the first and second phases of this Transcaucasian collection has convinced the excavator that the two series were genetically connected.[135]

The identity of the artists is in any case unknown, and the absence of recorded precedents in Transcaucasia to the already mastered technique of the first series argues against an autochthonous origin. The many parallels to the far-distant paintings of warriors in the Spanish Levant have gone unexplained, but if the estimated range of dates for both of these collections is correct, neither could have been altogether remote in time from the war described in the *Timaeus*. As that conflict was said to have involved all those living inside the Straits, its force may well have carried a kindred artistic style, if not the war itself, to the edge of the Caspian Sea.

It is also possible that one or both of these collections were actually commemorative art. The Egyptian priest claimed that the memory of the great war had been erased by time and circumstance long before Solon's day, but such an encompassing event must have been recalled for many generations around the postwar Mediterranean. The battle scenes of the Spanish Levant have in fact been seen by one analyst as commemorations of times past. Pericot Garcia has suggested that the Spanish artists were trying to evoke the memory of heroic warriors whose earlier successes in battle had been preserved in the oral tradition, and that "more emphatically in each progressive phase we find a commemorative aspect."[319]

We shall also find the warrior glorified, although by very different means, in Palestine and Syria, following unmistakable signs of hostilities in those lands in the last half of the ninth millennium B.C.

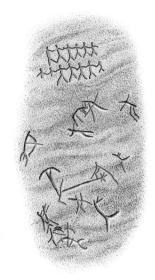

37 Kobystan, second series. Representations of dancers and a battle scene (*after Formozov, 1969*)

The War in the East

38 Near Eastern tanged,
notched, and tanged-and-
notched points, c. 8500
B.C.: (a) arrowheads from
El-Khiam, (b) Helwan
point, (c) Harifian points
(after Perrot, 1952; Prausnitz, 1970; Marks, 1973)

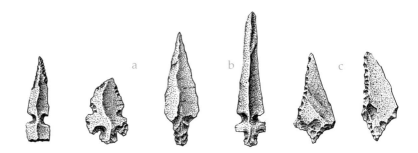

Tanged and Notched Points, Harifian Points, Jericho

map at figure 19

We earlier noted the desertion of most or all of the original
Natufian settlements of Palestine in the first half of the ninth
millennium and the subsequent appearance of tanged, notched,
or tanged-and-notched arrowheads in the few remaining or
reoccupied sites (fig. 38a). In Syria the Natufian-related settlement at Abu Hureyra was also abandoned midway in the ninth
millennium,[290] and a new site, soon to be stocked with several
types of arrowhead, was established at Mureybet on the Syrian
Euphrates.[68] The tanged-and-notched points at Helwan in Lower
Egypt (fig. 38b) have also been assigned to this period,[334] and
in the Negev desert this same mid-to-late ninth millennium
epoch saw the introduction of Harifian points (fig. 38c), arrowheads fashioned with either a pinched little tang or a triangular
base.[263]

Jericho's massive stone wall and tower are believed to have
been raised c. 8300 B.C. (fig. 39), presenting one of the biggest
puzzles in Near Eastern archæology. Investigators have reached
little agreement on the reason for these apparently defensive
structures, but as one prehistorian noted, whatever their ultimate purpose the tower and wall would seem to be proof of
the presence in the surrounding country of "potentially hostile
people, without whom the necessity to build these defences

would scarcely have arisen."[54] The expert design of Jericho's fortifications was cited earlier to demonstrate the need for presuming ancestral wall builders elsewhere in the pre-ninth-millennium Mediterranean. But while these may indeed have been Athenian, as suggested there, the possibility that Jericho's architects were Atlantic should also be considered. It is true that the Ur-Athenians had surrounded their Acropolis with a wall, and the Gravettian-type round houses within Jericho's walls do suggest a northern alliance. But the Atlantics were also wall builders. The ring islands and canals that encircled the temple of Poseidon were enclosed by "a stone wall all round, with towers and gates guarding the bridges on either side where they crossed the water" (*Critias* 115 – 16). Moreover, the Atlantics had hollowed out a great ditch around their most fertile plain to irrigate the summer planting (*Critias* 118), and at Jericho later in this period a huge ditch was hewn out of the natural limestone bedrock outside the wall — nine feet deep, twenty-seven feet wide, and possibly half a mile around — in the words of one observer, "a considerable feat in the absence of metal tools."[54] It may also be significant that the number of arrowheads found in this walled phase at Jericho was very small. One analyst has even suggested that these rare tanged-and-notched points may actually have been those of the invaders against whom Jericho was fortified.[89]

see pages 45 – 46

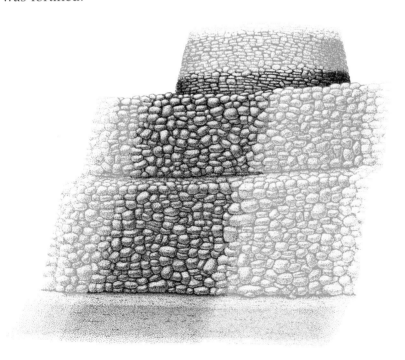

39 Artist's reconstruction of Jericho's tower and a section of the stone wall (*after Kenyon, 1957, 1960*)

The War of 8500 B.C.   63

The Destruction of Mureybet III

The allegiance of Mureybet, the most important Syrian site of this epoch, may be no less ambiguous. The strategic value of the settlement might have been enhanced by its location near what was later known as a traditional crossing point on the Euphrates river; but regardless of how one interprets its turbulent history, the importance of Mureybet, not only to Plato's narrative but to our general understanding of the sources of Neolithic culture, cannot be overestimated.

The first settlement at Mureybet was apparently burned around 8500 B.C. When rebuilt, tanged, notched, and tanged-and-notched points were added to the Natufian-related assemblage (fig. 40). After several strata of round houses (Phase II) comparable to those of Ain Mallaha and Jericho, Mureybet's tenth building level revealed the earliest permanent rectangular structures of record, marking the beginning of Phase III.[246] The two separate excavations at this site have not yet been fully integrated, but Cauvin's more recent work[66, 68] has uncovered a dazzling array of innovations that appear to date to the period in which Van Loon found rectangular architecture. These include: (1) the first documented ceramic receptacles (possibly ritual vessels, as their very small size precludes cooking or storage), (2) the earliest recorded wall paintings (one showing black chevrons on a white base), (3) a shift from gazelle-dominated faunal remains to a greater emphasis on cattle and wild ass (a change evidently prompted by cultural preference alone and accompanied by a notable decline in fish), and (4) the first clay female figurine known to the Near East (fig. 41), standing with arms under relatively small breasts in the classic pose assumed by numerous later likenesses around the eastern Mediterranean.[68]

The absence of recorded precedents elsewhere led Cauvin to propose an indigenous origin for Mureybet's new traditions. There are indeed signs of continuity with earlier levels: round houses apparently coexisted alongside the rectangular structures; projectile points continued to be present (fig. 42), although these did show an increase in both size and number in this third phase, and certain types of other tools persisted. But given the extraordinary quantity, quality, and apparent near-simultaneity of the innovations named above, some degree of external influence seems assured. Jericho's roughly contemporary wall and tower were also without known precedents, but few would pronounce them native inventions even though a continuity of

40 Arrowheads from Mureybet Ib, c. 8400 B.C. *(after Cauvin, 1979)*

41 Clay female figurine from Mureybet III. Height, two and one-half inches *(after Cauvin, 1978)*

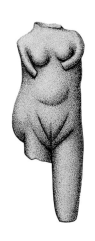

other traditions seems to have been recorded there as well. Furthermore, a new community of unknown origin, Tell Aswad I, was founded in the Damascus basin around 8000 B.C. (the approximate beginning of Mureybet's innovative third phase) without permanent architecture but displaying almost identical large projectile points.[70]

map at figure 68

Wherever they originated, Mureybet's new traditions seem to have brought trouble to the site. In Van Loon's excavation, Phase III ended with two disastrous fires following closely on one another. The next to last stratum was described as only about a foot deep, with evidence of having been "burned fiercely" in every part of the mound where it was encountered. Noting that the following level had experienced the same fate, Van Loon concluded that "the wholesale destruction in this and the next stratum suggests enemy action."[246]

Who was the enemy? There seems little doubt that the action at Mureybet was connected to the over-all pattern of hostilities (defense fortifications, numerous and varied types of projectile point) that characterized the Near East in this epoch. If these Near Eastern events were in turn related to the war described in the *Timaeus*, Mureybet's enemy theoretically could have been either Atlantic or Greek. For example, if the introduction of rectangular architecture and the other innovations marked an Atlantic intrusion into Asia, the destruction of Mureybet III might have signaled the triumph of the eastern alliance over the incoming adversary. But if, on the other hand, the new architecture, ceramics, wall paintings, maiden figurines, etc., announced the arrival of Greek peoples with a grander cultural assemblage than that of their Syrian allies, the twice-over burning of Mureybet may have been among the reverses suffered by the Athenians en route to final victory (*Timaeus* 25), or, given the relatively late carbon-14 dates for these rectangular-house levels (c. 8000–7700 B.C.), possibly postwar skirmishing.

Whatever the relationship of Mureybet's misfortunes to Plato's war (and the question will be raised again later in discussing the mythic correlates to that war), if the hostilities here and elsewhere around the Epi-Paleolithic Old World were in fact a record of the conflict described in the *Timaeus*, it was now over. Jericho's walled town was abandoned around 7600 B.C. (the tower had long since been blocked up); Harifian points were gone from the Negev by around 8000 B.C. In North Africa the Iberomaurusian culture also began breaking up at the beginning of the eighth millennium, to be replaced by Proto-Mediterranean peoples of unknown, apparently eastern, origin.[370] Europe's

42 Projectile points from Mureybet III, early eighth millennium B.C. *(after Cauvin, 1979)*

The War of 8500 B.C.   65

original tanged point complex began to disperse around 8000 B.C. as well;[224] most of the continent would remain at a Mesolithic stage of hunter-gatherer-fisher culture for the next several thousand years.

In the Near East, settlement activity almost ceased after the abandonment of Jericho, but not for long. The Neolithic Revolution was to take a sudden leap forward in the last half of the eighth millennium B.C.

Deluge and Survivors?

"What happened," asked John Wymer at the close of his 1982 text on the Paleolithic Age, "between 8000 and 6000 B.C. to create a completely new economy [the Neolithic way of life] and eventually destroy almost all trace of the old hunting societies?"[437] However one might reword it, this is perhaps the most important question in archaeology today.

Plato does not say how many years or possibly centuries may have passed after the end of the war before the "greatest of all destructions by water" (*Timaeus* 23) removed both former antagonists from the scene. All we are told is that the floods and earthquakes came "at a later time" (*Timaeus* 25). The archaeology of the northeast Mediterranean, however scant, suggests that the most likely time for such a cataclysmic event, if it did occur, would have been around the middle of the eighth millennium B.C. Franchthi Cave, the only Greek site known to this period, shows a stratigraphical confusion, and the excavator concluded that Franchthi may have been temporarily abandoned before a reoccupation in the last half of the eighth millennium.[199] (That the reoccupied cave was now somewhat closer to the coast was suggested to analysts by the numerous remains of the marine species *Cyclope neritea* which appeared in these new levels at Franchthi.)[362] At the Beldibi cave site in southern Anatolia, Bostanci noted a "pluvial period," a densely packed sterile layer extremely high in iron oxide from the washing action of heavy rains, immediately preceding a reoccupation of the cave in the late eighth or early seventh millennium (Phase B at Beldibi).[36]

map at figure 19

To the east, less severe signs of flooding have been recorded at both Mureybet and Jericho in the middle of the eighth millennium. The Euphrates river seems to have reached flood tide, with riverine species in Mureybet's pollen diagram indicating to Cauvin the undoubtedly high course of the waters at this time.[68] At Jericho, Kenyon found that the upper levels of the previously abandoned town had been deeply cut by a stream bed which left deposits of silt and gravel over part of the settlement. Noting the certain insufficiency of rainfall in Jericho's normal winter season to accomplish a cut of that depth, she concluded that the rushing stream must have been created by atypical "storm water."[209]

But perhaps the most compelling argument for dating Plato's deluge to the mid-eighth millennium is simply the number and nature of the newly founded settlements that appeared in the east around 75/7300 B.C. From Syria and Palestine to east Anatolia and the Zagros mountains, extraordinarily advanced communities emerged, seemingly out of nowhere. An inventory of their collective remains shows that virtually all of the elements upon which the civilizations of later ages would be based—complex hybrid grains, advanced architectural techniques, functional pottery, even the beginnings of metal work—were introduced almost simultaneously by this wave of new settlers.

Rectangular architecture was everywhere in evidence, but at no two sites were the buildings, or their contents, identical. For example, a honeycombed architectural complex using very long, plano-convex, mud bricks at the Iranian Zagros community of Ganj Dareh D housed an extensive pottery collection that was map at figure 68 elsewhere unknown.[368] The huge new settlement at Tell Abu Hureyra in Syria yielded a wealth of new plant domesticates in a setting of substantial mud-brick buildings with occasional black-plastered floors.[288] A new occupation of Jericho brought the fine red-plastered and polished floors that were to become a hallmark of seventh millennium sites throughout Palestine and Anatolia; here the red floors were found within stereotyped rectangular buildings made of cigar-shaped bricks.[210] Frequently associated with the "red-plastered-floor people" of this epoch were well-developed traditions of ancestor worship and elaborate weaponry, the earlier mentioned counterparts, perhaps, to the commemoration of ancestral warriors in the paintings of the Spanish Levant.

The details of this new era will be more fully explored in Part III, but one more of its vanguard settlements deserves special mention here. The east Anatolian community of Çayönü was also founded c. 75/7300 B.C., and revealed not only the earliest known copper items (a drill, straight pins, ovoid beads) but a settlement plan which far exceeded the expectations of the excavators for so early a site.[59] At least four different architectural designs included such unprecedented features as the use of internal buttresses, *farisi*-style entrances usually associated with later Aegean architecture, and a "brilliantly executed"[337] terrazzo floor which had been ground smooth and polished to set off parallel strips of white pebbles against a background of salmon pink stones.

In the words of the excavators, "The evolved comprehension of the art of building, which the Çayönü evidence yields, is truly remarkable. We ask ourselves, where are its forerunners?"[45] If the deluge of the *Timaeus* did indeed occur midway through the eighth millennium, the forerunners of Çayönü's architectural achievements and the other innovations of this time may lie, or may once have lain, to the west. Plato makes no mention of refugees from his inundated Greek nations, but no more logical source has yet been found for the unexpectedly skilled peoples who transformed the Near East in the last half of the eighth millennium B.C.

Summary: Sequence, Space, and Time

These were the major archaeological events from 10,000 to 7000 B.C. within the Straits of Gibraltar. It seems fair to say that, set beside Plato's tale, their sequence and spatial distribution mirror his account to an often astonishing degree of accuracy. Direct contradictions are rare, if one accepts the sparseness of remains in Greece as no less than would be expected from the Egyptian priest's description of the bone-deep devastation of the land (with or without the effects of the rising seas). Exaggeration also seems negligible, if we stay inside the Straits. But again, this is not to say that the priest's tale should be read verbatim as history, or that my own interpretation of the archaeology of this period relative to Plato's account is always, or even most often, the correct one. Without a more precise system of dating, the relationship of many of these events to the sequence sketched in the *Timaeus* and *Critias* must remain ambiguous, but this does not mean that they, or the remarkable correspondence over-all, can be ignored.

To summarize what has been presented so far, and leaving aside for the moment the problems associated with correcting carbon-14 dates:

"9,000 years ago" from the vantage point of the Egyptian priest, 9600 B.C. from ours, a divinely sired Atlantic race that wrote laws, raced horses, and controlled populations inside the Straits as far as Italy and Egypt, had succumbed to an all-too-human hunger for power that would eventually lead them to attack the peoples of Europe and Asia.

"9,000 years ago" in the archaeological record of western Europe (9600 B.C. in uncorrected radiocarbon years), a uniquely gifted Magdalenian culture which for several thousand years had graced Europe as far as Italy with an artistic tradition of uncommon excellence and unity, a devotion to the horse (which they apparently had harnessed), and possibly a system of written communication, was showing the first signs of decay. Magdalenian influence seems to have reached across much of Europe by this time; in the west their expanding population had already begun to show a greater interest in weaponry than art, a trend that would hold until the culture itself was dissolved into or replaced by groups who specialized in curved-back, and then tanged, points.

On the other side of the Straits, North Africa was occupied by a very different and far poorer culture than the Magdalenian, but the temporal and geographical limits of these Iberomaurusian assemblages were still remarkably faithful to those set by the priest for Atlantic domination. Africa was not among the lands mentioned in the priest's description of the war, and in fact, Iberomaurusian culture seems to have remained relatively stable until the unrest elsewhere around the Mediterranean was almost at an end.

"9,000 years ago" in the eastern Mediterranean (again, 9600 B.C. in uncorrected carbon-14 years), peoples of extraordinary artistic and technological expertise had already begun settling Palestine, for reasons as unknown as their origins. Some of these early Natufian sites yielded elements associated with the far west, but communities like the village at Ain Mallaha showed a stronger connection to central and east European (Gravettian) settlements of a much greater age. The abnormal scarcity of recorded Epi-Paleolithic sites on the Balkan peninsula led to the suggestion that those Natufians with apparent ties to an unknown advanced Gravettian tradition might have come from southeast European cultures of which we have no trace, perhaps from Plato's "Greek nations" themselves, which were later to be swept away in the floods. And in light of the violence manifested in Late or Epi-Paleolithic Ukrainian and Nilotic cemeteries, we further suggested that the Near East offered safe harbor at this time to peoples from several different localities who may have been displaced or disaffected by prewar Atlantic advances.

A thousand years later (c. 8500 B.C.), northern Europe and the east Mediterranean Levant were both awash in arrowheads, various types of tanged points which seem to be more plausibly linked to warfare than to the chase. The fortifications at Jericho, monumental works of unknown but not inexperienced architects, date to the same period. Battle paintings in the Spanish Levant and engravings of warriors at Kobystan also appear to belong to this general time frame, or, if later, may have been commemorative works of art.

The walled town at Jericho was later abandoned, apparently without incident (although contemporary Mureybet III was twice burned), and there is evidence of heavy rainfall here and at other northeast Mediterranean sites midway in the eighth millenium B.C. Shortly thereafter the Near East was enlivened by diverse groups of settlers whose "Neolithic achievements" show clear signs of having been developed elsewhere, although forerunners are not to be found in the archaeological record. As we shall see in Part III, at least one of these new communities fits Critias' description of ancient Athenian traditions well enough to suggest that the Neolithic Near East was in part a legacy of Plato's vanished Greek cultures.

If Plato's tale may be said to score high in terms of sequence and space, the element of time may be more contrary. From the first outward signs of Magdalenian decline around 9500 B.C. to the theorized 75/7300 B.C. date of the deluge seems a very long time for the historical enactment of Plato's brief narrative. If we break it down, however, it is not inconceivable that a millennium of growing antagonism between east and west should have preceded what appears to be an outbreak of war around 8500 B.C. But if the war itself lasted until the final destruction of Mureybet III, dated to around 7700 B.C., we are talking in terms of some 800 years of armed conflict.

It is possible, however, that the war officially ended around 8000 B.C., when both the Tanged Point Technocomplex of Europe and the Iberomaurusian culture of North Africa began breaking up. In this case, the burning of Mureybet's final levels may have represented either residual hostilities or an extended Near Eastern campaign. We would still have a 500-year war, c. 8500–8000 B.C., but considering the claim in the *Critias* of the long line of ancestral Greek names mentioned in the narrative,* and the apparently uneven course of the Athenian victory (*Timaeus* 25), such a span may not be altogether unreasonable.

---

* Critias stated that "Cecrops, Erechtheus, Erichthonios, Erusichthon and most of the other names recorded before Theseus, occurred, according to Solon, in the narrative of the priests about this war" (*Critias* 110). These names were then said to have been given to the descendants of survivors of the deluge, and thereby preserved long after the achievements of the earlier generation had been forgotten. As we shall see in Part II, the first three names were associated with autochthonous Athenian ancestors in popular Greek myth.

We might also expect some leeway from the notorious vagaries of carbon-14 dates, and from the still unknown path of the curve for correcting or calibrating radiocarbon dates that are earlier than 5000 B.C. If the calibration curve turns out to be regular, the intervals of time between existing carbon-14 dates would remain unchanged, and all dates of Late or Epi-Paleolithic age would uniformly receive an additional 600 to 1,000 years or more to accord with calendar time. But a recent summary of this question suggests that an irregular curve is also possible see Appendix B for the correction of dates earlier than 7000 B.C., in which case a point by point calibration would be required for carbon-14 dates in the period which concerns us here.[126] What this means to the present study is that not only the radiocarbon dates but also the intervals between those dates could be inaccurate representations of real time.

The Problem of Atlantis

If the archaeological correspondence to Plato's tale seems promising inside the Straits, the reverse is certainly true outside. Although several events in west European archaeology might seem to make more sense with an Atlantis "out there" (e.g., the distribution of the Magdalenian cave sanctuaries and the inexplicable grandeur, uniformity, and conservatism of their artistic canon), the ocean floor has yet to produce any sign of a huge sunken continent opposite the Straits of Gibraltar. Moreover, we are now assured that the mid-Atlantic ridge, long a favorite candidate of Atlantis-seekers, is actually rising rather than sinking, a volcanic phenomenon in process. Its elevated portions, such as the Azores plateau, are said to be the result of greater buoyancy of newly extruded volcanic material, rather than the remnants of sunken continental land areas.[177]

Another likely prospect was Rockall Bank, a broad submarine feature lying midway between Ireland and Iceland which has recently been discovered to have once been continental dry land.[383] Its geographical position would fit particularly well with the idea of an attack on Europe from the northwest, as might be suggested by the concentration of tanged points in that quarter. But as core samples from Rockall Bank are said to show three main periods of sinking — 55, 40, and 15 million years ago — its candidacy as Plato's Upper Paleolithic Atlantic continent must also be withdrawn.

We would seem to be left with only two alternatives: (1) to presume exaggeration on the part of one of the transmitters of the tale and situate a vastly shrunken Atlantis somewhere other than the Atlantic ocean, as the Thera proponents and a great many others have done in the past,[377] or (2) to presume outright invention and discard the idea of an historical Atlantis altogether, also a well-worn path. Unfortunately, either of these traditional approaches will allow the question of Atlantis to continue to obscure the main themes of Plato's account: the war and the ancient Athenian society. The so-called Atlantis controversy already ranks as one of the most unproductive arguments of our time, largely based even now on belief and disbelief, both of which have led to some unforgiveable overstatements of what is a minimum of scientific fact. Rather than participate, I would offer a third choice: to ignore the question of Atlantis for the present. There is more than enough to be done in testing the hypothesis that Plato's account of Mediterranean prehistory, prehistory inside the Straits, is basically accurate. If such an hypothesis should prove fruitful in light of what we do know, it can then be used to define and explore what we don't.

But to withhold judgement on Atlantis, or to leave room for exaggeration, is not to disregard all aspects of Plato's tale that seem impossible from our present point of view. It may be a change in our perception of what is, or was, possible that is wanted here. At the very least our perceptual field must be widened. To see what Plato or the Egyptian priest saw requires looking at the Mediterranean as a whole, rather than as the sum of the isolated regional divisions that specialization has tended to create. Tanged points, for example, are not in themselves necessarily indicative of all-out warfare, and the Tanged Point Technocomplex of Epi-Paleolithic northern Europe will probably continue to be dismissed as an economic adaptation until set beside its Near Eastern counterpart, and both placed within the general context of violent death, site abandonment, defense fortifications, and battle paintings that seems to characterize this epoch of Mediterranean prehistory.

If such a pan-Mediterranean perspective were achieved, the specialists would truly come into their own. Fitting together all of the pieces of this immensely complicated puzzle, for which Plato provides only a minimum of guidance, would require the special knowledge of not only archaeologists in all fields of expertise, but also anthropologists, paleoclimatologists, historians of religion and art, classical scholars and (as we shall see in the following section) mythographers — all those whose work touches on the early world. It would be a tremendous under-taking, but the developing of a more realistic framework of thought is obviously its own reward. Furthermore, if there is any truth at all to Plato's tale, as the evidence presented here certainly suggests, we might ask with Socrates: "Where shall we find an alternative if we abandon it?" (*Timaeus* 26)

II

Parallels to
Plato's Tale in Myth

43 Athena and Poseidon; detail from a black-figured vase of the sixth century B.C., painted by the Athenian artist Amasis (whose signature appears between the two figures). Athena holds a spear and, in a gesture that some see as menacing, raises her left hand against Poseidon, characteristically pictured with his trident. This scene has often been compared to descriptions in Greek myth and art of a dispute between Athena and Poseidon over possession of Attica. *(after Lenormant, 1844)*

Popular Greek Mythology

If parallels to Plato's tale are to be found in the archaeological record, might they not also be present in the literary record—the myths and legends—of the peoples most directly involved? Of the Greeks, for example, it was said in the *Timaeus* (23) that Solon's contemporaries knew nothing of the events 9,000 years earlier, and indeed the story the priest told is not repeated in popular Greek mythology as we know it. But that same mythic corpus is rich in challenges to the order of Zeus—by Titans, Giants, the monstrous Typhon—one or more of which could conceivably represent a time-blurred memory of the *Timaeus* war. Tales of an old enmity between Athena and Poseidon, gods of Plato's Greek and Atlantic combatants, may also owe something to the conflict described by the priest. The age of these stories is in each case unknown, but there is little doubt that each was part of an oral tradition long before being recorded by the poets of antiquity.[212]

We shall briefly explore these mythic contests, but before doing so, some of the problems with Greek mythology as a whole should be acknowledged. One of these has to do with the growing tendency among classical scholars to credit many of the myths with some degree of historical accuracy. As expressed by one author:

> The epic poets and mythographers embroidered and slanted much of their material, misunderstood more, and got a great deal plain wrong; but as often as not there turns out to be a solid substratum of fact underlying their fancies.[165]

But if some part of Greek myth does record actual happenings, one must ask not only which part, but also which version of that part. There are no standard models in Greek mythology; nor is there any assurance that the earliest known versions of the myths are necessarily more authentic than those recorded at a later time. A late-appearing myth may well have been taken from earlier literature that is now lost, or from the oral tradition, which was still very much alive throughout antiquity.[132] We know only that the existing sources (a few complete narratives, a great many literary allusions, and numerous illustrations of myths in vase paintings, sculpture, coins, etc.) can vary widely in describing the same event. Even the works of Homer and Hesiod, the earliest literary recordings of Greek mythology, often differ where they meet.

There are several possible explanations for this lack of consensus, the most obvious being simply the great age of many myths. Another is probably the slanting, embroidering, and misunderstanding of which the poets are accused in the quotation above. A third would be the different traditions from which the myths originally sprang, Greek (Indo-European) or pre-Greek, about which more will be said later.

Yet another source of mythic confusion may be the alleged tendency among the Greeks to attribute the deeds of an earlier hero or god to a later one of the same name. Forty-three heroes of the name Herakles are said to have been enumerated by Varro;[132] Cicero (*Nat. Deor.* III.16) and Diodorus Siculus (III.74) each counted several; but popular Greek tradition knew only one, the great Theban hero to whom it referred all deeds associated with the name of Herakles. Of the gods, three Dionysoi were said to have been hymned at Eleusis: first Zagreus, son of Persephone, then Bromios, son of Semele, and lastly Iacchos, the Eleusinian Dionysos (Nonnus XLVIII.958–68); but Greek mythology generally makes no distinction among them. The same is true of Apollo. Five different gods of that name were identified by Clement of Alexandria and Ampelius, drawing on a common source which is believed to have been Aristotle,[132] but all were one Apollo to most Greeks.

Another, more subtle cause of ambiguity in myth is the inevitable entanglement of abstract with concrete material. Myths may be metaphysical, historical, cosmological, mystical—the greatest probably include all of these dimensions. In Egypt, for example, Osiris was not only an historical figure (culture hero and one time king of Egypt) and the Lord of the Dead; he was also the "neter" of Nature, representing the cycles of death and rebirth to which the Egyptians believed all nature was subject and which are most clearly illustrated in the seed-plant-seed cycle of vegetation. The enmity between the historical Osiris and his brother Set is mirrored in the natural world in the struggles between Osiris as the orderly process of nature and Set, the demon of disorder (drought, flood, etc.). These two levels of conflict became confused even in the well-ordered theology of the Egyptians. We can expect no less from the Greeks.

Battles with demons or dragons are further open to interpretation as examples of the mystical dimension of myth. Some historians of religion see all such conflicts, which are known throughout the ancient world, as initiatory ordeals, with the dragon representing the animal nature of the hero himself that must be mastered in the process of self-transcendence. To others, however, the details of many of these dragon battles have suggested a record of actual warfare.[132] It seems certain in any case that while abstract themes were being historicized, the opposite process was also at work. Often, as Eliade remarked, "the real adversaries of the nation or the empire are imagined as monsters, and especially as dragons."[119]

One further thought should be kept in mind as we review some of the likelier correlates to the priest's tale in Greek mythology. Most if not all of these old stories were accessible to Plato himself. If the *Timaeus* and *Critias* account was indeed the child of Plato's fancy, the following myths may only reveal the sources of his inspiration.

Zeus Against the Titans, the Giants, and Typhon

Of the three mythic challenges to the authority of Zeus, the first was that of the Titans, the old gods whom Zeus and his brethren were to replace. As told by Hesiod in the *Theogony*, before Zeus came to power the sovereignty of the earth belonged to Kronos, who had wrested the throne from his father Ouranos by castrating him with a flint sickle. Kronos married Rhea, his sister Titan, but having been warned that he would himself eventually be overcome by one of his own children, he swallowed each of them as they were born: Hestia, Demeter, Hera, Hades, and Poseidon. Rhea then bore Zeus secretly in Crete and hid him in the Dictaean Cave. (The legendary Cretan armed priests, the Kouretes, are said to have performed a noisy dance at the birth of Zeus, with much clashing of arms to drown the cries of the babe from the ears of his father [Callimachus *Hymn I.* 51–53].)

Wrapping a stone in swaddling clothes, Rhea gave it to Kronos, who swallowed it thinking it was the newborn child. When Zeus grew to manhood, he tricked Kronos into disgorging both the stone and his elder brothers and sisters, then led his generation of gods in a war against the Titans (who in some versions were led by Atlas). The younger gods were victorious; the Titans were banished to a place at the end of the earth that was encircled by a wall whose bronze gates had been fixed by Poseidon (or, some say, to remote islands in the farthest west). Zeus assumed the throne in heaven; his brothers Hades and Poseidon are said elsewhere to have taken charge of the underworld and the sea, respectively. According to some sources, Zeus later freed the Titans and reconciled their differences.

Although certain elements in the Titanomachy do recall the details of Plato's tale (e.g., the leadership of Atlas, the locating of the Titans' place of confinement in the farthest west, Poseidon's contribution to its construction), the Atlantic kings of the *Timaeus* could not have been Titans if they were the sons of Poseidon, one of the new generation of gods. Moreover, Zeus seems to have been fully empowered at the start of Plato's narrative. If his battle for supremacy against the Titans did have an historical counterpart, it must presumably be sought in an earlier period of prehistory than the time specified for the war of the *Timaeus* and *Critias*.

More promising than the Titan challenge, though frequently confused with it,[270] is the assault of the Giants, "monstrous and huge births" brought forth by Earth to do battle with the new race of gods. The Giants were invulnerable to the weapons of the gods and could only be killed by one who was both god and mortal. Herakles, son of Zeus, was summoned forthwith; whenever a god wounded a Giant with an arrow, Herakles had to deal the death blow. After a desperate fight, the Giants were at last defeated. Some of their number are said to be buried under islands; the Giant Enkelados supposedly lies under Sicily, which Athena threw at him.

Here we have Zeus not only enthroned from the start, but many of his offspring—Dionysos, Apollo, and most prominently in several versions, Athena—fighting on his side. The leading role taken by the founding goddess of Ur-Athens in the battle with the Giants would add to the compatibility of that contest and Plato's war, as would the location, or rather locations, of the Gigantomachy. "Phlegra," which is named by some as the birthplace of the Giants as well as their battleground, has been variously sited from Spain to the Isthmus of Thrace. (See Apollodorus I.6.i, footnote 3 of the Frazer translation.)[140] The earthborn but more than human nature of the Giants also agrees with the unfortunate mixture of human and divine stock which characterized Plato's fallen Atlantic race.*

Particularly reminiscent of the *Timaeus* account is the assault of the twin Aloadai on Olympus, generally considered to be another aspect of the Giants' revolt. (The name of Ephialtes, one of the Aloadai, also appears among the names of the Giants.) Twin sons of Poseidon, the Aloadai are described in the *Odyssey* (XI.305ff.) as follows:

> Tallest they were of all that the fertile earth nurtured, and goodliest by far, next to the famous Orion; nine years old were they, and nine cubits was their breadth, but in height they were nine fathom. And they twain threatened to arouse the din of furious battle even against the gods in Olympus . . . but the son of Zeus, whom Leto Fairlocks brought forth [Apollo], destroyed them both.

Scholars have found it curious that some of the oldest traditions represent the Aloadai as beneficent beings, founders of cities and originators of the cult of the Muses. As one remarked: "Here we have no rebels against Heaven nor upsetters of the established order of the Universe, but rather some kind of culture-heroes or gods."[349] We are reminded of the earlier greatness and later temerity of Plato's Atlantic kings. They too had been sets of twins, sons of Poseidon, and the benefactors of lands beyond their own before challenging the order of Zeus.

But it is mainly through its association with the battle waged by Zeus against Typhon in the Near East that the Gigantomachy becomes plausible as a repository for memories of the Atlantic assault on Europe. Typhon (Typhoeus) has been linked with Porphyrion, the king of the Giants, and in some accounts it is said that the earth bore Typhon in vengeance for the defeat of the Giants. In most versions of the assault, Zeus has no difficulty overcoming the monster, using his lightning bolts to set Typhon on fire and render him helpless (fig. 44). But a more complex story, believed to derive from an earlier source,[132] was recorded by Apollodorus (I.6.ii–iii).

---

* This theme has also been compared to the Hebraic remembrance of a time when "there were giants in the earth . . . and also after that, when the sons of God came in unto the daughters of men, and they bare children to them, the same became mighty men which were of old, men of renown" (Genesis 6:4). Here the mixing of godly and human races appears to have led to the depravity and violence which were said to have been the cause of the Biblical deluge.

As he told it, Zeus initially put Typhon to flight with thunderbolts and a sweep of his adamantine sickle, but the monster
stopped and faced the god again at Mount Kasios on the north
Syrian border. As they grappled, Typhon wrenched the sickle
from Zeus, cut the sinews of the god's hands and feet, and
carried him across the sea to the Corycian Cave in Cilicia (the
southeastern coast of Anatolia). Recovering his sinews, and
taking up his thunderbolts, Zeus pursued Typhon first to Nysa
and thence to Thrace, where the monster made another stand
and heaved mountains heavenward. Zeus finally cast Mount
Etna upon Typhon as he fled across the Sicilian Sea and buried
him (as Athena had similarly buried the Giant Enkelados under
Sicily).

Typhon was known to Homer as well as Hesiod, but many
classicists assign a Near Eastern origin to the myth on the basis
of both geography and comparative mythology. The Hittites of
Anatolia, who had absorbed a great many of the traditions of
their Hurrian predecessors, knew the story of a stone giant
named Ullikummi who, supported on the shoulders of Ubelluri
(the Hurrian counterpart of the Greek Atlas), threatened to
destroy all mankind. Teshub, who is generally identified with
Zeus, went to the seaside and attacked the giant but was
defeated. It appeared that nothing would stop Ullikummi until
Ea, the god of Wisdom, suggested using the knife that had
originally severed Heaven from Earth to cut off the monster's
feet and send him crashing into the sea.[97] (Similarly, the sickle
used by Zeus against Typhon supposedly served earlier to cas-
trate Ouranos, who was also identified with Heaven, his wife
Ge with Earth.)[164]

Anatolia was not the only land named in the Greek Typhon myth that remembered similar events. On the northern coast of Syria, the mythology of ancient Ugarit (modern Ras Shamra) tells of an aquatic dragon known as Yam or "Prince Sea" who was accused by his younger brother, the Zeus-like Baal, of presumptuous accession to sovereignty among the gods. To confront Yam, Baal was given a pair of magic bludgeons made by the divine blacksmith, Koshar-wa-Hasis (just as Zeus confronted Typhon with thunderstones made by Hephaistos, also a divine smith). The first missed its mark; the second struck Yam, who sank to the ground. Baal assumed the throne of heaven and earth, while Yam continued to reign over the sea, and a third brother, Mot, remained lord of the subterranean world of the dead — an unmistakable analogue to the Greek brotherhood of Zeus, Poseidon, and Hades.[152] Moreover, when Baal dies (temporarily, like the Cretan Zeus) he is buried on Mount Saphon, which is believed to be the same Mount Kasios where Typhon removed the sinews of Zeus, as well as Mount Hazzi, home of the Hurrian Teshub.[97, 119] Modern scholars generally identify this peak with Jebel el-Akra, at the mouth of the Orontes River north of Ras Shamra. (See map at figure 68.)

We have noted the likelihood that some of the battles against dragons and demons described in ancient literature refer to initiatory ordeals, the contest against one's own lower nature. Others may have to do with the upsetting of the natural order by drought or flood. (As early as Aeschylus, the Greek Typhon was identified with the Egyptian Set, who was traditionally associated with catastrophic imbalances in nature.) But the geographical detail of the Zeus-Typhon conflict seems to argue for a more literal meaning, and some classicists see here the elements of a larger war.[132] Moreover, whether or not the Greeks imported the Typhon myth from the east, its associations are generally with the Gigantomachy, which is neither initiatory nor nature-oriented in its structure.

We would also point out that several of the archaeological events which in Part I suggested an historical base for Plato's account of the Atlantic attack on Asia fit the uprising of Typhon equally well. Most striking, perhaps, is the general coincidence of the geographical setting of Typhon's assault and the various signs of hostilities in the Epi-Paleolithic Near East. The violence at Mureybet III took place not far from the scene of Typhon's Syrian confrontation with Zeus. Ras Shamra or ancient Ugarit will itself be first settled in the seventh millennium B.C., by people with an assemblage related to that which was introduced

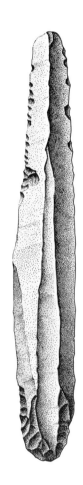

45 Single sickle-blade from Mureybet III, Syria, early eighth millennium B.C.; length, five inches (after Cauvin, 1979)

into Mureybet III early in the eighth. Whoever occupied Ras Shamra in the succeeding millennia, since the local gods and legends of ancient lands are known to have been frequently adopted by incoming peoples, it would not be surprising to find traces of the traditions of Ras Shamra's earliest settlers in later phases of her history, i.e., in Ugaritic mythology.

The presence of large, single-bladed sickles (fig. 45) along-side the weapons at Mureybet III and contemporary Palestinian sites further recalls the use of a sickle in the Zeus-Typhon battle. Sickles with multiple microflints hafted in horn had been known to the Near East since Early Natufian times (fig. 22), but the new long blades would presumably have made better weapons, symbolic or real. In any case, it is the introduction of a new type of sickle, at a time that also saw the raising of defensive fortifications and a sudden profusion of arrowheads in the east Mediterranean Levant, that catches our attention.

As the other weapon used by Zeus against Typhon was his thunderbolt, one notes with equal interest the appearance of a single polished greenstone axe at Mureybet III. Similar polished stone celts were known elsewhere in Syria and Palestine during this period (fig. 46); they were hereafter to enjoy a long and illustrious career in Old World archaeology. Ancient explanations show these implements to be universally designated as "thunderstones" and associated with the sky god (Zeus in Greece).[79, 31, 125] Among later Greeks, Neolithic celts were given the name of *astropelekia*, denoting thunderbolts, and greatly valued as charms. Their deeper religious significance is demonstrated by the engraving of Mithraic subjects on a serpentine celt from the Argolid (fig. 48), and by the claim that Pythagoras was purified by the thunderstone of Zeus in the Idaean Cave of Crete.[173] Five thousand years earlier, the first polished greenstone axes known to Greek archaeology were laid in a shrine at the sixth millennium settlement of Nea Nikomedeia, today judged ceremonial objects by their excavator.[346]

That polished stone celts already held special significance in the late ninth and early eighth millennia is suggested by the miniaturization of these forms in Near Eastern sites of this period.[14] Often pierced for suspension in the following epoch (fig. 47), these "axe amulets"[209] were the first of a long series of apparently sacred elements. (Many millennia later a Minoan grave at Phaistos yielded a small stone celt with a hole in the top, "doubtless worn as an amulet.")[79] If the ninth millennium valuation of stone celts already derived from an association with the thunderbolts of the sky god, their extraordinary spread in

46 Polished stone axe from Netiv Hagdud, Palestine, late ninth millennium B.C.; length, five inches (*after Bar-Yosef et al, 1980*)

both large and miniature forms after 7500 B.C. (detailed in Part III) suggests a continuation of his worship. As in the myth, the sovereignty of Zeus-Baal-Teshub seems to have been intact, after the late ninth and early eighth millennium hostilities in whose midst polished greenstone axes first appeared.

The Contest for Attica

A less famous Greek myth of conflict says nothing of the monstrous beings associated with the Giant-Aload-Typhon cycle, but it does describe an old disagreement between Athena and Poseidon, the gods of Plato's combatants. As we shall see later, Poseidon was generally as unpopular a figure in Greek mythology as Athena was beloved. In fact, the best known story about Poseidon appears to have been this tale of his defeat by the goddess in their contest for possession of Attica.[349]

Again there are several known versions of the myth. As told by Apollodorus (III.14.i), Poseidon struck the middle of the Acropolis with a blow of his trident to establish his right to the place. Athena planted an olive tree, summoning Cecrops (the legendary king of Athens) as her witness. When the two deities strove for possession, Zeus appointed the twelve gods as arbitrators. By their verdict, the land was adjudged to Athena, who then named the city Athens after herself, while "in hot anger Poseidon flooded the Thriasian plain and laid Attica under the sea."

Scholars have found it difficult to separate the story itself from the many monuments picturing the strife of Athena and Poseidon. The most famous of these is a now-destroyed frieze that apparently adorned the western pediment of the Parthenon (Pausanias I.24.v) and is believed to have been the inspiration for a late fifth century vase from Kertsch in the Crimea (fig. 49). Here the olive tree stands in the center between the two rivals. Athena holds her lance aloft, shield raised against Poseidon, who is striking downwards at either the roots of the tree planted by Athena or the snake (one of her emblems) that guards it. From the left Dionysos approaches with his companion leopard. In the opinion of one scholar:

> In the next moment the conflict between the gods threatens to ignite. Whether it actually comes to that or Zeus through his intervention causes a resolution, the viewer can have no doubts to whom the victory will go, as from the top of the olive tree Nike flees toward Athena.[345]

47 Miniature polished greenstone axes from (a) Netiv Hagdud, Palestine, late ninth millennium B.C. and (b) Jericho, late eighth or seventh millennium B.C.; length, one inch (*after Bar-Yosef et al, 1980; Wheeler, 1983*)

48 Roman celt in serpentine from the Argolid (*after Harrison, 1912*)

Another classicist concluded that the original dispute was indeed more likely a fight than a lawsuit:

> Why after producing their tokens are the gods depicted as strik-
> ing downwards? If Athena merely planted her olive tree, what
> then are we to make of her action with that spear?[79]

A third also admitted perplexity:

> It is very doubtful what he is striking and with what purpose,
> nor is it easy to say why she should be wielding her spear as
> she is after the olive tree has already been produced, nor why
> Dionysos with his panther and thyrsos should apparently be
> running to her aid.[128]

Although the story itself has been described by one mythographer as a local Attic legend,[349] the traditions of several other
regions of Greece reflect the same theme. At Argos, Poseidon
is said to have contested with Hera for possession of the Argolid;
when Inachos and his fellow judges decided in favor of the

great native goddess, Poseidon flooded the country. At Troezen, he strove with Athena for possession of the land until Zeus judged that both should hold it; for this reason or another, Poseidon flooded the region and made it unfruitful with his salt waters (Pausanias II.22.iv, 30.vi, 32.viii). Similar tales are known to Corinth, Aegina, Naxos, and Delphi.

The parallels to Plato's story are evident, extending even to the divine referendum called by Zeus in the Attic version of the legend, just as he had done at the breaking-off point of the see page 32 *Critias*. But the historical correlate to the strife between Athena and Poseidon is generally thought to have occurred long after the ninth millennium B.C. Poseidon's name is Indo-European, belonging to a family of languages that is composed of most of the European tongues (including Greek) as well as Iranian and Indic. The name Athena, on the other hand, is "pre-Greek," apparently derived from a language spoken by the native population of the Aegean before the coming of the Greeks. Many scholars believe, therefore, that the confrontation between the two gods represents a conflict between the cults of incoming Indo-Europeans and those of the indigenous peoples of Greece. And as the third millennium B.C. or thereabouts has been seen as marking the arrival of the Greeks in Greece, the contest for possession of Attica, if it did correspond to the intrusion of Indo-European cult, theoretically could not have happened before that time.

This long-held theory of a Bronze Age invasion of Greece by Indo-Europeans is currently under fire, however, as evidence accumulates of the continuity of certain Greek traditions from Early Neolithic times (the sixth millennium in Greece) down to the Christian era. What was once seen as an invasion from the north now appears to some investigators to have been more on the order of a gradual infiltration, which may or may not have involved a language change.[340] The original homeland of the Indo-European people as a whole, the date of their separation, and the timing of their migrations into their present territories are all complex questions about which there is essentially no consensus among scholars.[254] As there is no way of determining a language change from nonliterate archaeological remains, all that can be said with certainty about linguistic developments in Greece is that by Mycenean times (the second millennium B.C.), an early form of the Greek language—Linear B—was written in Greece.

It does seem likely, however, that a non-Indo-European language was indeed spoken at some earlier time in this part of the world. Several thousand loan words in the Greek language are believed to have been borrowed from a native pre-Greek tongue. Place names with -nth- or -ss- suffixes, also thought to be pre-Indo-European, have been recorded from Anatolia to southern Italy, with concentrations in central and southern Greece, Crete, and western Anatolia. As shown on the map at figure 50, these denser clusters of place names define approximately that area which one assumes would have been either occupied or directly influenced by Plato's Greek nations of the day. If these were indeed a "native race" (*Critias* 109), their language may well have been what we call pre-Greek, however long it outlived them.

If "pre-Greek" was possibly the tongue of Plato's vanished cultures, the oldest stratum of Aegean religion—variously designated pre-Hellenic, Pelasgian, or pre-Greek—may have derived from their cults. As we shall see later, worship of the Cretan Dionysos and of the Eleusinian goddesses Demeter and Persephone, with whom he was intimately associated, has been traced back to a pre-Indo-European horizon, beyond which point their ancestries are lost in time. Identified as Mysteries in the first millennium B.C., these initiatory Aegean cults had far more in common with Near Eastern traditions, particularly those of Anatolia and Syria, than with Homeric beliefs.[167] Like all of the mystery religions of antiquity, they held that the divine and the human spirit were essentially one, that man contained within himself the seeds of divinity and the potential for immortality. Whatever their tenets in earlier times (a question to which we shall return), the presence of well-developed prototypes of Demeter, Persephone, and a Dionysian child-god on a leopard among the icons at the sixth millennium Anatolian center of Çatal Hüyük suggests that the worship of these divinities was a great deal older than has been imagined.

see figure 104

For now, however, the point to be noted with regard to the contest for Attica is that the event illustrated on the Parthenon conceivably could have taken place long before the Bronze Age. Look again at the scene at figure 49. Like Athena, the olive with which she established her claim on Attica has a "pre-Greek" name, and olive trees were apparently known to Greece at least as early as the sixth millennium.[430] The horse held by Poseidon appears to have been harnessed in Paleolithic times. With proto-Dionysos and his leopard at Çatal Hüyük, the main elements in this representation were already on hand in the sixth millennium B.C., making it not inconceivable that the confrontation

see figure 9

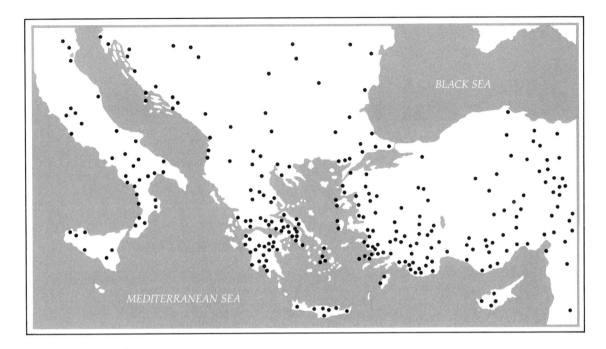

between Athena and Poseidon—or at least that confrontation which was portrayed on the Kertsch vase and thus, presumably, in the Parthenon frieze—took place even earlier.

Poseidon, Ancestral God of the Atlantics

A suggested etymology of the name Poseidon, "husband of earth" or "lord of earth" (*Posis Das*), has led scholars to conclude that the god may originally have possessed a universal sovereignty.[119] If so, his omnipotence had been lost by the time Greek myth, as we know it, was formulated. When Poseidon is mentioned at all, he is usually portrayed as violent or quarrelsome, with only the sea as his unchallenged domain.[164] As might be expected from the reports of Poseidon's flooding various parts of Greece, his epithets included *Prokystios*, the Flooder. He was also *Enosichthon*, the Earth-shaker, and all earthquakes were said to be his work.[167] Poseidon's intimate association with the horse was mentioned earlier (his main epithet was *Hippios*, He of the Horses), and the god was seldom depicted without the trident, his three-pronged fish spear (fig. 51).

Just when and how Poseidon, an Indo-European deity whose worshippers are believed by many prehistorians to have come

51 Sixth century clay *pinake* from Corinth, showing Poseidon with emblematic trident or fish spear seated atop a pair of horses (*after Farnell, 1909*)

see figure 8

from landlocked northern steppes, acquired his status as sea god is unknown, but the possible derivation of his characteristic fish spear from the Late Paleolithic harpoons might be a rewarding line of research. From an apparent origin in Magdalenian France and Spain, these barbed bone or antler implements continued to be present across north central Europe as late as the fifth or fourth millennium B.C. At this time the harpoons are known to have been used in the Kurgan culture of the north Caucasian steppes, which some investigators see as the ancestor of the Indo-Europeans.[158] As with the Magdalenians (and later Indo-European nations), horses were of great importance to the Kurgan people, who also carved heads of horses in stone and mounted them on rods for use as scepters. If Kurgan culture was in fact Indo-European, its parallels to Magdalenian traditions of horse reverence and harpoons would suggest that an earlier theory, which saw Upper Paleolithic western Europe as the proto-Indo-European homeland, may need to be retrieved.[225]

map at figure 85

Barbed bone harpoons were also known across Middle Africa, from the far west of the continent to the East African rifts, and while some are clearly more recent, the main extension of the African harpoons is said to have taken place no later than the seventh millennium B.C.[384] Those at Khartoum (fig. 52) reminded the excavator of Magdalenian models.[5] They now appear certain to have been fishermen's tools; we are advised by one specialist to imagine the Middle African spread of harpoons as originating in a "small but successful and hence assimilating group, wedded psychologically as well as economically to the waters."[384] Atlantic survivors? The relationship between the two harpoon streams north and south of the Mediterranean lands has not, to my knowledge, been explored; but the apparently Magdalenian ancestry of these implements, and their possible connection to the fish spear of Poseidon (whom we shall later find worshipped in Libya as well as Europe) allow at least the suspicion that the European and the African harpoons represent two lines of Atlantic inheritance.

Poseidon is also known in Greek myth for the gigantic or monstrous forms of his children and grandchildren, many of whom had homes at the "western edge of the world." The Cyclops Polyphemos, living on an island off the coast of Libya, was the son of Poseidon. Geryon, in whom the bodies of three men were joined, was Poseidon's grandson; his island, Erytheia, was placed by some authors off Gadira (Spanish Gades or Cadiz), by others off the Libyan coast. (Herodotus IV.8 put Geryon near Gades on an island "which lies on the Ocean beyond the Pillars of Herakles.") The career of the outsized Aloadai, twin sons of Poseidon, has already been summarized. Poseidon's offspring were also the frequent enemies of Greek heroes, particularly Herakles. After slaying the monstrous Geryon, Herakles felled Ialebion and Dereynus, sons of Poseidon, in Liguria (Apollodorus II.5.x). At Pylos he overcame the sons of Neleus, himself a son of Poseidon; in Libya he killed Antaeus, also a son of Poseidon. To another Greek hero, Perseus, fell the task of beheading Medusa, Poseidon's mistress. (Medusa and her sister Gorgons were usually situated in Libya, either beside the lake Tritonis or near the Atlas mountains, whence they would make destructive attacks on their African neighbors.)[132] And in the *Odyssey* it is Poseidon himself who consistently plays the part of antagonist to the heroic Odysseus.

In short, Poseidon was a rather unsympathetic figure in Greek mythology, his offspring and associates even more so. Plato could not, it seems, have chosen a more likely ancestral god for his obstreperous Atlantics. And yet, Poseidon is said to have fought on the side of the gods in the battle against the Giants, and although his children and worshippers are portrayed in myth as the enemies of Erechtheus, one of the autochthonous ancestors of the Athenians, an altar to Poseidon stood before the Erechtheum on the Acropolis. Classicists again find this ambivalence of the Athenians toward Poseidon suggestive of a "final reconciliation of two cults that were often in conflict at first."[128] And again the question is when. When were they first in conflict, and when were they reconciled?

52 Bone harpoon from the Sudanese site of Khartoum *(after Arkell and Ucko, 1965)*

Hephaistos and Athena, Patron Deities of Ur-Athens

The origin of Hephaistos, co-patron with Athena of Plato's warrior-guardians, is unknown to historians of religion. As one noted, he is clearly an archaic figure, but attempts to explain Hephaistos in terms of either Indo-European or pre-Greek traditions have failed.[119] Cicero (*Nat. Deor.* III.22) claimed that there were actually several Hephaistoi (Vulcanae), however, and enumerated them as follows:

> The first is a son of the Sky-God and was said to be the father by Minerva [Athena] of the Apollo whom the old historians claimed to be the protector of Athens. The second was a son of Nilus, whom the Egyptians call Ptah and claim as the guardian of Egypt. The third is a son of the third Jupiter and Juno [Zeus and Hera] who tradition says was the master of the smithy at Lemnos. The fourth was a son of Memalius and was lord of the volcanic islands around Sicily.

All but the first of Cicero's Hephaistoi were familiar aspects of the god in popular Greek myth. The association of Hephaistos with both Lemnos and the Lipari Islands near Sicily (once called *Hephaestiades insulae*) was known to all; volcanic fire, no less than the fire of the smithy and of the potter's kiln, was the ally of this divinity.[128] The identity of Hephaistos and the Egyptian god Ptah is also suggested elsewhere.[79] Ptah was one of the oldest and most venerable of Egyptian deities and, like Hephaistos, was considered the master of all transformations by fire, as well as architect and sculptor of the gods.[49] Both divinities were also the creators of wondrous weapons with which the gods defeated their enemies: Hephaistos the thunderbolts with which Zeus vanquished Typhon, Ptah the arms used by Horus, son of Osiris, against Set.

Of Cicero's first-named Hephaistos, however, the father by Athena of the Apollo who protected Athens, nothing is known (including the identity of the "old historians" named as Cicero's sources). Athena was conventionally a virgin goddess, Apollo the son of Zeus and Leto. But Cicero is consistent, and repeats this genealogy in identifying several Athenas, the first of whom is said to be the mother of Apollo, and several Apollos, the first of whom is said to be the son of Athena and Hephaistos and the protector of Athens.

In popular Greek mythology Hephaistos did father a son by Athena in a roundabout way, but it was not Apollo. The seed of Hephaistos' desire to wed Athena is said to have fallen upon the Earth, which was thereby fertilized. The child of this union was Erichthonios, who like Erechtheus was held to be one of the autochthonous Athenian ancestors. In the myth Earth (Ge) then gave over the newborn Erichthonios to Athena to nurture, as illustrated in the vase painting at figure 53, with Hephaistos looking on. It is here, in fact, that popular Greek traditions most clearly merge with Plato's tale. According to the *Timaeus* (23), Athena took over the seed of Greece from Earth and Hephaistos in founding the Ur-Athenian society, with the latter deity apparently retained as Athena's partner in the temple of the warrior-guardians on the Acropolis (*Critias* 109).

53 Detail from a red-figured *stamnos* from Vulci. Earth or Ge hands the infant Erichthonios, one of the autochthonous ancestors of Athens, to the goddess Athena. Hephaistos watches from the left; Zeus is pictured on the other side of the vase. *(after Lenormant, 1844)*

And here again we find the paradoxical relationship of Poseidon to the autochthonous Athenians. In more than one vase painting, this supposedly late-arriving, Indo-European god is portrayed as a "sympathetic observer" at the birth of Erichthonios.[128]

Parallels to Plato's Tale in Myth   93

Egyptian Myth and Archaeology

As the *Timaeus* tale was said to be Egyptian, it is in the well-conserved traditions of the Nile that we would expect to find its confirmation. Egyptian myth is well known, however, for its preference for abstract or metaphysical rather than historical themes; and whether for this reason or not, the narrative told Solon in Sais is nowhere recreated in surviving Egyptian texts. Moreover, the few sources which deal with the age of Egyptian traditions assign to them an even greater antiquity than did Plato's priest.*

It could be argued, however, that there were actually several different Egyptian traditions in the valley of the Nile. Apart from the distinction between Upper and Lower Egypt, which must have been even sharper before their political unification at the beginning of the Dynastic period, each Egyptian district or "nome" paid particular reverence to one or another of the gods, honoring him with a more prominent role in creation myths and theogonies. The claim of the Saitic priest in the *Timaeus* (23), that "the age of our institutions is given in our sacred records as eight thousand years," may therefore have referred specifically to the traditions of Sais, the Libyan nome of Lower Egypt, where we find Neith celebrated as patron deity from the earliest times (fig. 54).

In any event, the cult of Neith was among the oldest in Egypt. The earliest dynastic temple of which we have direct evidence

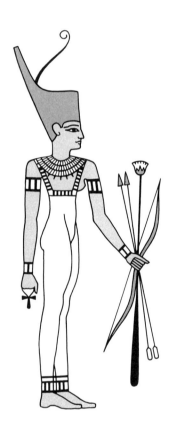

54 The goddess Neith, wearing the crown of Lower Egypt and holding her emblematic arrows and the lotus-headed scepter of Egyptian goddesses

* For example, fragments from writings attributed to Manetho, an Egyptian priest of the Ptolemaic period, have proven generally reliable with respect to the sequence of dynastic kings; but Manetho also claimed that prior to the time of the first mortal king, Egypt had been ruled by gods, demigods, and spirits of the dead for some 25,000 years (Frag. 1, Eusebius *Chronica*). Another reputable source, the Turin Papyrus, seems to record around 36,000 years of divine rule before Menes, the first mortal king: 23,200 years for reigns before the Shemsu-Hor and 13,420 years for the rulership of the Shemsu-Hor, usually translated as followers or worshippers of Horus,[414] presumably an older god than the more familiar Horus, son of Osiris.

is hers, and the age and importance of her worship can be seen in the names chosen by several First Dynasty queens (Merneit, Neithotep).[121] Her identification in the *Timaeus* with the Greek goddess Athena is supported by Herodotus (II.170) and Cicero, whose second Athena was "a daughter of Nilus, whom the Egyptians worship at Sais" (*Nat. Deor.* III.23). Like Athena, Neith was a goddess of war, although her emblem shows crossed arrows rather than the spear with which the Greek deity was associated.[29] Both were patron goddesses of weaving; both were considered to be androgynous; both were particularly distinguished by their creative intelligence.

In Saitic traditions and in the creation myth of Esna, "the house of Neith in the land of the south,"[49] Neith was even held to be the primeval creatrix. After first creating Egypt and its gods, she is said to have given birth to the sun god, Re. Placing him between her horns (like many Egyptian goddesses, Neith was occasionally portrayed as the cow of heaven), she swam with him to Esna and Sais. The journey supposedly took four months, during which time she visited many cities and annihilated the enemies of Re. On the thirteenth of Epiphi, according to the festival calendar of Esna, Neith arrived in Sais.[30] The event was commemorated annually; Herodotus (II.60) reported a Festival of Lamps, with great numbers of lights burning throughout the night "in honor of Athena at Sais."

Egyptologists agree that the Esna myth as a whole makes a trustworthy impression; it alludes to several very old themes and is considered to be in line with the traditional Egyptian way of thinking.[30] Quite unknown, however, is just how long before the earliest dynasties, which already knew her worship, Neith might have arrived in Sais. For Plato's priest, the date would have been c. 8600 B.C., one thousand years after the founding of ancient Athens by Neith-Athena (*Timaeus* 23); and a ninth millennium date for the advent of a war goddess in Lower Egypt would certainly not be contradicted by the appearance of the first projectile points known to Egypt at the site of Helwan near Cairo, one of the several types of arrowhead that blanketed the eastern Mediterranean from around 8500 B.C. But after Helwan, Egyptian archaeology shows not only Lower Egypt but all of the Nile valley to be "almost a blank" for the next four thousand years.[280]

Most Egyptologists feel that there was more to pre-dynastic Egypt than the archaeological record implies, however, and that the absence of pre-dynastic remains in the Delta and much of middle Egypt is, in the words of one, "certainly fortuitous and

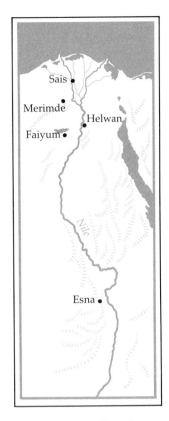

55 The Nile valley. Sites mentioned in the text.

see figure 38b

misleading."[58] As they point out, the most important settlements were probably always situated on the floodplain of the Nile; if the floodplain was indeed lower between 8000 and 5000 B.C., as has recently been suggested,[401] sites of that period would now lie buried under more recent deposits of alluvium. It has never seemed logical that the Nile valley would be almost uninhabited during a period when lands to the east and west of Egypt were experiencing great advances in population and cultural development. Moreover, the relative backwardness of the two Neolithic settlements which then do appear in fifth millennium northern Egypt (Faiyum and Merimde) is not what one expects of the times, and several archaeologists now suspect that both may actually have been marginal settlements, perhaps of Libyan bedouin as their northwesterly location suggests, rather than true representatives of the cultural level of fifth millennium Lower Egypt.[280]

map at figure 55

We shall later find suggestions of an "Egyptian" influence as early as the seventh or sixth millennium in the rock art of the central Sahara. And in Part IV we shall encounter Egyptian-style artifacts at Çatal Hüyük, in the company of ceramics whose technical resemblance to contemporary wares in the Sahara and the Sudan might suggest a Nilotic thoroughfare to the Mediterranean. But to turn the possibility that Plato's priest was correct in assigning a ninth millennium beginning to Egyptian, or Saitic, traditions into even a probability would require the up-to-date excavation of important Nilotic sites dated to this critical ninth to fifth millennium period, if indeed any can be found. With or without Plato's tale, this has been named "the greatest challenge for Egyptian archaeology in the future."[280]

The Mythic Art of the Sahara
and Sicily

Herodotus' record of his journey through Egypt in the fifth
century B.C. does not include the story told Solon in the *Timaeus*.
The Greek historian did find a venerable cult of Poseidon in
North Africa, however, a land which was supposedly once under Atlantic control: "Alone of all nations the Libyans have had
among them the name of Poseidon from the first, and they have
ever honored this god" (II.50). Herodotus also reported a
curious people living at the foot of a mountain they called Atlas
and from which they derived their name, "Atlantes" (IV.184).
Little else was said of the Atlantes, other than that they ate no
living creature and never had dreams. Maps based on Herodotus' account place them in the Hoggar region of the central
Sahara, not far from the recently discovered collection of rock
art in the massifs of Tassili n'Ajjer and Acacus. Most of these   map at figure 17
extraordinary works of art are far more ancient than Herodotus'
Atlantes, but their ancestry is equally obscure and the traditions
of their creators no less eccentric.

Before the disappearance of its water resources the Sahara,
already sand belt and waterless desert in Herodotus' time, is
believed to have been part of a "veritable garland" of rich vegetation stretching from the Atlantic to the Indus.[62] The earliest
phase of its rock art depicts a multitude of animal species that
once inhabited this region: Bubalis antiquus (a now-extinct giant
buffalo), Barbary sheep, giraffe, cattle, equid, rhinoceros. Known
as the *Large Wild Fauna* phase, these rock carvings are of unknown age; but as one art historian pointed out, there is no
reason to exclude the possibility that they are as old as the
painted slabs recently recovered in southwest Africa, which at
c. 25/23,000 B.C. are the earliest recorded examples of African
art.[249]

The following phase in the Sahara, the *Round Head* paintings,
shows little relationship to the animal engravings. In fact, the
leader of the Tassili expedition, Henri Lhote, found the Round

Head art so different from traditional forms of prehistoric art
that "we felt we were moving about in a world that bore no
relation to any other, a world apart."[242] Many hundreds of these
remarkable compositions have yet to be published, but already
famous are the depictions of beings whimsically named "Mar-
tians" by Lhote. The painting at figure 56 from Sefar is typical
of these portrayals; here several round-headed women seem to
be in a sort of procession, hands raised in supplication to a huge
central figure over ten feet high. Similar representations of these
enormous beings appear at Jabbaren, a name which, as it means
"the Giants," apparently was derived from the paintings.

Not all of these works portray monstrous beings. Late in the
Round Head period at Aouanrhet an exceptionally beautiful
scene includes the silhouette of a woman running or dancing,

with fringes falling from her knees, belt, and outstretched arms (fig. 57). Horns extend horizontally from either side of her head; a dotted area above was very tentatively interpreted as a cloud of grain falling from a wheat field. Her discoverers felt that this magnificent figure must have been either a goddess or a priestess, and saw a possible relationship to the Egyptian deity Isis, who, with Osiris, is credited in myth with introducing grain cultivation into the Nile valley.[242]

In fact, one of the many puzzles presented by the Tassili collection is how, at a time when the Nile valley seems almost deserted, so many of the Round Head compositions could show

57 The "White Lady" of Aouanrhet, Tassili n'Ajjer. Painted in yellow ochre outlined in white, her body is decorated with parallel rows of white spots and red lines. Height, approximately four feet *(after Lhote, 1959)*

Parallels to Plato's Tale in Myth   99

58 Tentative sequence of phases in Round Head art: (a) *Little Devils*, (b) *Evolved Phase*, (c) *Decadent Period*, (d) *Period of Egyptian Influence (after Lhote, 1959)*

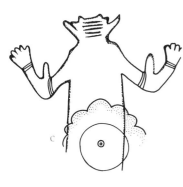

what appears to be an "Egyptian" influence. There are parallels in content as well as style. For example, Lhote found another of the paintings at Aouanrhet to be most readily interpreted in accordance with principles of Egyptian religion. As shown at figure 59, a woman with an elongated body and limbs gives the impression that she is floating in a liquid substance. Her arms are stretched out behind, pulling a man whose body is tightly flexed and apparently lifeless. The two middle figures may be unrelated to her, but a fourth, below in white, is drawn in the same style as the floating woman. This lower figure is shown emerging from an ovoid object marked with concentric circles, suggesting either an egg or a snail's shell. The red caps covering the heads of these figures are found elsewhere at Tassili in the company of Egyptian-like elements, and Lhote felt that this "obviously allegorical" painting might represent birth (below) and the voyage of the dead (above) as imagined by the ancient Egyptians. As he noted, "these figures are found in an art phase where Egyptian influences are marked. If we take into account beliefs held in dynastic Egypt—beliefs which must have had their origins in pre-dynastic times—it may be that this picture represents the voyage of the dead in the other world."[242]

Lhote has arranged the Round Head paintings into six phases, which he admits are quite tentative. The first two phases show small figures with round or horned heads (fig. 58a); clothing is a loincloth, and bows or a sort of pitchfork are often held by these *Little Devils*. The third and fourth phases, known as the *Martian* and *Evolved* periods respectively, show much larger and more robust round-headed figures of improving artistic quality (fig. 58b). In the fifth phase, the *Decadent Period*, these forms become coarse and heavy, with carelessly executed detail (fig. 58c and fig. 56, above). Gigantic size is also particularly characteristic of the Decadent Phase. In the sixth period, known as the *Period of Egyptian Influence*, the degenerative trend appears to have been overcome, and some of the finest paintings in the Sahara were produced (fig. 58d and figs. 57 and 59).

The purposes served by the Round Head paintings are as unknown as the identity of their creators. In view of the many supernatural elements in the art, Lhote felt that the painted rock shelters may have been sanctuaries for religious cult or initiation, and an art historian who has studied the Saharan works in detail believes that these paintings offer "countless hints" regarding the spiritual life of the artists. Mori sees the Round Head series as essentially mythic, expressing religious beliefs

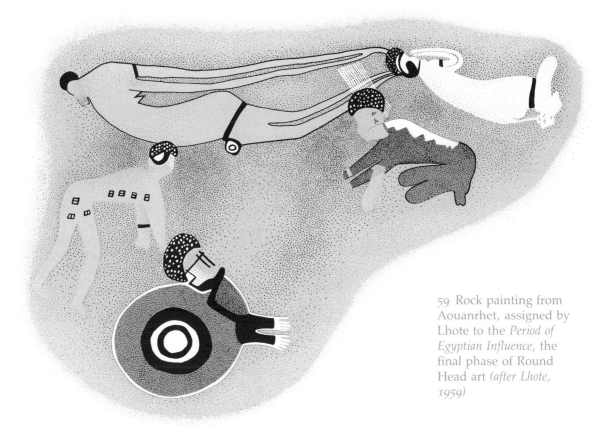

59 Rock painting from Aouanrhet, assigned by Lhote to the *Period of Egyptian Influence*, the final phase of Round Head art (*after Lhote, 1959*)

based upon a transcendent world that starts from man and is modelled on him—a world containing a swarm of creatures like him, who probably foreshadow by many millennia the multiform aspects taken on by the subsequent myths of the Mediterranean environment.[292]

Following Mori's lead, one is tempted to compare these exotic beings with creatures from Greek mythology, particularly the Giants and the monstrous Libyan offspring of Poseidon. Plato's tale may again be the key; the massifs of Tassili and Acacus are well within the "Africa up to Egypt" bounds of Atlantic colonization as defined in the *Timaeus*. Estimated dates, too, are not remote from Plato's chronology. Mori believes that the Round Head series began very early and ended before the seventh millennium B.C.;[291] others think it may have extended into the sixth millennium;[370] in either case Lhote's estimation that the Round Head period as a whole must have lasted for several thousand years would indicate at least an eighth or ninth millennium beginning for the series.

60 Engravings in the
Levanzo Cave, Sicily,
estimated to c. 8500–
8000 B.C. *(after Stern,
1969)*

A more specific clue to the timing of Round Head art may lie in the engravings of what seem to be counterparts of the monstrous creatures of Lhote's Decadent Phase in the Levanzo Cave, which is located on a small island off the western coast of Sicily (fig. 60). (As one analyst remarked, "it is odd that two widely separated ancient peoples should have such similar grotesque concepts.")[379] A date between 8500 and 8000 B.C. has been suggested for the Levanzo engravings.[280] If this estimation is accurate, the similar figures in the Decadent Phase of Round Head art in the Sahara presumably would fall within the same period, a period that was suggested in Part I as the time frame of Plato's war.

Coeval, apparently, with the Levanzo engravings were the rock carvings at Addaura Cave on the northern coast of Sicily, where naturalistic animals were rendered in a style similar to the bulls which were also depicted at Levanzo.[354] In addition to the animal engravings, Addaura Cave yielded a singular and still-controversial example of narrative art (fig. 61). At the top of this composition several human figures seem to be dancing around two recumbent males. Others look on, while another figure (outside the detail shown here) strides toward the group with a long spear. Some of the faces in the group seem to be covered by bird-beak masks; others appear to be surrounded by thick masses of hair. The two contorted figures in the middle register have been described by Bernabò Brea as follows:

> Though these were drawn one above the other, the artist probably intended us to imagine them lying beside each other. They face in opposite directions, in similar attitudes. One leans on his forearm, the other on his elbows, and both have their chests upright. The first at least is in an unnatural position, violently constricted, with his legs forcibly bent, so that his feet are near his buttocks; and although less clearly drawn, the second figure may probably have been in a similar position.[46]

Some critics see here a scene of torture, a "hanging" effected by the tying of feet to neck, with the ithyphallic aspect of both figures the result of strangulation. Others have suggested initiation ceremonies or propitiatory rites. As summed up by Sieveking, "two of the spectators have their arms raised, but whether to cheer or to castigate one cannot tell: the scene remains a mystery."[363]

The Addaura engraving is the last to be counted among the examples of narrative art known to the Epi-Paleolithic Old World. The Spanish Levant, Kobystan, and the Sahara, already discussed, house its only peers. If the theme of the Addaura engraving is indeed retribution, its only known analogues would be the scenes of execution pictured among the battle paintings of the Spanish Levant, in which a squad of archers is shown dispatching a lone figure. As the Spanish and the Sicilian rock art appear to be approximately contemporary, this engraving at Addaura Cave and the creatures resembling Round Head gods at Levanzo may together provide an important link between the scenes (and signs) of warfare in Epi-Paleolithic Europe and the Decadent Phase of Saharan art—between, from Plato's point of view, the effects of Atlantic corruption north and south of the Mediterranean Sea.

see figure 31

see figure 62

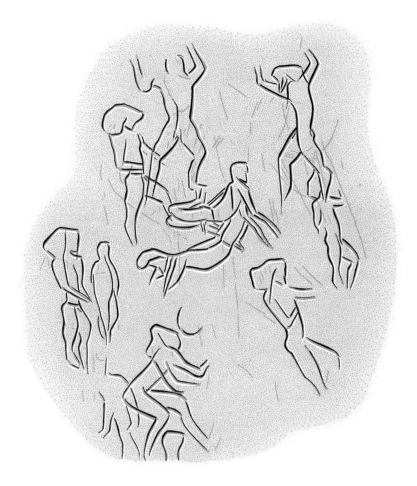

61 Detail from engraved scene in the Sicilian cave of Addaura, believed to be coeval with the rock art at Levanzo Cave *(after Sandars, 1968)*

Parallels to Plato's Tale in Myth   103

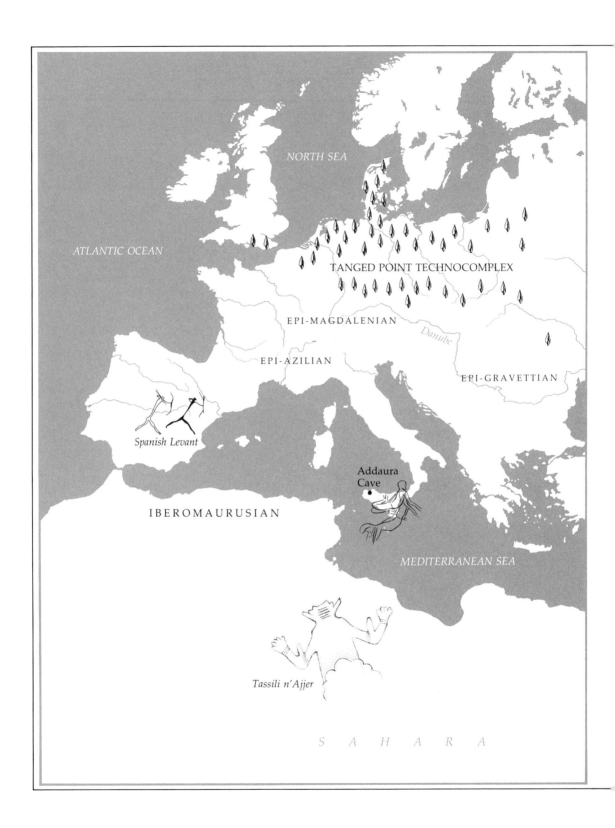

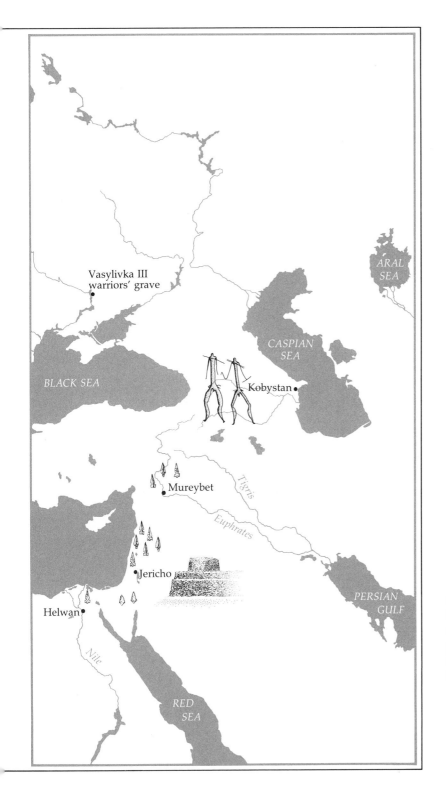

Vasylivka III
warriors' grave

ARAL
SEA

CASPIAN
SEA

BLACK SEA

Kobystan

Tigris

Mureybet

Euphrates

Jericho

PERSIAN
GULF

Helwan

Nile

RED
SEA

62 The Early Mesolithic
Mediterranean. Map
demonstrating the pro-
posed contemporaneity of
events described in Parts
I and II of this study

The Golden Age and
Indo-European Mythology

see figure 1a

With the Golden Age of Magdalenian Europe theoretically coinciding with the inspired reign of Plato's early Atlantic kings, a word should be said before we leave this section about the ubiquity of tales of a long-ago age of gold. What was referred to earlier as the old model or the existing framework of thought was not, of course, the first paradigm of prehistory. Like Plato's priest, a great many traditions have depicted human history not as an ascent from savagery to civilization, but as a descent, a descent from a superior humanity or an age of spiritual and material plenty, or both.

Primeval paradises such as that of Hesiod's Golden Race (and of Plato's *Statesman*), which knew neither arts, crafts, clothing, or governance, are obviously not to be compared with the presumably later and definitely civilized Greek and Atlantic races of the *Timaeus* and *Critias*. But another sort of Golden Age, of a more historical nature, was traditionally associated with the reign of a mythical king or god-king, not unlike Plato's semidivine Atlantic rulers. Indo-European peoples are among those who remember such a time, and the memory is believed to predate the splintering of the Indo-European unity. The Iranian Yima, for example, who was celebrated as king of the Golden Age throughout Persian literary history, appears as Yama in Indian texts as early as the *Rig Veda* and as the Giant Ymir of Scandinavian myth.[252] (All of these names are apparently derived from the Indo-European root *yemo*, "twin.") Typically, death and disease were unknown to the reign of this First King, and both people and herds throve and increased to the point that Yima was required to enlarge the world three times to accommodate their numbers (*Vendidad* II. 11–19).

The fall from grace of this sunlike monarch is variously explained. In one Iranian text the evil material existence seems to have been at fault (*Vendidad* II.22); another blames Yima for introducing falsehood to his mind (*Yašt* XIX.33). The oldest source

(*Yasna* XXXII.8) accuses him of giving the flesh of cattle to the people to eat (to make them immortal, according to a later annotation), which some have taken to mean the instituting of ritual animal slaughter or sacrifice.[442] But whatever his sin, or sins, Yima's punishment is generally described as the loss of the kingly Glory (*xvarenah*), which fled from him in the form of a bird. Caught up first by the god Mithra and then by two legendary Persian heroes (*Yašt* XIX.35–38), the Glory became, as one Iraniologist interprets the text, "the object of contest between Aryan and non-Aryan forces."[252]

Neither the date nor the domain of this Indo-European First King is specified, but the mythology surrounding Yima is believed to derive from an archaic stratum of oral folklore that considerably precedes the time of Zarathuštra, the prophet who reformed Iranian religion.[442] And if the Greeks were correct in assigning Zarathuštra to the seventh millennium B.C. (for which we shall find evidence in Part V), Yima theoretically could have lived and ruled no later than the eighth millennium, and possibly a good deal earlier. As for the location of his original rulership (presumably the proto-Indo-European hearth), Herbert Kuhn believed that the Indo-European peoples had already separated by Neolithic times, and that their unity should be sought in Upper Paleolithic western Europe.[225] If this theory has merit, as suggested in our earlier comparison of Kurgan harpoons and horse reverence with Magdalenian traditions, the see page 90 Golden Age of Magdalenian culture may have reflected the glory of Yima (Yama, Ymir) himself, and he in turn the benevolence of Plato's early Atlantic (twin) kings.

A rather sweeping proposition, to be sure, but there are one or two themes among the very rare examples of narrative art in the Magdalenian collection that seem particularly reminiscent of Iranian myth and rite. The first is shown at its best in the famous Shaft painting at Lascaux, described by one investigator as "the most striking scene in the entire cave."[229] The Shaft itself is sixteen feet deep and evidently was negotiated by means of a rope. At the bottom a small chamber is dominated by a painted panel some six feet long (fig. 63). Artistically the painting offers no challenge to the magnificent works in Lascaux's Axial Gallery; see figures 2, 6 many of the elements here are no more than sketched, without color or substance. At the center lies a bird-headed or bird-masked man drawn in stiff black lines. Below him a bird, also schematically drawn and with a head precisely like that of the man, is perched on a pole. On the right a bison rendered in an unusual style appears to be badly wounded. He too is

63 Scene painted in the shaft at Lascaux, 15,000–14,500 B.C. Early Magdalenian *(after Leroi-Gourhan, 1982)*

perhaps recumbent; large black loops believed to be entrails issue from his lower body, and his head is turned back in that direction. A line with a barbed hook, which may or may not represent the Bird-Headed Man's spear, lies across the body of the bison. To the left a rhinoceros is shown moving away from the scene. His belly, chest, and foreleg were never sketched in, and the six black dots under his upraised tail are of uncertain significance. Leroi-Gourhan believes that this animal may be irrelevant to the main drama,[238] but in the opinion of the Abbé Breuil, it was the rhinoceros, and not the fallen man, that was responsible for the goring of the bison.[262]

Countless numbers of human beings had apparently descended into the Shaft over the years, wearing and blackening the stone at the lip of the chasm. A great many bone points, all broken, and a number of small dishlike stone lamps lay below the painted panel. Presumed to have been ritual offerings, these objects add to the impression, generally shared by prehistorians, that this celebrated chamber played a central role in the religious life of those who visited Lascaux. The most intensive analysis of the cave to date has led its authors to conclude with respect to the Shaft:

> Though it is as yet too early to understand the real meaning of it, such consistency between the place, the wall decoration, and the whole assemblage invites us to see in this unity the heart of what was quite obviously a sanctuary.[240]

Too early or not, few prehistorians have failed to offer an explanation of the meaning of the Shaft painting (e.g., hunter slain by bison, shamanic trance; the man's rigid phallus could indicate either condition). None has been found convincing enough for a consensus, however, or for that matter, worthy of enshrinement at the heart of Lascaux. Hunting magic, at one time the answer to all problems in interpreting rock art, also seems to be an inadequate explanation; as Laming-Emperaire pointed out, it is difficult to see how the Bird-Headed Man, if indeed dead or wounded, could further the success of the hunt.[229] She found it more likely that figures such as these represent "mythical beings who were perhaps connected in some way with the history of the ancestors of the group." If Laming-Emperaire was on the right track, the scene portrayed here may find its closest surviving counterparts in Indo-European cosmogony. The composition in the Lascaux Shaft bears a provocative resemblance to the world-creating death of Gayomart (the Iranian First Man) and the Primordial Bull.

As told in the Persian *Bundahišn*, Gayomart and the bull lived in a state of divine bliss until the evil principle broke into the world, causing the death of the pair. When the bull died, its marrow flowed forth to create all the nourishing and healing plants; its semen was borne to the moon for purification and thence to the creation of all species of animals. From Gayomart's body came the metals (originally perhaps the mineral kingdom as a whole); from his own seed, purified in the sun, sprang the ten species of men.

We shall later find that the creation of the world out of the body of a primeval anthropomorph, or of a slain bull, was not limited to Indo-European traditions. But as Gayomart and the bull have close counterparts in Scandinavian as well as Vedic mythology,[72] many scholars believe that this theme, like that of Yima's reign, was known to the Indo-European unity. (In the Norse myth Ymir, who was also associated with a primordial bovid, is slain and the earth made from his flesh, the water from his blood, the mountains from his bones, etc. [*Gylfaginning* 6–8]; the sacrifice of the Vedic Purusa, a name which combines the Sanskrit words for "man" and "bull,"[244] was similarly generative [*Rig Veda* X.90.vi–xvi].) It has further been suggested that because of the greater conservatism of the Indo-Iranian branch of the Indo-Europeans, the eastern versions may more closely approximate the original myth.[243] And it is in fact the Iranian account which seems most faithful to the scene in the Lascaux Shaft.

Looking back at figure 63, we might first note that the bison is cousin to the wild aurochs and could as easily have represented the mythic Primordial Bull. Secondly, comparative studies of Eurafrican mythology have demonstrated the particular capacity of the rhinoceros for embodying the principle of evil,[190] and if the rhinoceros was indeed part of the Shaft composition, he may well have slain both man and bison. The pronounced ithyphallic condition of the fallen man could signify not only his moribund state but also the release of his seed, while the effluent from the lower belly of the bison may denote his own freed seminal substance, as well as or instead of his entrails. (The barbed line across the body of the bison is in any event oddly placed to be the man's spear and may depict a symbolic line of force.) The Persian association of the *xvarenah* with bird forms (as in Yima's loss of the Glory, above) suggests that the bird's head or mask on the fallen man and the bird perched below him may represent the immortal Glory which Gayomart himself possessed. Finally, and not of least importance, the slaying of the First Man and the Primordial Bull—the cosmogonic act itself—would have been an eminently appropriate subject for portrayal in the depths of the sanctuary at Lascaux.

The story describing the event depicted in the Shaft may have played a major part in the oral tradition during the Early and Middle Magdalenian periods; artistic variations on the man-bison theme have been found at three other European sites, dating from perhaps 17,000 to 12,000 B.C.[238] (Lascaux's paintings were executed in the first half of the fifteenth millennium.) In Persian mythology the death of the First Man did not prevent the celebration of a Golden Age; the resplendent Yima was said to be a descendant of Gayomart, five generations removed (*Bundahišn* XXXV). However telescoped mythic time may be, if the scene in the Shaft does represent the Indo-European cosmogony, the reign of Yima and the Magdalenian Golden Age may in fact have been one.

Accepting for the moment this hypothetical identity, we would expect the decay of art and culture in Late Paleolithic southwest Europe to have marked the fall of Yima (or of his line). It is in this light, perhaps, that one should view the next, and almost the only other, certain examples of narrative art in the Magdalenian collection, apparently rendered later in the Paleolithic period.[237] Of these two carved bone plaques, the one from Les Eyzies (fig. 64a) shows nine small silhouettes of human figures walking in file toward a bison. They either carry sticks or have

a

b

64 Magdalenian engravings on bone plaques from (a) Les Eyzies and (b) Raymonden, France (*after Marshack, 1972*)

been "struck through" by signs of unknown meaning.[265] The other, from Raymonden (fig. 64b), depicts the head of a bison, still attached to the spine, with the severed legs of the animal in front. On either side human figures have again been schematically drawn, one of which also appears to have lines extending from his chest. According to one prehistorian: "To regard this scene as depicting some magic rite connected with trapping, or the ritual interment of an animal, is altogether far-fetched. The men facing each other from either side of the animal's spine are obviously 'faithful' present at the ceremony."[260]

What sort of ceremony is not specified; we presume a sacrifice is meant. Nor is the reason why only now, possibly quite late in the Magdalenian day, does it seem to have been pictorially represented. If this is not merely an accident of recovery, these plaques may depict rites that had been newly instituted (or perhaps made public) toward the end of the Magdalenian era. We noted earlier that one of Yima's alleged sins was giving the flesh of cattle to the people to eat, which has been interpreted see page 107 as the establishing of ritualized slaughter of the bull. If the body of the dismembered bison at figure 64b had been ceremonially consumed by the men surrounding its remains, this was not a dissimilar ritual. Precise dates are lacking, but it is possible that these plaques were carved during the decline of prehistoric Europe's Golden Age. Did the ceremony they depict anticipate the end of Yima's reign?

Mithra and the Bull

The ceremonial consumption of a bull would later be typical of many of the initiatory cults of antiquity, among them the mysteries of the Iranian god Mithra, who in the eyes of some Iraniologists was closely connected to the Yima cycle of myth.[442] If, through the institution of animal sacrifice, Yima did intend to confer immortality upon his people (as claimed in the annotation cited above), it would agree with the purposes of the mysteries, which aimed at the divinizing, or the immortalizing, of the individual.

see page 107

The bull sacrifice in the Mithraic mysteries was apparently a re-enactment of Mithra's mythic slaying of the bull that he had captured in the wild. As reconstructed from Roman monuments, Mithra had seized a wild bull by the horns and ridden it until the animal was exhausted. He then carried the bull back to his cave, and, in a scene that was familiar throughout the Roman empire, Mithra slew the bull, grasping its nostrils with one hand and plunging a dagger into its side with the other (fig. 65). From the body of the dying animal emerged, according to one interpretation, all of the useful plants and herbs which cover the earth.[91] The similarity of this sequence to the murder of the Primordial Bull has not gone unnoticed, but it has also

65 Mithra slaying the bull. Roman statue of coarse-grained marble. The significance of the snake, dog, and scorpion that usually accompany these bull-slaying scenes is unclear; the sprouting of grain from the bull's shoulder (or often the tail) has been compared to the events that followed the death of the Iranian Primordial Bull. (after Vermaseren, 1956)

been observed that Mithra's deed recalls the eschatology as well as the cosmogony of the Iranians, who believed that the virtuous would be immortalized at the end of time through the sacrifice of a sacred bull by a *saošyant* (savior).[186] In this case, as one authority points out, "it could be said that initiation into the Mysteries anticipated the final Renovation, in other words, the salvation of the *mystes* [the participant]."[120]

Franz Cumont believed that the legends of which Mithra is the hero must have been created in an archaic epoch, and that the practice of consecrating mountain caves to the god was the heritage of a time when temples were not yet constructed.[91] It is true that the Mithraic mysteries were famous for the use of painted and decorated caves, a resemblance to Magdalenian traditions that is reinforced by the earlier-noted suggestions of see page 26 rites of mystical initiation in the Upper Paleolithic caves. Little is known of the prehistory of the Mithraic tradition; the possibility that it was a good deal older than has generally been suspected will be raised later by the several parallels to Mithraic rite and symbol in the sixth millennium shrines of Çatal Hüyük. But Mithra was associated in later antiquity with the Armenian river Araxes, not the French Dordogne, and one contemporary Iraniologist has suggested that the region west of the Caspian Sea — specifically the borderlands between northwestern Iran, Armenia, and the Caucasus — is in fact the most likely homeland of the Mithraic mysteries.[429] If the traditions surrounding this Indo-European god were possibly Magdalenian in origin, how did Mithraic (or proto-Mithraic) rites get from the painted caves of southwest Europe to the lands west of the Caspian Sea?

We mentioned earlier that Yima had found it necessary to "enlarge the world" three times during his reign in order to accommodate the increase in herds and men. If the extension of Middle to Late Magdalenian influence across Europe corre- see page 30 sponded to the mythic migrations of Yima's people, they would have spread first into Germanic lands and then as far east as the Russian site of Molodova V by the twelfth millennium B.C.; the solitary painted cave in the Urals may also date to this time. A thousand years later the Iranian cave site of Ali Tappeh on the eastern side of the Caspian Sea was occupied by people whose excellent bone work included finely eyed needles that the excavator compared to those of southwest Europe.[272] Had Yima's final expansion reached the Caspian Sea?

Let us look again at the first series of rock engravings at Kobystan, the earliest art of its kind in Transcaucasia and, from

see figure 36

the masterful quality of its execution, apparently the work of newcomers to this region. We suggested earlier that Plato's all-inclusive war might have carried these foreign bowmen and their artistic style, comparable in many respects to that of the Spanish Levant, to the shores of the Caspian Sea. The numerous representations of bulls at Kobystan have also been compared stylistically to those of western art,[135] and we can now further observe that the angular lines across the shoulders of the male figures of this first phase are not unlike the so-called "struck through" marks on the men of the Late Magdalenian plaques. If these large and deeply carved Kobystani figures do represent new arrivals in Transcaucasia, might they have been leaders in the last of Yima's line—and bearers of the bull-centered traditions of Mithra?

Lying just north of the Araxes river (the modern Aras) and above Iranian Azerbaijan, Kobystan is certainly not far from the reputed source of the Mithraic mysteries. It also falls within the region chosen by one prominent early Iraniologist as the most likely location of Eran-Vēj (*Airyāna Vaējah*), the legendary homeland of the Iranian people. (The Persian *Bundahišn* [XXIX.12] states that Eran-Vēj bordered on Azerbaijan, and James Darmesteter felt that the northern side of Azerbaijan best fitted the description in the text.)[92] We shall have a chance to explore these claims later when, in the sixth millennium B.C., peoples with ties to this region begin constructing permanent settlements in northern Mesopotamia, the remains of which yield pottery painted with designs (bull, scorpion, snake) reminiscent of Mithraic symbolism. We would only add here that the excavator of Kobystan believes that, whatever its significance, the area around these engraved rock surfaces continued to be held sacred throughout the remainder of prehistory and into historical times. Even today, there are six pagan sanctuaries in the vicinity, at which the Azerbaijanis offer small pieces of cloth in symbolic sacrifice.[135]

Summary

To close this section on myth we might briefly summarize these suggested links between Magdalenians, proto-Iranians, and Plato's Atlantics, again with the understanding that this is clearly an oversimplification of what must have been an extremely complex chain of events. As described in Part I, the archaeology of Upper Paleolithic Europe records a series of migratory movements out of western Europe, beginning as early as the initial expansion of Magdalenian culture in perhaps the thirteenth millennium B.C. Apparently welcome at first, as early Atlantic visitations would also have been, these migrating groups may have become increasingly aggressive as the decay of western culture set in, until we have the situation described by the excavator of the Ukrainian cemeteries as the forcing-out of native eastern Europeans, leaving Europe's first known collection of violent deaths in its wake. At this point the sequence intersected the warlike activities elsewhere in the archaeology of ninth millennium Europe and the Near East, theorized as the conflict described in the *Timaeus*.

In this second section, working backward from parallels to the Magdalenian harpoons and veneration of the horse in the later, apparently Indo-European, Kurgan culture of the Russian steppes, we revived an earlier theory that placed the proto-Indo-European homeland in Upper Paleolithic western Europe. The most important piece of Magdalenian narrative art, the painting in the Lascaux Shaft, fit the cosmogonic myth of the Iranians without undue stretching. We thus ventured to compare the Magdalenian epoch with the mythological Golden Age of Indo-European Yima, whose people, like the southwest Europeans, increased in number during his reign and expanded their range far beyond the boundaries of their original world. Two carved bone plaques of Late Magdalenian age were then offered as possible representations of the animal sacrifices attributed to Yima's last days. In the context of a cave-painting culture, these Magdalenian plaques seemed particularly suggestive of the traditions surrounding the Iranian god Mithra, whose followers also sacrificed bulls and whose later mysteries are known to have been celebrated in painted caves.

Looking then to Epi-Paleolithic Transcaucasia, and with the mythology of Yima's threefold expansion in mind, we found that the western connections of the Kobystani warriors and their bulls provided a means by which proto-Mithraic traditions might have been transferred to the region west of the Caspian Sea, believed to have been the homeland of the Mithraic mysteries. As Mithra was in one aspect a warrior god, our earlier proposal that these newcomers to Kobystan were associated in some way with Plato's war (the contest for Yima's lost Glory?) remains unaffected.

It may seem at this point that the theory of an Iranian connection to Magdalenian and Atlantic traditions is peripheral to our main theme. The plausibility of an historical foundation for

Plato's tale does not depend on the strength of the Persian component, or on the identification of the Magdalenian culture as proto-Indo-European. But the questions raised here will be helpful later, first in dealing with the Mithraic overtones in the bull cults of Çatal Hüyük and then in reconstructing the background of Zarathuštra. Furthermore, we are committed not only to trying to see the events of this epoch from Plato's perspective, but also to the construction of a whole picture, however broad and bare, from which future research can coherently develop or depart. If the speculative use of other mythologies seems a radical means to that end, the alternative, it now seems, is to treat the Magdalenian culture as an entertaining curiosity, a persistent anomaly without meaning or relevance to the course of human prehistory. The archaeological sciences have given us a great deal of valuable technical information but no real sense of the life and thought of these extraordinary Europeans. Indeed, as one authority on Upper Paleolithic Europe recently remarked, the more refined scientific research becomes, the further the Magdalenian experience seems to recede from our comprehension: "If there is any inherent point to the increasingly precise reconstructions of Ice Age landscapes provided by the pollen and bone specialists, or to the growing thoroughness with which the symbols of prehistoric art are recorded, it may be to bring home how strange and remote this world is to our imagination."[169]

Strange and remote it will undoubtedly remain, but not necessarily incomprehensible, if the resources of ancient literature are added to those of modern archaeology. The advisability of using both to reconstruct the Paleolithic world is perhaps most clearly perceived in the light of later, Neolithic, developments. As we shall see in the following section, the first great wave of Neolithic settlers appears to have brought to the Near East more than the material bases of the civilizations of the Bronze and later ages: a number of the spiritual bases—the mythologies—of those later civilizations seem to have been known as well to the men of what was, following Plato, the post-deluge period of prehistory.

III

The Neolithic Revolution:
Phase I

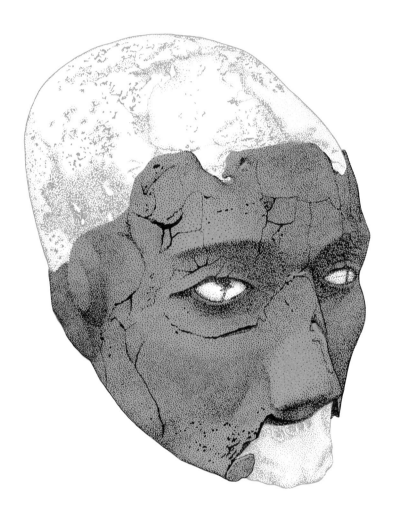

66 Plastered and painted skull from Jericho Pre-Pottery Neolithic B, late eighth or seventh millennium B.C. Believed to be evidence of ancestor worship, these skulls were given a lifelike appearance by the modeling of flesh and features with plaster, which was then painted a red-brown color. As shown here, pieces of shell were sometimes inserted into the eye slits. *(after Kenyon, 1957)*

The Hermocrates

ATHENIAN STRANGER: Do you believe that there is any truth in ancient traditions?

CLEINIAS: What traditions?

ATHENIAN STRANGER: The traditions about the many destructions of mankind which have been occasioned by deluges and pestilences, and in many other ways, and of the survival of a remnant?

CLEINIAS: Everyone is disposed to believe them.

ATHENIAN STRANGER: Let us consider one of them, that which was caused by the famous deluge. . . . Those who then escaped would only be hill shepherds—small sparks of the human race preserved on the tops of mountains. . . . Such survivors would necessarily be unacquainted with the arts and the various devices which are suggested to the dwellers in cities by interest or ambition, and with all the wrongs which they contrive against one another.

CLEINIAS: Very true.

ATHENIAN STRANGER: Let us suppose, then, that the cities in the plain and on the sea-coast were utterly destroyed at that time.

CLEINIAS: Very good. . . .

ATHENIAN STRANGER: After the great destruction, may we not suppose that the state of man was something of this sort: In the beginning of things there was a fearful illimitable desert and a vast expanse of land; a herd or two of oxen would be the only survivors of the animal world, and there might be a few goats. . . .   (*Laws* III.677–678)[203]

The eminent classicist Francis Cornford believed that the *Timaeus* and *Critias* were actually the first two parts of a planned trilogy, a project that Plato had abandoned midway through the *Critias* in order to write the *Laws*. As he saw it, Book III of the *Laws*, from which the passages above are taken, dealt with material originally intended for the third dialogue in the trilogy.[86]

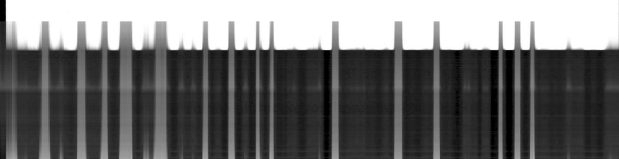

see Appendix A

Cornford's reasoning was as follows. At the opening of the *Timaeus*, three characters are introduced — Timaeus, Critias, and Hermocrates — who have together agreed to repay Socrates for his description on the previous day of an ideal society. Critias has chosen to relate the story told Solon by the Saitic priest; the Ur-Athenians would agree remarkably well with the citizens of Socrates' ideal state, which could thereby be transferred from the imaginary to the real world, as Socrates had requested (*Timaeus* 26). But first Timaeus is to describe the birth of the cosmos and the nature of man, the main themes of the dialogue bearing his name. The *Critias* dialogue then takes us through descriptions of Ur-Athens, Atlantis, and the initial degeneration that would eventually lead to war. At this point the story breaks off, but Critias' short preview at the start of the *Timaeus* indicates that he would have gone on to tell in more detail the story of the great conflict and of the subsequent catastrophe that overwhelmed both major combatants.

Why then was Hermocrates present? We are assured at the start of the *Critias* (108) that Hermocrates' turn to speak will come. Cornford suggested that Plato's original intent was to have him take up the story after the deluge and trace the re-emergence of Greek culture and its development into historical times. The trilogy, had it been completed, would thus have told the history of the world from the cosmogony to Plato's own epoch, "the most ambitious design he had ever conceived."[86] But there is no trace of a "Hermocrates" dialogue, and Cornford theorized that Plato gave up his original plan at the point where the *Critias* was interrupted and turned to writing the *Laws* instead.*

As we saw above, the third book of the *Laws* does indeed describe the recovery of a remnant of mankind after a great deluge. The surviving "hill shepherds" of the *Laws* are easily matched with the "unlettered mountain folk" who were left in Greece after the *Timaeus* deluge, and the Athenian Stranger shares the views of the Egyptian priest of the *Timaeus* with regard to the periodic destructions of mankind. But the "famous deluge" of which the Athenian speaks in the *Laws* seems unlikely to have been other than Deucalion's Flood, which to the Greeks of Plato's day was The Flood, while the disaster that overcame Ur-Athens was named by the Egyptian priest "the third terrible deluge before that of Deucalion" (*Critias* 112).

---

* Although Plutarch attributed the breaking-off of the *Critias* to the death of Plato (*Life of Solon*), modern scholars tend to believe that the *Laws* was his last work.

Still, Cornford's idea of a planned but unwritten dialogue in which the third man present describes post-deluge developments does make sense, whatever the reason for its abandonment. And it is quite possible that the Greeks typically compounded many deluge mythologies into one. (One mythographer believes that the number of different mountains on which Deucalion supposedly landed,* in Greece, Thrace, and Sicily, indicates that an ancient deluge myth was superimposed on a later legend of a flood in northern Greece.)[164] In any case, the account in the *Laws* apparently was meant to describe a cycle which had been repeated many times over; if not an authentic extension of the *Timaeus* and *Critias* dialogues, it still may be useful as a guide to post-deluge conditions per se, an example of Plato's views on what happens in Greece after any great flood. We are almost entirely on our own at this point and shall need whatever help Plato's other writings can lend to the archaeology of the times. For if Parts I and II of this study may be seen as an attempt to complete the unfinished *Critias* dialogue, Part III will try to recreate the first chapter in the story Hermocrates might have told: the story of the recovery.

* Warned by Prometheus that a great deluge was to be visited on the iniquitous Bronze Race, Deucalion built an ark for himself and his wife Pyrrha. When the waters subsided, the couple repopulated the world by throwing the "bones of their mother," the stones of Mother Earth, over their shoulders.

Greek Archaeology: 7500 – 5500 B.C.

see figure 26

This third section will take us from the middle of the eighth millennium, the theoretical time of the deluge, to the middle of the sixth millennium and the decline of the warrior tradition that informed Palestine and Syria during this two-thousand-year epoch. Greece herself played a late and very minor role in this period. With the exception of Franchthi Cave, the whole of the Greek peninsula was without recorded signs of life until the end of the seventh millennium B.C. But when open-air settlements did begin to take root, first in Thessaly around 6200 B.C., certain aspects of their remains suggest that Greek lands had not lain uninhabited prior to that time. As it is only in Greece that we are guided, however gently, by Plato, these initial Greek settlements should be briefly investigated before taking a closer look at the earlier and more impressive Near Eastern developments mentioned at the end of Part I.

The Civilization of Old Europe

> The survivors of this destruction were an unlettered mountain race who had just heard the names of the rulers of the land but knew little of their achievements. They were glad enough to give their names to their own children, but they knew nothing of the virtues and institutions of their predecessors, except for a few hazy reports; for many generations they and their children were short of bare necessities, and their minds and thoughts were occupied with providing for them, to the neglect of earlier history and tradition.
>
> (*Critias* 109 – 110)[232]

It was once the general belief among prehistorians that the earliest permanent settlers of Greece came from abroad. Immigrants from Anatolia or the Near Eastern Levant were thought to have arrived during the late seventh or early sixth millennium with a fully developed Neolithic culture—domestic plants and animals, permanent architecture, pottery, figurines—which was transplanted in its entirety to Greek soil. In favor of this theory, which many still hold, stands the scant evidence of human occupation in Mesolithic Greece and the presence in early Neolithic Greek sites of domesticated species (sheep and emmer wheat) whose wild progenitors apparently were not native to Greece and which were already domestic at this time in lands farther east.

Several archaeologists now believe, however, that the earliest Greek settlers were largely indigenous populations, and that animal husbandry and possibly the cultivation of plants were already known to Greece prior to, and independent of, foreign influence.[395, 417] The cattle at the c. 6200 B.C. Thessalian site of Argissa are the earliest certain domesticates of this species; pig and possibly goat were native to Greece and could have been locally domesticated. The same is true for several of the grains in Neolithic Greek sites. Wild oats and barley appeared at Franchthi Cave as early as 11,000 B.C., and the presence of domestic forms of both species in Neolithic levels led Jane Renfrew to remark of the earlier finds:

> Whether these species were already being experimented with as a source of food, and being brought into cultivation even at this early date is not clear, but the possibility must remain open, pending further finds from sites dating to this period in Greece.[343]

Furthermore, if Greece had been colonized by Near Easterners, one would expect to find many more stylistic similarities in tools, architecture, and other artifacts between the two regions than is actually the case. The rudimentary tool kits of early Greek sites were mainly composed of small unworked blades, whereas those of contemporary Anatolia and the Levant displayed a variety of retouched tools and finely worked projectile points that had no counterparts in Greece. As we shall also see in the following chapters, rectangular mud-brick architecture had now been standard in the east for over a thousand years, but the earliest Thessalian dwellings were oval shaped huts of wattle-and-daub (interwoven poles and twigs plastered over with mud), a building material that continued in use when larger rectangular structures were raised and mud-brick employed in parts of Greece. As for ceramics, the monochrome pottery in early Greek sites does show general similarities to the wares of the eastern Mediterranean, but there are important differences as well,[430] and it now seems that pottery actually appeared in both

Greece and the Levant at around the same early sixth millennium date.

In short, if some of the domesticated plants and animals, building and ceramic techniques, were either acquired or improved through contact with the east, a careful analysis of the existing data argues in favor of a largely independent Neolithic development of Greece.[430] Moreover, when painted patterns are applied to ceramic vessels later in the period, the individuality of local designs throughout Greece and the Balkans speaks even more clearly for the presence in these lands of heretofore invisible native populations.

Were these the descendants of Plato's slow-recovering herdsmen, the only survivors left in Greece after the floods? The aggregate of these Greco-Balkan traditions formed a unique cultural horizon which has been named by Marija Gimbutas the *Civilization of Old Europe* (fig. 67).[159] To be discussed in Part V, this bloc of related cultures eventually extended from the Aegean and Adriatic to the Danube, flourishing for more than two millennia on the mainland and conserved in the Minoan civilization of Crete until the middle of the second millennium.

67 Area occupied by the *Civilization of Old Europe*, a Neolithic Greco-Balkan complex of cultures believed to have been largely indigenous *(after Gimbutas, 1974)*

OLD EUROPE

According to Gimbutas, the temple world of Old Europe reveals "clear lines of architectural and religious influence that stretch through to the far later Minoan-Mycenean period and beyond to Greek and even Roman times."[161] If essentially a native development, as she too maintains, the Civilization of Old Europe may in fact represent the recovery, with however great an assist from abroad, of traditions all but lost in the deluge of the *Timaeus*.

The Near Eastern Vanguard:
75/7300 B.C.

We must go back now two thousand years, to the dawn of this epoch in the Near East and the possibility that other survivors, some more advanced than Plato's rustic herdsmen, found refuge outside Greece. As we recall from Part I, Near Eastern archaeology had revealed glimpses of higher levels of culture as early as the tenth millennium in the artistry and technological accomplishments of the Natufians, again in the late ninth millennium with Jericho's monumental wall and tower, and then early in the eighth millennium in the rectangular architecture and other innovations at Mureybet III. We were nevertheless unprepared for the sudden burst of settlement activity around 75/7300 B.C., which sent unexpectedly sophisticated architectural and agricultural skills into Anatolia, Syria, Palestine, and the southernmost reaches of the Zagros mountains of Iran. One could almost say that the Neolithic Revolution was accomplished overnight. After this abrupt introduction of new approaches to clay and stone, grain and metal, no significant change would occur in the Near East for almost two thousand years.

see pages 42–45

see page 64

The archaeology of this period is usually divided into two main cultural impulses: the *Pre-Pottery Neolithic B* peoples of Palestine and related sites in Syria and Anatolia,* and the *Zagros village* traditions of the Iranian and Iraqi mountains of that name. "PPNB" settlements generally were characterized by red-plastered floors, expertly worked arrow and spear heads, and a notable veneration of ancestors. In the considerably more modest Zagros settlements, projectile points were unknown, herding seems to have been more important than farming, and religious pursuits bore an odd resemblance to the later cult life of the Aegean.

---

* The earlier walled-town phase at Jericho approximately defines the Pre-Pottery Neolithic *A* period (c. 8500–7600 B.C.). Pre-Pottery Neolithic *B* is generally dated from around 75/7300 to 5800 B.C.

This division into two main traditions does help to bring a sense of order into what has suddenly become an extremely complex archaeological picture. But too much reliance on these categories tends to mask the extraordinary diversity from site to site within each of the major divisions, and to obscure the importance of several assemblages which fail to conform to either group. Differences are in fact never so pronounced as in the early days of this epoch. Of the several settlements founded in approximately 75/7300 B.C. — Çayönü, Ganj Dareh D, Jericho PPNB, Abu Hureyra, Alikosh, and the expansion of Tell Aswad — no two were similar enough to suggest more than the

68 The Near East, 7500–5600 B.C. Sites mentioned in the text

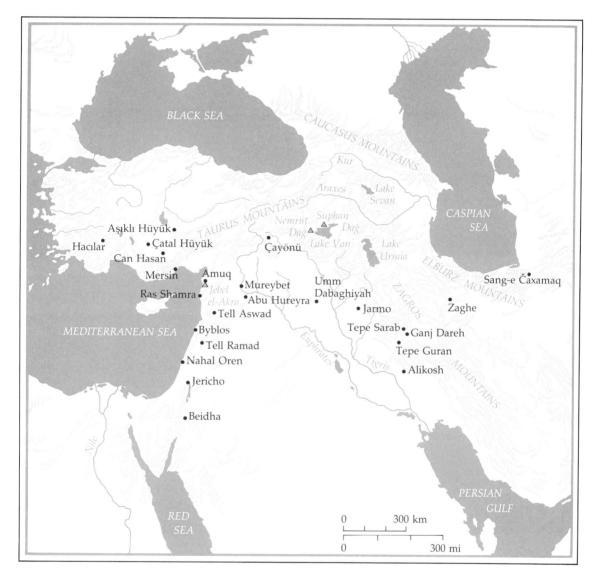

The Neolithic Revolution: Phase I   127

sharing of a common, and in each case unknown, ancestor from which both had long ago diverged. As notable as the numerical increase in sites undoubtedly was, this variation in previously developed cultural expressions was even more remarkable. There were, in other words, not only a great many new people in the late eighth millennium Near East, but a great many different new people.

The following survey of the most significant of these new sites, some of which were introduced briefly at the end of Part I, will illustrate this point. What Plato's account might tell us about their origins will also be discussed here, but the range and depth of the spiritual life of these Neolithic settlers will not be fully appreciated until we come to the well-preserved site of Çatal Hüyük late in the seventh millennium. Here virtually all of the known traditions of the day met in an outpouring of religious art that for the first time makes explicit what is presumed to have been either implicit or ill-preserved at these earlier sites. The wealth of symbolism in the shrines of this Anatolian center has enabled archaeologists, in the words of one, "to approach as near as ever possible to an insight into the minds of prehistoric peoples without written records."[54]

As we shall see in Part IV, these particular prehistoric minds seem to have been engrossed by religious themes which the excavator of Çatal Hüyük found remarkably similar to those of Minoan Crete and the oldest stratum of Greek religion and mythology.[275] Mellaart's views have since been shared by several colleagues,[97] a consensus which suggests that the residents of Çatal Hüyük (like their apparent kinsmen in the Civilization of Old Europe) may have been descended from survivors of the *Timaeus* floods. But a closer look at the Çatal collection will also reveal influences that seem distinctly African or Egyptian, and others that recall the religion of ancient Iran. It might be unwise at this point, therefore, to theorize that all or perhaps even most of the people in the Neolithic Near East were Greek.

Çayönü

This said, we can turn first to what is perhaps the most Greek-like of the new settlements in the late eighth millennium Near East. With a founding date of around 75/7300 B.C., Çayönü map at figure 68 opened the epoch in Anatolia that Çatal Hüyük would close two thousand years later. And although much smaller in size and considerably less well-preserved, Çayönü was nevertheless clearly designed by people no less skilled than the creators of the Çatal community.

The settlement lies in the east Anatolian foothills of the Taurus mountains, on a tributary of the Tigris river and within range of several obsidian flows and the copper deposits at Ergani. The unexpected familiarity of the residents of Çayönü with the working of (presumably cold-hammered) copper was mentioned in Part I; investigators have found it equally surprising that copper products apparently were discontinued after their brief appearance there. With the exception of a stray bead or two, worked copper was not visible again in the Near East until the early levels of Çatal Hüyük. If this was a craft that the founders of Çayönü brought into the Taurus, it apparently did not long survive the transfer.

see page 67

Çayönü's architects fared better than her would-be smiths, and it is in their uncommon skill that we find the most promising analogies to Plato's Greeks. Parallels between Çayönü's building plans and Critias' description of the layout of the Athenian Acropolis will not be exact; there was, for example, no defensive wall at Çayönü. But it appears certain that her architectural designs, for which precedents do not exist in the archaeological record, were no less specialized and differentiated than those attributed to Ur-Athens.

We are told in the *Critias* that the Acropolis was far more extensive before the deluge and covered with soil. Craftsmen and husbandmen lived on its lower slopes; the warrior-guardians were quartered higher up around the temple of Athena and Hephaistos. The structures raised by this ranking class were then described as follows:

> On the northern side they built their common dwelling-houses and winter mess-rooms, and everything else required by their communal life in the way of buildings and temples. . . . [They] aimed at a balance between extravagance and meanness in the houses they built, in which they and their descendants grew old and which they handed on unchanged to succeeding generations who resembled themselves. In the summer they abandoned their gardens and gymnasia and mess-rooms and used the southern side of the Acropolis instead. (*Critias* 112)[232]

Turning to Çayönü, we find that the several building plans were originally believed to represent sequential phases: first a Grill Plan, then a Broad Pavement Plan, then a Cell Plan, and lastly a Large House Plan. Such a rapid overturning of architectural styles would in itself have been quite unconventional

The Neolithic Revolution: Phase I   129

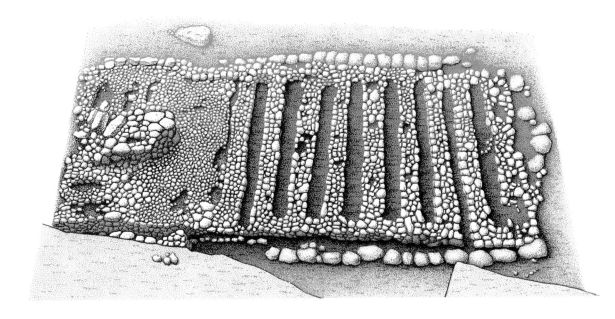

(Jericho in this period yielded twenty-five consecutive levels of
stereotyped rectangular dwellings), but the excavators' recent
decision that the several plans at Çayönü must have coexisted
to some extent is even more contrary to existing ideas about
undifferentiated early settlers.[59] The details of these plans are
summarized below:

1. The *Grill Plan* consisted of a grid of narrowly parallel stone
walls (fig. 69), upon which wooden beams and then floors seem
to have been laid. The purpose of such an extensive foundation
is unknown; several analysts have suggested that it was a means
of raising the floors of the buildings above off the winter-damp
ground,[280, 337] and the excavators see indications of the "absolute
need for dry floors and a corresponding comprehension by the
builders of how to achieve them."[45] Trash-filled pits and open-
air hearths which were once thought to represent an earlier
phase of occupation are now believed more likely to have been
the result of outdoor activities undertaken by the inhabitants of
the Grill Plan structures.

2. The *Broad Pavement Plan* featured smooth flagstone floors and
the use of tall upright slabs of limestone, together with the first
recorded examples of internal buttressing. One structure, known
as the "flagstone building," was floored with large flat stones
measuring up to five feet in length; the remains of two standing
stones opposed the buttresses on the back wall. The "terrazzo
building" mentioned in Part I yielded a true terrazzo floor, in
which two pairs of white-pebbled lines, positioned relative to

the buttresses along the walls, were set into a ground of salmon pink limestone particles. Analysis has shown that five different limestone fabrics were used in preparing this floor; once the mortar had set and hardened, the whole surface was carefully polished.[45] Another of these stone-paved structures included a corner entranceway that was compared to the *farisi* of later Aegean architecture, a device which allows more light to enter the building than conventional doorways. The floor of this particular structure had been covered with an even layer of coarse sand; a water channel ran the length of the south wall, with a two-foot-wide podium along the other sides.

3. The *Cell Plan* consisted of mud-brick superstructures which were supported by high stone foundations divided into six or eight small compartments (fig. 70). The contents of these cubicles suggest that each may have served as a storage room

70 Cell Plan foundation at Çayönü. Openings in the stone walls may have been passageways between "cells." *(after Redman, 1978)*

for the specialized materials used by Çayönü's craftsmen. One compartment contained a large number of ground and polished stone celts; another held a collection of marine shells; elsewhere caches of obsidian implements were laid: obsidian blades, points (including a few arrow or spear heads), and tools whose large size suggested ritual objects to an excavator.[337] Two small clay house-models in these deposits have been compared to similar items in Neolithic Greco-Balkan settlements,[160] and Çayönü's "two-in-one" figurine (fig. 71), which presents an ideal male-female image, has been likened to forms in the Bronze Age sculpture of the Cyclades.[446]

4. The *Large Room Plan* featured single-room structures, one measuring approximately 15 by 27 feet, without interior partitions. Evidence from the preserved portion of one of these large buildings points to the preparation of vegetable foodstuffs. Basalt handstones, pestles, and fragments of a stone quern were found alongside a storage bin.

The excavators of Çayönü have agreed that more work will be necessary to determine the extent to which these architectural designs overlapped in time. But whatever additional information is gathered in the future (the site is still under excavation), Çayönü's building and settlement plans have already been judged "far beyond and outside the customary form for this phase."[59] Assuredly not invented on the spot, might these unprecedented architectural forms have once been Greek?

Possible counterparts of the Athenian structures named in the *Critias* are not hard to find among the remains of this east Anatolian settlement. The internally buttressed, terrazzo- or flagstone-floored buildings of the Broad Pavement Plan, which the excavators believe must have served "some very special nondomestic purpose,"[40] may well have been temples; the building with sand-strewn floor and water channel might answer to one of Critias' gymnasia. The superstructures of Çayönü's Grill Plan, elevated against the winter damp, could be compared to the Athenian winter quarters; the Large Room Plan, with its evidence of food preparation, may be akin to the common dining or mess rooms named in the *Critias*. As for the apparently ceremonial objects in obsidian that were found among the storerooms of the Cell Plan, the association of this volcanic glass with the Greek god Hephaistos, Athena's reputed partner on the Acropolis, is very old and widely known. The presence of his cult at Çayönü would not be surprising in light of the copper work here, which would also have come under the patronage of Hephaistos as divine smith.

71 "Two-in-one" clay figurine from Çayönü (*after Redman, 1978*)

see page 92

But however fascinating an exercise, the comparison of Çayönü's artifacts and architecture with possible Athenian analogues can only be speculative at this point. More certain, and more important at present, is simply the recognition that Çayönü's settlement plan was equally as complex as that described in the *Critias*, and that her architectural forms were undoubtedly the products of a long prehistory. A millennium or more of prior development would not be an extravagant claim for these techniques. And wherever that development might have taken place, as Çayönü's excavators have pointed out, it is not in the record of known sites.

see page 68

Ganj Dareh D

The same may be said of Ganj Dareh D, founded, like the settlement at Çayönü, around 75/7300 B.C. Situated in a small valley of the Iranian Zagros some 1,400 feet above sea level, Ganj Dareh's origins are equally mysterious, but her traditions were very different from those of Çayönü. What sets this new Zagros community apart from her contemporaries and predecessors is primarily the ingenious use of clay.

map at figure 68

Architecturally, clay was used to form two types of very long bricks, one plano-convex, the other a sausagelike shape. *Tauf* or *chineh*, clay mixed with straw and laid in sun-dried layers, was also used at Ganj Dareh (as it is today in the Zagros); walls, floors, and ceilings of the honeycombed rectangular chambers created by these several techniques were then plastered over with clay. Large clay plugs grooved for gripping with the hand were fitted to the occasional round "portholes" which had been cut through the walls. Prefabricated slabs of clay with bevelled edges had also been fitted into the walls, forming partitioned cabinets or boxes. Clay was used again to raise the rims of large stone mortars, some of which had been provided with clay pedestals.[367-369]

Most remarkable of all, however, were Ganj Dareh's clay vessels. These ranged in size from thick-walled storage jars of over a hundred liter capacity, to "bread bowls" and even miniature goblets. The excavator believes that the larger containers were probably only sun-baked, but the smaller ones, including one vase made of two hemispheres joined together, evidently had been fired. Small animal figurines, one depicting a bearded goat, were also modeled in clay at Ganj Dareh, as were miniature geometric forms: spheres, cones, pyramids. Both types of clay object were also known to Çayönü; both will be ubiquitous in the Near East during this epoch. The animals have been interpreted as ritual offerings or toys, while the geometrics are believed to have been "counters," mathematical devices perhaps used in trade computation.[360]

Goats appear to have been herded at Ganj Dareh. Hoofprints believed to be those of the goat were found on bricks, which, together with a concentration of immature goats in the faunal sample, suggests a controlled herd. Sheep may also have been kept; their special standing at Ganj Dareh is demonstrated by the presence of a pair of ram's skulls with scimitar-shaped horns set one above the other in the wall of a plastered, possibly consecrated, niche. Just where these potter-herders gained their experience in the arts of permanent settlement is unknown, but if the founders of Ganj Dareh D were in fact the survivors of a lower-lying community that was lost in the floods, the absence of projectile points here and in other Zagros villages of this epoch may mean they had also escaped a war which seems to have left a lasting memory in Palestine and Syria.

Jericho: Pre-Pottery Neolithic B

Dating from around 7300 B.C., the Pre-Pottery Neolithic B occupation of Jericho lasted through some twenty-five building levels of large rectangular houses whose design remained so constant that Kenyon concluded that Jericho's architecture had been stereotyped during a long period of previous development elsewhere.[208-210] A well-preserved structure which resembles the *megaron* style of building associated with later Greek architecture may have been a shrine (fig. 72). Lime-plaster floors had been stained several shades of red, or left white, and given a burnish that was still hard enough to be scrubbed down for photographers. A herringbone pattern had been painted on one of the floors. Einkorn and emmer wheat and two-row barley were domestic, goat and possibly sheep were herded,[74] but in contrast to earlier settlements in the Levant (and to contemporary Zagros sites), there is no evidence of the consumption of fish, snails, fresh-water mussels, or birds.[17] One is reminded of the sharp decline in fish that accompanied PPNB-related traditions into Mureybet III.

The new occupants of Jericho apparently saw no need to erect a defense complex like that of the PPNA town (an existing structure is believed to have been a terrace wall rather than a

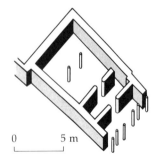

0   5 m

72 Plan of *megaron*-type shrine at Jericho PPNB (*after Mellaart, 1975*)

protective device),[289] yet the PPNB collection of weapons was far superior to the scarce points of the earlier phase. The tanged and winged arrowheads known as Jericho points (fig. 73) were fashioned from mauve, honey, and salmon colored flint; a distinctive type of retouch known as "pressure-flaking" was often employed.[90]

The miniature axe amulets described earlier also belong to this period at Jericho, as do practices attributed to ancestor worship. Individual human skulls had been preserved in Near Eastern sites as early as Ain Mallaha and again in the walled PPNA phase at Jericho, but this custom was carried to its most elaborate extreme at Jericho PPNB, where the faces and features of several male skulls had been reconstructed with plaster and paint (fig. 66), complete with a black moustache on one individual.[381] It was this combination of an intensified veneration of ancestors and a superabundance of fine weaponry, typical of PPNB sites in this period, that was suggested earlier as a possible Near Eastern counterpart to the commemoration of ancient warriors in the battle paintings of the Spanish Levant.

Tell Abu Hureyra

We noted in Part I that the Natufian-related community of round houses at Abu Hureyra was abandoned midway in the ninth millennium, shortly before the appearance of the first recorded arrowheads elsewhere in Syria. A thousand years later, again around 75/7300 B.C., a huge new settlement was founded at Hureyra, with large, multi-roomed, rectangular, mud-brick buildings present from the start. Their design, like the black-plastered floors found in these early levels, persisted throughout the 1,500 year life of this PPNB-related settlement.[288-290]

A wealth of agricultural advances was also evident in the earliest deposits at Abu Hureyra: hulled and naked six-row barley, oats, chick-pea, and horse bean, as well as emmer and einkorn wheat. The successful cultivation of six-row barley in particular implies a knowledge of irrigation techniques. Sheep and goat appear to have been herded, and if gazelle were controlled as well (for which there is some evidence),[289] the percentage of hunted animals in Hureyra's faunal sample would be negligible. Yet here again the most numerous tools on the site were arrow and lance heads. Somewhat crudely fashioned in the early years of this period, the projectile points became increasingly more refined; with the better weaponry came red

73 Jericho points, from Pre-Pottery Neolithic B levels at Jericho *(after Crowfoot-Payne, 1983)*

plastered floors to join the black, and one floor painting of a red sunburst on a black background.

Polished greenstone axes were present during all phases of Neolithic Hureyra, some of them miniaturized and pierced for suspension. Burials had been wrapped in woven matting before interment beneath the floors or between the buildings, and red ochre was scattered over many of the bodies, a custom that dates back to Upper Paleolithic times. Ochre was also applied to some of the skulls, which were frequently detached and buried separately although not plastered as at Jericho.

Tell Aswad II

As mentioned in Part I, the site of Tell Aswad in Syria's Damascus basin was first settled early in the eighth millennium, approximately contemporary with the introduction of rectangular architecture and other innovations into Mureybet III. The large projectile points and single sickle blades of Aswad I were similar to those of Mureybet III, but her architecture was impermanent and her grain morphologically domestic (emmer wheat, which, other than two-row barley, was the only domesticated grain known to the PPNA period). If there was an attack on Aswad comparable to the destruction of Mureybet, the absence of permanent architecture left it unrecorded.

Around 7300 B.C. the settlement at Tell Aswad was greatly enlarged (Aswad II).[78] Again the structures were not preserved, but agricultural activities were significantly improved. Not only was six-row barley added to the domestic grain bin, but also the earliest known samples of a free-threshing hexaploid wheat tentatively identified as club wheat.[445] The absence of on-site developmental stages both here and at Abu Hureyra suggests that these complex new grains were imported, but similar species have yet to be recorded at any known earlier site. Crop rotation also seems to have been introduced into Aswad at this time, with the pollen diagram showing phases of legumes between sproutings of cereals.[239]

And here again the pattern of arms elaboration was repeated. Aswad II saw the introduction of several new types of arrow and spear or lance heads (fig. 74). Leaf shaped points, long thin Amuq points, and Jericho points joined the tanged Byblos point which was known earlier at Aswad I, and which now began to show the ornamental pressure-flaking that became increasingly popular in the Levant during this epoch.[70]

74 Weaponry from Tell Aswad II: (a) Byblos point, (b) Jericho point, (c) Amuq point, (d) leaf point *(after M.-C. Cauvin, 1974)*

The Origin of Pre-Pottery Neolithic B

With Jericho, Abu Hureyra, and Tell Aswad II firmly grounded in the agricultural way of life, and with no evidence of hostilities during this period, the care and attention given to the crafting of weapons at these and related communities clearly exceeded economic or political necessity. To give another example, domestic goat accounted for almost 90% of the faunal remains at the seventh millennium PPNB settlement at Beidha in Jordan, yet an astonishing variety of some twenty different types of arrow and lance heads was recorded.[213] We shall later find many of the weapons at Çatal Hüyük to be nonutilitarian, with spear or lance heads offered in the shrines or buried unused with the dead. Given the similarity of other traditions at Çatal Hüyük to those of PPNB peoples—in crops, architecture, the use of red plaster and ornamental painting, the preservation of skulls[282]—it seems likely that the Çatal cult of the warrior was also shared by the weapon-makers of Syria and Palestine, perhaps from the start of this period.

c

d

If so, did the Pre-Pottery Neolithic B glorification of both warrior and ancestor spring from, and commemorate, the events of Plato's war? We have noted that PPNB traditions, however diverse, apparently were related to those that were introduced into Mureybet III early in the eighth millennium. The subsequent destruction of that Syrian site was seen in Part I as either a final phase of the *Timaeus* war or a display of residual enmity. Our question then—were the rectangular architecture and other innovations at Mureybet III more likely Greek or Atlantic?— may therefore be replaced now by the question of the identity of the Mureybet-related PPNB peoples who began settling Syria and Palestine in the last half of the eighth millennium. The likelihood that they were refugees from flooded Aegean lands seems lessened now that we know that red-plastered floors and projectile points will not appear in the earliest recorded settlements of Greece herself. Moreover, PPNB tools as a whole were largely macrolithic, those of Greece largely microlithic. It may thus be the case that PPNB equals Atlantic, rather than Greek, survivors.*

It is also possible, however, that these large and richly agricultural PPNB settlements were inhabited by a different sort of Greek survivor than those who stayed at home. It was said

---

* One recalls, for example, the grandly macrolithic blades of the Magdalenians; but harpoons are nowhere to be found in PPNB settlements, and in fact the rarity of fish in many PPNB sites may indicate a proscription on aquatic creatures.

75 (opposite) Near
Eastern and Aegean
sites named in the
text: approximate
chronologies

see page 119

map at figure 68

see page 44

see pages 84–85

in the *Critias* (109) that only a rustic mountain race was left in post-deluge Greece (a claim which is certainly not contradicted by the simplicity of the earliest Greek settlements). The vanished centers of culture, if such did exist, must therefore have been situated in the stricken river valleys and on the coast. Mountain and valley folk may have shared some of the same traditions, but, as observed in the *Laws*, surviving hill shepherds "would necessarily be unacquainted with the arts and the various devices which are suggested to the dwellers in cities." And it is among the civilized valley people that the role, or the class, of the warrior would have been most clearly defined.

Pre-Pottery Neolithic B peoples might therefore have been refugees from the valleys, rather than the hills, of Greece or her near neighbors. The six-row hulled barley that first appeared at Abu Hureyra will be the main crop of valley cultures all the way down to historical times;[178] presumably it originated in one as well. Then, too, red-plastered floors emerged very early in Anatolia, Greece's closest neighbor to the east: first in the central sector at Aşıklı Hüyük which, although incompletely excavated, is believed to date to the last half of the eighth millennium,[398] and a little later perhaps at Hacılar in western Anatolia,[279] a region which may itself have been flooded.

Furthermore, although Jericho's PPNB traditions were once believed to represent a complete break with those of the PPNA walled town of round houses, a more recent trend in archaeological thinking sees PPNB as possibly a more highly evolved variant of the earlier culture.[13] Several Levantine sites of this period yielded PPNA-type round houses in contexts that were otherwise typically PPNB (e.g., Beidha and Tell Ramad), and we are reminded that it was in a round house at Ain Mallaha that the first use of red plaster was recorded. This ability of the two traditions to blend implies that they were at least not inimical. If Pre-Pottery Neolithic A peoples were indeed Greek-allied, as suggested in Part I, Pre-Pottery Neolithic B may represent an influx of more advanced kinsmen from flooded lands to the west.

It was Greece, after all, who won the war. The prosperous, warrior-glorifying, ancestor-worshipping, PPNB settlers of the late eighth and seventh millennium Levant do not look like vanquished peoples. Furthermore, if the polished greenstone axes of the earlier period were in fact already associated with the thunderstones of the sky god, their consistent presence in PPNB sites of this new epoch suggests a continuing allegiance to his order.

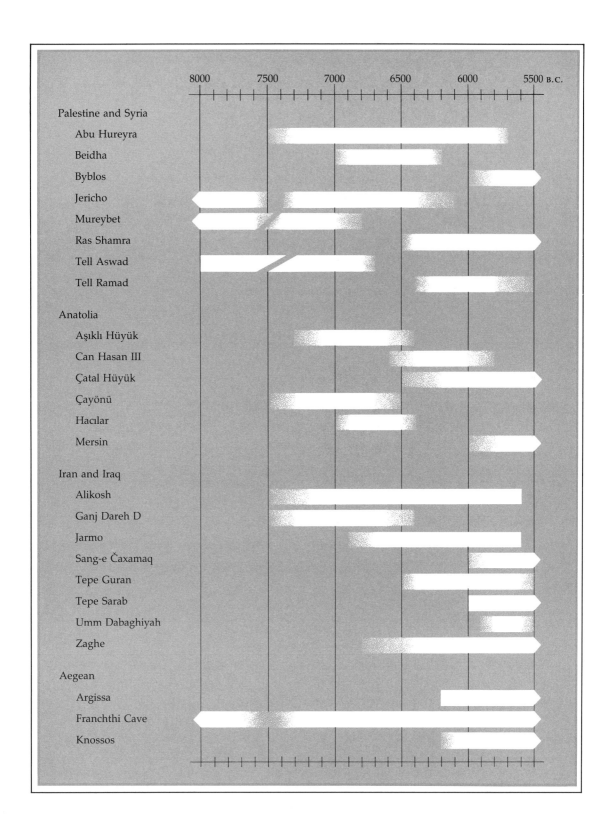

The Neolithic Revolution: Phase I   139

Zagros Village Culture

see page 133

Although the traditions of the warrior seem to have carried the day in the Levant, they ultimately may have been less influential on the course of prehistory than the more modest developments in Iran and Iraq during this theoretically post-deluge era. The early potters of Ganj Dareh D in the Iranian Zagros were described above. Approximately contemporary with the founding of that all-clay settlement, a small new community appeared in the Deh Luran plain to the south, marking the beginning of the 2,000-year-long occupation of the site of Alikosh.[188, 189] (Carbon-14 dates from Alikosh were exceptionally erratic, but its founding is generally placed somewhere between 7500 and 7000 B.C.)

map at figure 68

Surprisingly, obsidian from Nemrut Dağ near Lake Van, some 500 miles to the north in easternmost Anatolia, was present in the first phase at Alikosh, linking that settlement to a greatly expanded "obsidian network" that may have been responsible for both consolidation and change in Zagros village traditions during this epoch.

In the first phase at Alikosh, small huts were constructed of slabs of clay cut directly out of a natural deposit in the floor of the plain. Far more primitive than the mud-brick and tauf architecture of Ganj Dareh, these rectangular structures were no less unprecedented in the Zagros. Also new to the region

76 Reconstruction of marble bowls from Jarmo. Height of taller vessel, four inches (*after L. S. Braidwood et al, 1983*)

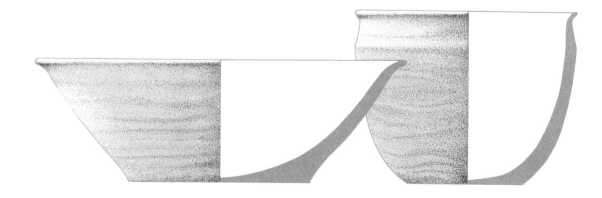

were the domestic grains at Alikosh: emmer wheat and two-row barley. Sheep and goat appear to have been herded; as at Ganj Dareh most of the goat remains were those of immature animals. (Only a third of the flock at Alikosh reached the age of three years.) Small clay figurines of goats may again have been of ritual significance.

Of Ganj Dareh's pottery, however, there was no trace at Alikosh. Nor will clay vessels be known elsewhere in the Zagros for almost a thousand years. Investigators have suggested that the singular exclusion of Ganj Dareh from the above-mentioned obsidian network may have substantially reduced her opportunities for contact with other Zagros villages of this epoch, all of which imported the Nemrut Dağ type of Vannic obsidian found at Alikosh.* It should be noted here that the means by which obsidian was distributed are still a mystery, as permanent settlements dating to this period have not been recorded in the region around Lake Van. We shall later find evidence, however, that this juncture of the Taurus and Zagros mountain ranges was probably home to a number of nomadic or seminomadic peoples at this time, groups whose traces would be largely undetectable to the archaeologist. The site of Çayönü also lies within this general area; it too imported Vannic obsidian; and if, as suggested earlier in examining Çayönü's architectural ingenuity, that east Anatolian settlement was founded by refugees from the floods of the *Timaeus*, this same mountainous region may have been chosen by survivors who would only later turn (or return) to a sedentary way of life, and who meanwhile played an active role in the distribution of obsidian.

In any event, the appearance at Alikosh of a second type of obsidian from the Lake Van region (believed to be from Suphan Dağ) seems to have roughly coincided with the enlargement and stabilization of that site around 6800 B.C. At approximately the same time, the settlement of Jarmo was founded in the Iraqi Zagros, with obsidian from both Vannic sources among her artifacts. Jarmo's tool kit (largely microlithic) and carved stone "bracelets" (fig. 77) have been compared to those of Alikosh, but the settlers of Jarmo built multi-roomed, tauf-walled structures and at least one stone foundation complex that resembles a miniature version of Çayönü's Grill Plan.[41] And it is here that the stone bowl industry that distinguished the Zagros villages of this epoch is displayed at its best (fig. 76). Cups, bowls, and

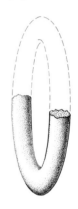

77 Fragments of stone "bracelets" from Jarmo, Iraq; seventh millennium B.C. *(after L. S. Braidwood et al, 1983)*

map at figure 68

see figure 69

---

* Analysts find one of the most interesting aspects of the obsidian trade to be the evidence it affords for "the widespread and early traffic in ideas and commodities, of which obsidian itself was by no means the most important."[342]

The Neolithic Revolution: Phase I   141

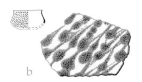

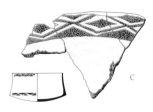

78 Red-on-cream painted pottery from Tepe Guran, late seventh and early sixth millennium B.C.: (a) archaic painted ware, (b) "tadpole" or "Jarmo ware," (c) "Sarab ware," (d) red burnished bowl with concave base, four and one-half inches high *(after Mortensen, 1963)*

dishes were characterized by finely polished thin walls, crisp profiles, and a variety of treatments of the lip. Primarily marble or alabaster, the stone used in these vessels had been selected and worked so that its natural veining gave a decorative effect to the finished product.[43] Investigators have expressed surprise at this very high level of craftsmanship, further noting that "mere usefulness does not furnish an adequate explanation for the tremendous elaboration that the stone bowls underwent."[41] Phallic images were also fashioned from stone at Jarmo; a central drilling suggests that they had been mounted on small sticks, presumably for ceremonial use. The question of what sort of rites might have involved both phallic symbols and fine vessels will be raised a little later.

The Ceramic Zagros

Stone bowls were present in Zagros villages throughout this epoch, but their eventual replacement by ceramic wares was anticipated in the last half of the seventh millennium. As noted above, the isolated potters of Ganj Dareh seem to have lived and died without heirs at the end of that settlement (perhaps 6500 B.C.). The tradition may only have gone into the hills, however, for the next recorded development of ceramics took place at a site just west of Ganj Dareh.

In 6400 B.C. Tepe Guran was no more than a group of wooden huts around outdoor hearths. Domestic goat dominated the faunal remains; agricultural equipment and grain were not present. After a few aceramic strata, a grayish brown, chaff-tempered pottery appeared at Guran. It was followed by finer buff wares occasionally decorated with simple patterns in "fugitive" red paint (paint that was applied after the vessels had been fired), the earliest known examples of painted pottery in the archaeological record (fig. 78a).[293]

Only after the development of ceramics to this point (c. 6200 B.C.) did Tepe Guran begin to take on the aspect of a permanent farming village. Agricultural tools—mortars, pestles, querns—and domestic barley, marble bowls and stone phallic images suggest some sort of contact with Jarmo. (Both varieties of Vannic obsidian were now also present at Guran.) The new mud-brick architecture, simple terrazzo floor, and occasional use of red or white plaster on walls and floors may indicate an inheritance from the superior Çayönü tradition as well, although the site of Çayönü itself apparently had been deserted by this time.

In any case, the borrowing between Tepe Guran and Jarmo seems to have been reciprocal. The next phase of pottery at Guran, decorated with an arrangement of oblique blobbed lines (fig. 78b) was introduced into the heretofore aceramic settlement at Jarmo. Following this "tadpole ware," ceramics at Guran were adorned with horizontal bands of lozenges, triangles, and chevrons (fig. 78c). The final phase saw red burnished bowls with concave bases (fig. 78d). Pottery somewhat similar to these last two types appeared in the uppermost levels at Alikosh as well.

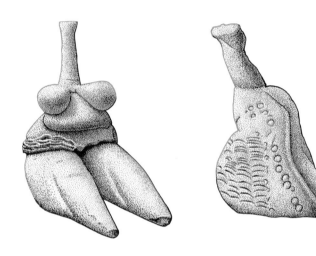

79 Clay female figurines from Tepe Sarab, Iran, early sixth millennium B.C. *(after Redman, 1978)*

More exact counterparts of the Guran wares were present at Tepe Sarab, a new settlement founded around 6000 B.C. to the north of Tepe Guran.[293] Sarab was without permanent architecture, but her kinship to other Zagros communities is attested by the presence of well-crafted stone bowls, domestic barley, and similar microlithic tools. Several fine, seated, full-breasted clay figurines, not unlike earlier and less well-preserved models at Jarmo and Ganj Dareh D, were also recovered at Tepe Sarab (fig. 79). Here one type of figurine had been made in six separate parts and then pegged together with sticks,[360] a technique that has otherwise been recorded only in Early Neolithic Greece (the Macedonian site of Nea Nikomedeia).[346] Sheep and goat were apparently domestic at Sarab, but here as elsewhere in the Zagros, faunal remains show that such animals as wild cattle, boar, and leopard were still objects of the hunt.[34]

One wonders why. At this stage of cultural development the Zagros-wide affection for the chase seems somewhat questionably related to economic need. The leopard, for example, must have been prized more for his skin than for his edible meat.

"Stab marks" on the figurines of wild boar at Tepe Sarab suggest that the boar hunt may have been ceremonial. But the most important clue to the nature of Zagros hunting may lie in the report that the remains of the wild cattle at Sarab (where the preliminary faunal analysis was exceptionally detailed) were exclusively those of mature wild bulls.[34] These were surely not the easiest of their species to be taken, and the analyst found it equally curious that the bulls at Tepe Sarab apparently had been carried back to the settlement intact, rather than butchered where they fell for easier hauling. Was this the logic of a ritual?

One cannot help but recall, particularly in an Iranian context, the mythical capture and carrying of the wild bull by the Persian god Mithra, and the sacrifice of a bull by his followers. If, as suggested in Part II, proto-Mithraic traditions were already present west of the Caspian Sea at this time, they could easily have percolated down into southwestern Iran by way of the obsidian network. But there may also have been Greeks in this obsidian-rich region west of the Caspian, if the founders of the extraordinary settlement at Çayönü were in fact survivors of the floods. And in Aegean traditions, the ceremonial consumption of a whole wild bull would later be associated with the cult of the Cretan Dionysos, Zagreus. The etymology of the Greeks made the name Zagreus mean "Mighty Hunter," but modern scholars have found a more likely source of the word in the name of the peak from which the mountain range between Assyria and Media takes its name: Mount Zagron.[79, 166] As we shall see below, both readings of the name Zagreus may be correct, and the worship of this Mighty Hunter as old as the first permanent settlements in the Zagros mountains.

see page 112

see pages 129–33

Zagreus and the Zagros Religion

As mentioned in Part II, the Cretan cult of Dionysos apparently belongs to the oldest, pre-Greek, stratum of Aegean religion. When we meet this Cretan deity in the Orphic religion of the first millennium B.C., he is Zagreus, son of Zeus (by Persephone, Zeus's own daughter by Demeter) and the intended heir to his throne. As at the birth of Zeus, the Cretan Kouretes are said to have danced and clashed their weapons when Zagreus was born. The babe then "climbed upon the heavenly throne of Zeus and brandished lightning in his little hand, and newly born, lifted and carried thunderbolts in his tender fingers" (Nonnus

VI.165–69). But the Titans, or the Giants,[172] lured Zagreus away with toys—among them a top (or a bull roarer), knucklebones, a mirror, "jointed-dolls"[166]—and then set upon him with their daggers. Seeking to escape by assuming various animal and other forms, Zagreus was finally overcome in the guise of a bull and his body torn to pieces and devoured. Zeus destroyed the villains with his thunderbolts, and according to some, Athena rescued the heart of Zagreus and brought it to Zeus, who placed it in a sculpted image of the child, causing Zagreus to come to life again.

The Cretan Zeus was himself a dying god (slain by a wild boar in some accounts)[79] and often difficult to distinguish from his son Zagreus.[172] But however the Cretan deity was called, classicists have found evidence in all periods, from the Minoan-Mycenean seals down to Strabo, that the religion of Crete was "ecstatic and mystic, devoted to a god who was born, lived as a babe and youth, and died, who also appeared in taurine form; a religion of dancing, drums and omophagy; in short, all that we mean by Dionysiac."[168] The mystical quality of the cult is evident in a fragment from Euripides' *Cretans*, the confession of an initiate (recorded by Porphyry, *De Abstin.* IV.16)[166] that provides our main source of information, however meager, on the rites of Zeus-Zagreus:

> Pure has my life been
> Since the day I became
> Initiate of Idaean Zeus
> And herdsman of night-wandering Zagreus;
> And having accomplished the raw feasts,
> And held torches aloft to the Mountain Mother,
> Yea, torches of the Kouretes,
> Was raised to the holy estate and called Bakchos.

The age of this Dionysian cult is quite unknown. The myth of Zagreus apparently was first given literary form by Onomacritos in the sixth century B.C., but scholars find that the legend itself "bears the stamp of great antiquity."[139] Was it as old as the seventh millennium B.C.?

We have seen suggestions of the consumption of a whole wild bull in Zagros villages, a ceremony known in Crete as the *omophagia*, the raw feast accomplished by the initiate in Euripides' fragment, presumably a re-enactment of the mythic death of Zagreus. We have also noted the predominance of immature goats in Zagros faunal samples, an indication that the kid, a favorite offering to Dionysos (the god who is most often associated with the goat in Greek traditions, and who is frequently referred to as *Eriphos*, the kid)[316] may have been sacrificed by Zagros mountain peoples as well. The leopard which was also present in Zagros remains was closely linked to Dionysos, designated by one author "the oldest clearly pre-Hellenic attribute of the god."[94] Leopards will be found flanking counterparts of Tepe Sarab's seated female figurines in slightly later Anatolian settlements, the earliest recorded examples of a type later to be known as the Mistress of the Animals and identified with the Mountain Mother of the Aegean—the goddess to whom Euripides' initiate held torches aloft.

see figures 108, 110

The carved stone phalli in Zagros assemblages, while not typical of Crete, were elsewhere patently Dionysian; the cult vessel, the *kantharos*, was the special property of that god. Of the toys most often named as those offered to Zagreus by the Titans, several were present in Zagros sites. Knucklebones were at Jarmo, seen as game pieces by the excavators;[43] a "jointed doll" is an accurate description of the pegged-together female figurines at Tepe Sarab; and as for the mirror, we shall find magnificently crafted obsidian mirrors among the shrines of contemporary Çatal Hüyük, where the earlier-mentioned stone statuette of the child-god on a leopard is one of that site's many analogues to Cretan deities.

see figure 104

It may of course be argued that the presence of paraphernalia associated with the Cretan cult of Zagreus in seventh millennium Zagros villages does not necessarily mean that the aims of these early rites were those of the later ones. To become a Bacchos, as did Euripides' Cretan initiate, was to become a fully realized, immortal being. Although historians of religion generally agree that the mystery religions of antiquity were based on archaic rituals, most believe that the status of these cults as vehicles of personal transcendence was not achieved until the first or possibly the second millennium B.C. This may be true; the question will be more fully explored later; but for now, if we may take one wall painting out of its context in a late shrine at Çatal Hüyük, this "dance of the hunters" suggests that rebirth into the mystical brotherhood of Zagreus may have been available to Neolithic man as well.

The shrine which contained the painting shown at figure 81 was one of the two "Hunting Shrines" at Çatal Hüyük. Dated to around 55/5400 B.C., they would have been contemporary with late levels, or perhaps a time just after the abandonment, of the Zagros villages. The scene was described by Mellaart:

With the exception of two figures in the bottom register, a drummer and a bowman with raised sling, all the figures are shown proceeding to the left in three super-imposed rows. The three figures in the middle row . . . are larger in size and the first is painted half red, half white, and is headless like the third figure which is all white except for a leopard-skin on the shoulder. The middle figure wears a white loin-cloth as well as a leopard-skin (pink with black spots) in which all figures except two naked acrobats are dressed. Similarly all figures wear berets of leopard-skin. They are armed with bows and slings. . . . It appears that the dance takes place around the central figure in the middle row. . . .[278]

81 Wall painting from the Level III "Hunting Shrine" at Çatal Hüyük, c. 5400 B.C. *(after Mellaart, 1966)*

Mellaart found it extremely unlikely that the entire population of Çatal Hüyük, or even all of the males, wore leopard skins. He assumed that the dancers here were actually a small segment of the community who were entitled to this ceremonial dress: "in other words, the priesthood." With the added note that the absence of a head in Çatal painting apparently was an artistic convention for depicting otherworldly beings (dead or divine), what we have here is a prominent central figure escorted by two spirit companions into the midst of armed, dancing, leopard-skin-clad priests.

We know from the myth that the birth of Zagreus was celebrated by an armed dance of the Kouretes, the divine warrior-daemons of Crete. As at the birth of Zeus, they raised a great hubbub, "the din of drums and war-like dancing and clashing of arms," around the newborn child.[166] Given the known tendency of initiatory cults to imitate, or recreate, in their ceremonies of rebirth the events surrounding the birth of their god,[118] one expects the armed dance of the Kouretes to have been

The Neolithic Revolution: Phase I   147

played out at the rebirth of an initiate into the cult of Zagreus. In light of the numerous parallels to other Cretan traditions which have been recorded at Çatal Hüyük (to be detailed in Part IV), it seems quite possible that the central figure of this Çatal scene, emerging with otherworldly escorts into the circle of armed dancers, anticipated Euripides' Bacchos by five thousand years.

The Origin of Zagros Village Traditions

If the birth (or rebirth) of Dionysos was already being celebrated in the Zagros mountains long before it was made visible on the walls of Çatal Hüyük, the question of how these rites got to Anatolia may be less challenging than the question of how they first came to the Zagros. Although certain elements of Zagros village assemblages can be traced to the Epi-Paleolithic sites of this region (microlithic tools, carved stone "bracelets"), more than one archaeologist has found a "conspicuous lack of continuity" between Zagros village traditions as a whole and those of the impermanent campsites which heretofore characterized this mountainous country.[43, 189] And the break in continuity first occurred with the founding of Ganj Dareh D and Alikosh in the last half of the eighth millennium, the dawn of our theorized post-deluge period.

At the same time, as we saw above, the newly founded settlement at Çayönü was linked by Nemrut Dağ obsidian to the first phase at Alikosh. Continued contact between the Çayönü tradition and Zagros villages was suggested by Jarmo's version of a Grill Plan and the terrazzo floor at Tepe Guran. Recall-
see pages 130–32
ing the several temple-like structures at Çayönü, one assumes the presence there of religious traditions which, like the unprecedented architectural designs themselves, were brought in with the founders. Çayönü's copper products and the apparently ritual objects in obsidian earlier prompted the suggestion that an Hephaistos-type god may have been worshipped at this Taurus foothills community. Might these hypothetical Greek survivors have also carried the religion of Dionysos into the Taurus, and ultimately, along with their superior building skills, down the Zagros chain?

Or were the dionysian elements in Zagros religion older than the Neolithic villages, and associated with a prototype of the Iranian god Mithra? The possibility that Mithraic traditions were
see pages 113–14
already present north of the Zagros in Epi-Paleolithic times was

raised above, and goats as well as bulls are known to have been offered to Mithra in antiquity. (In the *Mihr Yašt* he is worshipped with small cattle [sheep, goats] as well as large, and winged birds [*Yt.* X.119].) If the mysterious heap of fifteen mature wild goat skulls accompanying the wing bones of a great many vultures at one Epi-Paleolithic Zagros site was indeed a sacrifice, as the evidence suggests,[372] offerings to Mithra may have been made in the Zagros as early as the ninth millennium B.C. Furthermore, very recent excavations have established definite connections between the Neolithic Zagros villagers and the earliest known settlers on the Iranian plateau. And it is here, at the site of Zaghe, that we find the next recorded collection of wild goat skulls, this time on the walls of a surprisingly complex painted shrine (fig. 82).

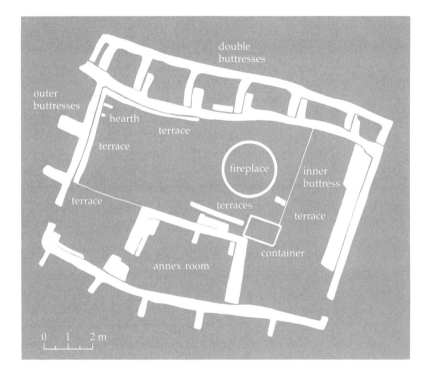

82 Plan of the painted shrine at Zaghe, central Iran (*after Negahban, 1979*)

Zaghe and Sang-e Čaxamaq, which lies farther east in the Gurgan plain, are the only two known permanent settlements dating to this period east of the Zagros mountains. Excavations are incomplete at both sites, but preliminary reports from Zaghe show the presence of microlithic tools and ceramics which, although of higher quality than the Zagros pottery, were apparently of the same family.[299] (As at Guran and Sarab, buff wares

map at figure 68

The Neolithic Revolution: Phase I   149

with fugitive geometric patterns in red were accompanied by monochrome red vessels.) Zaghe's use of red plaster on interior wall surfaces also recalls the upgraded phase at Tepe Guran, but there was nothing so grand as the shrine at figure 82 in any of the Zagros villages. Supported by several types of buttress, the walls of this large mud-brick building had been painted red, with a meander pattern of six alternating black and white stripes forming a low decorative band.[298] A circular fireplace occupied the center of the room; Zagros (or Zaghe) type pottery was liberally set about; and above the meander, some eighteen sets of horns and skulls of the wild goat had been fixed to the walls.

The evident superiority of Zaghe's pottery and architecture to those of the Zagros villagers suggested to the excavator that the latter were actually the rural cousins of their more sophisticated contemporaries on the Iranian plateau.[299] Where the plateau people came from is no better known than the origin of the Zagros village founders, but we recall Darmesteter's suggestion that Eran-Vēj, the ancestral Iranian homeland, was see page 114 to be found on the northern side of Azerbaijan. Immediately northwest of Azerbaijan lies Lake Van, the obsidian source for the Zagros villages. It is not yet known whether obsidian was also present at Zaghe, but a few samples of the volcanic glass were recorded at Sang-e Čaxamaq,[269] the other north Iranian settlement currently under excavation.* Although the source of Sang-e Čaxamaq's obsidian has not been reported, the nearest flows would again be those of the Azerbaijan-Armenia-Lake Van region west of the Caspian Sea. If this region is indeed to be associated with Eran-Vēj, it may have been not only the source of obsidian, but the source of Iran's earliest settlers themselves, both on the plateau and in the Zagros mountains.

It seems clear in any case that permanent communities were the exception rather than the rule of life throughout Iran in this epoch. Just how rich and varied the nomadic tradition was at this time will become evident in the following period, when a number of hitherto unknown peoples with well-developed traditions of their own suddenly turn to farming the plains of Iran and Mesopotamia. These developments, and a fuller treatment of the possibility that there were already Iranians (i.e., Indo-Europeans) in seventh millennium Iran, will be covered in Part V.

* Of the two mounds at Sang-e Čaxamaq, the older western tepe apparently was founded early in the sixth millennium. Several of its rooms, while less elaborately decorated than the shrine at Zaghe, suggested sacred precincts to the excavator.[269]

The Decline of PPNB and Zagros Village Culture

The conservatism of western sites during this era has been observed. Although the number of PPNB and related settlements greatly increased during the seventh millennium, the tradition remained essentially unchanged. Plastered skulls appeared again at Tell Ramad and Beisamoun late in the period. Weapons continued to be more finely crafted, and newly founded settlements such as Ras Shamra (ancient Ugarit) on the Syrian coast yielded lance or spear heads of excellent quality.[77] The only real innovation was a curious sort of "white ware" made in Syria by hardening lime plaster in basket molds.

see pages 83–84

As their name implies, Pre-Pottery Neolithic B peoples were not potters, and the chaff-tempered red or red-on-buff painted pottery of the east either failed to reach, or was not accepted by, most of these western sites. Jericho, for example, remained "staunchly aceramic" until her abandonment.[280] Early in the sixth millennium, however, an excellent dark monochrome pottery appeared in the upper levels of several of the remaining PPNB sites, just before they too were deserted. Apparently not of the Zagros line, the source of this fine, grit-tempered, hard-fired ware will be sought in the next chapter.

Widespread desiccation has been suggested as the cause of the decline of PPNB. Rainfall appears to have decreased on the Syrian steppes as temperatures rose toward their postglacial maximum, and there are indications that man himself may have degraded the vegetation in settled areas.[290] Signs of economic stress were also recorded in the Zagros mountains, again possibly the result of drought. The final phase at Alikosh showed a decrease in agricultural activity accompanied by an increase in herding and the gathering of wild plants,[189] and it has been suggested that the lake of the Deh Luran plain may have shrunk, receding from the village at Alikosh until farming was no longer viable. Whatever the reason, by 5500 B.C. Alikosh, Jarmo, and Tepe Guran all lay deserted.

If drought did cause the decline of both PPNB and Zagros village traditions, one is reminded of the remarks of Plato's Saitic priest regarding the periodic destruction of humanity: "There have been and will be many different calamities to destroy mankind, the greatest of them by fire and water. . . ." (*Timaeus* 22). We are now almost two thousand years from the theorized date of the deluge, and if water (flood) was the agent of destruction midway in the eighth millennium, fire (drought) may have taken its turn in the middle of the sixth.

Dark-faced Burnished Ware

map at figure 68

One further cultural expression dating to this period should be mentioned before we view the convergence of all of these Neolithic traditions at Çatal Hüyük. Twenty miles north of Beirut, the site that would later be famed as the Phoenician city of Byblos was first settled around 5900 B.C., with the monochrome ceramics which were now finding their way into late PPNB levels elsewhere present from the start. Known as "dark-faced burnished ware," this hard-fired, grit-tempered pottery ranged in color from black to dark brown, gray, and red. Examples at Byblos were frequently globular or hemispherical (fig. 83b) and occasionally combed all over with a cardium (cockle) shell.[107] Expertly crafted spear and arrowheads, stone maceheads, and polished greenstone axes were also a part of this *Byblos Early Neolithic* culture, which reached around the coast from Lebanon to the new Cilician settlement of Mersin. Round-based, dark burnished bowls were also among Mersin's earliest ceramics; again shell-impressed patterns included the "rocker-stamping" shown on the sherd at figure 83a.[151]

The several connections between Byblos Early Neolithic and PPNB suggest that some part of the population of these new coastal communities may have been former inhabitants of inland PPNB settlements, seeking refuge in areas where the effects of drought would presumably have been less extreme.[280] But the superior ceramic technique may actually have been independent of either culture. Cardium-impressed monochrome pottery has been found at otherwise quite primitive sites in Corsica and along the coasts of Italy and southern France, again dating to the first half of the sixth millennium.[147, 327] Similar wares, often rocker-stamped with a cockle shell, reached northernmost Morocco as well.[63]

If distribution by sea seems assured, the source of this widespread ceramic technique remains a mystery. The presence of similar wares in the sixth millennium Sahara and Sudan has not gone unnoticed by archaeologists, but as Sahara-Sudanese pottery is usually found more than five hundred miles from the Mediterranean coast, it is generally assumed to have been an unrelated tradition. This may certainly be the case; the isolated development of ceramics in tenth millennium Japan offers a convincing precedent for the independent invention of pottery. But the evident contemporaneity of Sahara-Sudanese ceramics and those of the northern Mediterranean coast, plus some remarkable parallels in fabric, shape, and decorative technique, call for a closer look at the African potters.

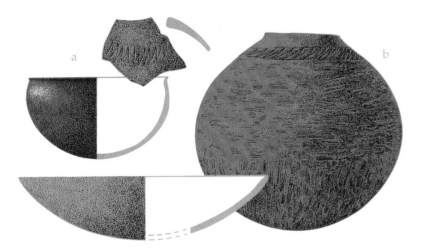

83 Ceramics from the Byblos Early Neolithic culture: (a) round-based bowls and sherd from Mersin showing the "rocker-stamp" motif that appeared at several early sixth millennium Mediterranean sites; (b) globular bowl from Byblos, combed with a cardium shell. Height of Byblos bowl, twelve inches. *(after Garstang, 1953; Dunand, 1955)*

Sahara-Sudanese Neolithic Ware

The massifs of Tassili n'Ajjer and Acacus have already given us the enigmatic Round Head paintings illustrated in Part II. At the end of the seventh millennium, and perhaps coinciding with the final phase of Round Head art,[62] a fine, grit-tempered, dark monochrome pottery appeared at several sites in this region of the Sahara. Round-based, often near-spherical, the African wares ranged from black to red-brown in color; incised or impressed decoration was common. As shown at figure 84, many of the bowls at Amekni were decorated with a motif which bears a striking resemblance to the rocker-stamped designs around the Mediterranean coast.[60] Moreover, carbon-14 dates show the advent of these ceramics in the Sahara (5950 B.C. at Ouan Tabu, 6100 B.C. at Amekni) to be either contemporary with, or only slightly earlier than, the wares of the Byblos Early Neolithic cultural province.

see figures 56–59

The Neolithic Revolution: Phase I   153

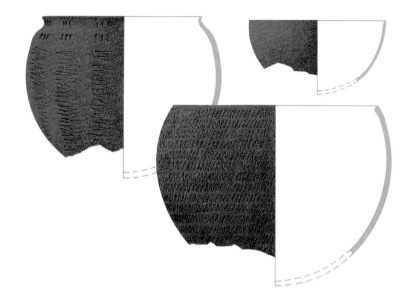

84 Reconstruction of round-based bowls from the Saharan site of Amekni, late seventh or early sixth millennium B.C. Impressed designs resemble the rocker-stamp motif of Mediterranean wares. Height of largest bowl, fourteen inches. *(after Camps, 1982)*

Similar pottery dated to around 6000 B.C. has been recovered in the Nubian region of Nabta Playa (fig. 85), some 60 miles west of the Nile near the Egyptian-Sudanese border.[421] Here it was associated with domestic barley and possibly domestic cattle, a properly Neolithic context, while to the south in the Sudan it was used by hunter-gatherer-fisher folk at the Nilotic complex of Khartoum. There the grit-tempered wares displayed rocker-stamping as well as the more common wavy-line motif.[73] Sherds of this pottery, which is now generally known as *Sahara-Sudanese Neolithic* ware, have been found in the foothills of the Ethiopian escarpment and as far south as Lake Turkana, which appears to have been connected at that time to the Nile system.

The origin of these African ceramics is unknown. Very recent excavations at Ti-n-Torha in the Libyan Sahara have uncovered Sahara-Sudanese type pottery with one carbon-14 reading of 7100 B.C.,[16] which, if a reliable date, would suggest a western seniority. The context in which the Ti-n-Torha wares were found reminded the excavator of the old Iberomaurusian assemblages, with a microlithic industry of backed bladelets accompanied by occasional bone harpoons. Harpoons were also present at Khartoum, and if these fish spears were indeed of Atlantic ancestry, see figure 52 one might be tempted to theorize a similar origin for the ceramic technology, which, like the harpoons, appears to have been diffused across Middle Africa to a number of different local peoples[329] (fig. 85).

But Sahara-Sudanese pottery was not consistently associated with harpoons by any means,[384] and if the round-based, rocker-stamped, African ceramics were indeed of the same family as the similar wares across the Mediterranean, the most logical means of reaching the sea from the Sudan would have been down the Nile. We noted earlier the conviction among Egyptologists that the scarcity of early Neolithic material in Egypt is misleading, and that settlements situated on the flood-plain between 8000 and 5000 B.C. would have been buried by more recent deposits of alluvium. One authority finds it "hardly credible" that the most fertile valley in North Africa should not have played some role during a period that saw so many important developments to the east and west.[280] If these several opinions are to be heeded, one cannot overlook the possibility of Egyptian involvement in the distribution, if not the development, of Sahara-Sudanese pottery.

see pages 95–96

85 Distribution of harpoons and Sahara-Sudanese Neolithic ware across Middle Africa *(after Sutton, 1974; Camps, 1975)*

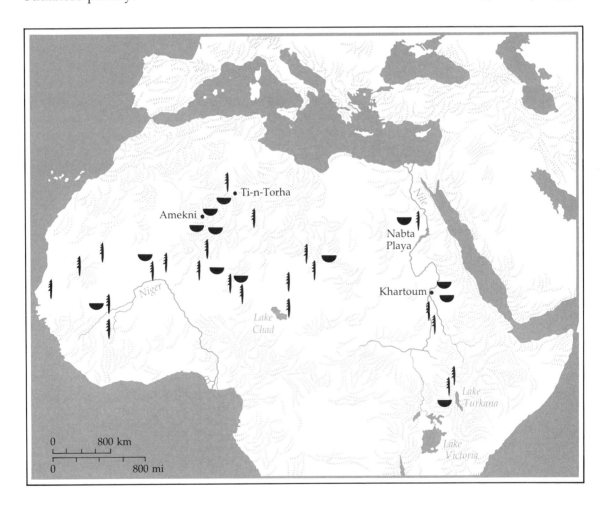

Such a proposal is wholly speculative at this point, and will remain so until significant sites of this period are unearthed in the Nile valley. But there are several arguments in favor of Egypt's participation in the spread of these ceramics. For one thing, the oldest known pre-dynastic pottery in Upper Egypt, undated by carbon-14 but apparently no later than the fifth millennium, was already an exceptionally fine monochrome ceramic product whose entire surface occasionally was combed before the pot was burnished and fired. This *Badarian* pottery is considered a possible descendant of the Khartoum wares of the Sudan,[6] but as the level of Badarian culture was much higher than that of Khartoum, the influence may well have gone the other way. In either case it is logical to assume that any important pre-Badarian sites which might have existed in Egypt would also have known an earlier version of the Sudanese ceramics.

The same conclusion could be drawn from the archaeology of the Sahara where, as mentioned above, one authority believes that the spread of Sahara-Sudanese pottery was possibly coeval with the last stages of Round Head art.[62] It was this final phase, we recall, that produced the magnificent horned goddess and other themes which led Lhote to designate this "the Period of Egyptian Influence."

see page 100

Nor would it be surprising to find Egyptians at Early Neolithic Byblos. Egypt is known to have maintained an almost continuous interest in the politics, commerce, and religion of Byblos throughout the Bronze Age, identifying the goddess of the city, the "Lady of Byblos," with Hathor, one of the oldest known Egyptian deities.[138] That this relationship with Egypt might date back to the earliest settlements within the Byblos Neolithic tradition is suggested both at Mersin (where the excavator found some of the finest Neolithic pottery to be comparable in shape and design to the Badarian wares of Upper Egypt)[151] and at Çatal Hüyük, where we shall find several parallels to the traditions of pre-dynastic Upper Egypt accompanying Byblos-type pottery into the early sixth millennium shrines. There are, moreover, several mythological accounts which characterize the Egyptians as world travelers from the most ancient times, and among them is Plutarch's description of the recovery at Byblos of the coffin of Osiris.

As Plutarch told the story (*De Isid.* 356–57), Osiris was locked in a chest by the malevolent Set-Typhon, who pushed the coffin into the river to be carried out to sea. The chest came ashore at Byblos; a tree grew up around it hiding the coffin from view;

the tree was subsequently cut down and used as a pillar in the house of the king of Byblos. The dejected Isis wandered everywhere in search of the chest, and finally learning its whereabouts, proceeded forthwith to Byblos. Disguised, she became nursemaid to the king's son, whose mortal parts she attempted to burn away in the fire by night (an evident initiatory motif). When discovered and her identity revealed, Isis retrieved the coffin and set sail for Egypt.

It should be noted that the similarity of Isis' behavior at Byblos to that of Demeter under similar circumstances at Eleusis* has led many scholars to question the authenticity of some of Plutarch's details (although not that of the general theme of the wanderings of Isis, which are also mentioned in Egyptian texts, or the plausibility of Egyptian contact with Byblos). The confusing of concrete with abstract elements also seems likely. But if the broad outlines of Plutarch's story do record an historical event, the visit to Byblos may have taken place as early as the first settlement at that site, or shortly thereafter. We know that in one of his aspects Set was the embodiment of all that is unseasonal or disorderly in nature, and Plutarch later remarked that "the so-called shutting up of Osiris in the coffin seems to symbolize nothing other than the concealment and disappearance of water," a time of severe drought (*De Isid.* 366). We also know that Byblos was founded shortly before the closing down of PPNB sites from Syria to the Sinai by what is believed to have been widespread desiccation. A centuries-long drought has been recorded from around 6000 B.C. in the Sahara as well, during which time many low-lying areas are believed to have been abandoned.[365] If these various reports are in fact documenting Plutarch's death of Osiris, the early sixth millennium spread of dark monochrome ceramics to the north Mediterranean coast may have charted the path of the wandering, sea-borne, Isis— or "Isis," as symbolic of African peoples.

In the Near East, dark-faced burnished ware reached as far inland as the steppes of Syria and northern Iraq, and the curious activities which accompanied its presence at the Iraqi site of

---

* In the *Homeric Hymn to Demeter*, the goddess pauses at the residence of the king of Eleusis in her search for her daughter Persephone, who was carried off to the underworld by Hades. Like Plutarch's Isis, the disguised Demeter accepts the position of nursemaid to the king's infant son, whom, to make immortal, she holds in the fire each night. But when Demeter is found out, she remains at Eleusis, demands that a sanctuary be built, and retires within its walls. Still grieving for the lost Persephone, she withholds the sprouting of the grain until her daughter is returned to her for at least part of the year.[32]

map at figure 68

Umm Dabaghiyah may strengthen the possibility of a ceramic tie to Africa. Estimated to the first half of the sixth millennium, Umm Dabaghiyah is the type-site for a small group of villages that are the first known settlements in the Jezireh steppe.[215-217] The origin of their founders is uncertain; a soft, chaff-tempered, regional pottery was produced at Umm Dabaghiyah, but the presence in the earliest levels of both a variant of dark-faced burnished ware and Byblos-type projectile points suggests a fundamental connection to Syria and the coast. Flint, stone, and the more advanced species of food plants apparently were imported into this saline steppe. Domestic sheep, goat, cattle, and pig must also have been imports, but the more surprising aspect of Umm Dabaghiyah's faunal sample was the very high percentage (68%) of the bones of the wild ass.* It seems that the primary purpose of this settlement, and that for which it presumably was founded, was the capture of this desert and steppe-dwelling animal.

The wild ass dominated the art of Umm Dabaghiyah as well. The several wall paintings recovered at this site have been compared to those of contemporary Çatal Hüyük, but the majority of the murals preserved at Umm Dabaghiyah portray the wild ass (fig. 86, a and b). With small clay forms of this animal also applied in relief to ceramic containers, a more-than-economic valuation of the wild ass seems certain.

We are reminded that in Egypt the ass was traditionally a major "Set-animal." Lord of desert lands as well as the principle of desiccation, Set already commanded a large following in Upper Egypt at the beginning of the dynastic period,[121] and according to Plutarch, animals associated with Set were always more carefully tended and worshipped in times of dryness. He further remarked:

> Should a long and severe drought occur, bringing with it an excess of deadly diseases or other strange and unaccountable calamities, the priests lead off some of the sacred animals quietly and in silence under cover of darkness, threaten them at first and try to frighten them. But should the visitation continue, they consecrate the animals and slaughter them, intending thus to inflict a kind of chastisement upon the spirit.   (De Isid. 380)

In the best of times the dry reaches of the Jezireh steppe were inhospitable to settlers. If drought was now widespread, one

---

* Originally thought to be the onager or Asiatic wild ass, *Equus hemionis*, the early Holocene equids of this region have recently been found to bear a greater similarity to the African wild ass, *Equus asinus*.[105]

86 Fragments of wall
paintings portraying the
wild ass at Umm
Dabaghiyah, Iraq, early
to mid-sixth millennium
B.C. (after Kirkbride, 1975)

can see why Umm Dabaghiyah was first temporarily, and then
finally, abandoned within only a few centuries of its birth. But
why such a region was chosen for settlement in the first place
is still a mystery. The excavator of Umm Dabaghiyah has suggested that the purpose of her site was to serve as a tanning
and trading center for the skins of the wild ass. Might it instead,
or in addition, have served as a center for the sacrifice of Set-
animals?

Let us look again at the murals from this site. Kirkbride felt
that the fragment pictured at figure 86a might record the beginning of a wild ass stampede into hunting nets:

> Although the animal's stylized leg appears to be still, the tail is
> flying and ear turned back. Behind it are two strange, perhaps
> terrorizing, totem-like human figures, while above it the lower
> limbs of a man, apparently jumping, could represent one of the
> hunter reinforcements keeping the herd on the right line.[216]

As she further remarked, the second of these paintings (fig. 86b)
"also appears to show the animals at speed and under pressure.
Despite the still legs, necks are stretched, ears back and tails
flying."

The possibility that these were actually terrified animals
standing in place (with "still legs") rather than a stampeding
herd is strenghtened by a seldom-noticed frieze in one of the
late shrines at Çatal Hüyük, approximately contemporary with

The Neolithic Revolution: Phase I   159

the end of Umm Dabaghiyah. There we find seven wild asses accompanied by seventeen gesticulating human figures, one of whom, as shown at figure 87, appears to be leading the animals.[277] No interpretation has been offered for the Çatal scene. Is it possible that these gesturing men were trying to frighten asses that were being "led off under the cover of darkness"? Might this painting, as well as those of Umm Dabaghiyah, depict the Egyptian custom of ritually threatening Set-animals in time of drought, as described by Plutarch above? The Çatal frieze is dated to around 5500 B.C., which would have been close to the theorized peak of desiccation in the Near East—and only a few centuries after dark-faced burnished ware was introduced into the shrines of Çatal Hüyük.

It is to this old Anatolian site itself that we must now turn for what is essentially a summary, as well as the culmination, of the events of this 2,000 year long, theoretically post-deluge, era of prehistory.

87 Detail of a frieze at Çatal Hüyük (Level V, c. 5500 B.C.) in which wild asses, accompanied by gesticulating male figures, appear to be led by a man in a loincloth (after Mellaart, 1966)

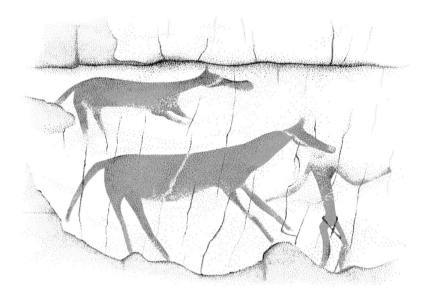

I V
Çatal Hüyük:
6200–5300 B.C.

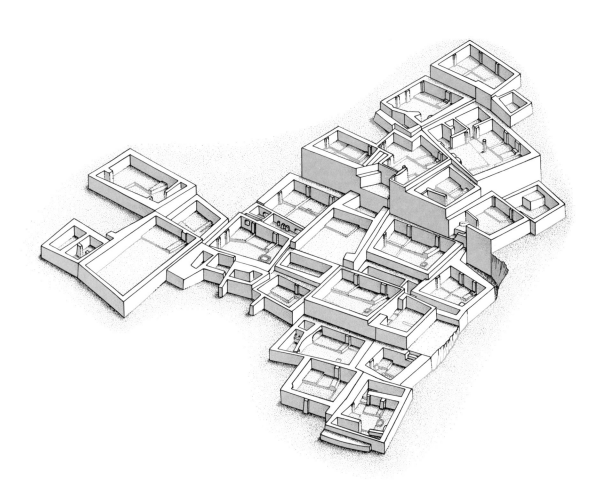

88 Isometric view of a section of Level VI at Çatal Hüyük
(pronounced *cha*-tal *hoo*-yook), c. 5600 B.C. Each of the abutting
shrines and houses had its own walls; entry was accomplished
through an opening in the flat roof. The truncated walls of previous
structures were used as foundations for each successive building
level, and in several instances similarly decorated shrines were built
one above the other, suggesting a continuity of cult. *(after Mellaart, 1963)*

"A Premature Flash of Brilliance and Complexity"

The huge settlement at Çatal Hüyük was spread over thirty-two map at figure 68 acres of the Konya plain of central Anatolia, accommodating perhaps five to seven thousand persons at peak levels. Only one acre of the Çatal mound has been excavated to date, but the wealth of material recovered from that acre alone has, in the words of one archaeologist, "astonished the world."[215] The many wall paintings and relief constructions, the excellent textiles, the polished obsidian mirrors and jewelry, the elaborate burial arrangements—all suggest a luxurious standard of living that fit no one's expectations for a Neolithic community.

A large collection of stone statuettes had no counterpart in contemporary sites. As one art historian remarked:

> They are not at all what one might have expected to find—stone sculpture for one thing, the earliest known in Anatolia; in two instances a facial type that anticipates Cycladic marble "idols" of the third millennium; a twin figure; leopard ladies; the relief pairs of figures—all strongly suggestive of divinities known from the monuments of later times.[413]

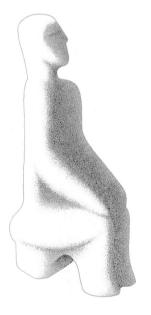

The regal male in white marble at figure 89 is one of those resembling the Cycladic sculpture of the Bronze Age.

Pressure-flaked obsidian spearheads, frequently found buried unused with the dead or offered in the shrines, have been designated "easily the most elegant in the Near East" (fig. 90).[278, 25] Lead and copper beads and pendants were also present, and a lump of slag at Level VI suggests that copper was now being extracted from its ore.[300] What has been described as a highly organized trading system brought tabular flint from Syria, seashells from both the Red Sea and the Mediterranean, fir from the Taurus mountains, raw copper probably from Ergani across

89 Male statuette in white marble from Level VI, Çatal Hüyük. Height, eight and one-half inches (*after Mellaart, 1963*)

Çatal Hüyük: 6200–5300 B.C. 163

the Euphrates, lead from the Cilician Gates — as well as mineral pigments, obsidian, greenstone, white marble, limestone, and basalt from sources nearer the site.[278]

Whether these imports were trade or tribute is another question. The extraordinary number of richly adorned shrines led Mellaart to the conclusion that Çatal Hüyük was probably the spiritual center of the Konya plain.[280] Up to fifteen shrines were present in a single building-level in the excavated area, each apparently the cult center for three or four of the surrounding houses. This abundance of religious structures suggested to Mellaart that his excavation had tapped the priests' quarter, and separate facilities for artisans and husbandmen are presumed to exist elsewhere on the mound in what appears to have been a stratified society of full-time specialists. But just how, and why, this "premature flash of brilliance and complexity," as another prehistorian described Çatal Hüyük,[337] was ignited in the sixth millennium b.c. remains one of the great puzzles of prehistory.

Çatal Architecture and Interior Design

The excavated portion of the Çatal mound consists of thirteen building-levels above a thick layer of still-unexplored material between these known strata and virgin soil. Figure 88 shows the honeycombed arrangement of the settlement plan. Both houses and shrines were usually some fifteen by twenty feet in size and were often adjoined by a smaller storeroom or shaft. Interior walls had been divided into sets of panels by timbers placed vertically and horizontally; these were plastered over and sometimes painted red. A curious corbeling technique brought the two upper panels forward toward the center of the room, each thus overhanging the panel below.

These structural details, as well as the most common interior design, are shown at figure 91. A square platform up to eight inches high usually occupied the northeast corner of the room, with a longer platform on the east wall ending in a narrow bench about a foot in height. Burials were generally confined to the area beneath these two platforms, although they occasionally intruded into the space under the center floor in the crowded levels of VII and VI, when as many as 32 burials were known to a single shrine. Floors were plastered white, sometimes covered with woven straw mats, and in early levels often stained

90 Obsidian spearpoint from Çatal Hüyük (after Mellaart, 1964)

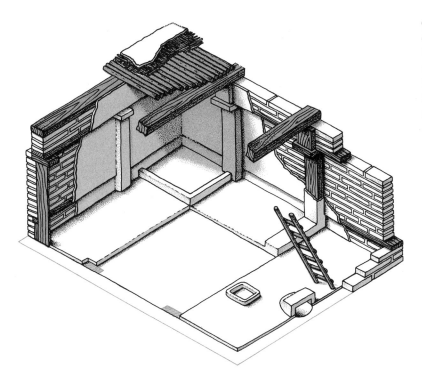

91 Diagrammatic view of interior of a typical building at Çatal Hüyük, showing platforms, bench, hearth, oven, and the ladder leading to the roof (after Mellaart, 1964)

red. Along the south wall a ladder led up to the opening in the roof, the only entranceway.

The excavators have designated this south side the kitchen area, as it was often provided with a raised hearth, a domed oven, and a built-in mortar or a raised grinding slab.[277] Granaries, or rooms containing a number of grain bins, appear to have been shared by several shrines. No explanation has been offered for the presence of so much "kitchen equipment" and grain in what were patently religious structures, and one wonders if the preparation of a sacred bread or porridge, so common in the cults of later antiquity, might already have been known at this site. We are told that the barley grown in the Rarian plain at Eleusis was used only in sacrificial contexts;[172] in Egypt the grain sown in the Field of Osiris was made into ceremonial cakes.[51] The mortars and grinding slabs placed near Çatal shrine hearths also bring to mind the archaic Indo-Iranian ritual of pressing a consecrated plant in either a stone mortar (the Iranian *haoma*) or a stone grinding slab (the Indian *soma*) before offering its juice to the fire. Both of these ceremonies, which will be described more fully in Part V, also included the preparation of a sacred bread.[104]

Çatal Hüyük: 6200–5300 B.C.   165

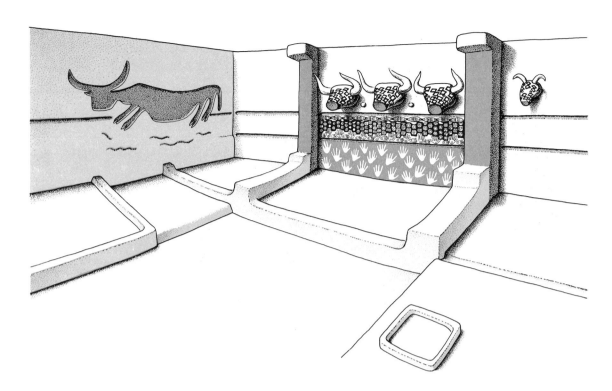

92 Çatal Shrine VI.8;
restoration of north and
east walls. A detail from
the mural below the
bulls' heads is shown at
figure 97. *(after Mellaart,
1963)*

Techniques of Shrine Decoration

In spite of the many murals, Çatal shrine walls were usually
plain white, with accents of red limited to the plastered timbers
and occasional grooves and niches. All interiors apparently were
replastered at least once a year; individual paintings may have
been plastered over as soon as their ritual function was complete. The same wall might then be repainted with a different
composition at a later time, with many layers of white plaster
accumulating between the two. The range of pigments used by
the Çatal artists was unmatched in the Near East (although
equaled or surpassed in the Round Head art of the Sahara);
azurite, malachite, manganese, and galena gave shades of purple, yellow, brown, blue, and black, in addition to the reds,
oranges, and pinks of ochre, haematite, and cinnabar.

Modeled plaster constructions, projecting in relief from the
surfaces of the walls, were a second type of shrine ornamentation. Figure 92 shows this technique in a composition with
three bulls' heads and one of a ram (right) from Shrine VI.8.
A third type of decoration was accomplished by cutting out
silhouettes of animals from the deep accumulations of plaster

on the walls (fig. 92, left), a curious use of interior surfaces that Mellaart believes may have been carried over from the techniques of rock art.

The added dimension in these cutouts and relief constructions would have been particularly effective in the lamp or torch light that may have provided the main illumination, day and night, for these abutting chambers. Courtyards were scarce in all but the uppermost levels, leaving the roof entry as the only sure source of exterior light. It has been suggested that small high windows may have been present in the south and west walls, made possible by stepping the roofs, but no building has survived to a height that could prove or disprove this theory, and it is possible that a cavelike gloom was considered desirable by the architects. The numerous stalagmites and stalactites that had been brought from caves into these precincts led Mellaart to conclude that the shrines of Çatal Hüyük were dedicated to chthonic gods, and another scholar has suggested that Çatal cult activities were once celebrated in a cave.[97] Caves were in fact used for religious ceremonies into historical times. The Cretan Zeus was honored in the Idaean Cave (where Pythagoras was said to have been purified by his thunderstone);[79] the Anatolian goddess Kybele was mistress of a cave cult; caves were even constructed artificially for use in Mithraic rites in the days of the Roman empire. When neither man-made nor natural caverns were available, the worshippers of Mithra sought out basements and crypts.[435]

Burial Customs

The intensity of the conflagration that destroyed Level VI.A at Çatal Hüyük left the burials beneath the floors of that peak stratum remarkably well-preserved, revealing funeral arrangements as elaborate as they were diverse. Most of the Çatal burials were secondary; skeletal remains had been laid on mats, placed in baskets, or more commonly, wrapped in fabric, skins, or fur.[276] One characteristic type of shroud consisted of several layers of woven cloth bound by a netlike fabric of twined construction.[56] No agreement has been reached on the raw material used in these extraordinarily fine textiles,[353] and both fiber and wool may have been present. Felt was also found among the burials, as were traces of string skirts and fringed garments, and it is assumed that some of the Çatal dead were clothed before burial. Toggles made from antler in male graves may

93 Carved wooden vessels from Çatal VI burials and shrines (after Mellaart, 1964)

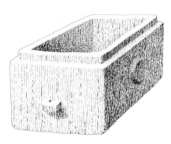

Çatal Hüyük: 6200–5300 B.C.   167

have served to fasten cloaks; bone pins apparently clasped women's garments near the shoulder.

Although the majority of the dead lay in a contracted position, others were extended, and several in Levels VIII and VII were seated upright.[277] When gifts were present, males were often accompanied by either a polished stone macehead, a flint dagger, or obsidian spearheads. Also present in male burials were occasional copper finger rings (worn by women as well), bone belt hooks and eyes, and clay stamp seals. Females might be given jewelry (great numbers of beads were made into necklaces, bracelets, armlets, and anklets, frequently up to eight strands wide), cosmetic palettes for grinding pigments, baskets with "rouge" (red ochre mixed with fat), and obsidian mirrors, which Mellaart feels may have served both ritual and cosmetic purposes.[281] Wooden containers (fig. 93) were found in burials as well as shrines. Here as elsewhere red ochre was occasionally applied to the dead, but unique to Çatal Hüyük was the use of blue and green paint on the bones of several burials in Levels VII and VI. Bright blue pigment was found in the neck region of ten skeletons, both male and female, while green paint had been applied to the "eyebrows" of one female skull and to the bones of a male. The substitution of a ball of fine cloth for the brain in one skull at Çatal VI may or may not point to Egyptian practices of mummification;[278] it seems clear in any case that the belief in an afterlife was no less secure at Çatal Hüyük than along the ancient Nile.

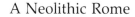

94 Clay stamp seals from Çatal VI–II (after Mellaart, 1967)

A Neolithic Rome

Çatal Hüyük has been called the Rome of her day, an urban center of power, religion, and religious art.[279] Like Rome, she also seems to have served as a magnet for almost all of the known traditions of the time. The heads of bull and ram, first seen at Mureybet in Syria and Ganj Dareh D in southwest Iran respectively, were both attached to the walls of Çatal shrines from the earliest levels. (Originally modeled in plaster with plaster horns, these wall constructions began using the horns of real animals in the peak levels VII and VI, as shown in figure 92.) The leopard we met in the Zagros was represented in wall constructions, stone sculpture, and the leopard-skin garments of dancers in the Hunting Shrines. The PPNB ancestor cult is recalled by the display of human skulls on the platforms of

95 Reconstructed fragment of a *kilim* painting from Level VI at Çatal Hüyük *(after Mellaart, 1962)*

several Çatal shrines, and cowries had been inserted into the eye sockets of one skull as in the plastered skulls at Jericho PPNB. The miniature greenstone axes of Palestine and Syria were also present among Çatal burials, and larger ones offered in the shrines. Geometric wall paintings recall those at Mureybet III and in the painted shrine at Iranian Zaghe, although Çatal designs were considerably more complex (fig. 95);* a comparison of the figurative paintings to those at Umm Dabaghiyah has already been made. The stamp seals introduced at Çatal VI (fig. 94) were also known at the contemporary Greek site of Nea Nikomedeia (termed "a European link with Çatal Hüyük" by its excavator),[347] as were the bone belt-hooks that accompanied several male burials at Çatal Hüyük (fig. 96), possibly used as clasps on the leopard-skin waistbands shown on the dancers in the Çatal Hunting Shrines.

In short, archaeologists from the Aegean to Iran have found Çatal Hüyük a plentiful source of symbolic contexts within which to view more intelligently the artifacts from their own sites. There are in addition enough archaic survivals underlying the numerous contemporary references for Mellaart to have concluded that Çatal Hüyük was descended from "an Upper Paleolithic culture, probably Anatolian, of which hardly anything is known."[278]

* Border designs reminiscent of stitching on two of the geometric murals at Çatal Hüyük, together with the skill shown in the weaving of the burial shrouds, led Mellaart to conclude that *kilims*, the colorful woven mats found today in Turkey, were already being made on the Konya plain as early as the seventh millennium B.C., and that these Çatal murals were inspired by kilim designs rather than the reverse.

Çatal Hüyük: 6200–5300 B.C.   169

If Çatal traditions may be said to reach backward into Upper Paleolithic times, their forward reach seems to have extended into the Bronze Age and beyond. Mellaart is only one of several prehistorians who have found the religion and mythology implied in Çatal symbolism to be remarkably similar to that of Minoan Crete and the oldest stratum of Greek religion and myth. Although some three thousand years separate Çatal Hüyük from the Minoan civilization, he feels that the numerous

96 Polished bone belt-
fastener from Çatal VI
(after Mellaart, 1964)

symbolic parallels indicate a common ancestry for the two cultures.[275] Mellaart's assessment has been complemented by the work of Marija Gimbutas, who sees Minoan Crete as the inheritor of the traditions of the Civilization of Old Europe, the Neolithic Greco-Balkan complex with which Çatal Hüyük was see pages 124–25 in part contemporary and kin.

If the same unknown ancestor did sire the traditions of Çatal Hüyük, the Civilization of Old Europe, and Minoan Crete—an ancestor dating to Upper Paleolithic times—Plato's vanished Athenians or the other Greek peoples of their day would seem likely candidates for the role. But to see Çatal Hüyük as the possible heir of Plato's Greeks, and that alone, may be to miss part of her significance to the Neolithic period. This great Anatolian settlement was apparently a thriving center of cult life, one whose shrines were enriched by decorations and statuary which recall the later mystery religions of Iran and Egypt as well as the Aegean and Anatolia. We have already seen one Çatal painting that is reminiscent of a celebration of the rites of rebirth into the cult of the Cretan or Orphic Dionysos (fig. 81). We shall find other images that bring to mind the initiatory traditions of the Iranian god Mithra, the Eleusinian goddesses Demeter and Persephone, the Anatolian Kybele, perhaps even Osiris of Egypt. Throughout these chambers, symbols of transformation are profuse. So much so, in fact, that the frieze below the bulls' heads at figure 92 may be seen as a depiction of the purposes of Çatal shrines as a whole.

There were actually two paintings here, one superimposed on the other after a lapse of time. The first suggested to Mellaart the life cycle of the bee in a honeycomb, with closed cells on the left from which bees emerged to fly freely in a field of flowers on the right.[278] The later painting, a section of which is shown at figure 97, continued the honeycomb pattern, but now wingless chrysalises seem to sway from branches, while creatures resembling butterflies replace the bees. As Mellaart noted, the process of metamorphosis appears to have already impressed Neolithic man.[275] Indeed, if the Greek identification of the human soul with both bee and butterfly was known to sixth millennium Anatolia, this scene of metamorphosis in the central panel of one of the great shrines at Çatal Hüyük would suggest that the freeing of the soul in life, the rebirth of the living individual onto a higher plane of being, was the goal toward which Çatal rites were aimed.

Background of the Mysteries

Before exploring the evidence of initiatory activity in these Neolithic shrines, a word should be said about the limits of our knowledge in this field. As Eliade has remarked: "The Eleusinian mysteries—like Dionysianism and Orphism in general—confront the investigator with countless problems, especially with regard to their origin and, hence, their antiquity. For in each of these cases we have to do with extremely archaic rites and beliefs . . . [whose] roots go deep into prehistory."[118] The same may be said of the mysteries of Egypt and Persia, and everywhere the problems of age and origin are compounded by our very limited access to the content of the rites themselves.

97 Detail from the scene of metamorphosis below the bulls' heads in Shrine VI.8 (figure 92), Çatal Hüyük (*after Mellaart, 1963*)

As participants were invariably pledged to secrecy, almost all of the available information comes from either veiled literary references or the polemics of detractors, obviously not the most reliable of sources.

We noted earlier that while historians of religion generally do accept a long prehistory for these cults, most feel that they only became instruments of personal transcendence under the demands of individualism in the first millennium B.C. Before this latter-day search for salvation, eons of collective agricultural rituals are believed to have preceded the Eleusinian mysteries of Demeter and Persephone, ancient shamanic traditions to have anticipated the rites of Osiris and the Orphic Dionysos-Zagreus.[118] That is, an archaic ritual is presumed to have existed first, to which a mystical meaning was later attached by the theologians of the high civilizations. Orpheus, for example, was said by one classicist to have taken "an ancient superstition, deep-rooted in the savage ritual of Dionysos, and lent to it a new spiritual significance."[172]

But others have suggested that the Orphic religion of first millennium Greece and Crete was actually a revival as well as a reform, a revival of an earlier and possibly purer faith than the degenerate Dionysianism that confronted Orpheus. Cornford argued that this type of mystical religion, like the gods it served, was perpetually reborn, that it had been reborn "a thousand times."[85] The Greeks would have agreed, or at least those would who believed with Aristotle that "every art and philosophy has probably been repeatedly developed to the utmost and has perished again" (*Metaphysics* XII.8.xxi). And the evident decadence into which many of the mystery religions, including Orphic cult practices, had fallen by Greco-Roman times[10] can only reinforce the idea that superstition and "magic" characterize not a more archaic period of religious thought, but the final phase in a religious cycle.

Is it not then possible that the great initiatory themes of antiquity had already known, if not a thousand, more than one cycle of decay and renewal before their pre-Christian corruption? Our survey of the shrines of Çatal Hüyük will suggest not only that prototypes of the mystery religions of many lands were present at this Neolithic site; the complexity of symbolic forms, plus the unmistakable decadence revealed in the dense and overgrown iconography of Level VI in particular, indicate that some of these cults were already at the exhausted end of one cycle by the middle of the sixth millennium B.C.

The most useful historical analogue to take with us into this prehistoric site may indeed be Rome, therefore, specifically the Rome of those centuries just before and after the birth of Christ, when the cults of almost all of the foreign deities of the day— Dionysos, Isis, Mithra, Dea Syria, Kybele—came together in a burst of syncretism that confused and blended divinities once held to be distinct. A similar confusion was discernible in the Near East, where the collapse of the Persian empire had dissolved all existing barriers, religious as well as political. As Franz Cumont described the eastern situation:

> Heterogeneous races had suddenly come in contact with one another, and as a result Hither Asia passed through a phase of syncretism analogous to that which is more distinctly observable under the Roman Empire. The contact of all the theologies of the Orient and all the philosophies of Greece produced the most startling combinations.[91]

Was this a unique phenomenon, or had the Near East passed through similar phases of dissolution and syncretism at earlier points in its history? We have observed the collapse of Neolithic cultures in Syria, Palestine, and the Zagros mountains during the first half of the sixth millennium B.C. Migrants from these dying communities may well have contributed their spiritual traditions as well as their bodily numbers to the exceptionally crowded conditions in Levels VII and VI at Çatal Hüyük (c. 5700–5500 B.C.). The breakdown of religious distinctions is suggested by the melding and overlapping of these diverse traditions in the Çatal shrines. That the races too met and mixed is indicated by a uniquely high percentage of Alpine Brachyce-phalic physical types intermingled at Çatal Hüyük with the two Proto-Mediterranean strains known earlier in the Near East,[4] and again by the presence of a group of black men among the otherwise pink-skinned celebrants in the Hunting Shrine murals. A convergence of foreign cults is further implied by the stylistic diversity of the Çatal statuettes. Not only do these figures evoke deities later associated with the Aegean, Iran, and Egypt, but they were sculpted in very different styles, none of which had much in common with the Çatal home style.

The following survey of the shrines and their contents will illustrate this point. As Levels VIII to VI seem to mark the peak of shrine ornamentation as well as foreign influence, it is this period which takes priority in any review of Çatal Hüyük, including our own.

Level VIII and the Çatal
Vulture Theme

see figure 83

A local pottery was present in the earliest excavated levels at Çatal Hüyük, a medium-fired, thick-walled, buff ware tempered with straw. Its fabric was quite unlike that of the fine hard-fired ceramics which first appeared at Level VIII and which, by Level VII, had largely replaced the earlier ware.[277] This new pottery lacked the combed and rocker-stamped designs of the dark burnished wares of the coast, but the grit-tempered, thin-walled excellence of Çatal bowls identify them as products of the same technique. The dating of Level VIII to around 59/5800 B.C. puts the advent of this new ceramic technology at Çatal Hüyük approximately coeval with its appearance elsewhere in the northeast Mediterranean.

Level VIII also saw the first of the magnificent flint daggers that would be the most frequent accompaniments to male burials from VIII to VI, and to one female burial at VII. While the obsidian spearpoints at Çatal Hüyük are known for the quality of their bifacial retouch, the flint daggers had intentionally been worked on one face only (fig. 98). After an allover grinding and polishing, a controlled parallel ripple-flaking gave the weapons a finely serrated edge.[276] As noted by the excavators, a similar technique would be used two thousand years later on ceremonial flint knives in pre-dynastic Egypt, where those in the painted tomb at Hierankopolis were judged "the zenith of the flint-knapper's art."[7] The haft of the dagger pictured here, carved in the form of a snake with pointillé scales, is considered to be the finest bone artifact at the site.[399]

Level VIII also yielded two shrines with possibly related initiatory overtones. One, the first of the Çatal vulture shrines, contained a painting of what may have been an archaic descent into hell; the other, a burial that had been accorded honors appropriate for those capable of descending, and returning.

The latter chamber, known as the Red Shrine, apparently was constructed for the specific purpose of housing the remains of a brachycephalic male (originally believed to have been those of a female);[399] the only other burial was that of a small child in a basket. Floor, platforms, and benches of this extraordinary shrine were all covered with red plaster. Paintings (ill-preserved) and bulls' heads adorned the walls; a raised platform decorated with chevrons and abstract figures marked the grave. A molded porthole in the shaft which connected this chamber to a larger, perhaps more public, room allowed a person standing in the shaft to see into the Red Shrine.

The apparent object of reverence, the male buried beneath the painted platform, was seated upright; a polished macehead of white-veined blue limestone and several fine beaded necklaces accompanied his remains. The intentional inclusion of a great many skulls and long bones of the common house mouse with this elaborate burial puzzled the excavators, but if this animal already carried his archaic association with the healing arts, the Red Shrine mice may offer a clue to the talents of the heroic figure with which they were buried. In ancient Crete, for example, the mouse was particularly associated with Apollo Smintheus, whose epithet is a pre-Greek word apparently derived from the Cretan word for mice. Although Smintheus is said to have been Apollo's "specifically Cretan epithet,"[433a] the cult of Apollo Smintheus is known to have been celebrated in Anatolia as well. (Many scholars see Anatolia as the homeland of Apollo himself, who generally was known in antiquity as the Averter of Evil [*Apotropaios*], particularly the evil of physical disease.) If the connection between the mouse and the god of healing was possibly as old as Çatal Hüyük, the man with whom the Red Shrine mice were buried may well have been a valued physician. In any case, the event portrayed on the walls of another Level VIII shrine, if not already mythic during the lifetime of this uniquely honored individual, may record one of his accomplishments.

Only the east wall of Shrine VIII.8 survived, but it provides us with the earliest narrative painting recovered at Çatal Hüyük. As shown at figure 99, two large black vultures have been portrayed facing one another across two small human figures. One of these figures, drawn with a triangular shaped head, swings a black sling and brandishes what may have been a club or a mace.[278] The figure beside him lies on its left side in the flexed position common to many Çatal burials; the absence of a head identifies it as dead or otherworldly by this site's artistic

98 Flint dagger with carved bone handle from a male burial at Çatal VI. Length, ten inches (*after Mellaart, 1967*)

99 Damaged wall paint-
ing in black and red from
Çatal Shrine VIII.8 *(after
Mellaart, 1964)*

conventions. Later murals show headless human forms under attack by vultures, and Mellaart believes that these scavenger birds may have been among the agents of excarnation for the secondary burials at this site. He accordingly suggested that the man with the sling and mace (?) at figure 99 may have been protecting a corpse from attack by the two vultures. But if excarnation by vultures was a traditional preliminary to burial at Çatal Hüyük, one wonders why this living figure would be interfering with accepted practice. Might he instead have been guiding the soul of his companion through the regions of the dead, or perhaps returning it to the land of the living?

The legendary healers of antiquity were often accomplished initiates, whose concern for the health of the human soul was not limited to its earthly existence. If the soul of an individual could not be revived, the physician's initiatory experience of death enabled him, in some traditions, to lead it safely through the land of the dead. Journeys into the underworld for the purpose of healing, guiding, or retrieving a lost soul were undertaken by the heroes of high civilizations as well as shamanic societies. Both Herakles and Theseus made such descents in Greek mythology; the efforts of Orpheus to retrieve the lost Eurydice are well known. Orpheus was also a great healer, incidentally, and Eliade has observed that in fact Orpheus combined exactly those functions — physician, bard, civilizing hero — that fall to the shaman in primitive society. As he further remarked, however, these similarities do not imply that Orpheus was a shaman, but rather that "the mystical experience appears to generate similar heroic or superhuman capacities which are apparently universal and timeless."[114]

The heroic figure painted on a shrine wall at the huge urban center of Çatal Hüyük was no more likely a shaman in the strict sense than was Orpheus, but he too may have participated in this seemingly universal experience. Look again at the vultures facing one another at figure 99. In initiatory myths the entrance to other worlds traditionally is guarded by two related but opposing forces. The hero of such tales must pass between two rocks that may clash together at any moment, between the two halves of an eagle's beak, between sleepless "razor-edged lightnings" (or snakes or dragons). As one scholar noted: "Whoever would transfer from this to the other world, or return, must do so in the uni-dimensional and timeless 'interval' that divides related but contrary forces."[81]

Once he knows the way between the planes of life and death, the individual may penetrate these regions for his own purposes, be they healing or the conducting of the souls of the dead. But it is only through the experience of his own death and bodily dissolution that this mobility is attained. In many traditions this death-in-life experience is facilitated by masters of initiation, who "kill" and "dismember" the candidate in order that he may be reborn into a higher state of being. To visualize one's own death at the hands of demons or spirits, to see one's body reduced to the state of a skeleton, is a very old initiatory practice.[116] That it may have been known as early as the sixth millennium is suggested in a Level VII vulture mural at Çatal Hüyük, which shows human legs protruding from beneath the bodies of vultures (fig. 100). This painting led Mellaart to theorize that men in vulture garb had participated in Çatal funerary

100 Çatal Shrine VII.21, reconstruction of west and part of north wall. Several human skulls were found on the platforms of this vulture-bull shrine. *(after Mellaart, 1967)*

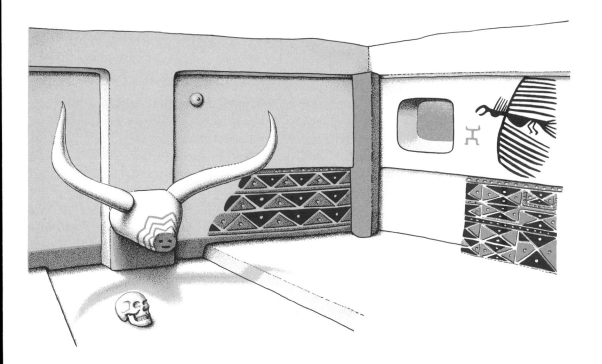

rites.[278] He may be correct, but if vultures were indeed responsible for reducing the Çatal dead to skeletons, it is also possible that these vulture-men were masters of initiation, playing out the "death" of the Çatal neophyte.

Attached to the west wall of the shrine at figure 100 was a huge plaster head of a bull that had been given actual horns measuring some six feet across. The anteroom of the same chamber yielded a rather crude stone statuette of a muscular young male (fig. 101) seated on a bull whose head is said to be modeled in the style of the bull's head inside the shrine. This sculpted figure is the earliest recorded example of an iconographic type later to be known as the Master of the Animals and to enjoy a very wide range as an initiatory exemplar. The Cretan Zeus, the Phrygian Sabazios, and the Syrian Baal were all pictured standing on the bull;[79] the Persian god Mithra was portrayed in Roman art as riding it. (Although more commonly depicted killing the bull, Mithra is shown in several monuments mounted on the animal, either in the act of capturing the bull or victoriously seated on its back.) In the cultural amalgam at Çatal Hüyük, a Master of Animals might have been the prototype of any one of these gods; but in the immediate context of vulture, bull, and ancestor worship—and an expressed reverence elsewhere on the site for the mace, the dagger, and the weapons of the warrior—this youthful bull rider seems most closely kin to Mithra.*

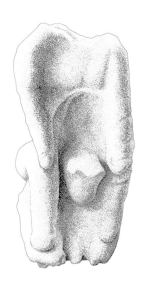

101 Youthful male figure on bull from the anteroom of Shrine VII.21; white calcite, six inches high *(after Mellaart, 1963)*

Mithra and the Magi

Other than the mythic associations noted in Part II, what little is known of the Iranian Mithra shows him to be a warrior's ideal as well as the god of contracts. In Persian texts (*Yašt* X) he has "a thousand well-made bows," "a thousand arrows with feathers of vultures," "a thousand lances of sharp blades," "a thousand axes with two bits," "a thousand maces cast in the yellow metal." His mace was as prominent in Iranian religion as the flint dagger with which he slew the bull. Initiated Zoroastrian

see pages 112–13

* Although a mastery of the animals, particularly of the bull, traditionally symbolized the mastery of one's own animal nature, a more literal mastery of the bull may once have been demanded, especially if the imitation of a mythic deed were involved. Mellaart's discovery of signs of "goring" in at least one of the burials at Çatal Hüyük[281] might mean that efforts to re-create such feats as Mithra's single-handed capture of the wild bull, if indeed attempted, were not always successful.

178   Plato, Prehistorian

priests were given the *gurz*, the mace of Mithra, which had the head of a bull at one end; but Iraniologists have found nothing in the form, use, or symbolism of this weapon to suggest that it was Zoroastrian in origin, and the ceremonial mace, like Mithraic worship itself, is believed to predate the prophet Zarathuštra.[186]

The ceremonial nature of both the flint dagger and the mace at Çatal Hüyük has been demonstrated. And though Çatal maceheads were of polished stone, a mace cast in yellow metal (a solid cast-copper macehead) was found in early fifth millennium levels at the Anatolian site of Can Hasan. Of the other Mithraic weapons described above, only the "axe with two bits" is missing from the arms deposited in Çatal shrines and graves, and if the double-axe is meant here, its image appears in a wall painting at Level VI. Moreover, the religion of Mithra was, according to one Iraniologist, "to its innermost core an ancestor cult."[308] And it is in the vulture-bull shrine at figure 100 that evidence of the veneration of ancestors (several human skulls displayed on the shrine platforms) was most pronounced at Çatal Hüyük.

see figure 112

We noted earlier that the Mithraic mysteries are believed to have originated in the borderlands of northwest Iran, Armenia, and the Caucasus. Northwestern Iran was also an historical stronghold of the Iranian Magi, with whom Mithra is frequently associated. A sacerdotal caste distinguished by their traditional exposure of the dead to vultures, the Magi are known to have established centers in Anatolia as well as Iran; Strabo (XV.3.xv) reported a large body of Magi maintaining eternal fires on the altars of Cappadocian shrines. The age and origin of this priestly, often itinerant people are no better known than the history of the Mithraic rites at which they are said to have officiated.[427] As we shall see later, it is possible that forerunners of both were present in central Anatolia in the sixth millennium B.C.

Egyptian Vultures

Vulture and bull were also linked in Egypt, however, and it may be that some part of what we have interpreted as proto-Mithraic traditions at Çatal Hüyük was African instead. The Apis Bull of Memphis, for example, was often portrayed in Egyptian art with vultures over the fore and hind legs.[51] The vulture itself was particularly associated with Upper Egypt, where it served as the emblem of the south from earliest dynastic times.

The vulture goddess Nekhebit was both guardian of Upper Egypt and tutelary deity of Hierankopolis, and although she appeared in later art in the form of a woman with a vulture head or headdress, in the archaic period she was always portrayed simply as a vulture.[121]

Nekhebit was also considered the mother of the Pharoah (the Egyptian letters *mwt* may be read as either "mother" or "vulture") and was often shown in the mortuary temples of the Old Kingdom nursing the king after his rebirth.[50, 138] The "two pendulous breasts" with which she suckled him are mentioned in the *Pyramid Texts*, and one wonders if a similar idea might have inspired the modeling of a woman's breasts in plaster on the wall of a Level VI shrine at Çatal Hüyük, each of which contained the complete skull of a vulture, its beak protruding slightly from the open nipple. In any event, if the vulture theme did enter Çatal Hüyük at Level VIII with the pre-dynastic-style flint daggers and possibly Sahara-Sudanese-related ceramics, as the excavations to this point suggest, the chance that some of this Anatolian vulture symbolism was actually African cannot be ruled out.

The Çatal Leopard Theme

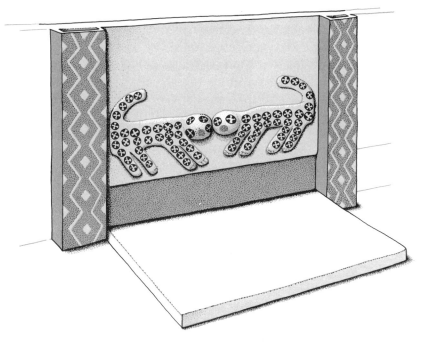

102 Level VI Leopard
Shrine (VI.44), north
wall. Two leopards in
relief, each approximately
three feet long, face one
another between deco-
rated pillars. (after
Mellaart, 1967)

Like the vulture, the leopard traditionally was associated with
death and rebirth. The Greek Dionysos and the Egyptian Osiris,
both connected with chthonic funereal themes, were assigned
the leopard in their respective lands. We have already noted
this "clearly pre-Hellenic" attribute of Dionysos. In Egypt the
wearer of the skin of the leopard was said to possess special
powers in dealing with the souls of the dead; in the ritual performed to bring about the resurrection of the dead (which included the slaughter of a Bull of the South), the Sem priest is
pictured wearing a leopard skin over white linen garments.[50]

see page 146

Level VII saw the first identifiable leopards in relief at Çatal
Hüyük, although an ill-preserved pair of heraldic animals at VIII
may also have been of this species. Those pictured at figure 102
are from the Level VI Leopard Shrine. They had been decorated

many times over, first with black rosettes on a white background, then by several applications of lemon yellow with black spots, and finally covered with several layers of whitewash. Their position face to face again presents the image of related but opposing forces. Numerous offerings of grain were found on the platform in front of the leopards, along with a basalt statuette of a mature female figure (fig. 103) that Mellaart saw as a possible prototype of Demeter, the Greek goddess of grain.[275]

The same goddess is evoked by another group of statuary at Level VI, in which two women and a small boy with leopards bear a striking resemblance to Demeter, Persephone, and either Iacchos (the Eleusinian Dionysos) or Zagreus, the Cretan Dionysos with whom the goddesses were also associated (fig. 104). These three images were modeled in a different style from the matron in the Leopard Shrine, and were accompanied by the figure of a seated, priestlike male (fig. 105) wearing a leopard-skin beret similar to the headgear worn by many of the dancers in the Hunting Shrines of Levels V and III. One of these later paintings was introduced in the discussion of Zagros religion (fig. 81). The others will be described below, although it takes us temporarily outside the limits of Levels VIII to VI, in order to see the Çatal leopard theme as a whole.

103 Female statuette in black stone from the Çatal VI Leopard Shrine. Height, six inches *(after Mellaart, 1963)*

104 Group of three statu-ettes with leopards from Çatal Shrine VI.10. The female figures, in brown and blue limestone, are approximately four inches high; the male child on leopard, in brown lime-stone, measures two inches. *(after Mellaart, 1967)*

The Hunting Shrines

All four walls of the Level V Hunting Shrine had been decorated, showing a variety of animals—bull, stag, boar, bear, wolf—surrounded by lively human figures wearing loincloths with stiffly projecting animal skins at the waist. The men are sometimes armed with bows or clubs, but there are no signs of any animal being shot or killed. Suggested instead are festivities: dancing, brandishing of weapons, and acrobatic feats.[277]

On the west wall a group of pinkish red men with black hair and beards are exuberantly teasing a stag (fig. 106). Dressed in a combination of leopard skins and what may be black goat skins, they cling to the animal's tongue, tail, nose, and antlers. The north wall is dominated by a huge bull surrounded by human figures, several of which have been painted black (fig. 107). Some of the men around the bull wear the skins of long-tailed animals; those in front are wearing leopard skins. Large harlequin-type figures similar to the one above the bull are shown headless in the later Hunting Shrine, and Mellaart wondered if these several bichromatic figures might not represent super-human beings, possibly revered ancestors or deities.[277]

In the northeast corner another large red stag was again surrounded by men in leopard skins; below, the tail and tongue of a wild boar were being pulled by several others. Another boar and a bear were being similarly treated on the east wall, and in the next panel dancers were apparently in motion around a richly dressed figure, poorly preserved. As Mellaart described the scene: "arms wave, leopard skins swing, and one man carries an unidentified object which may have been a musical instrument, such as a set of pipes. . . . It is difficult to see where the dancers begin and the pursuers of the animals stop."[277]

The Level III Hunting Shrine was more modest. Only deer and bull were represented, the latter accompanied by a group of men that included the headless bicolored figures mentioned above. The scene on the east wall was shown in the earlier discussion of Zagros village traditions, where the Çatal depiction of armed, leopard-skin-clad men dancing around a central figure was compared to the armed dance of the Cretan Kouretes at the birth of Zagreus, or perhaps at the rebirth of a candidate into the mystical brotherhood of Zagreus. As noted there, initiatory cults tended to imitate in their ceremonies of rebirth the events which had surrounded the birth of their god.

105 Seated male statuette in white marble from Shrine VI.10. Height, four and one-half inches (*after Mellaart, 1963*)

see page 147

106 Detail from the west
wall of the Hunting Shrine
at Level V, showing indi-
vidually characterized,
bearded men in leopard
skins teasing a stag
(after Mellaart, 1966)

The death of the god, too, was often recreated in cult, and
it may in fact have been the death of Zagreus-Dionysos that
these other vignettes describe. Although Mellaart named these
two chambers Hunting Shrines — and the murals do show men
armed with bows, clubs, and axes — he feels that no actual hunt
was portrayed here and that these paintings are more likely to
have been pictorial records of myths and legends belonging to
the religious traditions of Çatal Hüyük. He cites no particular
myth or legend, but we recall that in the Cretan myth, when
see page 145 Zagreus was set upon by the enemies of Zeus, he assumed the
shapes of several different animals before finally being captured
and consumed in the form of a bull. It therefore seems possible
that the festive chasing-around after the many beasts in these
Hunting Shrines was actually a dramatization of the efforts of
the Titans to capture the ever-transforming Dionysos. One wonders if the great bull, the central figure in each of these shrines,
was eventually devoured by the participants in these rites, as
was the bull-formed Zagreus. Or were these paintings merely
illustrations of the myth, rather than the record of an actual
playing-out of the trials of the god?

In either case some of these enthusiastic armed dancers may
have been representations of those the Cretans called Kouretes.
The name (from *kouros*, youth) was given to Cretan initiates as
well as to the legendary Cretan daemons, and it is said that
warlike dances were performed in Crete at regular intervals by
the young warrior-Kouretes in celebration of the actions of the
divine warriors who danced at the births of Zeus and Zagreus.[166]

If the often-individualized figures in the Çatal Hunting Shrines were indeed real men, the bichromatic figures that the excavator saw as possibly superhuman beings could have depicted the divine Kouretic daemons, already legendary at the time of Çatal Hüyük. As Mellaart has observed, the tradition that inspired these paintings was not formed overnight and may well stretch back to the end of the Upper Paleolithic era.[277]

see figure 81

But Kouretes, mythic or real, may not have been the only group portrayed by the diversely costumed figures on these walls. Learned Greeks knew of several other troops of daemons in the Aegean; Strabo relates the Kouretes to the Satyroi and Silenoi (animal-tailed companions of Dionysos in Greek art) as well as to the Korybantes, the Kabeiroi, the Idaean Daktyloi, and the Telchines, all of whom were said to be represented as

> a kind of inspired people and as subject to Bacchic frenzy, and,
> in the guise of ministers, as inspiring terror at the celebration of
> the sacred rites by means of war-dances, accompanied by uproar
> and noise and cymbals and drums and arms.   (X.3.vii)

Just as the Kouretes bore the torches of the Mountain Mother in Crete, the Korybantes were attendant on Kybele, the great Phrygian goddess who, like her Cretan counterpart Rhea, was also a Mountain Mother.[128] The parallelism of Cretan and Phrygian (northwest Anatolian) cult was in fact so close that one cannot tell whether the final representation of the feline theme at Çatal Hüyük is more likely to have anticipated Rhea or Kybele.

107 Scene from the north wall of the Hunting Shrine at Çatal V. A large bull is surrounded by animated male figures, several of which are painted black (after Mellaart, 1966)

The Mistress of the Animals

The tails of leopards or lions extend up the back and over the shoulders of the seated female at figure 110, recovered from Level II. Presumably the portrayal of a goddess, this clay figurine is the first recorded example of a type known in later traditions as the Mistress of the Animals.[446] No less widely celebrated than the Master of the Animals, the Mistress was largely identified with the Mountain Mothers of antiquity. Lions and leopards were especially consecrated to Kybele; Rhea is often shown seated between two lions in Greek statuary.[128] It is perhaps not important which name she bore at Çatal Hüyük. Rhea, Kybele, and such regional counterparts as the Cappadocian Ma are believed by many scholars to have been one and the same goddess, a deity of the pre-Greek populations of the Aegean and Anatolia.

And of the Zagros mountains as well? Earlier we saw seated, corpulent, clay female figurines in Zagros assemblages (fig. 79) that included the remains of the leopard, the wild bull, and other elements which were reminiscent of Aegean cult. Should the origin of the Anatolian Mistress or Mountain Mother, and of the dionysian rites over which she traditionally presided, be sought in the east? Or is it possible, as suggested in Part III, that a native Aegean cult took refuge in the Zagros or Taurus highlands after the floods? A collection of artistically superior analogues (fig. 108) of the Çatal Mistress was found in contemporary levels of a new settlement at Hacılar in western Anatolia (a community that is considered part of the Greco-Balkan Civilization of Old Europe described earlier). Lying just to the south of ancient Phrygia, Hacılar's well-developed, apparently local, traditions suggest that if the worship of Kybele-Rhea was in fact transferred at some point to the Zagros, she had not been forgotten by the peoples of the Aegean.

The same goddess may have inspired the settling of Crete. An ancient legend credits the Kouretes and Korybantes with the founding of Knossos and the establishment there of the cult of Kybele (Eusebius *Chronica* 22,26,42). Carbon-14 dating shows Knossos, which is the earliest recorded settlement on Crete, to have been founded around 6100 B.C., coeval with early levels at Çatal Hüyük. The presence at base level of sheep, goat, cattle, and pig, as well as the most advanced grains of the day, has led archaeologists to conclude that the founders of Knossos arrived by sea with already domesticated animals and crops.[280] And as the same domesticates were present slightly earlier in Anatolia,[143] a west Anatolian point of departure is believed likely.

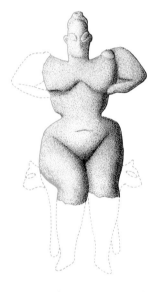

108 Hacılar "Mistress of the Animals," height of preserved portion, four inches *(after Mellaart, 1970)*

In the two following levels at Knossos rectangular dwellings were constructed of kiln-fired bricks, an unexpected and unprecedented building material that was later replaced by pisé.[123] A fragmented clay female figurine has also been recorded, but the most remarkable find in Knossos' first three strata was an exceptionally fine marble statuette of a youthful male figure (fig. 109), the earliest known example of an Aegean type later to be known as the *kouros*.

Similar statuary did not appear again among the excavated material from Neolithic Knossos, but the tradition that produced this piece of sculpture may have formed the basis of the Minoan civilization of the third and second millennia B.C. Investigators are now tending to downplay the role of foreign influence in the development of Minoan culture, finding its foundations instead in "slowly but firmly matured indigenous traditions."[433a] If this is true, might the Cretan Kouretes have been there all along, the founders of Knossos as the legend claims? Neither the archaeology of early Knossos, the counterparts to Kouretic traditions already noted at Çatal Hüyük, or the several other Çatal parallels to Minoan Crete to be described below would argue against such a proposal.

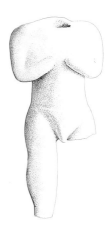

109 Marble figurine from Knossos, Crete, early sixth millennium B.C. Height, three and one-half inches (*after Theocharis, 1973*)

110 Çatal "Mistress of the Animals." Clay figurine from Level II. Height, six and one-half inches. (*after Mellaart, 1963*)

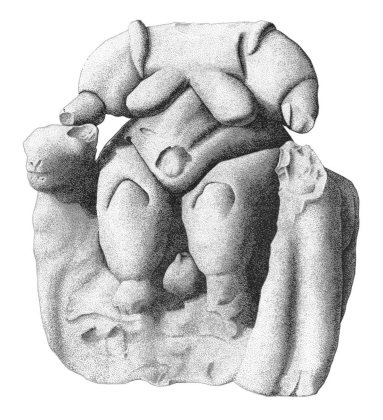

Çatal Hüyük: 6200–5300 B.C.   187

Peak Levels VII and VI
at Çatal Hüyük

Level VII yielded the earliest traces of the Çatal "bull pillars" (fig. 111, left), single mud-bricks topped with the actual horns of a bull (bucrania), which several analysts have compared to the Cretan horns of consecration. Although these single pillars continued to be present in levels up to II, the multiple-horned "bull benches" also shown at figure 111 were known only to Level VI. Mellaart described the shrine pictured here as follows:

> This impressive building, evidently dedicated to "the cult of the wild bull," bore no wall paintings or reliefs. It was decorated with two huge bucrania set on the edge of the northeast corner platform, and with an even more impressive row of seven horn cores of Bos primogenius set in the bench at the southern end of the main platform. Six of these were at the same level and the seventh raised above it, like a serried row of stylized bulls heads, one behind the other, in awesome splendor.[275]

111 East end of Çatal Shrine VI.61, showing several bull pillars and a bench into which seven pairs of aurochs' horns had been set (*after Mellaart, 1963*)

In other shrines at Level VI, three and five pairs of bulls' horns had been similarly set into the raised benches. All of these

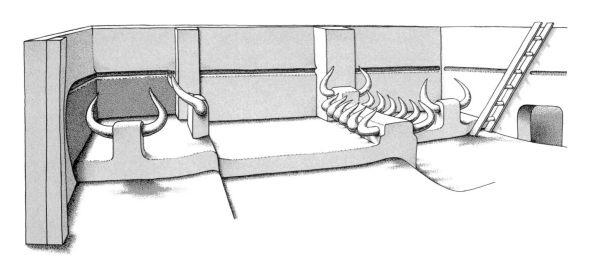

structures have been seen as possible healing couches, comparable to the *abata* that were used during a spread of malaria in Greco-Roman times (a particularly apt comparison if the anemia that seems to have afflicted some 40% of Çatal residents, creating an overgrowth of the spongy marrow space of the skull, was in fact caused by malaria as has been suggested).[4]

In Crete the horns of consecration were often shown framing the symbol of the double-axe, a favorite Minoan motif. Nothing has been found preserved on the bull-pillar pedestals at Çatal Hüyük, but the earliest known representation of the double-axe itself formed part of a mural in a shrine at Level VI (fig. 112).

Frequently represented elsewhere in the coming epoch, the double-axe was to become one of the most popular symbolic forms known to prehistory, and its meaning (or meanings) among the most controversial. According to one scholar, the twin-bladed axe between the horns of Minoan bulls was to be associated with the god Dionysos.[111] Others have suggested that its form signifies the union of earth and heaven, or the coincidence of opposites, the initiatory goal. Most recently an M.I.T. scholar in archaeo-astronomy proposed that the double-axe was actually associated with the Precession of the Equinoxes,[95] a startling new interpretation to which we shall later return.

To the right of the double-axe in figure 112 is a form which Mellaart calls a "wheeled cross," painted here in purple and orange manganese to which a sparkling mineral had been added.[275] When this branching cross motif appears in Greco-Balkan pottery designs, Gimbutas finds it symbolic of the perpetual renewal of the cosmic cycle.[160] She sees the four arms of the cross as representing the four seasons of the year and the four cardinal directions of space, with the branching extremities emphasizing the dynamic movement of the whole. About the wheel in the center of this cosmic cross, more will also be said later.

112 Painted panel from Çatal Shrine VI.A.66 with double-axe, wheeled cross, and a bull's head in relief *(after Mellaart, 1963)*

A Veiled Goddess and
the Queen of the Underworld

The same mural shows several small figures above the right arm of the cross, the largest of which are a steatopygous female, an archer, and a stylized goddess-form. The last named is frequently encountered in Levels VII and VI of Çatal Hüyük before disappearing with the fire at VI.A. No definite sign of sex is indicated in her numerous images, but the occasional swelling of the stomach in relief treatments and the birth-giving position of the legs have led the excavators to see this deity, or the several deities represented by this form, as female. Most of these icons were defaced when the shrines were abandoned and rebuilt, but evidence of some sort of an extension on either side of the head suggested horns to Mellaart, or perhaps the horned hair style of a small figurine at Neolithic Hacılar.

In Shrine VII.23 the goddess was alone in the chamber (fig. 113). Concentric circles on her stomach were seen by the excavators as possible indications of pregnancy. She is described as apparently wearing a netlike garment and holding up a black, red, and yellow veil of the same pattern. Both garment and veil have been compared to the netlike weave of the Çatal shrouds of the dead.[276] A similar goddess-form appeared in silhouette beside a *kilim* mural at Level VI, and these various associations with woven fabric led Mellaart to see in this veiled figure a possible prototype of Athena, the Greek goddess of weaving. He may be right; the inscription below the statue of Neith at Sais stated that no mortal has ever seen through her veil,[30] and the Neoplatonist Proclus (*Commentary on the Timaeus*) claimed that the veil of Athena was the essence of that divinity, "the last image of the whole contrariety of things." An unmistakable initiatory motif, the many-colored veil of the goddess is seen by some as representing the ever-changing world of nature, in Platonic terms the perceptible world of becoming, behind which the real lies hidden. It is said that only the initiate, "mortal no more," penetrates the veil of visible forms, perceiving the spirit that it conceals as well as suggests.

Mellaart's comparison of the veil of the Çatal deity to the burial fabrics at this site recalls as well the goddess Persephone, who as queen of the underworld was credited in Greek myth with weaving the shrouds of the dead. (Persephone was also described as "horned" in antiquity,[94] and her offspring Zagreus a "horned child" [Nonnus VI.165].) We have seen suggestions

113 The veiled goddess. Relief construction from east wall of Çatal Shrine VII.23, painted in black, red, and yellow on a white ground. Height, approximately two feet (*after Mellaart, 1964*)

of her prototype in Çatal statuary (fig. 104); Mellaart believes that the same goddess may have formed one half of a monumental plaster relief on the west wall of Shrine VI.14 (fig. 114), which he sees as a representation of a twin-formed deity, possibly the mother and maid of Aegean mythology.[275] (Classicists have noted, in fact, that on the oldest vases and terracottas Demeter and Persephone appear almost as twin sisters: "without the aid of the inscriptions the mother would not be known from the daughter.")[128] Here Mellaart sees two heads, two bodies, a single pair of horizontally placed arms, and a single pair of upturned legs, giving an impression of twins that is reinforced by the presence elsewhere of a twin-formed statuette (fig. 117c).

Beneath the right-hand figure of this construction had been modeled an enormous bull's head with a smaller head on its brow. If the abstracted twin form does depict prototypes of Demeter and Persephone, Cretan myth would suggest that the great bull was most likely Zeus and the smaller head Zagreus. Zeus occasionally took the form of a bull in Aegean mythology; Zagreus was supposedly a horned child; and the placement of the two animal heads below one of the twin figures recalls the mythic coupling of Zeus with Persephone to produce Zagreus,

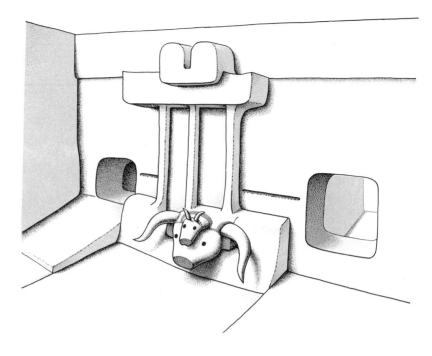

114 Relief construction of a stylized twin goddess with large and small bulls' heads, from the west wall of Shrine VI.14 at Çatal Hüyük. Height, seven feet *(after Mellaart, 1963)*

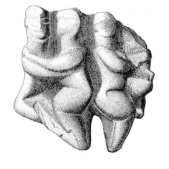

115 Gray schist plaque from Çatal VI; on the left an embracing couple, on the right a mother and child. Height, four and one-half inches *(after Mellaart, 1967)*

with whom he evidently was identified in cult. A similar theme, anthropomorphically stated, may have inspired the carved schist plaque at figure 115, recovered from a house at Level VI.

This Twin Goddess shrine also contained a good deal of weaponry, and we recall that the Kouretes who served the cult of Zagreus were traditionally armed priests. Each of the three main types of weapons that differentiated important male burials at Çatal Hüyük was represented here: four flint daggers below the left leg of the twin figure, several obsidian lanceheads in front of the bull, polished stone maceheads elsewhere in the chamber. All have been judged probable offerings to the deities represented in the huge wall construction, but the shrine was not lacking in other icons. A three-horned bull bench, several bull pillars, two wall-mounted rams' heads and one bull's head, all modeled around the horn cores of real animals, left little space on the east side of the room. Even the south wall, usually empty above the hearth, was now decorated (a ram's head).

Mellaart has compared the Twin Goddess relief to the even larger construction that dominated Shrine VI.10, and it is possible that Persephone's prototype figured in this composition as well. His tentative reconstruction at figure 116 shows the stylized goddess-form apparently giving birth to another horned child; this time a small ram's head had been positioned just below her body. Within the doorlike frame supporting the goddess were set three superimposed bulls' heads. On either side cavernous niches had been cut into the walls. These and the several limestone concretions that seem to have been brought into this shrine from caves suggested to Mellaart an orientation toward the underworld: "a chthonic cult of the Great Goddess as mistress of the underworld."[275]

A large plaster ram's head with two sets of actual horns occupied the north wall of this shrine, a place usually held by the bull. Elsewhere at Level VI, a "ram pillar," a pedestal topped with the horns of the ram rather than the bull, made a solitary appearance. These new treatments of the ram, plus the apparent birth of the ram expressed monumentally in Shrine VI.10 (fig. 116), suggest that the bull's partner (or opponent) may have enjoyed a heightened status at Level VI, just before the fire which would effectively put an end to many of the practices of the preceding three hundred years.

116 Reconstruction of an early phase of Shrine VI.10 at Çatal Hüyük, west and north walls. A goddess-form gives birth to a ram above three bulls' heads. Height of panel, twelve feet (after Mellaart, 1964)

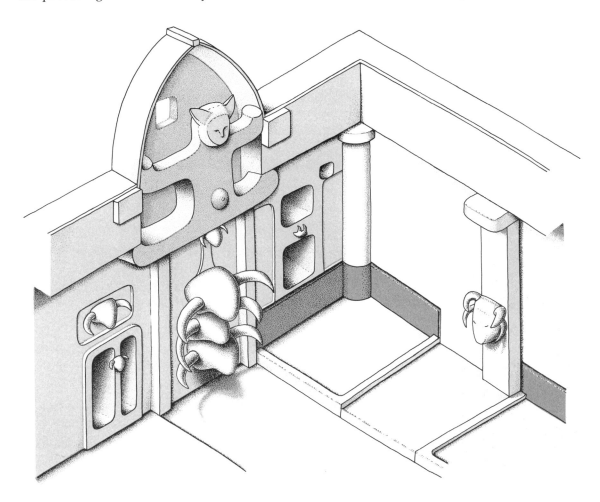

The Çatal Statuary

The largest collection of stone statuettes also came from Shrine VI.10. The two women and a boy with leopards and the priestly male with leopard-skin beret were shown above (figs. 104 and 105); the earlier-mentioned twin statuette was also a member of the VI.10 group, carved in white marble with two torsos and two heads but only one pair of arms and legs (fig. 117c). A rather monkish-looking figure, robed and hooded, belongs here as well (fig. 117a), as does a bearded male in a cloak, seated serenely on the back of an animal which may have been either an ox or a bull (fig. 117b). Two other bearded and similarly mounted figures were found in the Leopard Shrine of this level, and if all of these mature males were meant to be gods, they would not be unlike later portrayals of the bearded Zeus or the bearded Dionysos, carried on the backs of bulls in Greek vase paintings.[79]

But the identification of these stone figures is less important at this point than the recognition of the stylistic diversity of Çatal sculpture as a whole. Even the statuettes placed together in a single shrine such as VI.10 often seem artistically unrelated, a phenomenon which Mellaart found doubly curious in light of the presence of a definite Çatal style in wall decoration. The suggestion made earlier, that these disparate pieces had been brought into the shrines of Çatal Hüyük with an influx of foreign cults, is no less plausible now that some fraction of the variety of symbolic forms at this site has been explored. But another factor to be considered is the condition of some of these statuettes. Several were described as "already old, worn, and broken" when recovered by the excavators; the younger female in the triad with leopards had been mended at least once. Mellaart believes that some of these figures may have been considerably older than the context in which they were found:

117 Stone statuettes from Çatal Shrine VI.10: (a) hooded figure in black stone; height, three inches, (b) bearded male seated on bull or ox, dark blue limestone; four and one-half inches, (c) opposite, twin figures in white marble; six and one-half inches *(after Mellaart, 1963)*

> The feeling that many of them are ritual heirlooms—like Romanesque sculptures in a Baroque church—is enhanced by the very fact that many of them show marked signs of wear and tear. Not a few show ancient breaks or are worn smooth.[275]

As almost all of the stone statuettes were found in the ruins of the great fire at Level VI.A, these long held and handed-down pieces were probably abandoned at that point only because of the need for hasty evacuation of the site. Similar images, and in fact male statuary as a whole, did not appear again after the fire.

Where, then, had they originated, these old and worn "heirlooms" that often bear a striking resemblance to personages in the earliest known stratum of Aegean mythology? Were they, or models from which they had been copied, possibly an inheritance from Plato's vanished Greek cultures? Anthropomorphic sculpture in the round was generally associated with the Gravettian tradition of central and eastern Europe (and Greece) in Upper Paleolithic times. In the Near East, the only earlier recorded examples of human figures carved in stone belonged to the Natufians of Palestine and the inhabitants of Mureybet III (where rather crude stone figurines accompanied the clay maiden-goddess shown in Part I), both of which peoples were earlier credited with possible Aegean connections. But if some part of the Çatal stone statuary was indeed a Greek legacy, one wonders where the tradition had been preserved during the centuries following the post-war floods. Neither PPNB nor Zagros village sites have yielded stone figurines. Should we then look to Crete, or rather to the unknown, possibly west Anatolian culture that founded Knossos and produced the only other male stone statuette of this period, the *kouros* at figure 109? Or was the tradition maintained in Greece itself, as might be suggested by the presence of two anthropomorphic stone carvings, however more primitive, in the base level of one of the Early Neolithic settlements in Thessaly?[430]

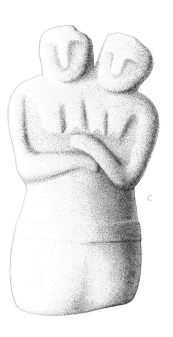

It is also possible that some of the stylistically varied statuettes at Çatal Hüyük were brought into the site by more easterly peoples of whom we have no trace until this mid-sixth-millennium date. As we shall see later, the symbolic use of rams' and bulls' heads, double-axe, and wheeled cross were all known to the *Halafian* culture which began settling northern Mesopotamia in the last half of the sixth millennium. One eminent Near Eastern archaeologist has suggested that Çatal Hüyük may in fact have been a westerly variant of Halaf.[42] Apparently former nomads or seminomads, the Halafians are believed by some investigators to have come from the high country east of Çayönü, near the obsidian-rich region of Lake Van, a region which we earlier proposed as a possible refuge for survivors of the *Timaeus* floods. Anthropomorphic stone sculpture is rare in Halaf sites, but a related group of new agriculturalists to the south down the Tigris buried the only other large collection of stone statuary dating to this period (all female) in a cemetery at the base level

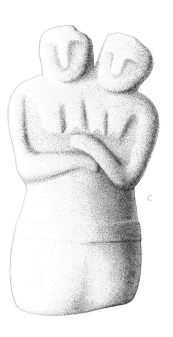

see figures 23, 41

of Tell es-Sawwan around 5500 B.C., and thereafter modeled only in clay.[311] This was only one of the signs of the new epoch now taking form in the Near East, and it may be that a conscious effort was underway to put aside the ways of the old.

Signs of Decadence Before the Fire

see figure 100

Prior to Level VI, no structure at Çatal Hüyük had been burned; both shrines and houses stood until they became uninhabitable before being rebuilt. In Levels VIII and VII up to 120 layers of plaster had accumulated on the shrine walls, causing them to lean precariously under the weight.[277] The condition of the vulture-bull shrine pictured earlier was described by the excavators as "appalling," with every wall near collapse and the kitchen end of the building littered with animal bones.[276]

The shrines of Level VI had also acquired 100–120 layers of plaster (VI.B) before part of the settlement was destroyed by fire. Some of the houses were rebuilt after this minor fire and the extremely crowded conditions alleviated somewhat by the installation of courtyards, but the major shrines were only re-modeled, not rebuilt.[277] It was at this point (Level VI.A) that the ram pillar mentioned earlier was erected, joining the other special treatments of that animal which were instituted at VI.B. But if the apparently higher status of the ram at Level VI did represent the encroachment of a solar impulse on the chthonic-lunar themes that had prevailed at Çatal Hüyük since Level VIII,* it was not yet strong enough to transform the site.

Layer upon layer of plaster continued to accumulate in the remodeled shrines; more than 60 layers were added in VI.A to the 120 of VI.B to bring the total number of applications of plaster (and perhaps years of life) at Çatal VI to almost 200. The many replasterings caused the floor of Shrine VI.10 to rise almost two feet, giving the bulls' heads the appearance of sinking into the floor, but no effort was made to adjust them. Burials in this same shrine became so numerous that they could no longer be contained beneath the platforms, and some intruded into the space below the floor. Mellaart also noted that less care seems to have been taken to leave earlier burials undisturbed; bones and skulls were found rearranged, funeral gifts scattered.[278]

---

* In antiquity the ram was usually associated with the sun, the bull usually with the moon, although there were sun-bulls as well.[79]

This combination of carelessness, conservatism, and a taste for monstrous iconography tells a familiar story. If the conflagration at VI.A had not completely destroyed the Çatal shrines, their own encrusted weight of tradition (and plaster) must eventually have brought them down. It seems clear that some of the cults represented in these rooms were not at the beginning, but at the overripe end of their spiritual impulse, at least for this era. When a much smaller settlement was built over the ruins of the VI.A fire, the number of shrines was greatly reduced; the monumental wall constructions were gone, and most of the chthonic themes seem to have vanished with them. By Level II, as we shall see shortly, Çatal Hüyük was a thoroughly reformed site with an altogether different orientation.

Patterns of Reform

How many cycles of decay and renewal these chthonic cults had already experienced before appearing at Çatal Hüyük may never be known. If some of these traditions did originate in Upper Paleolithic contexts—e.g., in the painted caves of Magdalenian Europe or among vanished Greek or Anatolian peoples—one suspects that they were given a fresh start, perhaps a recombination of elements, in the confusion that would have followed mid-eighth-millennium floods. But if their pre-Çatal development remains uncertain, their future course, or how many times the mystery religions would be revived and again decay before entering history, is certainly not unknowable, if this was in fact the pattern of religious prehistory. A major challenge for prehistorians could be the charting of their respective cycles of rebirth.

There are, fortunately, a few ancient models from which one might work. One, the earliest attested example of religious reform in Greece, comes to us with the enigmatic figure of Orpheus, the legendary musician whose song could tame wild beasts, move stones and trees, and even abrogate the laws of Hades in his descent in quest of Eurydice. However mythicized Orpheus had become by the sixth century b.c., he is generally believed to have been a real person, a religious leader whose teachings were to influence Plato as well as Pythagoras. Little is known of the life of Orpheus; some scholars believe he was born in Thrace; others see Crete as the home of Orphism, if not of its founder, perceiving in Crete that "strange blend of Egyptian and primitive Pelasgian which found its expression in Orphic rites."[172] It is unlikely that he lived before the late second millennium b.c.,* but it will nevertheless be worth our while to consider the Orphic reform, insofar as it is known, before examining signs of a similar phenomenon in the upper levels at

* Diodorus Siculus (VII.1) put Orpheus at around 1300 b.c.; others have dated him to as late as the sixth century b.c.[432]

Çatal Hüyük. We obviously cannot hope to do justice in this space to an extraordinarily complex system of thought which many scholars place at the root of Greek philosophy. But as it is the religion of Zagreus-Dionysos with which Orpheus is commonly associated, and as he is said to have revealed the "true spiritual meaning of the old religion,"[166] a brief review of Orphic principles may enlarge our understanding not only of the general pattern of religious reform, but also of the doctrines that informed the Cretan, and possibly the Çatal, brand of mysticism.

The Orphic Religion

What Orpheus found, in Crete or Thrace or both, was a form of Dionysian religion that evidently sought transcendence through maddening music, dance, wine, and, at the pitch of excitement generated by these devices, the rending of certain animals. What Orpheus did, it is said, was to replace the licentiousness of this cult with asceticism.[166] Retaining the Dionysian idea that man might become god, Orphism held that abstinence and purification rather than physical intoxication were the means by which divinity was to be achieved. Not only was the drunkenness of the Thracian cult denounced, but also its excesses of animal sacrifice.[172] The Orphic ideal, in short, was a Dionysos "tamed, and clothed, and in his right mind—in a word, Apollinised."[85]

Although he is most often associated with Dionysos, Orpheus is said to have been a priest of Apollo, whom he accounted the greatest of gods and identified with the sun.[172] The reforming principle is itself considered to be Apollonian.[85] To transform orgiastic rites through order and reason, to bring the solar principle to the lunar, to emphasize the unity (monotheism) rather than the diversity (polytheism) of god—these are all traditional ways of expressing the spirit of reform. The elevation of fire above the other elements is also Apollonian (and Orphic); according to Plutarch:

> God's transformation into fire is called Apollo by reason of its unity, or Phoebos by reason of its pure and unpolluted character; but as to his turning into wind, water, earth, stars, births of plants and animals, and his ordering of the universe in general, they hint at his suffering and transformation by speaking of a certain rending-asunder and dismemberment; they call him Dionysos, Zagreus. . . .   (*On the Ei.* 388–89)

As mentioned above, both Plato and Pythagoras are believed to have been deeply influenced by Orphism.[166] Although Plato deplored the superficial practices of the Orphic priests of his day (*Republic* 364), his own thinking, like that of the Pythagoreans, is often indistinguishable from Orphic principles. But then again, the Orphic-Platonic world view is also indistinguishable from the principles underlying many of the great religions of antiquity. The belief in a spiritual creation which precedes and informs the material one, for example, is found not only in Plato and Orphism but also in the doctrines of Egypt and India. In Iranian religion as well, every terrestrial phenomenon has an invisible transcendent prototype, not unlike a Platonic Idea.[113]

Belief in reincarnation was also widely shared. For the Orphic, worldly existence was pictured as a wheel, a ceaselessly revolving round of lives from which the soul sought release. The gold plates from Orphic graves in Italy announce:

> I have flown out of the sorrowful, weary wheel
> I have passed with swift feet to the diadem desired.
> I have sunk beneath the bosom of the Mistress, Queen
>   of the Underworld.
> And now I come a suppliant to holy Persephone,
> That of her grace she send me to the seats of the
>   Hallowed—
> Happy and blessed one, thou shalt be god instead
>   of mortal. . . .

In Plato's *Phaedo* (70) an "old legend" states that the souls of men exist in another world after they leave this one, and then "come back here again and are born from the dead." Herodotus (II.112) claimed that the Greeks borrowed the idea of metempsychosis from Egypt, that the Egyptians were the first to assert that the soul of man was immortal, born and reborn in a series of incarnations. But aside from the distances involved, any borrowing on the subject could as easily have come from India, where the motif of the fall of the spirit into the circle of existences, the "revolving wheel," is well-documented in Brahmanic texts. In the *Upanishads*, for example, those seeking release from the cycle of lives are advised:

> He who tears up the snare of greed, cuts down delusion, and
> disparages anger, transcending the elemental powers and their
> objects, may enter Brahma's palace, whence he can look down
> upon the revolving wheel as may the charioteer upon the turning
> wheels of his vehicle.   (*MU* VI.38)

Reincarnation in a mortal body, impassioned and imperfect, causes the soul to forget much of what it knows.[166] The forgetful soul is often likened in these traditions to one asleep, disoriented and oblivious of the reality it once knew. Plato's parable of the cave (*Republic* VII.514) deals with this theme, and in the sense that initiation is an awakening from conditioned existence, Socrates has himself been called a master of initiation,[118] a "midwife" of souls (*Theaetetus* 150) who could deliver from men that which was already known to them but forgotten. To become a Bacchos, in Platonic terms, the individual must re-collect all that he has experienced between lives in the world of Ideas. (Pythagoras is said to have recalled past lives as well [Porphyry, *Vita Pythagorae*].)

Fully awake, recollected, the initiate transcends time. In the *Corpus Hermeticum* (XI.20) the neophyte is instructed: "Raise yourself above all time, become Aion [Eternity], then you will understand God." The Orphic too recognized a god of Eternal Time—Aion or Chronos Ageratos, Undecaying Time—and it is particularly here, in the Orphic divinization of Time, that we meet many of the specific parallels to Iranian religion that have led scholars to suspect that the Orphics, and Plato, borrowed their religious ideas from the Chaldean Magi.

The Magian Time God

Like Plato, for whom Time was a "moving image of Eternity" (*Timaeus* 37), the Magi gave their Time god two aspects. *Zurvān akarāna*, Infinite Time or Eternity, was the model in whose image Limited Time, or "time of the long dominion," was made. No purely Zervanite text has survived that would enable scholars to reconstruct Magian religion with confidence, but here again there are indications of a belief in reincarnation. Porphyry (*De Abstin.* IV.16) stated that the Magi were divided into three grades, and all held that there is a transmigration of souls; "and this they also appear to indicate in the mysteries of Mithra." In any case, Time was zodiacally conceived, and a late Armenian text is often quoted as representing the Zervanite view of celestial influence on earthly events:

> All welfare and adversity that come to man and the other crea-
> tures come through the Seven and the Twelve . . . for the twelve
> signs of the Zodiac and the seven planets rule the fate of the
> world and direct it. (*Menok-i-Xrat* XIII.12–14)

This may be an overly fatalistic expression, however, for in the Persian *Zatspram*, possibly a more trustworthy Zervanite source, the planets are treated as integral and harmonious parts of the universe, analogous to the different parts of the human body as macrocosm to microcosm. So too in the Iranian *Bundahišn*, where the Seven and the Twelve are compared to the hands and feet of man.[440] It may therefore be the case that the attitude of the Magi toward the visible heavens was closer to that of Plato in the *Timaeus*, where he advises us to

> see the revolutions of intelligence in the heavens and use their untroubled course to guide the troubled revolutions in our own understanding, which are akin to them; and so, by learning what they are and how to calculate them accurately according to their nature, correct the disorder of our own revolutions by the standard of the invariability of those of god.   (*Timaeus* 47)

Plato's further encouragement to exercise the divine part of ourselves if we would attain immortality (*Timaeus* 90) would also have been approved by the serious religious thinkers of Iran, who held that man's spiritual destiny was in his own hands, that whatever influence might be exercised by Fate, or the Seven and the Twelve, was limited to the material sphere alone.[440]* Thus could *Zurvān akarāna*, Eternity, have been the god of the Mithraic candidate, whose objective was to transcend the material estate, rise above Fate, and operate outside Time as we know it.

Persian religion and the teachings of the Magi will be more fully discussed in Part V. Here we need only observe the similarities that modern scholars have found between the Orphic and Iranian systems of belief. In Cornford's frequently quoted words: "Whether or not we accept the hypothesis of direct influence from Persia on the Ionian Greeks in the sixth century, any student of Orphic and Pythagorean thought cannot fail to see that the similarities between it and Persian religion are so close as to warrant our regarding them as expressions of the same view of life, and using the one system to interpret the other."[85] Parallels extend not only to doctrine (e.g., the divini-

---

* The Neoplatonists were explicit on this point:
  Not everything in nature is bound by fatality. There is another principle of the soul higher than all nature and all genesis, through which we can unite with the gods, rule the cosmic order, and participate in eternal life and in the action of the supercelestial gods. According to this principle, we are capable of our own deliverance. (Iamblicus *On the Mysteries* VI.7)

zation of Time, the pre-existence of spiritual archetypes to the material creation of the world, the elevation of fire over the other elements) but also to such mythic traditions as the dismemberment of the world soul in the form of a bull. If the rending of the bull-formed Zagreus in the Orphic myth did represent the partition of the divine into its various cosmic manifestations, as claimed by Plutarch above, it closely parallels the death of the Iranian Primordial Bull, which gave rise to the plant and animal kingdoms of earth.

see page 199

see page 109

Seeking to account for these similarities, some scholars have placed Iranian influence at the root of Orphism and Greek philosophy. Pythagoras is said to have journeyed to the east and been nourished by the science of the Magi;[20] Plato is thought to have been influenced by Zervanism; Orphism is described as "almost exclusively based on oriental ideas."[307] All of this may be true, but the view that saw Orphism as a revival as well as a reform should not be forgotten. And if images of a Mountain Mother, Kouretes, a Zagreus-like child god with leopard, and a Queen of the Underworld were present at Çatal Hüyük, the main characters of Orphic myth and rite were already assembled in Anatolia in the sixth millennium—and already intermingled with an Iranian, or at least a seemingly Mithraic, element that informed certain other Çatal shrines.

see page 172

Leaving aside for the moment any further speculation on how Orphism came to be so like the religion of the Magi (which we should be in a better position to approach after discussing Zarathuštra in Part V), we might return at this point to the question of whether these symbols at Çatal Hüyük bore the same meaning that they would possess in Orphic circles of the first millennium B.C. That is, was the Çatal pantheon merely a collection of primitive deities who five thousand years later would be given a profoundly spiritual significance by Orpheus, or did these ancient prototypes already embody principles that were reactivated in the first millennium—and surely more than once in the interim?

It would seem from the foregoing sample of Çatal cult life that rites of mystical initiation were indeed practiced in these shrines. The presence, in particular, of a veiled goddess and a Master of Animals among symbols emphasizing metamorphosis and the coincidence of opposites is difficult to interpret in any other terms. But while an intense concern for the life of the soul after death is implied by Çatal burial customs, the presence or absence of a belief in the reincarnation of that soul cannot be determined from the remains of a nonliterate culture.

see pages 167–68

We can, however, and perhaps should, confront the possibility that a Time god similar to the Orphic and Zervanite deities was worshipped at this sixth millennium site. For those committed to finding the origins of astronomy in Babylonian civilization, such an early date for a deity with zodiacal attributes is unthinkable, but many Iraniologists have admitted the possibility of a very remote antiquity for the god Zurvan.[440] What is more, the M.I.T. archaeo-astronomers argue convincingly for a much earlier recognition of such zodiacal phenomena as the Precession of the Equinoxes than anyone had previously thought possible.[355] Dechend and her associates have found evidence of an awareness of the Precession, the changing zodiacal position of the rising sun at the spring equinox, in some of the oldest fragments of art and myth of both ancient and primitive cultures. In the opinion of these investigators, the recognition of the Precession of the Equinoxes first occurred in the Near East at approximately 5000 B.C. and subsequently spread throughout the archaic world and into the recesses of primitive and ancient mythology.

If, as Dechend further claims,[95] the symbolism of the double-axe is to be associated with this phenomenon, its presence at Çatal Hüyük's sixth level may mean that her estimation of c. 5000 B.C. as "Time Zero" is more than a millennium too late, in terms of calendar time. Çatal VI is carbon-14 dated to around 5500 B.C., and we are now close enough to the official calibration curve for archaeologists to presume from its trajectory that 800 to 1,000 years must be added to sixth millennium carbon-14 dates to bring them into accord with calendar time,[280] which would put the true date of the double-axe painting—and possibly the recognition of the Precession of the Equinoxes—at around 65/6300 B.C.

It is also possible that the interaction of the Seven and the Twelve, the planets and the constellations, was the subject of a second painting at Çatal Hüyük, this time from Level VII (fig. 119). As Mellaart described Shrine VII.8 (which had earlier housed a vulture mural):

The main panel in the southwest corner shows two rows of hands with the fingers pointing towards the right, framing a pattern of alternate red and black geometric "ladders and squiggles," not unlike some of the net pattern found on the goddess in Shrine VII.23 [the veiled goddess], and perhaps likewise of textile origin. Seven red hands line the bottom of the panel and twelve alternate red and black hands the top. . . .[276]

We noted earlier that the *Bundahišn*, a Zervanite-tinged Iranian text, compares the Seven and the Twelve to the hands and feet of man. Moreover, the netlike pattern of weaving between these rows of seven and twelve hands at Çatal Hüyük is itself a traditional symbol for the connections between the heavenly bodies. In the words of the *Tao Te Ching*, the "net of heaven" (in the Wilhelm translation, the network of planets and constellations)[431] "is wide-meshed but lets nothing through" (LXXIII.179). It was as impenetrable for the uninitiated as the veil of the goddess.

If a similar design appeared in first millennium Mesopotamia, there would be no question of its zodiacal connotations. We are now in the sixth millennium, however, and the possibility that a Time god with zodiacal attributes was already worshipped at the Neolithic site of Çatal Hüyük is thoroughly at odds with the conventional framework of thought. But later we shall find that the religion of the Magi is believed to have preceded the birth of Zarathuštra, and if the Greeks were correct in dating the prophet to 6,000 years before the death of Plato, some form of what we call Zervanism must have been observed in the last half of the seventh millennium B.C. (in calendar time). *If* the Greeks were correct. Perhaps this question too is better left until after the discussion of Zarathuštra.

119 Painted panel from Çatal Shrine VII.8, showing twelve hands above and seven hands below, connected by a netlike pattern *(after Mellaart, 1964)*

Çatal Hüyük: Levels V–I

The fire that swept through Çatal Hüyük at Level VI.A was extraordinarily intense. Mellaart felt that it must have smoldered a very long time to have penetrated more than three feet beneath the level of the floors, carbonizing the earth, the bones of the dead, and their burial gifts, and arresting all bacterial decay.[278] When the settlement was rebuilt, much smaller now and more open, it was evident that the fire had destroyed far more than the superstructures of the Çatal community.

As mentioned earlier, the number of shrines and the clutter of their contents were greatly reduced. The massive wall constructions were no longer erected, nor were the multiple-horned bull benches of Level VI. Single bull pillars occasionally were used in these upper levels, but the horns were now smaller. The flint daggers of Levels VIII to VI were gone, and although obsidian weapons were still made, their size increasingly diminished until by Level II the industry showed definite signs of decay.[278] With only one human skull also reported in these post-conflagration strata (at Level V), it would seem that the twin cults of ancestor worship and glorification of the warrior, characteristic of the eastern Mediterranean for 2,000 years, were either dead or dying. The memory of Plato's war may have gone with them.

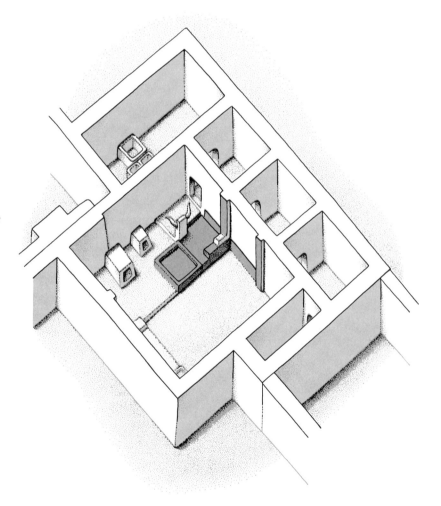

120 Isometric view of the Level II shrine at Çatal Hüyük, showing the large square hearth and its adjoining platform, a pair of ovens, and a single bull pillar (after Mellaart, 1963)

The change at Çatal Hüyük is perhaps nowhere more clearly illustrated than in the simplicity of the only shrine at Level II (fig. 120). The two platforms and bench were still situated along the east wall, but no burials were found beneath them as in earlier levels. Walls were undecorated, except for the use of red plaster. The center of attention was now the fire in the raised hearth. The large square hearth had been provided with a curb, a low bench, and a platform, all of which were covered with burnished red plaster; a pair of ovens was placed nearby; a single bull pillar was fixed to the platform adjoining the hearth.[275] All was order and serenity. Were it not for a scattering of clay female figurines, one might almost say "Apollonian."

Little is known of the topmost levels (1 and 0) at Çatal Hüyük, which are badly eroded. The settlement was then abandoned, around 5300 B.C., for a new location across the river. Çatal Hüyük West has not yet been excavated, but soundings show that geometrically painted pottery was present in the lowest levels, as it had been in the upper strata (from III) of the old site, and as it would be throughout the Near and Middle East in the coming epoch. Mellaart's description of this new era in Anatolia, known as Early Chalcolithic, expresses the magnitude of a change that was almost universal:

> Technologically, painted pottery, usually red on cream with lighter coloured monochrome and plain wares, replaces the dark burnished ware; the chipped-stone industries lose their weapons and are reduced to blades; spindle whorls replace scrapers as hunting declines with the domestication of sheep, goat, pig, now added to that of dog and cattle. Copper occurs, but still mainly for trinkets, such as beads and pins. Maces and sling-stones are the only weapons. The dead are buried outside the settlement, and archaic features such as red floors, roof entry, secondary burial, ochre graves, become far fewer. Figurines are preferably made of clay rather than stone. The date of its beginning is roughly the middle of the sixth millennium in carbon-14 terms.[280]

Characteristic of this new epoch was a massive settling down of presumably nomadic peoples from northeastern Iran to Mesopotamia, creating the greatest single increase in agricultural settlements known to any period of prehistory. Domestic plants and animals were everywhere in evidence; scarcely a site was without the hexaploid, free-threshing grain known as bread wheat. Irrigation would have been necessary for its cultivation at many of these new sites, which frequently were situated in regions unsuitable for dry farming.

As noted above, when mid-sixth-millennium carbon-14 dates are corrected to calendar time, the dawn of this new impulse will be dated to approximately 65/6300 B.C. With Iran the center of action, it seems more than fortuitous that this date should almost precisely coincide with that given by learned Greeks for the birth of Zarathuštra, the Iranian prophet whose reforms were as much economic as spiritual. To settle, to plant—particularly in those places which could be made fertile only by the efforts of man—to raise cattle large and small: these were the imperatives of Zarathuštra's economic reform. Orthodox Zoroastrian tradition dates him to 628 B.C., but many western scholars find that far too recent a time for a prophet whose teachings reflect a period when Iranians were still largely nomadic herdsmen. Some feel that the second millennium is a more likely setting for Zarathuštra. Few would go as far as the Greeks. But as we shall see in the following section, at no later time in Iranian prehistory would the transition from nomad to settler be as abrupt, wide-reaching, or profound as it was in the (carbon-14 dated) middle of the sixth millennium B.C.

V

The Neolithic Revolution:
Phase II

121a During the last half of the sixth millennium B.C., the influence of the Halafian culture spread from Mesopotamia and the Iranian frontiers westward to Syria, parts of Anatolia, and possibly Greece. The vessel above and those pictured in the margins of the following pages are hand-built products of the Halafian potters at Arpachiyah (Iraq), whose skillfully fired ceramics far surpassed the later wheel-made pottery of Babylonia. Framed by checkered patterns or bands of light and dark triangles, the centerpieces of these shallow bowls usually form either a multipetaled rosette or some variation of the cross. *(after Mallowan and Rose, 1935)*

The Background and Teachings
of Zarathuštra

> [Zarathuštra] is said to have been older than Plato by 6,000 years;
> some say that he was a Greek, or a man of that nation which
> came from the Continent on the other side of the great water.
> He is said to have learnt universal wisdom from the Good Spirit,
> that is from the excellent understanding. His name translated
> into Greek means Astrothutes, a "star-worshipper."

The passage above appears among the scholia preserved in
the margins of the *Alcibiades I*, attributed to Plato. As the Iraniologist Wilhelm Geiger pointed out in his analysis, with one
exception all of the statements made here were reliably documented in antiquity. For example, Pliny (*Nat. Hist.* XXX.3–4)
stated that both Aristotle and Eudoxus believed that Zarathuštra
lived 6,000 years before the death of Plato. Plutarch (*De Isid.*
369) claimed that Zarathuštra "the Magian" lived 5,000 years
before the siege of Troy (estimated in his day to the late second
millennium), a measure which was also used by Hermodorus,
a follower of Plato (Diogenes Laertius I.2). By either standard
of reference, Zarathuštra would have been "older than Plato by
6,000 years."

That the prophet was said to have learned wisdom from the
Good Spirit is also true. Ahura Mazda, the supreme god, included Good Mind (Vohu Manah) among his immortal aspects,
and it was through the medium of what might be called this
"excellent understanding" that Zarathuštra is said to have received his revelation. Ahura Mazda is also associated with Spenta
Mainyu, the beneficent spirit of Iranian religion, whose opposite
number is Angra Mainyu or Ahriman, the destructive spirit.
Although Zarathuštra himself is generally believed to have
preached what one Iraniologist described as a pure monotheism
against a dualistic background,[442] the tension between these two

forces of light and darkness would later harden into the rigid dualism for which the Zoroastrian religion is renowned.

As for the name Zarathuštra (Greek Zoroaster) meaning a "star-worshipper," Diogenes Laertius (I.8) wrote that Dinon, an historian living near the end of the Persian empire, had stated in the fifth book of his *History* that the literal interpretation of the name Zoroaster was star-worshipper, an interpretation that was shared by Hermodorus.

Geiger completed his own analysis of the scholium with the following remarks:

> Quite unique stands the statement—He was a Greek or one of those who came forth from the Continent on the other side of the great sea. This last expression is very obscure; it sounds too mysterious to designate the Greeks of Asia Minor. Is it perhaps some reminiscence of the passage of primitive man to the six keshvars* . . . ? Or of the Atlantis?[155]

This curious distinction between Greeks and those who came from the continent on the other side of the great sea, if the latter are indeed to be associated with Plato's Atlantics, would also agree with the early date of Zarathuštra's birth. If the prophet did live and teach 6,000 years before Plato, theoretically his ancestry could still have been traced to the Greek or Atlantic peoples of the *Timaeus* and *Critias*. The Indo-European root of the Iranian language might favor an Atlantic line of descent, but at this point the question of Zarathuštra's ancestry is less important than the claim that he lived in the latter half of the seventh millennium B.C. To explore that very unorthodox idea, we must go first to the *Zend-Avesta*.

see pages 106–11

Dating the Avesta

Perhaps three-fourths of the original *Zend-Avesta*, the sacred texts of the Zoroastrian religion, is believed to be lost. What remains consists of three main types of scripture: (1) the *Gāthās*, seventeen hymns attributed to Zarathuštra himself and often addressed directly to Ahura Mazda, (2) a group of *Yašts*, songs in praise of archaic divinities usually associated with one or another aspect of nature, and (3) the *Vendidad*, which is largely

---

* A reference to the Iranian belief that the world is divided into seven realms, or *kešvars*, the largest of which is inhabited by man.[38]

a collection of religious and moral precepts and purifications. The Avesta was not written down until the Sassanian period (the third to seventh centuries A.D.), before which time these texts had been handed down orally by countless generations of Iranian priests.[185] Because the words themselves were believed to have effective power, their verbatim preservation was considered essential. The surviving scriptures are therefore relatively uncorrupted, but they are written in a dead church language that presents innumerable problems to the translator.

Zarathuštra's *Gāthās* are particularly obscure, with hardly a verse finding an agreed-upon translation. For several reasons these lyric hymns are believed to be considerably more ancient than the *Yašts* and the *Vendidad*, which together comprise the so-called Younger Avesta. Not only do the *Gāthās* appear to be a good deal older linguistically than even the oldest parts of the Younger Avesta,[37] but the same characters who speak and act with immediacy in the Gathic hymns are represented in the Younger Avesta as belonging to a remote past. As one Iraniologist remarked, to go from the *Gāthās* to the *Yašts* or the *Vendidad* is to go "from the land of reality to the land of fable. [We leave] . . . in the one a toiling prophet, to meet in the other a fantastic demi-god."[285]

Most telling, perhaps, is the difference in the state of the religion. In the *Gāthās* the followers of Zarathuštra are struggling for existence, often oppressed and endangered. His denunciation of old gods and old ways, his economic imperative to settle and farm the land, apparently were not well-received by certain nomadic peoples, and several Iraniologists have found suggestions of bloody conflict in the Gathic hymns. In the *Vendidad* a different view unfolds. The danger is past; the church is firmly established, and sacrifices, recitations, and purifications which require minute observances under priestly surveillance occupy considerable space[154] (at whatever cost to the original vision of the prophet).

But the evident seniority of the *Gāthās* should not detract from the antiquity of the Younger Avesta itself. The *Fravardin Yašt*, for example, contains references to Iranian peoples who were apparently unknown to the earliest Achaemenid records of the sixth century B.C. And with the single exception of "Ragha," believed to be ancient Rayy near Tehran, no allusion is made to a known Iranian city or village. Moreover, the practices described in parts of the Younger Avesta are still those of simple agriculturalists and herdsmen. Stone mortars and pestles and the ritual flint knife, implements associated with Neolithic times, were still in use; arrows and spears were often flint-tipped. We seem to be as much in the Stone as in the Bronze Age, and if the Younger Avesta, or some part of it, does belong to a Late Neolithic stage of culture, the *Gāthās* must have been composed even earlier.

Earlier still was the polytheistic religion that Zarathuštra reformed. Before the coming of the prophet, the Iranian people apparently had worshipped a pantheon of gods who personified physical phenomena: sun, moon, earth, fire, the winds, the waters. These ancient divinities of nature are hymned in the *Yašts* of the Younger Avesta (as is the god Mithra), and it is generally agreed that although the *Yašts* were collected later, many of them reflect traditions which are actually older than the *Gāthās*. Some Iraniologists feel that Zoroastrianism was forced to assimilate these popular deities to its creed,[19] but others have argued that Zarathuštra himself was instructed to respect the ancient faith and not to undo entirely the archaic forms of worship, particularly the reverence for fire, which was to play such a prominent role in Zoroastrian rites. The prophet was not to be the founder of a new religion as much as the restorer of an old one, a faith whose purity had been defiled by what one early Iraniologist termed "disorderly idol worship."[174]

Zarathuštra was himself a priest as well as a prophet, evidently trained in the religion he would later reform. He refers to himself in the *Gāthās* as a *zaotar*, a fully qualified priest, as well as a *vaedemna*, one who knows, an initiate possessing divinely inspired wisdom.[38] It is possible that his own name was then given to the heads of the Zoroastrian priesthood. A much-disputed passage in the Avesta (*Y.*XIX.18) mentions a hierarchy of five leaders, the uppermost of which was evidently known as the *Zarathuštrōtema*. Suggested translations of this term as "high priest" and "greatest or highest Zarathuštra" may mean that *Zarathuštra* as well as *Zarathuštrōtema* was a priestly title, a generic term.[154]

A generic use of the prophet's name might also explain the occasional indications in ancient literature that there was more than one historical Zarathuštra. Pliny, for example, when referring to the Zarathuštra born 6,000 years before Plato, remarked that "it is not so clear whether there was only one man of this name, or another one later on" (*Nat. Hist.* XXX.3). The existence of more than one Zarathuštra could in turn be responsible for the vast difference in the dates assigned to the prophet by (1) the Sassanians, who placed him in the sixth century B.C., (2) modern Iraniologists, some of whom would add 500 to 1,000 years to that date, and (3) learned Greeks, who added 6,000. It could also explain why Iraniologists hold such conflicting views regarding the historical milieu of the prophet. At one extreme Zarathuštra has been described as a primitive ecstatic, a kind of "shaman";[307] at the other, as the worldly familiar of Chorasmian kings and court politics.[182]

Zarathuštra's Homeland and Associations with the Magi

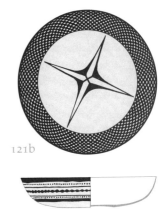

121b

The location of the prophet's birth is no less controversial than its date. As the dialect of the Gathic hymns seems to belong to the northeastern group of Iranian languages, some Iraniologists situate Zarathuštra in the eastern part of Iran.[252] Others follow ancient Persian traditions and put his native home in the west, in Ragha (Rayy) near Tehran or farther northwest in Median Atropatene (modern Azerbaijan),* theorizing that the prophet then traveled east in the course of his teachings.[442, 195] Zarathuštra's ancient association with the Magi might also argue for a western base, if not birthplace, of the prophet. Although Magi were known throughout Iran and Mesopotamia, and have been reported as far afield as Egypt, Ethiopia, and the Aegean, their homeland was traditionally placed in western Iran, specifically Azerbaijan.[38] (A very old Magian center was located near Lake Urmia.)

Iraniologists have found the problem of the Magi to be one of the most compelling, as well as one of the most difficult, in the history of the ancient world: "associated with the highest speculation and the most base charlatanism; the mixed resources of religion and magic; a mysterious origin and an authority that endures across the succession of beliefs."[20] Portrayed as sorcerers in popular fable, the Magi were recognized by the more serious Greeks and Romans (Dio Chrysostom, Apuleius) as dedicated servants of the gods. They were everywhere the reputed masters of learning, credited in ancient times with

* As mentioned earlier, the region around Azerbaijan was identified in the Persian *Bundahišn* with the legendary homeland of the proto-Iranian people, Eran-Vēj; elsewhere in the *Bundahišn* (XX.32) Eran-Vēj is named as the birthplace of Zarathuštra. See Jackson's Appendix IV[194] for a complete list of the Persian accounts of the prophet's homeland.

initiating the "cosmological science,"[20] the study of not only the heavens but also the elements and kingdoms of earth.

According to Herodotus (I.102) the Magi were a Median "tribe," but many Iraniologists now consider it more likely that they were a sacerdotal caste, and of indistinct ethnic origin.[284, 442] By all accounts their way of living was ascetic; personal ornament and the wearing of gold were prohibited; their bed was made upon the ground, their food limited to cheese, herbs, and coarse bread (Diogenes Laertius I.6–7). Both fire and water, and both celestial and chthonic gods, apparently were worshipped by the Magi. Their practice of exposing the dead to vultures was mentioned earlier; according to Strabo (XV.3.xx), "the Magi are not buried, but the birds are allowed to devour them."

see page 179

Plutarch's reference to Zarathuštra as "the Magian" led one eminent Iraniologist to conclude that the Magi, and their Zervanite religion, must have existed before the birth of the prophet.[428] Another found the mention of the "twin spirits" in the *Gāthās* to be additional proof that Zervanism was already known in Zarathuštra's time.[19] (In the Zervanite theogony, Ahura Mazda and Ahriman, associated with Light and Darkness, were the twin sons of Zurvan, god of Infinite Time.) We might note that these conclusions are theoretically independent of the time of the prophet's birth, which Plutarch himself, in naming Zarathuštra a Magus, placed 5,000 years before the siege of Troy.

see page 211

But if there is some evidence that the Magi were older than Zarathuštra, there is little certainty about their relationship to the prophet. Several Iraniologists believe that the Magi were originally opposed to Zarathuštra,[295] and that the teachings of the prophet may have been directed not only against excesses within the nature cults of his day, but against certain Zervanite principles as well.[19] As one scholar saw it, Zarathuštra "abolished the worship of Time or Fate," concentrating instead on man's active participation in the struggle between the creative and destructive spirits.[103] Others have suggested that the Magi continued to preach a Zervanite doctrine while joining themselves to the Zoroastrian reform,[37] or that the Magi accepted the prophet "probably as they had absorbed other teachings."[145]

Here again the possibility of more than one Zarathuštra, and more than one set of relations with the Magi, should be considered. But if the original prophet was himself a Magus, as claimed in antiquity, it is difficult to see how he could have been unsympathetic to all forms of Zervanism. Perhaps the religion of the Magi was indeed in want of reform.

The Old Iranian Religion

The ancestors of Iranians and Indians (or Indo-Aryans, to be more precise) both called themselves *āryas*, and the similarity of many of their traditions has led scholars to conclude that the two were originally a single people, an Indo-Iranian branch of the larger Indo-European family of nations. As mentioned earlier, the date of the severance of these more easterly peoples from the Europeans, the lands they inhabited before moving into their present territories, and the time of the separation of Iranian from Indo-Aryan populations are unknown elements. It was once thought that the original split in Indo-Iranian traditions had been caused by Zarathuštra's reforms. The word *deva*, for example, means "god" in the *Rig Veda* (the oldest Indo-Aryan religious text) but translates as "demon" (*daēva*) in Avestan; and one finds several Vedic divinities demonized in the Younger Avesta. But scholars today generally believe that the two peoples had already separated before the coming of the prophet, and give the name Old Iranian to the popular religion that he reformed.

As noted earlier, Mithra and the "nature gods" hymned in the *Yašts* appear to belong to this ancient stratum, as do the legends surrounding Yima in the *Vendidad*, our source in recounting some of the activities of this Iranian First King in Part II. The comparison of other archaic survivals in the Younger Avesta with material from the Vedas reveals two further, particularly important features of the Old Iranian religion, both of which played leading roles in the Zoroastrianism of later times.

see pages 106–14

The first of these conserved traditions centers around the pressing of a consecrated plant (Iranian *haoma*, Vedic *soma*) whose juice was thought to exhilarate and heighten the powers of the drinker. A ceremonial mortar and pestle, emblematic of the Zoroastrian priesthood, were used to pound the *haoma*; the juice was then collected and filtered through a ring around which three, five, or seven hairs of the sacred bull had been woven.[104] In India the analogous *soma* plant was beaten on a grinding slab before the pulp was put into a vessel and water poured over it. While the juice of the *haoma* was only "shown" to the fire, some of the *soma* juice was offered to various deities by pouring it into the fire from wooden containers of different shapes. Both rituals, as mentioned earlier, included the preparation of a sacred bread.

see page 165

The symbolic use of a ring entwined with bull's hair in the Zoroastrian ceremony has suggested to scholars that the sacrifice of a bull was once part of the *haoma* ritual. Some have further concluded that an excess of animal sacrifice was partly responsible for Zarathuštra's apparent denunciation of the *haoma*.* As the *haoma* ceremony was to be one of the most important Zoroastrian rites down through the ages, these Iraniologists feel that what Zarathuštra actually condemned was not the ritual as such, but an orgiastic perversion in which the wanton slaying of cattle accompanied the abuse of intoxicating plant substances.[103] And as Mithra was traditionally associated with animal sacrifice in general, and with bull sacrifice in particular,[186] these theorized excesses are most frequently attributed to the worshippers of that ancient god.[442]

121C

The second principle of particular importance to both Old Iranian and Vedic religion, and again conserved by Zoroastrians, is the association of fire with the concept of a universal order: *aša* in Iran, *rta* in India. At once cosmic, liturgical, and moral, this ordering principle was held to govern every aspect of existence, from the rhythms of the cosmos and the workings of nature to the conduct of men.[39] In India the highest sky as well as the fire altar was the seat of *rta* (from the verb "to fit"), a term that is used several hundred times in the *Rig Veda*.[119] In Iran the fire was protected by Asha, Right Order; the righteous man was *ašavan*, possessing *aša*, an upholder of the right order of things. Zarathuštra himself would claim to have seen into that order, vowing "while I have power and strength, I shall teach men to seek the Right [Asha]" (*Y.XXVIII.4*). The priests of the old religion had apparently fallen away from *aša*, a dereliction that in itself defines falsehood or deceit, and missionaries were sent to spread the word of the prophet not only to Iranians but also to "those who seek Asha in other lands" (*Y.XLII.6*).

The origin of this very old concept, which has been compared to the *tao* of China and the Egyptian *maat*, is unknown. If, as some scholars believe, it was derived from an observation of the regular movements of the celestial bodies,[131] one wonders what the relationship might have been between the popular concept of *aša* and the attentiveness of the Magi, fire-worshippers themselves, to the changing patterns in the sky.

* In the *Gathas* (*Y.XLVIII.10*) the prophet asks:
  When, O Mazda . . . wilt thou smite the filth of this intoxicant, with which out of enmity the pagan priests deceive, and with which, by their will, the evil rulers of the land deceive us?

The Message of the Prophet

From these observations alone, it is clear that the teachings of Zarathuštra were conservative as well as original, retaining large elements of the religion (or religions) of his day. According to one Iraniologist:

> In a way Zarathushtra not so much innovated as restored the traditional hierarchy, which a certain form of cult, encouraged by certain rulers, had deranged. These war-like rulers, who "to please the people," like fabulous Yima, sacrificed bulls and distributed their flesh, were to be held in check.[103]

see page 107

In the view of some scholars, the practices of Zarathuštra's time included not only an excess of animal sacrifice, idolatry, and the abuse of intoxicants, but also—and perhaps not unrelated to these—an overvaluation of the spiritual domain. As one authority points out,[185] the Indian Brahman traditionally sought salvation in the renunciation of earthly life and the subjugation of the body, with little or no concern for the material world. The same may once have been true of the ancient Iranians. In any case, the aim of the prophet was to secure the material as well as the spiritual welfare of the "Good Creation," to restore the belief in the sanctity of the material world, and ultimately, it is said, to restore the earth to its original state of perfection.[38] The ethics of Zarathuštra's followers were the ethics of life in this world; their prayer: "May we be those who will renew this existence" (Y.XXX.9).

The renovation was to be accomplished through husbandry. Zarathuštra is not presented as the inventor of agriculture; in Persian tradition that distinction goes to more ancient kings.[185] He is, however, said to have been the first to put the husbandman at the center of his religious system, over the priest and warrior. The cultivation of the earth was looked upon by Zarathuštra's followers as a kind of worship: "He who cultivates corn [grain] cultivates righteousness." Among the places in which the earth is most joyful is "where one of the faithful sows the most corn . . . where he waters ground that is dry or drains ground that is too wet" (Vendidad III.1–3).

The functions of warrior and priest were either diminished or transformed. Scholars generally agree that one of the most difficult aspects of Zarathuštra's reform must have been the abolition of the warrior function as such, and the transformation of the man of arms into a "purified crusader in the service of the true religion."[106] The ideal of the Indo-Aryan warrior was Indra, pictured in the *Rig Veda* (IV.42) as an arrogant, strife-provoking warrior, drunk on songs and *soma* but bountiful to his followers, from whom he demanded abundant offerings.[38] Indra is not mentioned in the *Gāthās*, but in the Younger Avesta he is demonized as one of the *daēvas*. His Iranian counterpart, the god Mithra in his warrior aspect, is also absent from the Gathic hymns, but as noted above, a very old *Yašt* was dedicated to him, and some Iraniologists believe that Mithra was already the warrior god of the Iranians before the time of Zarathuštra. Like the *haoma* sacrifice, Mithra was to play a prominent role in the Zoroastrian religion of later times. If his exclusion from the *Gāthās* was indeed intentional, it may be that the worship of Mithra was at that time suffering excesses like Indra's and had thus become a target of the prophet's reform.*

As for the priest of Zarathuštra's religion, as one scholar pointed out: "There is no room for sacerdotal functions as a really integral part of such a man's gospel; and of ritual and spells we hear as little as we expect to hear after studying the life and work of religious reformers in other parts of the world. Ritual has its place, but it is not in the first fresh dawn of a religion that it is going to live."[295] The Gathic priest would more likely have been found on the road or in the fields, or both. Zarathuštra's reform was vigorously missionary in spirit, committed to bringing the word of the prophet to all mankind. If the cultivation of the earth was an important part of that message, missionary priests would presumably have been as well-versed in agricultural technique as in religious dogma. Zarathuštra himself prays in the *Gāthās* for the skills of the husbandman: "I who as priest would learn by the Best Spirit how to practice husbandry" (Y.XXXIII.6). Irrigation, fertilization, cattle breeding, would have been part of a missionary's wisdom. He may also have been an architect and builder, if one Iraniologist's picture of the movement as a whole is correct: "With the spread of the new doctrine, the increase in settlements goes hand in hand. When a hitherto nomadic tribe becomes converted to the Zoroastrian religion, it abandons its former unsettled mode of living, builds permanent dwellings, and cultivates the fields."[153]

* Zaehner found many of the traits of the Vedic Indra in the Iranian Mithra.[442] In the *Mihr Yašt* this "warrior with strong arms" smashes the skulls of the *daēvas* and cruelly exacts pains from those who lie (*Yt.*X.7).

There would in any event have been little requirement for the liturgical services of Zarathuštra's priests, at least not at first. Those who receive the message of the prophet are invited to hear with their own ears, without intermediary, and to judge for themselves the truth of the teaching. In the famous *Gāthā of the Choice* (Y.XXX), the individual is urged to choose for himself either the path of Asha (Right Order) or the path of the Druj (Deceit):

> Hear with your ears the highest truths I preach
> And with illumined minds weigh them with care
> Before you choose which of two paths to tread,
> Deciding man by man, each one for each. . . . [385]

He who chooses to continue the old ways may lose the blessing of Armaiti, guardian of the earth and protectress of herdsmen and farmers.[38] He will certainly fall out of harmony with Asha. But the choice is his to make freely, without priestly intervention.

It is in this evident affirmation of free will that Iraniologists find the most striking contrast to the astrological fatalism expressed in certain late texts attributed to Zervanism. And yet Zarathuštra himself prays in an earlier stanza that propitious results may be discerned "in the lights" (Y.XXX.1), which one scholar interpreted to mean the heavenly bodies.[285] In any event, the prophet is generally credited with being the first to teach that each man must bear the responsibility for the fate of his own soul, as well as share in the responsibility for the fate of the world.[38]

see page 201

Faithful to this vision of man as God's ally, and to the basic monotheism of the *Gāthās*, was Zarathuštra's replacement of personified gods by qualities of the person. The Entities or Amesha Spentas (Holy Immortals) that surround Ahura Mazda are at once divine and human: Vohu Manah (Good Thought), Asha (Right Order), Khshathra (Sovereign Power), Haurvatat (Immortality), Ameretat (Wholeness or Integrity), and Armaiti (Right-Mindedness or Humility). Aspects of Ahura, they are also virtues of the perfected man.[366] By cultivating these qualities in himself, the individual could realize his own likeness to the divine, and, as each Entity was to be associated with the protection of some particular aspect of creation (Haurvatat, water; Ameretat, plants), his commitment to the stewardship of the earth—one of the principal tenets of the Zoroastrian religion—was secured as well.[39]

The Neolithic Revolution: Phase II   221

The Eschatological Expectation

To close this brief review of some of the teachings attributed to Zarathuštra, a word should be said about Friedrich Nietzsche's characterization of the prophet. Nietzsche claimed that in writing the prose poem *Thus Spake Zarathustra*, he had created the exact opposite of the historical prophet, of whom he apparently had only fragmentary knowledge and whom he denounced elsewhere as the first moralist.[303] This supposedly antithetical figure then served as the prototype of Nietzsche's ideal man, his free and unconditioned, self-ruled *Übermensch*. The unforeseen ironies of this portrayal cannot be explored here, but if Nietzsche did set out to create Zarathuštra's opposite, he was conventionally correct in having his fictional prophet announce the doctrine of "eternal recurrence," Nietzsche's own version of the ancient view of earthly events as cyclic, repetitious, and essentially meaningless. For the historical Zarathuštra is generally held to have been the first to conceive of the world's course as both progressive and purposeful.[371]

121d

In contrast to the idea that time is circular and history an endless series of cycles—the Eternal Return of Hindu and later Greek (and Nietzschean) formulations—Zoroastrian time is linear. The world had a beginning and a midpoint and will have an end, a final goal which gives meaning to all that went before. In the beginning Ahura Mazda created a perfect world which was subsequently marred by the penetration of the evil principle into every domain. Midway in the course of history Zarathuštra came to offer (or to remind men of) the opportunity to collaborate in the work of redemption, in the restoration of perfection toward which all creation is striving. At the end of time another *saošyant* (savior) will appear and lead the forces of light in an ordeal by fire, in which a flood of molten metal will burn up the last vestiges of evil, leaving the good unharmed.*

But with half the world's course theoretically still to be run at the time of Zarathuštra, scholars have found indications in

---

* The parallels between Zoroastrian and Judaeo-Christian traditions have often been noted; the role of the savior and the optimistic end point of time are not the only similarities between the two. Some scholars attribute the resemblance to Zoroastrian influence on the Hebraic matrix;[37, 252] others believe that Zoroastrianism and Mosaism are independent prophetic religions, springing from separate though similar revelations.[371] Dating Zarathuštra to the seventh millennium B.C. would obviously call for a fresh approach to this question.

the *Gāthās* that the prophet believed that the end of the world was imminent, and that the renewal of a world destroyed by fire would take place within his lifetime.[103, 119] The prayer, "May we be those who will renew this existence," is seen as an indication that Zarathuštra's followers also believed that the crisis would come in their own time, allowing them personally to contribute to the triumph of Ahura Mazda over evil.[286]

Two observations may be relevant here. First, we know that the destruction of the world by fire, as by flood, is a common mythological theme;[113] and while some of these conflagration myths may pertain to the ultimate fate of the earth, others seem more descriptive of historical catastrophes, comparable perhaps to the periodic cleansing of the earth described by the Egyptian priest in the *Timaeus*. Second, the M.I.T. archaeo-astronomers tell us that for the ancients, the "end of the world" actually meant the end of a world-age, in terms of the Precession of the Equinoxes:

> What actually comes to an end is *a* world, in the sense of a world-age. The catastrophe cleans out the past, which is replaced by a "new heaven and a new earth."[355]

When the sun no longer rose at the vernal equinox in the zodiacal constellation which had framed it for some two thousand years, the "old world" had come to an end.

In this light one cannot help but be struck by the fact that the late seventh millennium date given by the Greeks for the time of Zarathuštra very nearly coincides with astronomers' estimates for the end of the age of Cancer and the dawn of Gemini, c. 6480 B.C.* If this is not pure coincidence, and if an awareness of the Precession of the Equinoxes did in fact exist see page 204 in the last half of the seventh millennium, the more immediate "end of the world" foreseen by the prophet may well have referred to the end of a world-age, the age of Cancer. Dating to this same period (c. 57/5500 B.C. in uncorrected carbon-14 years) would have been the height of the drought which is thought to have caused the death of PPNB and possibly Zagros village culture, a sufficiently destructive "fire," perhaps, to ready the material world for renewal.

* M.I.T. reckoning begins our present age of Pisces with a superior conjunction of Saturn and Jupiter in 6 B.C. Allowing the conventional 2,160 years for each preceding age, the beginning of the age of Aries would have been around 2160 B.C., that of the age of Taurus c. 4320 B.C., of Gemini around 6480 B.C., the beginning of the age of Cancer around 8640 B.C. and so on.

A Look Back at Çatal Hüyük

Before exploring the archaeology of Iran and Mesopotamia in the new world-age, we might briefly review the changes in the upper levels at Çatal Hüyük, which date to the earliest years of this era. As we recall, the number of shrines and the extravagance of their icons were greatly reduced after the fire at VI.A. A corresponding reduction in the priestly corps, if not a change in its function, was evident by Level II with its single plain shrine. By that time the Çatal weapons industry had also visibly declined; the status of the warrior was presumably diminished

along with it. The number of bulls' horns used in levels above VI.A was considerably smaller, indicating a brake of some sort on the slaughter of those animals whose horns had crowned the bull benches and wall constructions of Levels VII and VI. Strata below VI had also yielded analogues to the warrior-oriented, ancestor-worshipping cult of Mithra, particularly in the symbolic context of vulture, bull, and bull-riding Master of Animals. The presence of the "Seven and Twelve" mural in a vulture shrine at Level VII added to the suspicion that the Zervanite religion of the Magi, which may also have been that of the Mithraic mysteries, was already known to central Anatolia in the sixth millennium B.C.

see figure 119

It is possible that the change at Çatal Hüyük actually began before the VI.A fire, when, after the partial burning of Level VI.B, a more open settlement plan was adopted. As Mellaart noted, a whole series of shrines was given up at this time, and only three new ones took their place.[276] Level VI.A also yielded several symbols which were not known to the excavated portion of earlier strata, among them the double-axe and wheeled cross. Where these elements originated is quite unknown, but as both would be popular pottery motifs in Iran and Mesopotamia in the coming epoch, they may well have come from the east. If Zarathuštra did live 6,000 years before Plato, the estimation of Çatal VI to around 65/6300 B.C. in calendar time (carbon-14 dated to c. 5500 B.C.) makes it not inconceivable that the bearers of these new ideas were emissaries of the prophet himself, announcing reforms which would not be fully accepted at this tradition-weighted center for several centuries. But whoever did come to Çatal Hüyük, or when, one fact is certain. The manifest change in the upper levels of that site coincided with a complete transformation of Mesopotamia and Iran (fig. 122).

see figure 112

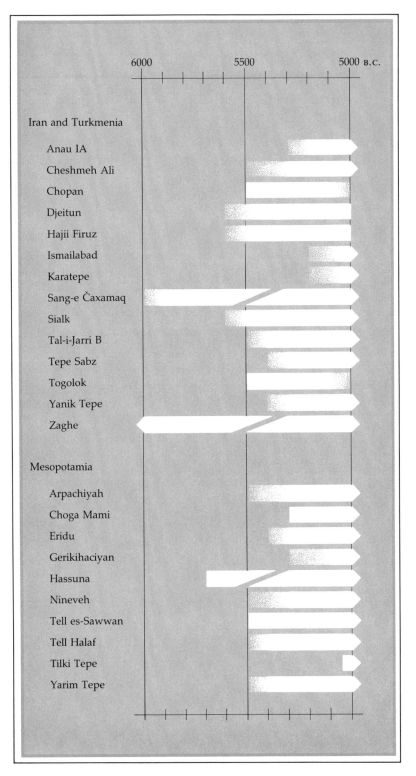

123 Sites named in the text, tentative chronologies based on uncorrected carbon-14 dates. (Although many archaeologists add 800 to 1,000 years to sixth millennium carbon-14 dates to bring them closer to calendar time, official calibration is still unavailable for this period.)

Iranian Archaeology:
5500 – 5000 B.C.

Central Iran: the Sialk/Cheshmeh Ali Culture

As noted earlier, only two settlements with permanent architecture have been recorded east of the Zagros prior to 5500 B.C.:
Zaghe on the north Iranian plateau, and Sang-e Čaxamaq in the
Gurgan plain to the east. Although excavations at both sites are
incomplete, each seems to have undergone a change midway
in the sixth millennium, accompanied at Sang-e Čaxamaq by a
move from the old western tepe to a new site slightly further
east. At Zaghe we recall that the earlier settlement knew mud-
brick and tauf construction, the use of red plaster, and a red-
on-cream painted pottery similar to that of the Zagros villages.
In the new phase Zaghe's building techniques apparently were
unchanged, but her pottery now bore the black or chocolate
brown designs of the *Cheshmeh Ali* culture, a tradition which
was to dominate the Iranian plateau for centuries to come, and
leave a lasting imprint on the art and technology of prehistoric
Iran.

Our best information about the new plateau culture comes
from Tepe Sialk to the south. Although architecture was impermanent at base level (Sialk I,1, dating to around 5500 B.C.)
agriculture is assumed to have been practiced from the start.
(Modern techniques for the recovery of plant remains were unknown at the time Sialk was excavated, but sickles were present
and at least one grain, barley, was identified.) Miniature mortars
and pestles, which would be popular items in Iranian sites of
this period, were made in pottery as well as stone at Sialk I.
Fine ovoid maceheads were also present, occasionally engraved
with chevrons and believed to have served ceremonial purposes.[280] Most remarkable of all, however, was a bone knife
handle (fig. 124) that had been carved into the form of a male

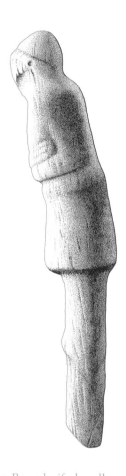

124 Bone knife handle
from Sialk I. The bowing
figure, whose face is
missing, wears a conical
hat and a belted garment
that reaches his knees.
(after Ghirschman, 1938)

figure with hands and arms "reverently folded across the front of the body in an attitude of obeisance which is already astonishingly Persian."[257]

Ties to the older Iranian traditions at Zaghe and the Zagros villages are suggested by the presence of carved stone "bracelets" and a monochrome red pottery with concave bases, but the painted decoration on buff-colored wares in Sialk's first stratum was black rather than red (possibly the result of higher firing temperatures, which are known to darken iron-oxide-based pigments). Red wares decorated in black appeared in the next level of Sialk I. Designs on both the black-on-buff and black-on-red ceramics were exclusively geometric; the interior surface of both types of vessel was frequently used as decorative ground, in one known instance for a double-axe motif (fig. 125).[157]

The next phase, Sialk II, saw the appearance of rectangular houses made of tauf with mud-brick foundations and occasional red walls, which recall the architecture and interiors of Zaghe on the northern plateau. Geometric patterns continue to dominate the painted pottery; alternating dark and light cones form an encircled Maltese cross; another cruciform design resembles

125 Black-on-buff and black-on-red ceramic vessels and sherds from Sialk I, central Iran, c. 5500–5000 B.C. (after Ghirschman, 1938)

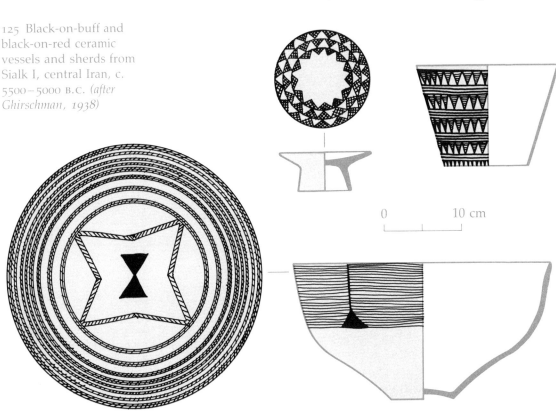

0   10 cm

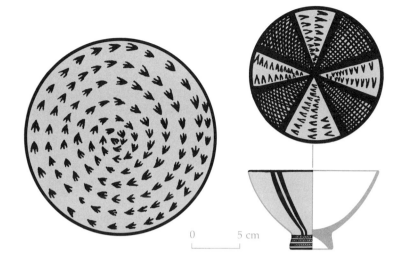

126 Black-on-red bowls
and sherds from Sialk II,
c. 5000–4500 B.C. *(after
Ghirschman, 1938)*

a fringed swastika (fig. 126). Stylized animals appear as well on
the ceramics of Sialk II, primarily goats whose shape reminded
the excavator of the double-axe,[157] and birdlike forms trace the
pattern of a spiral.

The pottery of this second phase at Sialk was nevertheless
rivaled by the black-on-red wares of sites to the north in the
region around Tehran (Ismailabad, Karatepe, Cheshmeh Ali itself), about which unfortunately little is known. Here stylized
goats were painted in rows or in whirl-patterns, and shapes
included goblets or bowls on fenestrated pedestals. The ceramics at the site of Cheshmeh Ali in particular were described by
one analyst as "decidedly more mature" than those elsewhere
on the plateau during this period,[253] and though carbon-14 dates
are lacking, the reported likeness of the pottery at Cheshmeh
Ali's base level to that of the first phase at Sialk[361] suggests that
this more northerly settlement may also have been founded as
early as the mid-sixth millennium.

In any case, as another investigator has pointed out: "If the
presence of a more highly developed repertoire of designs and
ceramic forms may be interpreted as meaning that a site is close
to the focus of a culture, we could consider that Cheshmeh Ali
is nearer the center of this culture than Sialk."[273] From the excavations at Zaghe we now know that the northern plateau had see pages 149–50
an architectural advantage over Sialk as well. This combination
of a greater maturity in both ceramics and building techniques
suggests that the north Iranian plateau may in fact have been
the home base of the tradition that inspired the founding of
Sialk.

To the south in the province of Fars, the plain of Persepolis was also first settled midway through the sixth millennium. Information is again limited, but black-on-buff pottery is known to have been present in the lowest levels of *Tal-i-Jarri B* and in ten other surveyed mounds of the region. Linked by one archaeologist to the ceramics of Sialk I,[23] by another to the pottery of southwestern Iran[96] (to be described below), the wares of this culture nevertheless show an individuality of design which suggests that wherever the ceramic technique originated, the settlers themselves were native to Fars.

Southwest Iran: The Sabz Phase

see page 151

For some years, perhaps centuries, after the abandonment of Alikosh and related sites of the Zagros village tradition, southwestern Iran was only sparsely settled at best. Then, at some point between 5500 and 5000 B.C., a burst of new activity brought permanent settlements into the region in force. As described by Frank Hole and Kent Flannery:

> Midway through the sixth millennium, peoples in certain areas of southwest Iran went through a rapid and crucial transition which was to set them clearly on the path toward population expansion and urban life. The three major innovations of that period were (1) the beginnings of competent irrigation, (2) the beginnings of cattle domestication, and (3) the use of a full range of cereals improved either by mutation or hybridization.[188]

"What eludes us still," they added at a later writing, "is a clear-cut picture of its origins."[189]

Archaeological survey has recorded at least 34 villages dating to this period in the Susiana plain alone. Hole and Flannery found it hard to believe that so many farmers and herdsmen had suddenly descended on the plain, but sites of earlier age have yet to be discovered in Susiana. Most of our information about this period in southwest Iran comes from the excavations at Tepe Sabz, a new settlement just north of Alikosh in the Deh Luran plain. Here domestic cattle joined the sheep and goat of the earlier Zagros village tradition (and wild cattle disappeared from the faunal remains); bread wheat, six-row hulled barley, and flax all made their first appearance in this region. The flax seeds have been judged too large for plants raised on rainfall alone, and Hole and Flannery noted that in fact many settlements of this period, known as the *Sabz phase*, had been situated

map at figure 122

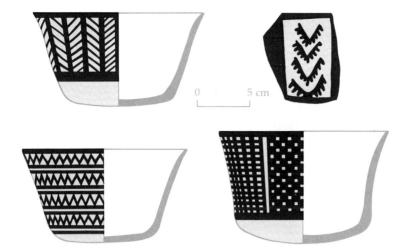

127 Black-on-buff ceramic
vessels from the Sabz
phase in southwestern
Iran, late sixth millen-
nium B.C. (after Hole et al,
1969)

to take advantage of the small stream channels coming down
from the mountains as sources of irrigation water.[189]

Vestiges of the older Zagros tradition included such items as
carved stone "bracelets," now wide bands of stone with a number of grooves running parallel to the edges, but the tool kit
was significantly changed, reflecting what the excavators saw
as a shift away from an earlier preoccupation with hunting. The
quantity of flint tools was greatly reduced (for the first time
fragments of flint were outnumbered by sherds of pottery); a
decrease in hide-working tools was matched by an increase in
spindle whorls, suggesting, with the cultivation of flax, that the
skins of wild animals were now being replaced by woven cloth.
Plain blades and sickle blades, trimmed to fit into slots in a
handle or haft, were the principal implements of the Sabz phase.

A few of the stone bowls so popular with their predecessors
were also made by these new settlers, and sherds of a soft-fired,
monochrome red or pinkish tan pottery reminiscent of the final
phase at Alikosh were here as well. But the majority of Sabz
phase vessels were hard, sand-tempered, buff-colored ceramics
of superior quality. And while certain of their shapes and designs suggest an evolution out of the old Zagros village line of
pottery, the paint decorating these buff wares was now dark
brown or black rather than red (again attributed to higher firing
temperatures), and applied in what the excavators described as
a "broad-line, free-hand manner, with a great deal of individualism."[189] Chevrons were still prominent, now often arranged in
pierced vertical rows ("fir trees"); more common was a reserve
screen or "checkerboard" also known at Alikosh. Schematized
birds ("vultures") were among the new motifs (fig. 127).

see figure 131

The Neolithic Revolution: Phase II   231

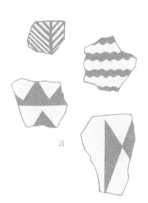

Seeking the origin of the several changes recorded in the Sabz phase, one might look east to the black-on-buff pottery traditions of the Iranian plateau, with which, as we saw above, these slightly later ceramics of southwest Iran appear to share certain elements of design. One might also look to the north, where a pair of extraordinary cultures known as *Samarra* and *Halaf* were spreading rapidly across the plains of central and northern Iraq in the last half of the sixth millennium B.C. Before investigating these new Mesopotamian cultures and their possible relationship to Iranian developments, we shall briefly review contemporary events in northeast and northwestern Iran.

Northeastern Iran: the Djeitun Tradition

128 (a) Red-on-cream ceramic sherds from the Djeitun culture of Turkmenia and northeastern Iran, mid-to-late sixth millennium B.C., (b) black-on-red sherds from Anau IA *(after Masson and Sariandi, 1972)*

b

The *Djeitun* culture of northeast Iran and Turkmenia is generally dated to the middle of the sixth millennium, coeval with Sialk I on the plateau. It is represented by ten excavated sites, of which Djeitun itself is the best known.[266, 267] The reported presence of bread wheat, barley, and a very high percentage of sickle blades (set in straight bone hafts like those at Sialk) identify the members of this culture as farmers. They may have been irrigators as well; Djeitun lies on the delta of a large mountain stream between the Kopet Dagh and the Karakum desert, and archaeologists have observed that irrigation could have been effected by damming up the small rivulets of the stream.[280] Domestic sheep and goat were known from the start; domestic cattle appear in later phases of the Djeitun culture; a decrease over time in the number of bones of wild animals again suggests a diminishing interest in the hunt. Here as elsewhere in Iran during this epoch, arrow and spear heads were virtually unknown, with slingstones the only recognizable weapons.

The dwellings at Djeitun were free-standing, mud-brick structures whose interior walls and floors occasionally were coated with red plaster. A large rectangular hearth was often fronted by a narrow platform. Unlike the ceramics of the Iranian plateau, Djeitun's painted pottery was still a rather primitive, red-on-cream, soft-fired ware (fig. 128a), comparable, in the eyes of the excavator, to that of the Zagros villages. But the newly miniaturized mortars and pestles known at Sialk I were here as well.

map at figure 122 A similar assemblage at Sang-e Čaxamaq East shows the Djeitun culture extending as far west as the Gurgan plain of Iran. This new settlement at Sang-e Čaxamaq was larger than the earlier western tepe and yielded several elements, including miniature mortars and pestles, that were absent from the older community.[269] Red-on-cream wares similar to those of Djeitun were produced in the early levels at Sang-e Čaxamaq East, but the upper strata here, and new settlements elsewhere in the northeast (Anau IA), show a stronger connection to the black-on-red ceramic styles of the plateau (fig. 128b).[268]

see pages 149–50

Northwest Iran: Hajii Firuz

The earliest known settlements in Azerbaijan, comprising the *Hajii Firuz* culture, are also dated to the mid-to-late sixth millennium.[110, 439] Bread wheat and barley, domestic sheep, goat, pig, and dog are reported among the remains of the two excavated sites of this culture: Hajii Firuz in the Solduz valley south of Lake Urmia, and Yanik Tepe to the east of the lake. As at Djeitun, both villages were composed of free-standing, mud-brick houses, "solidly and in some places massively built"[52] at Yanik Tepe, with raised hearths and traces of red stained or plastered floors. Alabaster bowls and "bracelets" at Yanik Tepe suggest connections to the earlier Zagros village tradition, as do certain aspects of the pottery of this culture (fig. 129a). Comparisons have also been made to the chevron-dominated ceramics of the Hassuna culture of northern Mesopotamia, to be described later.[412]

Earlier sites have not been discovered in Azerbaijan, and it is believed that Hajii Firuz, Yanik Tepe, and the handful of other mounds dating to this period in the Urmia basin were founded by settlers from another region. Contact with the Iranian plateau is suggested by the presence at Yanik Tepe of a ceramic sherd (fig. 129b) bearing a design identical to one from the third level of Sialk I. (A similar motif appears on contemporary Samarran pottery in Mesopotamia as well.) But if the settlement at Yanik Tepe was not entirely outside the main stream of events during this epoch, the Hajii Firuz culture as a whole showed such a pronounced conservatism that one excavator believes that these people may have moved into the Urmia basin to avoid the sweeping changes that were now taking place on the Mesopotamian plains.[412] For whatever reason, their culture remained essentially unchanged until the end of the sixth millennium, at which time both Hajii Firuz and Yanik Tepe apparently were abandoned, leaving Azerbaijan without known settlements for what may have been several centuries.

a

b

129 Sherds from the Hajii Firuz culture of northwest Iran (Azerbaijan), mid-to-late sixth millennium B.C.: (a) red-on-cream pottery from Hajii Firuz, (b) dark brown-on-red sherd from Yanik Tepe (compare figure 125) *(after Voight, 1983; Burney, 1964)*

The Neolithic Revolution: Phase II   233

The rapidity of material progress elsewhere in Iran provides a striking contrast. In the southwest the early fifth millennium saw further increases in the number of new agricultural sites in Susiana,[189] while in the northeast a chain of perhaps twenty settlements now stretched along the foothills of the Kopet Dagh and into the Gurgan plain.[267] Shrines had begun to appear in the larger northeastern communities; flint tools were gradually being replaced by copper. On the plateau, copper was already being cast into molds at Tepe Gabristan, where a recently discovered workshop for coppersmiths, complete with crucible, kiln, and molds, has been dated to the early fifth millennium B.C.[250] By this time, as noted above, the Sialk/Cheshmeh Ali plateau pottery had begun to display the ornamental animal motifs which were to give Iranian art its most distinctive trait (fig. 130).

The end of the fifth millennium would see the first recorded use of the potter's wheel at Sialk, an innovation which, like the advances in metallurgy, was then to spread westward from Iran into southern Mesopotamia, and not, as was once supposed, the other way around.[280] As we shall see later, Iranian influences on the west may actually have begun as early as the mid-sixth millennium B.C.

The Time of Zarathuštra?

Before turning to the archaeology of the west in this epoch, we might ask how well events within Iran itself agree with what is known of Zarathuštra's reforms. We should first note, however, that the whole of this country is sorely underexcavated for the Neolithic period. Most of eastern Iran is archaeological *terra incognita* in this time frame, and critical plateau sites such as Cheshmeh Ali are greatly in need of up-to-date excavation. But even with the limited information at hand, it is possible to speak of a genuine transformation of Iran in the last half of the sixth millennium B.C.

As noted earlier, the numerical increase in permanent settlements was proportionately greater during this 5500–5000 B.C. span than at any other time in prehistory. And while an agricultural kinship is attested by the bread wheat which found its way into the far reaches of Iranian territory during this era, and a technological relationship suggested by the black-painted, hard-fired ceramics which were almost as ubiquitous, regional differences in the designs on those wares indicate that these were primarily local populations. The composition of their tool kits, many still in the process of change, further the impression that these settlers were former hunter-herdsmen who had been pursuing nomadic or seminomadic patterns of existence. But why so many, already possessing developed traditions of their own, should suddenly have chosen the life of a farmer—and often on land that required irrigation—remains a mystery to prehistorians.

The miniaturization of mortars and pestles in Iranian sites of this period (larger ones were known as well) suggests that these implements had acquired a special significance in the last half of the sixth millennium B.C. We know that the mortar and pestle were ritual objects in Zoroastrian religion, used to press the sacred *haoma*. In the *Vendidad* the priest of Zarathuštra is identified by his possession of the mortar. Zoroastrian priests were also invested with a mace, and although the marble maceheads at Sialk were adorned with chevrons rather than the bull's head of the later Mithraic *gurz*, their use was as patently ceremonial. The added presence at that plateau site of an "astonishingly Persian" carved figure testifies to the antiquity of the Iranian tradition, and to its continuity (or its periodic recurrence) from this epoch onward.

see page 179

In such a context one ventures to suggest that the carved stone "bracelets" at Sialk and other Iranian sites of this period were actually the rings which, entwined with animal hair, symbolically filtered the fluid from the *haoma* plant in Zoroastrian rites. As mentioned above, some form of the *haoma* ritual seems to have been known to the Old Iranian religion before Zarathuštra's reforms, and was perhaps associated with the excesses of animal sacrifice condemned by the prophet. The carved stone bands were among the oldest and most tenacious of the Zagros traditions; they may always have played a part in the *haoma* ceremony; or, as the introduction of a much wider and cylindrically grooved version in the Sabz phase (fig. 131) coincided with the first appearance of domestic cattle in southwest Iran, the use of rings wrapped with the hair of the bull may have replaced the slaying of that animal in the last half of the sixth millennium B.C.

see pages 217–18

see pages 141, 148

But cult and ceremony had little place in the *Gāthās*, and if ritual objects were present, shrines were rare in the earliest Iranian settlements of this period. When identifiable religious structures do appear, as at Yasa Depe early in the fifth millennium (fig. 132), the similarity of their wall paintings to the pottery designs of this era confirms the religious nature of the latter. In both we find an emphasis on contrast, sharp definition, and the alternation of otherwise identical light and dark geometric forms that recalls the strong dualism underlying Zoroastrian doctrine—a duality made explicit, perhaps, in the double-axe form at the center of a Sialk bowl (fig. 125). And in the "whirl-patterns" of the plateau pottery, one senses a momentum no less vital (and no less progressive, if the spiral at Sialk may be so interpreted) than that which suddenly thrust Iran into the forefront of material progress in this epoch.

Furthermore, if the higher firing temperatures of these black-decorated ceramics possibly were related to the advances in metallurgy, the "molten metal" to which Zarathuštra refers in

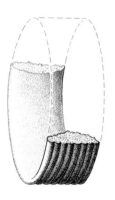

131 Fragment of a stone "bracelet" from the Sabz phase in southwestern Iran *(after Hole et al, 1969)*

132 Plan of shrine and
one of its wall paintings,
Yasa Depe, Turkmenia;
fifth millennium B.C.
(after Mellaart, 1975)

the *Gāthās* (Y.XXX.7, XXXII.7) may in fact have been known to
Iran in the middle of the sixth millennium B.C. The discovery
of the copper workshop at Tepe Gabristan has moved recorded
knowledge of the smelting and casting of copper, once thought
to have been acquired around 4000 B.C., back at least 500 to
1,000 years. A cast-copper macehead at Can Hasan in Anatolia
is also dated to the early fifth millennium, and a process developed to this degree in both Anatolia and Iran seems certain
to have been discovered several centuries earlier. Indeed, if the
identification of copper slag at Level VI of Çatal Hüyük holds see page 163
up, molten metal was known at least as early as the mid-sixth
millennium B.C., the date of the advent of black-on-buff ceramics
on the Iranian plateau.

At the same time, as we saw above, an intensification of
efforts to improve plant and animal species by the techniques
of domestication was evident throughout Iran and, as we shall
see later, across the Mesopotamian plains. Adding the work
with metals to these qualitative changes would mean that significant steps toward the transformation, or what might be seen as
the perfecting, of the animal, vegetable, and mineral kingdoms
of nature were taken around 5500 B.C., the date, when corrected
to calendar time, assigned to Zarathuštra by the Greeks.

If this was in fact the time of Zarathuštra, and the Neolithizing
of Iran a response to the prophet's word, the place of his birth
still presents a puzzle. As noted earlier, the dialect used in the
Gāthās has suggested to many Iraniologists that Zarathuštra was
born in northeastern Iran. Others have placed his home on the see page 215
plateau at Ragha (Rayy), the only recognizable city-name in the
Avesta, theorizing that he then traveled east in the course of
his teaching. (The governor of Ragha was said to be the only
one who was both lord of the province and the *Zarathuštrotema*,

The Neolithic Revolution: Phase II   237

indicating to one Iraniologist that Rayy was "plainly the seat of the religious government.")[194] Surveying the archaeology of this period, one would conclude from the richness of the Sialk/ Cheshmeh Ali tradition, and its lasting effect on Iranian culture, that the plateau did indeed play a critical role in the development of Zarathuštra's vision. We should not be surprised, perhaps, to find that the mound which has been named Cheshmeh Ali lies immediately adjacent to the ruins of the ancient city of Rayy itself.

But if the Iranian plateau was a center of Zarathuštran activity in the sixth millennium B.C., it may not have been the birthplace of the prophet. Passages in the *Gāthās* indicate that Zarathuštra's teachings were not well-received among his own people (although they later became faithful adherents), and he had to journey elsewhere to gain acceptance (*Y*.XLVI.1). It is presumed that the home he left was also a permanent settlement at that time, and for those who believe that the prophet came from the northeast, the excavation of the older mound at Sang-e Čaxamaq see pages 149-50 offers proof of the existence of northeast Iranian settlements dating to the early sixth millennium B.C. Further support for the idea of a northeastern homeland for Zarathuštra may be found in the relative backwardness of the Djeitun culture, of which the younger community at Sang-e Čaxamaq was a member. As noted above, the archaic red-on-cream pottery was not superseded here until late in the sixth millennium.

The far northwest has also been claimed as the birthplace of the prophet, however, and one Iraniologist who believed that Zarathuštra's home lay in Azerbaijan specified "the neighborhood around Lake Urmia,"[194] which rather precisely defines the location of the sites belonging to the Hajii Firuz culture of the mid-to-late sixth millennium B.C. These early Azerbaijanis were as conservative as the Djeitun peoples, if not more so, and it is possible that the settlement at Hajii Firuz was older than its see figure 123 current dating to around 5500 B.C. (The excavators were prevented from reaching virgin soil by the water table in the Solduz valley.)[412] Then too, if Eran-Vēj, the ancestral Iranian homeland, see page 114 did border on Azerbaijan, as claimed in the *Bundahišn*, the weight of ancient tradition in this region could explain both the apparent resistance to change of the Hajii Firuz culture and the hiatus in settlement activity which seems to have followed its disappearance. Alternatively, if Eran-Vēj actually lay east rather than west of the Caspian, as some Iraniologists believe,[156] these northwest Iranian settlers may instead represent particularly conservative groups of Magi, already occupying an area that would later house several Magian strongholds.[38]

see page 215

In any event, what was happening to the south and west of Azerbaijan during this period suggests that the message of the prophet was more enthusiastically received in Mesopotamia, where a host of heretofore unknown peoples of diverse backgrounds began settling the Tigris basin in the last half of the sixth millennium. As we shall see in the following section, it may not be insignificant that this same east Mesopotamian region was included among the otherwise largely Iranian "good lands and countries" which were said in the Avesta to have been created by Ahura Mazda himself (*Vendidad* I).

Mesopotamian Archaeology:
5500 – 5000 B.C.

Hassuna-Samarra

Prior to 5500 B.C. the only permanent settlements of record on the Mesopotamian plains belonged to the *Hassuna* culture, known to us from local elements at Umm Dabaghiyah and scattered sites elsewhere in early sixth millennium Iraq. The earliest Hassuna painted pottery, like that of the old Zagros village settlements with which it was partly contemporary, was red-on-cream with simple geometric designs; parallel lines often formed what has been described as an overlapping chevron pattern.

map at figure 122

Midway in the sixth millennium, the painted decoration on the ceramics at the site of Hassuna changed from a uniform red to a spectrum ranging from dark reddish brown to almost black. Local designs continued, but several new elements appeared, among them the first use of pattern on the inside of a bowl (a cruciform arrangement of crosshatched zones).[245] These wares were nevertheless modest in comparison with the richly decorated, primarily dark brown-on-buff, *Samarran* pottery that

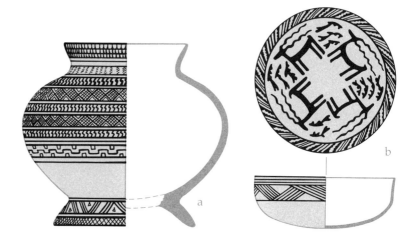

133 Chocolate brown-on-buff Samarran ceramics from (a) Tell es-Sawwan and (b) the site of Hassuna, mid-to-late sixth millennium B.C. *(after al-A'dami, 1968; Lloyd and Sefar, 1945)*

134 Reconstruction of a
dwelling at Level IV of
Hassuna, northern Iraq
(after Lloyd and Safar, 1945)

appeared in the following strata at Hassuna (fig. 133b). The
introduction of these superior imports coincided with a further
upgrading of Hassuna's tauf-walled houses, now substantial
multi-roomed structures (fig. 134), and the beginning of the
spread of permanent agricultural settlements to all parts of the
region.[309]

The Samarrans themselves chose to settle farther south, on
the margin and outside the dependable rainfed farming zone.
With bread wheat, six-row barley, and flax among the plant
remains at the Samarran communities of Tell es-Sawwan and
Choga Mami, it is not surprising to find the first certain evidence
of irrigation canals at the latter site.[312] The added presence of
domestic cattle at Choga Mami suggested to the excavator that
the ox-drawn plow may already have been used for cultivating
the fields. Mud-brick architecture, the earliest known to Mesopotamia, was present at both Tell es-Sawwan and Choga Mami;
beneath the complex of multi-roomed buildings at the base level
of Tell es-Sawwan an extraordinary cemetery had been laid, in
which the dead were accompanied by a great many alabaster
vessels and figurines.[311] As mentioned earlier, similar items did
not appear again (later levels knew only ceramic wares and clay
figurines), and these stone pieces appear to be the relics of an
earlier tradition, presumably nomadic or seminomadic in nature. Where that tradition originated, and why it changed, are
unknown.

see pages 195–96

The painted pottery of the Samarrans reveals an interest in
the circle, the cross, and most prominently, the principle of
motion. Not only the whirl-patterns on the shallow bowls but

135 Cruciform patterns on (a) the pottery of Eridu in southern Iraq, late sixth millennium B.C., and (b) Samarran ceramics *(after Braidwood et al, 1944; Mellaart, 1975)*

also the taller vessels, with their horizontal bands of flowing designs, give an illusion of movement (fig. 133a). Negative or "reserve" techniques, in which the background is filled with paint so that patterns appear as light in a dark field, were also known to the Samarrans. The use of a similar technique in Iran provides one of the points of comparison that have led analysts to place the Samarran culture coeval with the first three levels at Sialk on the Iranian plateau (Sialk I,1-3).[108] But unlike the Sialk ceramics, whose designs seem to have been exclusively geo-

see figure 125

metric during this period, the patterns on Samarran pottery included stylized forms from nature—wild goats, deer, birds, scorpions—whose counterparts evidently did not appear on the wares of the Iranian plateau until the following and later periods. The numerous Samarran swastikas (traditionally a solar symbol)[163] and whirling animal tetrads also seem to have preceded similar designs on plateau pottery, but again the lack of more precise information about the early levels at Cheshmeh Ali and other sites on the northern plateau leaves the question of seniority somewhat ambiguous.

What is more certain is that the impact of Samarran culture on Mesopotamia was comparable to that of the Sialk/Cheshmeh Ali tradition on Iran. Although Samarran settlements were generally confined to a band across central Iraq, the influence of these people reached north, south, and, as we shall see later, apparently far to the west as well. In the north the excavators of Yarim Tepe I found the coming of the Samarrans "clearly an important landmark in the development of Hassuna settlements,"[283] and a deep sounding at Nineveh revealed ceramics with Samarran motifs in the earliest levels of that ancient site.[320]

map at figure 122

In the south Samarran influence has been noted at Eridu, the first recorded settlement in the land later to be known as Sumer. Estimated to the late sixth millennium, the lowest strata at Eridu yielded mud-brick architecture and fine painted pottery whose chocolate-colored cruciform patterns are distinctly reminiscent of Samarran designs (fig. 135).[310] Connections between the Samarrans and the Sabz phase in southwest Iran have also been detected.

see pages 230–32

But in spite of their similarities, the differences between these several contemporary cultures left one authority with "the distinct impression that each area displays an essentially local though not an isolated development."[314] Joan Oates believes that a number of different ethnic groups were probably represented among these new Mesopotamian settlers, some of whom may earlier have been hunters or food-gatherers whose traces are less susceptible to archaeological detection. Why these various peoples now chose a sedentary way of life, where they got the architectural and agricultural know-how, and what might have been the nature of their relationship to the Iranian plateau, are still unanswered questions.

Some may in fact have chosen not to settle. As Oates further points out, "we should certainly consider at least the possibility that already in the sixth millennium there may have been no-madic herdsmen contemporary with, and probably in some sort of economic relationship with, the settled villages, a pattern which is well-established by the time of the earliest written records."[313] That this relationship between settler and nomad was not entirely harmonious in the sixth millennium may be indicated by the presence of a defensive ditch and buttressed fortification wall at Tell es-Sawwan, and a massive mud-brick tower guarding the entrance to Choga Mami.

Halaf

In the upper levels of Tell es-Sawwan there appeared a new type of painted pottery, an import from northern Mesopotamia which, like the Samarran wares, was to spread far beyond the boundaries of its home territory. This distinctive *Halafian* pottery was decorated in lustrous black or red-brown paint on an apricot or cream-colored slip. Similar in many respects to Samarran wares, the ceramics of Halaf were nevertheless the products of a different tradition, again perhaps a different ethnic group, than their Mesopotamian contemporaries. Yet the Halafians too were now farmers, of essentially the same crops (including bread wheat) that were cultivated farther south.[184] Carbon-14 dates are missing for the early Halaf period, known mainly at Arpachiyah,

136 Halaf miniatures (wheeled cross, bull's head, sickle, double-axe) from Arpachiyah, Iraq, late sixth millennium B.C. *(after Mallowan and Rose, 1935)*

but estimates range within the last half of the sixth millennium for the beginning of these peoples' settled life. As we shall see, certain elements of Halafian culture were undoubtedly a good deal older.

The Halafians entered our discussion earlier in connection with Çatal Hüyük. The bulls' and rams' heads that dominated the shrines of Çatal Hüyük appear on Halafian painted pottery; the wheeled cross and double-axe of the Çatal VI mural were carved into amulets or seals at Arpachiyah (fig. 136). Lead and copper appear to have been worked in both cultures, and in fact the excavators of Arpachiyah concluded that the Halafian "cream bowl," with its sharply beveled base and flaring neck (fig. 137), was almost certainly a copy of a metal type, although none was found.[258] Closely packed rectangular houses were also typical of the earliest levels at Arpachiyah,[184] although the Halafians are better known for their round structures, to which rectangular annexes were often attached in a keyhole pattern that resembles the later *tholoi* of the Aegean. But in general the Çatal-Halaf parallels are so numerous that in spite of the great distance between the two cultures (750 miles from Konya to Mosul by road), Robert Braidwood concluded that Çatal Hüyük was a westerly variant of the Halafian tradition.[42]

see figure 140

137 Halafian "cream bowl" from Arpachiyah, decorated in black glaze paint on an apricot-colored slip *(after Mallowan and Rose, 1935)*

Distance was in fact of little concern to these people. By the early fifth millennium, Halafian settlements extended from the hills east of the Tigris to Lake Van (Tilki Tepe) in the north and west to the western bend of the Syrian Euphrates, creating what has been termed "one of the most homogenous prehistoric cultures anywhere in the world."[231] As we shall see later, their influence reached the Mediterranean coast and even, in the opinion of several analysts, central and southern Greece.

The lustrous painted pottery of Halaf was dominated in all phases by geometric patterns. Like the Samarrans, Halafian potters occasionally portrayed the figures of animals, and here the stylized heads of bull and ram appear as well (fig. 139j), but far more common are minutely detailed panels of purely geometric designs (fig. 138). The frequency of checkered patterns is notable. Often both dark and light checkers contain a motif, such as a quatrefoil or a St. Andrew's cross; pairs of dark and light triangles inside other squares form fields of positive and negative images of the double-axe. As shown in the series of Halafian vessels that opened this section (fig. 121 a-d), these checkered designs were used as a border or frame for interior polychrome centerpieces which have yet to be surpassed in the ceramic arts. Indeed, in spite of its noted homogeneity of style, the ceramics of Halaf were largely individual works of art, with no one piece the exact replica of another.[258] The use of highly ferruginous clays allowed Halafian potters to fire their products at very high temperatures; firings apparently were controlled so that precisely the desired colors would result and each color stand out distinctly. As one analyst remarked, the Halafians "worked for contrast in a way that artists of the preceding and following periods did not."[163]

More than one prehistorian finds in Halaf the most beautiful pottery ever made in Mesopotamia.[351] Few would deny that the symbols decorating these wares were primarily religious. Was it the religion of Zarathuštra?

To carry the question further, were most if not all of the various peoples who chose to settle eastern Mesopotamia in the last half of the sixth millennium inspired by the vision of the prophet? The widespread abandonment of what was apparently a nomadic or seminomadic existence for the more demanding life of a farmer, the frequent choice of land which must be artificially watered for such an enterprise, and the ceramic connections of these groups to similar and contemporary efforts in Iran have found no more plausible explanation. Nor could one find a more coherent expression of Zarathuštra's concept of "pure monotheism against a dualistic background"[442] than in the masterfully unified, rosette-centered and checker-framed, interior designs of Halaf vessels. A celebration (or a resanctifying) of the Good Creation may have been the basis for the interest shown by Mesopotamian potters in the form of the cosmic cross as well (figs. 121b and 135).

And yet the appearance, however occasional, of traditionally chthonic themes — bull, snake, leopard, "dancers" — on the pottery of the Halafian (and a peculiarly demonic figure on that

138 Geometric patterns common to Halafian painted pottery (after Mallowan and Rose, 1935)

139 Naturalistic themes
on (a–c) Samarran and
(d–i and j, opposite)
Halafian ceramics *(after
Oates, 1969; Mallowan
and Rose, 1935; Merpert
and Munchaev, 1973)*

of the Samarran) leaders of the Mesopotamian movement are
not at all what one expects of early Zarathuštran religion. The
prophet supposedly denounced the nature cults of his day, and
naturalistic themes do indeed seem to be missing from the
ceramics of the Iranian plateau in the first centuries of this era.
But we know from the *Yašts* of the Younger Avesta that while
the dionysian aspects of the Old Iranian religion may have been
tamed or transformed by Zarathuštra's reforms, they were never
entirely eradicated (if that was in fact the prophet's intent). One
Iraniologist has suggested that elements of these ancient cults

were instead "exalted into a far higher sphere and penetrated with its spirit."[155]

The same would have been true of the worship of Mithra, which is also believed to predate the time of Zarathuštra and which plays such a prominent role in the Zoroastrian religion of the Younger Avesta. As noted above, scholars have theorized that the followers of this ancient warrior god were at some point transformed into "crusaders" in the service of the prophet's reform. The identification of Mithra with the sun (several Iraniologists believe that he was originally associated with the waters)[156] may date to the same period.

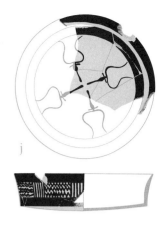

In Parts III and IV of this study we found suggestions of dionysian rites on both sides of Mesopotamia in the preceding epoch: to the east in the Zagros villages, to the west at Çatal Hüyük, where the parallels between Mithraic traditions and those of the Cretan Dionysos-Zagreus were shown to be numerous. We now find similar animal (and animal-tailed human) motifs, as well as the scorpion and snake that appear with the see figure 65 bull in later Mithraic iconography, on the excellent pottery of the Halafian and Samarran peoples of late sixth millennium Mesopotamia (fig. 139), frequently stylized and accompanied by symbols—rayed circles, swastikas, dot-centered circles—which art historians interpret as solar references. (One analyst found that in the darkness which surrounds this nonliterate period of Mesopotamian prehistory, "solar forms provide the greatest illumination.")[163] Might we then conclude that the cults of Çatal Hüyük were not the only chthonic organizations to be Apollonized in this epoch?

In their search for the origins of Halaf, investigators have noted the importance of obsidian to the people of this culture. Continuing the age-old use of the Nemrut Dağ source at Lake Van, the Halafians also imported a new type of obsidian which is believed to have come from the foot of Mount Ararat, just south of the Araxes river in ancient Armenia. The proximity of this obsidian-producing region west of the Caspian Sea to the apparent homeland of the Mithraic mysteries was observed earlier. The possibility that the adjacent east Taurus highlands once served as a refuge for Greek survivors of the *Timaeus* floods has also been raised. Before tracing the impact of Halaf on lands farther west, we might therefore look first to this west Caspian corridor and the question of Halafian origins. For it is here that the connecting link between Greece and Iran, between Plato's tale and the time of Zarathuštra, seems to lie.

The Halafian Homeland and the Obsidian Connection

James Mellaart has suggested that the Halafians came from the north, perhaps from the mountains around Lake Van, where their ancestors may have been involved in the obsidian trade. A number of very large cores of obsidian from both Nemrut Dağ and Mount Ararat were found alongside Halaf pottery of the highest quality at the settlement of Tilki Tepe, just south of Lake Van, and the prominence of obsidian here and in other Halafian sites was seen by Mellaart as a possible key to the origins of this culture:

map at figure 122

> The northern location of the Halaf sites also tends to suggest that in origin their occupants were hill people who had ventured into the plain in pursuit of agriculture and stockbreeding like their Hassuna neighbors, but who were loath to sever their connections with their old homeland and native building tradition. . . . Could it be that the Early Halaf settlers had come originally from the mountains between the Assyrian steppe and the Lake Van area, where for thousands of years, from Epipaleolithic times on, they had engaged in the obsidian trade? Once settled on the northern edge of the plain they might still have controlled the trade with their relatives to the north. . . .[280]

His references to "relatives to the north" and the "native building tradition" are based in part on the similarity of Halafian round houses to the dwellings in the earliest agricultural settlements in the Kur and Araxes valleys of Transcaucasia.[283] Some of these northern structures also had rectangular or curvilinear annexes like the Halafian "tholoi"; many were partly subterranean with a few steps down at the entrance, recalling the ancient round-house traditions of Natufian Ain Mallaha and the walled town of Jericho. What little is known of these Russian sites confirms the presence of domestic cattle, sheep, goat, and dog;[54] bread wheat has been reported in the Kur valley. A soft-fired local pottery was also present, and it is generally believed that these early Transcaucasian settlers were indigenous peoples from the surrounding hills. The reason for their switch to sedentary farming is unknown, but it is not inconceivable that they were influenced in this decision by contact with the Halafians (whose superior ceramics were found at both Tegut in the Ararat plain and Kültepe in the Araxes valley),[54] particularly if these contacts represented the return of the Halafians to the vicinity of their ancestral hearth.

see figure 140

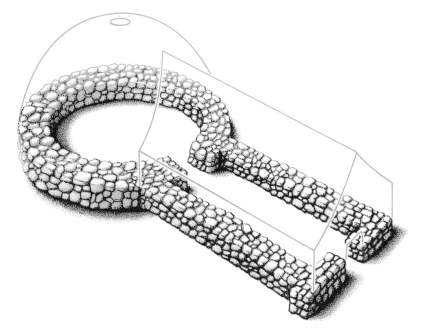

140 Stone foundation
walls and hypothetical
outline of Halaf structure
at Arpachiyah. The "key-
hole" design of these
buildings has been com-
pared to the form of the
much later *tholoi* of the
Aegean *(after Mallowan
and Rose, 1935)*

But if the ancestors of the Halafians were involved in the
obsidian trade, as Mellaart further suggests, these lands between the Black and Caspian Seas may not always have been
home to their culture. Although a few samples of Nemrut Dağ
obsidian were known to Epi-Paleolithic northern Iraq,[373] the so-
called obsidian trade route to and from Lake Van did not become
genuinely significant until around 75/7300 B.C. when, as noted
earlier, the newly founded settlement at Çayönü in eastern Anatolia was linked by Nemrut Dağ obsidian to the newly founded
settlement at Alikosh, some 500 miles to the south. Nemrut Dağ see pages 140–41
obsidian was known to all later Zagros villages as well as to
contemporary settlements in Syria. It therefore seems plausible
that most of its distributors assumed that role only with the
establishing of this greater obsidian network, which, at the mid-
point of the eighth millennium, coincided with the beginning
of our theoretically post-deluge epoch.

The founding of an Halafian settlement at Gerikihaciyan, just map at figure 122
east of the old site at Çayönü, has raised the possibility of a
connection between the ancestors of Halaf and the settlers of
Çayönü. As in Halaf sites, copper was worked and obsidian
used extensively at Çayönü; analogues of Çayönü's "two-in-
one" figurine have been found among Halafian remains.[446] If
the earlier east Anatolian settlement was in fact founded by
Greek refugees from the floods, as was suggested in our com- see pages 128–33
parison of Çayönü's architectural diversity to the description of

Ur-Athens in the *Critias*, the ancestors of the Halafians may have been kinsmen who had also taken refuge in the Taurus mountains, but as nomadic or seminomadic herdsmen rather than permanent settlers.

A Halaf-Greek equation could also account for the presence of activities similar to those of the Cretan cult of Dionysos in Zagros villages of the seventh and early sixth millennia. It was suggested in Part III that the religion of Dionysos may have been transported to eastern Anatolia by survivors of Plato's flood-ruined cultures, and thence down the Zagros chain. We now find the bucrania and double-axes associated with Aegean cult on the pottery of Halaf, along with animal-tailed human figures that recall the leopard-skin-clad dancers in the Çatal Hunting Shrines, our theoretical prototypes of the Cretan Kouretes. The excavators of Arpachiyah had in fact seen "definite Cretan connections" in the Halafian bull cult long before Çatal Hüyük was uncovered,[258] and if the ancestors of Halaf were distributing Vannic obsidian to the Zagros villages, they might well have spread the worship of Dionysos to the same communities. Furthermore, identifying the Halafians as descendants of Greek refugees would not in any way diminish the likelihood that they were now converts to, and bearers of, the message of Zarathuštra. The *Fravardin Yašt* names several groups other than *aryas* who were found receptive to the word.

see page 148

On the other hand, we have also observed how prominently this region west of the Caspian Sea figured in the traditions of Iran, and it may be that the early distributors of Vannic obsidian were of proto-Iranian rather than Aegean descent. Here lay, according to various sources, the ancestral hearth of the Iranians (Ēran-Vēj), the home of the Mithraic mysteries, the strongholds of the Magi. Here too lies Kobystan, whose rock carvings of warriors and bulls raised the possibility that proto-Mithraic traditions were already present in Transcaucasia as early as the ninth millenium B.C., a proposal which was supported by the seemingly Mithraic symbols at sixth millennium Çatal Hüyük. The dating of Zarathuštra to the middle of the sixth millennium would also put the Magi, who supposedly preceded him and whose connections to Mithra are evident, back into the seventh millennium at the latest. It seems unlikely that the association of obsidian with fire was lost on the peoples of this era; its distributors may well have included a fire-worshipping caste (or tribe) who, like the Magi of later ages, presided over sacrifices in a wide range of sites in and around the Zagros mountains (Herodotus I.132).

see figure 36

A third possibility would see descendants of both groups, both proto-Iranians and Greeks (whom we should perhaps be calling pre-Greeks to identify the antediluvian inhabitants of the Aegean), represented among the distributors of Vannic obsidian in the late eighth and seventh millennia B.C.* The combination of Late Paleolithic migrations from western Europe and eighth millennium floods in the Aegean and Anatolia could have brought any number of diverse peoples into the high mountain plateaus west of the Caspian, described by one Iraniologist as "a refuge area par excellence."[145] And it may have been here, long before their meeting (or re-encounter) at Çatal Hüyük, that the religion of the Magi and the tradition later to be known as Orphic became so similar that modern scholars would consider using the one system to interpret the other.

see pages 202–3

To which of these strains, proto-Iranian or pre-Greek, the ancestors of Halaf (or of Samarra) might have belonged remains a question for future research. The only certainty at this point is that their descendants' zeal for contact with other peoples, if not missionary in its fervor, was certainly no less intense.

* As mentioned in Part III, there were two types of Vannic obsidian in Zagros village sites, one from Nemrut Dağ to the west of Lake Van, the other believed to have come from Suphan Dağ to the north. As each entered the archaeological record at a different time, and under different circumstances (Suphan Dağ obsidian did not appear until the founding of Jarmo and the enlarging of Alikosh around 6800 B.C. and almost vanished after the middle of the sixth millennium), each may actually have been borne by a different set of "traders."

The Halafian Impact on the West

We know that the bearers of Zarathuštra's message went forth to "those who seek Asha in other lands" (*Y*.XLII.6), converting both Aryans and non-Aryans to the way of the prophet. Asia Minor and Greece are named among the successful missionary fields in legendary Persian accounts.[194] If the Halafians were now followers of Zarathuštra, the extent of their influence on the archaeology of the late sixth millennium B.C. suggests that *aša*-seeking peoples were in fact to be found from the Euphrates to the Aegean.

The Levant

In the opinion of one observer, the Halafian impact on foreign lands was largely the work of individuals who "peacefully invaded a wide area and mingled with the local population."[351] If so, the Halafian invasion of Syria and Lebanon was apparently

141 Greek and Near Eastern sites mentioned in the text.

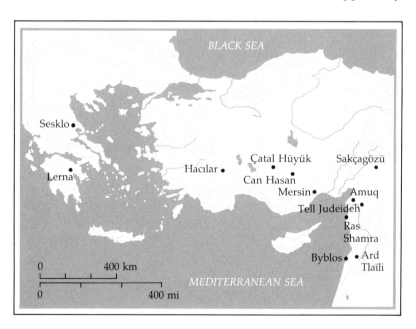

as thorough as it was peaceful. Very few settlements in these lands failed to show some sort of response to the coming of Halaf. At Tell Judeideh local painted wares imitated Halafian imports in design; at Sakçagözü II Halaf pottery appeared along with some Samarran wares; at Ras Shamra the Halafian impact caused the disappearance of the traditional pattern-burnished ceramics.[280]

map at figure 141

Not only pottery, but in some cases the chipped stone industry changed as well. In northern Syria the Amuq tradition of very long, thin, bifacially-flaked lanceheads came to an end, transformed into long blades with parallel edges. Even in conservative Byblos an increase in the Vannic-Armenian types of obsidian associated with the Halaf culture was accompanied by a marked decline in projectile points. And in the Beqa'a valley of Lebanon, the lower levels of Ard Tlaïli yielded bread wheat and six-row barley, crops not previously known to this region, along with a pottery collection that included imported Halafian wares. As Kirkbride described the situation, "by 5000 B.C. the north and central Beqa'a had been saved from the semi-nomads and become part of the Halaf sphere, albeit an outpost."[214]

Anatolia

The Halafian invasion of Anatolia may not have been so peaceful. At Mersin the first clearly Halaf ceramic motifs appeared around 5000 B.C. (fig. 142); shortly thereafter the settlement was destroyed by fire. A mass of human remains was found in the wreckage.[151] Mersin's excavator suggested that here the spread of Halaf was accompanied by an assault on the unfortified village (and one is reminded of the merciless treatment given to the impious by Mithra in the Younger Avesta). But it is also possible that local nomadic peoples had taken to raiding communities whose new orientation was perceived as threatening. When the settlement was rebuilt, other than an increase in Halaf inspired or imported ceramics, which may represent reinforcements from the east, the integrity of Mersin's culture seems to have been intact.

142 Mersin, Level XIX; sherds of imported Halaf pottery (after Garstang, 1953)

143 Imported Halafian sherd from Can Hasan (after French, 1962)

The Neolithic community at Can Hasan to the northwest was also destroyed by fire around the turn of the fifth millennium, three building levels after the appearance of painted pottery (red-on-cream followed by black-on-buff). A sherd of imported Halafian ware (fig. 143) was unstratified, but a shaft-hole macehead of cast copper was recovered from the burned level.[143] As

The Neolithic Revolution: Phase II   253

see page 237

mentioned earlier, this unprecedented metal object was approximately coeval with the earliest evidence of the smelting and casting of copper on the Iranian plateau.

On the Konya plain, Mellaart noted with curiosity that while no building below Level VI at Çatal Hüyük had been destroyed by fire, every level thereafter was burned, usually after only 40 to 50 layers of plaster had been applied to the walls.[276] And it was this pivotal sixth level (c. 5500 B.C.), we recall, that saw the first Anatolian depictions of both the double-axe and the wheeled cross, forms which characterized Halafian culture from the earliest years of its settled life.

In southwestern Anatolia the Neolithic settlement at Hacılar was also burned several times in the last half of the sixth millennium.[279] Little is known of Hacılar's earliest building levels (IX to VII, dating to perhaps 5500 B.C.), but a fire at VI left well-preserved remains which included small pendants of bulls and bulls' heads that are not unlike those at Halafian Arpachiyah.

see figure 136

Bulls' heads were also applied in relief to the fine monochrome pottery of Hacılar VI, as were images of scorpions and wild goats. Occasional painted wares were also present, decorated with regional red-on-cream or white-on-red designs, and it was at this level that the excellent representations of the Anatolian

see figure 108

Mistress of the Animals were discovered, superior to the Çatal Mistress but apparently depicting the same, presumably local goddess, the prototype of Kybele-Rhea. Unlike Çatal Hüyük, however, Hacılar yielded no projectile points, and although one plastered bull's head was found at Level VI (without actual horns), no other decoration was known to these whitewashed interiors. It seems evident that Hacılar's early levels are only to be compared with the reformed upper strata of the Çatal mound, and one wonders if the initial impulse for change which seems to have reached Çatal Hüyük as early as Level VI might not have continued westward at that time. If so, the settling of Neolithic Hacılar could represent another mid-sixth-millennium grounding of local, formerly nomadic peoples who with their regional traditions intact, perhaps even renewed, created their own distinctive response to its imperative.

Painted pottery dominated the following levels at Hacılar. Decorations consisted of highly stylized animal and human motifs or geometric patterns which used to advantage the effects of positive and negative painting (fig. 144a). At Level II the site was again destroyed by fire; only half the settlement was then rebuilt, and it too was burned shortly thereafter. At this point Hacılar may have either changed hands or received reinforcements. New forms of pottery were introduced, one the counter-part of a Samarran effigy vase; ceramic designs included interior cruciform patterns which also recall the wares of contemporary Mesopotamia (fig. 144b). The settlement itself now resembled a small fortress, with blocks of rooms radiating from a central courtyard. Hacılar I was nevertheless unable to hold its own, and after the settlement was again destroyed, it was not rebuilt. In the Konya plain the relocated site of Çatal Hüyük West was also abandoned early in the fifth millennium after what may have been a destructive fire;[279] the violence at Mersin was noted above. If Anatolia had indeed been a successful missionary field, as claimed in the Persian accounts, it was maintained at great cost.

144 Hacılar painted pottery: (a) reddish brown-on-cream wares from Level II, (b) dark red-on-ivory bowl from Level I, c. 5000 B.C. (after Mellaart, 1970)

Greece

As we saw earlier, permanent settlements were already known to parts of Greece at the end of the seventh millennium B.C. The earliest ceramics were largely monochrome; the relatively small percentage of painted wares — simple geometric patterns in red on a white or cream ground — may have been a local development. In any event, the painted pottery of central and southern Greece is said to have undergone a complete change late in the sixth millennium, and among the new ceramics was a type known as *Neolithic Urfirnis* which has frequently been compared to Halafian wares.[417]

see pages 122–25

The Neolithic Revolution: Phase II   255

Often decorated in lustrous dark brown paint on an apricot-colored slip, Neolithic Urfirnis has been ranked among the finest achievements of the prehistoric potter (fig. 145). Its similarity to Halafian ceramics extends, according to one team of analysts, to fabric, shape, glaze paint, and decoration.[415, 321] They believe that the sudden and abundant evidence of Neolithic Urfirnis in the eastern part of the Peloponnese and central Greece should be attributed to the arrival of a Halaf-inspired population from the Near East, probably coming by sea from Syrian or Cilician ports. Others have argued, however, that the ceramic parallels are more likely the result of a transfer of technique than of people. In Theocharis' opinion, the migration of sizeable populations from abroad would have left "much deeper traces which, at present at least, cannot be detected in the architecture, in the figurines, or in the economy."[395]

145 "Neolithic Urfirnis" pottery from southern Greece, late sixth millennium B.C. Patterns are painted in dark brown on a reddish or apricot-colored slip. (after Theocharis, 1973)

The question of how many Halafians came to Greece is less important to us than the fact that they came at all, that the influence of Halaf apparently did reach as far as the Greek peninsula in the last half of the sixth millennium B.C. But if Theocharis is right about the local character of the Greek figurines, a question raised here in Part I may be resolved. Among the figurines of this period in southern Greece was a standing clay female, more slender and graceful than prior Greek models. As shown in the example from Lerna (fig. 146), this *kore*-type figurine is remarkably like the ceramic maiden-goddess at Mureybet III, her senior by more than two thousand years.

see figure 41

The similarity of Mureybet's figurines to later images in the Aegean was noted earlier in discussing the possible sources, Greek or Atlantic, of the rectangular architecture and other innovations that accompanied these standing female figures in Mureybet's critical third phase. If the Lerna *kore* was in fact a local deity, as Theocharis suggests, and possibly the product of a revitalized tradition of great age, the newcomers at Mureybet

III and the related PPNB peoples who settled Palestine and Syria in the last half of the eighth millennium could now be more surely theorized as Greek. Other scholars believe, however, that the *kore* figurines, like their Neolithic Urfirnis pottery companions, were part of the Halafian gift to Greece;[417] and somewhat similar, though always seated, clay models do appear in Halaf sites in Mesopotamia. But in any event the goddess may not have been foreign to the Peloponnese. If the ancestors of the Halafians were themselves Greek, as seemed possible in our earlier discussion of the origins of Halaf, their descendants may only have returned the *kore* to her native land.

The Fulfillment of Old Europe

The end of the sixth millennium also saw a significant increase in the number of agricultural settlements in northern Greece, apparently stimulated by influences from Mesopotamia or Anatolia or both. At this time the painted pottery of Thessaly showed great development and change, including the introduction of interior cruciform and whirl patterns (fig. 147) that analysts find comparable to eastern designs (fig. 148). Of these Thessalian ceramics one prehistorian remarked: "Surely there is continuity and some hold-over of older types, but it is equally clear that something new is happening. Very probably, what is new is caused by a foreign impulse with Samarran relationships."[417]

Yugoslavian Macedonia was first settled at this time (with painted pottery and bread wheat among the earliest deposits), Bulgaria a little later, and so on, until all of southeast Europe was acquainted with the agricultural way of life. Thus was the Civilization of Old Europe fully extended (fig. 67), but if its largely indigenous character seems indicated by such factors as the individuality of local pottery designs, the reason for the successful spread of this agricultural complex, and the nature of its relationship to the east, remain unclear. Ruth Tringham's observations regarding the evident economic stability of southeast Europe's hill people before the advent of farming were mentioned in the opening pages of this study. She feels that many of these culturally Mesolithic groups may already have controlled dependable resources such as red deer and pig which, together with fish and tended forest plants, would have provided a subsistence base fully as nutritious and reliable as the grain-sheep-goat-cattle agricultural system that eventually replaced it. But if the adoption of a farmer's life offered no

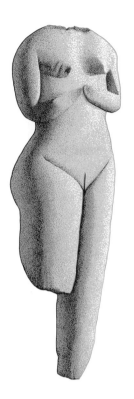

146 Clay *kore* figurine from Lerna, late sixth millennium B.C.; height, seven and one-half inches *(after Theocharis, 1973)*

147 Dark red-on-cream pottery from Thessaly, region of Sesklo, late sixth millennium B.C. *(after Theocharis, 1973)*

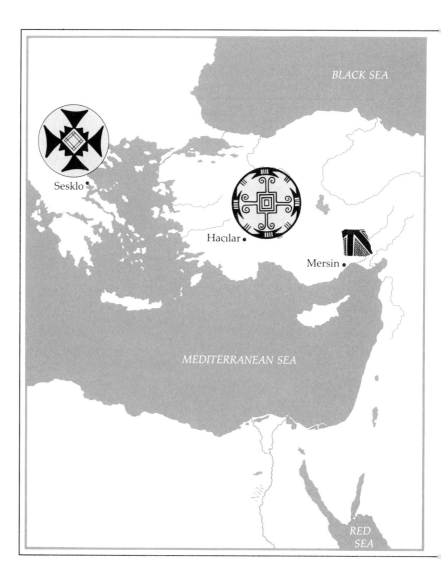

148 The distribution of related ceramic designs and techniques in the late sixth and early fifth millennia B.C.

economic advantage to these people, then how, she asks, and why, was the change to the new economy achieved? Although her colleagues find reason to believe that the earliest agricultural villages of southeast Europe were composed primarily of local peoples, Tringham points out that the idea of a continuing population from Mesolithic to Neolithic would mean

> that such a population changed from a successful economy based on forest mammals, fish and forest plants to an entirely different one, very suddenly and very drastically, without any apparent transition. A virtual "overnight" change like this is untenable in cultural ecological terms, *unless some very special factors were involved*.[403] [Emphasis added]

258   Plato, Prehistorian

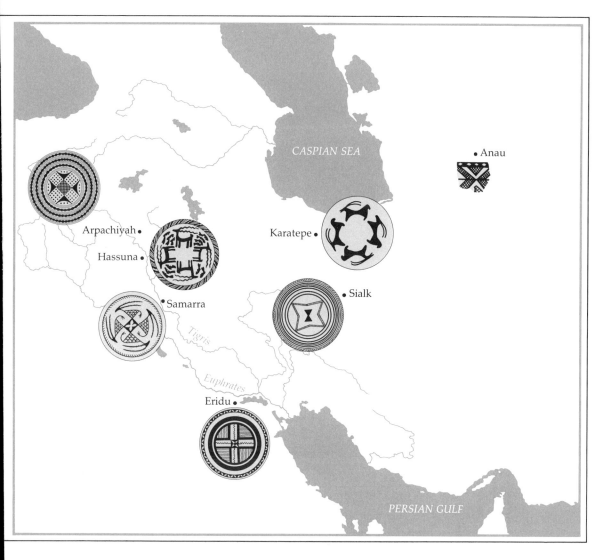

"He who cultivates corn cultivates righteousness" (*Vendidad* III). Should the agriculturalizing of southeast Europe—and eventually the entire continent—also be laid at Zarathuštra's door? The switch to settled farming in southeast Europe was no more sudden or illogical than similar phenomena in contemporary Iran and Mesopotamia. Were seekers of *aša* also to be found across Europe? We noted earlier the universality of this concept of an encompassing moral order (*aša*, *rta*, *tao*, *maat*) that see page 218 governed the conduct of men as well as the rhythms of the cosmos. The extent to which it occurs in the traditions of ancient and primitive peoples is well documented; indeed, it is Eliade's conviction that the main difference between the man of traditional society and the man of modern society lies in the fact that

The Neolithic Revolution: Phase II   259

"the former feels himself indissolubly connected with the Cosmos and cosmic rhythms, whereas the latter insists that he is connected only with History."[113] If the beliefs of the indigenous populations of Europe already included such a principle, the change to settled farming may not have required the renunciation of their own spiritual traditions. For their leaders to be persuaded that the Righteous Order had changed, that the way of *aša* now lay in cultivating the earth, may in itself have been sufficient cause for the European commitment to farming.

After Halaf

The Halafian occupation at Arpachiyah apparently ended in violence. As described by the excavators, the Mesopotamian settlement was destroyed midway in the fifth millennium in an "orgy of smashing," with cups, saucers, plates, and bowls deliberately hurled against the walls of the potter's shop before fire was set to the whole.[258] The identity of the attackers is unknown, but if the Halafians were among the bearers of Zarathuštra's reforms, their main opposition should have come see page 217 from those whose gods were demonized in the Younger Avesta. Among these Avestan demons or *daēvas* were the Vedic divinities Indra and the twin Nāsatyas, and it may not be fortuitous that these same gods would be worshipped in the Mitanni kingdom that occupied northern Mesopotamia three thousand years after the Halafian demise.

In the second millennium a treaty was drawn up at Boğazköy in Anatolia between the Mitanni king and the ruler of the Hittites in which several Vedic gods, including Indra and the Nāsatyas, were mentioned among the Mesopotamian divinities. Scholars now consider it unlikely that these Indo-Aryan deities migrated west from the Punjab, and the Boğazköy inscriptions usually are taken as an indication that some part of the proto-Indo-Aryan people had moved down into the Near East from an archaic homeland on the Russian steppes.[252] How long before the date of the Boğazköy treaty this movement occurred is unknown. As noted earlier, the timing of all Indo-European see page 87 migrations, or waves of migration, is today more controversial than ever before. But if Zarathuštra did live in the sixth millennium B.C. (in uncorrected carbon-14 years), there were Indo-Europeans in sixth millennium Iran. And if Indo-Aryan cousins of these early Iranians were already present in the Near East at this time, those who were not persuaded by the message of the prophet may have kept to their nomadic ways for millennia to come, raising havoc (and occasionally uniting) with the settled populations of Anatolia, Syria, and Mesopotamia.

We have noted the apparent need for defensive structures at the Samarran settlements of Tell es-Sawwan and Choga Mami. The violence in late sixth and early fifth millennium Anatolia has also been observed. If any of these events, including now the destruction of Arpachiyah, were possibly the work of Indo-Aryan "daēva worshippers," they may have encouraged the merging of western forms of early Zarathuštran religion with those of the east. It is perhaps not by chance that the same period which saw the disappearance of first Samarran (c. 4900 B.C.) and then Halafian culture (c. 4400 B.C.) from Mesopotamia also saw the enrichment of the ceramics of central and southwestern Iran with motifs from nature that are almost identical to those on the earlier pottery of these more westerly peoples. On the plateau at Sialk, we recall, it was only after several centuries of purely geometric decoration that animals began to appear on the pottery: at first mainly the stylized goats shown earlier (fig. 126) and then, as the fifth millennium progressed, the wealth of more naturalistically rendered creatures that were to give Iranian art its characteristic profile. As shown at figure 149, the resemblance of these plateau motifs to Halafian and Samarran designs extends to both animal (leopard, goat, snake, scorpion) and human forms ("dancers").

see page 243

see pages 253–55

149 Forms from nature on the ceramics of Sialk III, central Iran, from c. 4500 B.C. *(after Ghirschman, 1938).* Compare figure 139.

We noted earlier that the worship of Mithra, and of certain Iranian nature gods who are also believed to predate Zarathuš-tra, was missing from the *Gāthās* but had been incorporated into the Zoroastrian religion of the Younger Avesta. It was also suggested that either Halaf or Samarra, or both, may have been western conservators of Old Iranian traditions that had been transformed rather than superseded by the vision of the prophet. If this were the case, the later and lasting success of nature themes on the pottery of the plateau, motifs that appear to imitate those on the earlier ceramics of the west, might mean that the ancient cults had moved from the periphery to the center of Zoroastrian religion by the middle of the fifth millennium B.C.

see pages 214, 220

At this time, with the rise of the related 'Ubaid culture that followed and in many ways continued the Halaf tradition in Mesopotamia, Iran became part—and perhaps the origin—of a vast *oikoumene* which extended across Iraq into Syria and again, in the eyes of some investigators, into parts of Greece as well.[417] Distinctly inferior to Halafian ceramics, the pottery of 'Ubaid nevertheless bears many of the same motifs; its spread through Iraq and lands farther west in the last half of the fifth millennium equaled or surpassed the sphere of Halafian influence. As there are unmistakable ceramic ties between 'Ubaid and both central and southwestern Iran, it has been suggested that the bearers of what we call 'Ubaid culture moved out of Iran and into the region of Sumer at some point in the fifth millennium B.C.[320] Others see 'Ubaid as an indigenous south Mesopotamian development, growing out of the Samarra-influenced Eridu culture of late sixth millennium Sumer.[309] But however 'Ubaid arose, its disappearance at the end of the fifth millennium saw the emergence (or the reinstatement) of regionally differentiated cultures in northern and southern Mesopotamia that appear to have been much less closely connected to Iran.[320]

see pages 242–43

To explore these post-Halaf developments in any detail would take us beyond the limits of this study. And the question of whether 'Ubaid represents a still later phase of Zarathuštran activity in the west (more dogmatic now than inspired), or possibly an early expansion of the Sumerian-speaking people who would later dominate southern Iraq,* is again a subject for more

---

* It has been suggested that the region of Sumer was already inhabited by a mixed population in Neolithic times, among which may have been the ancestors of the Sumerian-speaking people of the Bronze Age. How long before their first written records the speakers of Sumerian became the cultural leaders of southern Mesopotamia is unknown.

specialized research. We would only note that after 'Ubaid, a
unified cultural sphere of like proportions would not be known
again in western Asia until the spread of the Assyrian empire.[320]
And the Zoroastrian religion, heir to the vision of a world faith,
entered history identified with the Iranian people alone.[38]

Jener entwerfende Geist, welcher das Irdische meistert,
Liebt in dem Schwung der Figur nichts wie den wendenden Punkt.

Rilke, *Sonnets to Orpheus*

264   Plato, Prehistorian

Epilogue

The Legacy of Zarathuštra

If other gods or local traditions prevailed outside Iran, they did little to halt the momentum of Zarathuštra's economic reforms. The spread of the agricultural way of life and the acceleration of material progress seem everywhere to have been associated with increases in population and, in some regions, with the development of cities. We earlier quoted Hole and Flannery on the mid-to-late sixth millennium transition to settled farming in southwest Iran, which was to set certain peoples there and in Mesopotamia "clearly on the path toward population expansion see page 230 and urban life." The full extent of that transition may never be known; the most important prehistoric centers of northern Iraq apparently lie buried and inaccessible under the huge mounds of ancient cities (the deep sounding at Nineveh was mentioned see page 242 above), and information on the early periods in southern Mesopotamia is extremely scarce.[309] It is nevertheless clear that events set in motion in the middle of the sixth millennium would lead, however circuitously, to the urban civilizations of Susa, Babylon, and beyond.

Few prehistorians living in today's all too well-populated and urbanized world now see this decisive last phase of the Neolithic Revolution as an unmixed blessing. The present drain on nature's resources, in some areas beyond her capacity for renewal, seems a very high price for what was once hailed unquestioningly as the progress of human culture. But if the progressive world view can be traced to the time of Zarathuštra, so too can the idea of man's responsible stewardship of the earth, the evident basis of that view and the only lasting solution, perhaps, to the modern dilemma. To close this study we might briefly explore this paradoxical legacy, beginning with the question of what, exactly, Zarathuštra did say, and to whom.

As noted earlier, the obscurity of the language of the *Gāthās*, the fragmented state of the Avesta as a whole, and the numerous inconsistencies in more recent Persian texts have left many of Zarathuštra's teachings a matter of conjecture. Although Iraniologists generally believe that the religion of the *Gāthās* differed significantly from the Zoroastrian faith of later times, there is little agreement about the precise nature of that difference. As one pointed out: "It is impossible to tell, on the one hand, how much of the Later Avestan doctrine is but a fuller definition of ideas already implicit in Zarathuštra's teaching, and, on the other, how much is merely accretion, due to centuries of oral repetition, copying, commentary, and deliberate interpolation."[366] The problem is obviously compounded if there were millennia rather than centuries of accretion. Moreover, if the writers of antiquity were correct in calling Zarathuštra a Magus, the Zervanite religion of the Magi, later to stand in a heterodox relationship to the Zoroastrian church, once felt the influence of the prophet and should be included in the search for his original views. Indeed, one of the many unsolved problems facing Iraniologists today is why, among the Greeks, Zervanism was always associated with the name of Zarathuštra.[19]

The source of that association, if authentic, will most likely be found in the esoteric or mystical dimension that many scholars see in the *Gāthās*. (One has theorized that Gathic religion was actually a private cult for initiates, separate and distinct from popular forms of Iranian religion.)[287] We noted earlier that the concept of the Entities, aspects of Ahura Mazda as well as qualities of the virtuous man, potentially would allow an individual to realize his likeness to God. References to "secret doctrines" also appear in the Gathic hymns (*Y*.XLVIII.3), but if these had to do with such Magian principles as a reverence for Endless Time or a cycle of lives, they were not to survive in orthodox Zoroastrianism, which found no place for metempsychosis and preferred the single and final to the cyclic in both world and man.[425] *

see page 221

* One notes, however, that although Zoroastrianism, like Christianity and Judaism, gives history a purpose and a final end, traces can be found in all three religions of the idea that periodic regeneration is necessary, and that the world may be destroyed and renewed a number of times before the final consummation.[113] It might also be argued that the whirl-patterns decorating Iranian and Mesopotamian pottery in the late sixth and early fifth millennium express cyclical rather than linear-progressive movement (or, as might be suggested by the spiral at Sialk, a combination of the two types of motion), in which case Nietzsche's portrayal of Zarathustra as an advocate of the cyclic view of history may have been truer than he intended.

Some scholars have attempted to explain the gulf between Zervanite and Zoroastrian principles by theorizing that the Magi deviated from the teachings of Zarathuštra as time went on.[284] This may be true; the Magian tradition presumably knew its own cycles of decay and renewal. On the other hand, what we know of organized religions and their resistance to change suggests that the Zoroastrian priesthood may have betrayed the Magian principle of cooperation with the changing quality of Time, by literalizing and conserving forms whose immediacy had been lost. As one Iraniologist described the situation in the Younger Avesta: "The Entities were reduced to mere deities which were even separated into male and female. Nevermore was their name used to designate a human faculty."[104]

But regardless of the ways in which both Zervanism and Zoroastrianism may have changed over the millennia, their differences are likely to have always been in some part the differences between inner and outer, or esoteric and popular, forms of religious experience. The initiatory schools of antiquity were often at odds with orthodox views. Just as the religion of the Magi was only tolerated as an "ascetic wing" of the Zoro-astrian church,[440] the Hermetic Aion cult was either unknown or ignored in orthodox Egyptian texts,[111] and official Greek religion knew nothing of a cycle of rebirths or a god of Undecaying Time.[167] The Orphic idea that all men contained the seeds of divinity, that man might become god, was heresy to Homeric belief, which saw gods and men as two essentially discrete categories of being.

It is this widespread initiatory tradition, centered on man's potential divinity, that has seemed indispensable here to the interpretation of prehistoric art and symbolism. Its immense antiquity has been suggested at several points; its source re-mains a mystery. Either or both of Plato's superior races could have been instrumental in developing the techniques of tran-scendence. It might also be argued that if human beings do possess the capacity to alter radically their mode of being, to become god (or god-like) is a potentiality which, as Huxley maintained, "man, as man, has always had it in his power to realize."[192] Indisputable in any event would seem to be the num-ber of reaffirmations of man's latent divinity across time and space by exceptional individuals who apparently spoke from their own experience, and whose influence on the course of history has been profound.

If Zarathuštra was evidently one of these exceptional men, Plato, six thousand years later and surrounded by a different set of historical circumstances, was surely another. It is difficult to doubt the authenticity of Plato's experience of a reality beyond the senses, or his capacity to rise, like the guardians of his ideal state, "out of the sea of change and lay hold of true being" (*Republic* 525). Although he avoided explicit descriptions of this Intelligible world, what Plato did write has been credited with influencing Christian, Islamic, and cabalistic forms of mysticism, as well as establishing the bases for two thousand years of rational western thought.[144] But Plato was also a man of his time and, like Socrates, saw a need to counter the arguments of the materialists and the relativizing Sophists of the day. In the *Timaeus* he shows the universe to be, not the result of random forces, but a purposeful creation — a living creature with mind in soul and soul "woven right through from the center to the outermost heaven" (*Timaeus* 36). And it was through the educated contemplation of that divinely ordered cosmos, and the reproduction in one's own nature of its harmonies (manifest in music, mathematics, and astronomy) that the qualified individual of Plato's time could discover the truth of his being, his very likeness to the divine.

The historical situation of Zarathuštra, on the other hand, called for the healing of the Good Creation itself, for the restoration of faith in the inherent sanctity of the material world. He too saw the cosmos as the work of a divine architect, but Zarathuštra advocated the perfecting of the earth as well as the individual, through man's collaboration with that creator. The way to God for his own inner circle of disciples is therefore likely to have been rather more active than contemplative, and centered on an intimate knowledge of the transformative possibilities in all nature, not merely one's own. Historians of religion have in fact commented on the emphasis the prophet placed on the religious value of accurate knowledge of this world:

> To be sure, it is not a matter of abstract science in the modern sense of the term, but of a creative thought that discovers and at the same time creates the structures of the world and the universe of values that is their correlative.[119]

That is also a fair definition of a practice known to the medieval world as alchemy, a much misunderstood predecessor of natural science that some have associated with the so-called Hellenized Magi.[26] Popularly identified today with attempts to turn lead "magically" into gold during the Middle Ages, the alchemic tradition was a great deal older and apparently directed toward something more: in the words of one medieval adherent, "how Nature may be seen and recognized as coming from God, and God in Nature."[117] Traces of alchemical thinking have been detected in Zoroastrian orthodoxy;[84] they are far more pronounced in Zervanism. There are, in fact, enough parallels in the *Gāthās* to the alchemic world view to suggest that Zarathuštra's contribution to the inner school of religious experience was to bring the Magian religion down to earth.

The Alchemical Idea

To approach the Gathic hymns as an early, perhaps the earliest, statement of the alchemical idea may be the surest way to grasp both their meaning and the contradictory nature of Zarathuštra's legacy to the modern world. Certainly this should be included among the several directions for future study that would emerge with the dating of the prophet to the sixth millennium B.C. Everywhere related to a mystical tradition (in India with yoga and Tantrism, in China with Taoism, in Hellenistic Egypt with gnosis),[117] alchemy shared with those traditions the perception that the whole of the phenomenal world participated in one fundamental, interconnected, and ceaselessly changing activity. The alchemist went further, however, and assigned a goal to this ever-transforming continuum. For him all of nature's kingdoms—mineral as well as plant, animal, and human—were moving toward an ultimate state of perfection, a "maturation" which the alchemist, through his ability to transmute material substance, could assist. In so doing he was himself, ideally, transformed.* As Eliade has noted, "alchemy prolongs and consummates a very old dream of *homo faber*: collaboration in the perfecting of matter while at the same time securing perfection for himself."[117]

How old was that dream? Man's intervention in natural processes is at least as old as the earliest crossing of plant species and selective breeding of animals, but the alchemists worked primarily with mineral substances. Was their art as old, then, as the first transmutations by fire of ores into metal? In China

---

* The creating of gold may have been largely symbolic. Gold represented perfection in every sphere and corresponded to immortality in the alchemical texts of India. It is said that the Alexandrian alchemists were aware from the beginning that in seeking to perfect metals they were pursuing their own perfection.[117]

the archaic initiation rites and mysteries of the smiths are known to have formed an integral part of the traditions inherited by alchemy and Taoism.[117] Does this mean that the symbolic or mystical dimension of alchemy, the so-called inner work, was a late addition to more primitive rites? Or was the commitment to the perfecting of both earth and man actually the basis for the development, if not the discovery, of metallurgy—a spiritual motive which may have been lost and regained several times prior to the emergence in late antiquity of what is called alchemy?

The writings of the alchemists say only that they built on what went before, on a divinely inspired tradition of great age.[24] Many scholars find the origin of that tradition in the Hermetic schools of second and third century A.D. Egypt, but others see Hellenistic Egypt as merely the inheritor of a body of knowledge which had long been incubating in Mesopotamia under the influence of the Magi.[134] Not only do certain historical references suggest a Babylonian seniority,* but the principles of Magian religion parallel those of the alchemists in many respects. One doctrine attributed to Zervanism, for example, states that Ahura Mazda came into being when fire and water were joined, and in Hermetic traditions it is this same conjunction of fire and water which, as Corbin observed, forms the "symbol par excellence" for the alchemical operation when seen as the divinizing of man.[84] The coincidence of opposites is in fact one of the great themes of alchemy, representing to some investigators its ultimate goal.[24]

see pages 201–3

Reminiscent as well of Zervanite principles is the alchemist's belief that the planets and constellations are bound up with earthly events: "nothing occurs below which does not have its correspondence above, and conversely."[24] The idea of correspondences is basic to alchemical thought; not only the heavens but the elements and kingdoms of earth find analogues in the various parts of the human body, the identity of macrocosm

---

* In ancient texts it was "Ostanes the Magus" who taught Democritus the art of alchemy, possibly the same Ostanes that King Xerxes supposedly sent to teach alchemy to the priests of Egypt.[134] And in cuneiform tablets from seventh century B.C. Nineveh, a prescription for the ritual construction of a furnace for minerals refers to the ores as "embryos," a favorite alchemical analogy based on the idea that the fire of the furnace assists in the perfecting, or the maturing, of mineral substance. A comparable document from Egypt in the Hellenistic Age has convinced some investigators that Egyptian alchemy was connected to Babylonian practices of far greater age.[112, 344]

and microcosm that we earlier saw reflected in Indo-European cosmogonies. It is noteworthy, however, that in the alchemic tradition these are ties of *interaction*. In contrast to the unilateral control accorded the Seven and the Twelve in the fatalistic view associated with possibly decadent forms of Zervanism, man himself can influence the cosmos. From the alchemical point of view, he can

see page 109

see page 201

> lift the world from its hinges, at first to be sure only the world in himself, but does this not correspond to the world outside?
>
> Thus alchemy becomes a universal potentiality. Its aims extend to every sphere of being; ultimately transcending the possibilities in nature. Its final goal is a transcendent perfection.[24]

Again we cannot hope to deal adequately in this space with an extremely complex system of thought and experience which many see as an (unwitting) precursor of modern science, others as a continuation of the mystery religions of antiquity, but of whose actual operations very little is known. Our purpose is only to draw attention to the general likeness of the alchemic idea to the spirit of the *Gāthās*, and to what plausibly may have been Zarathuštra's effect on Magian religion. Whether or not one follows the Greeks in crediting the prophet with an interest in the heavens, his hymns are permeated with an alchemical attitude toward the earth. Zarathuštra's emphasis on the value of efficient knowledge of this world has been mentioned; no less ardently than the alchemists did his followers seek to collaborate in the perfecting of the material domain. To describe the alchemist as "the brotherly savior of Nature"[117] is again to identify the prophet's disciple. From Gathic times onward, the responsibility for the welfare of the earth was to be shared by man.

see page 212

That molten metal, the basis of much alchemical symbolism, interested Zarathuštra is also evident in the *Gāthās* (Y.XXX.7, XXXII.7), and whatever its significance in Iranian eschatology, the glowing metal of these early hymns appears to offer the blessings of immortality to the virtuous man, now. We noted earlier the likelihood that the smelting of copper was known as early as the middle of the sixth millennium, coeval with and possibly related to the achievement of higher temperatures for the firing of ceramics. At the same time, improved species of grain and the breeding of cattle, large and small, began to spread rapidly across Iran and Mesopotamia. We were thus allowed to observe that efforts toward the transformation of three of the

see pages 236–37

four realms of nature—mineral, plant, and animal—seem to have been greatly accelerated around 5500 B.C., the date (when corrected to calendar time) assigned to Zarathuštra by the Greeks. If, as suggested in the *Gāthās*, the prophet's interests extended to transmutations in the human realm as well, it may indeed have been he who laid the foundations of the alchemical idea, and gave Magian religion its own science of the earth.

The ancient dream dies hard. It has in fact been found, stripped of its spiritual content, at the base of the progress-centered ideologies of the modern age. A remarkable passage from Eliade's *The Forge and the Crucible*, the most accessible contemporary work on alchemy, deserves quoting in full:

> We must not believe that the triumph of experimental science reduced to nought the dreams and ideals of the alchemist. On the contrary, the ideology of the new epoch, crystallized around the myth of infinite progress and boosted by the experimental sciences and the progress of industrialization which dominated and inspired the whole of the nineteenth century, takes up and carries forward—despite its radical secularization—the millenary dream of the alchemist. It is in the specific dogma of the nineteenth century, according to which man's true mission is to transform and improve upon Nature and become her master, that we must look for the authentic continuation of the alchemist's dream. The visionary's myth of the perfection, or more accurately, of the redemption of Nature, survives, in camouflaged form, in the pathetic program of the industrial societies whose aim is the total transmutation of Nature, its transformation into "energy."

If Eliade's perception is correct, one might ask if the distortion of the alchemic idea is unique to the modern epoch. Is this the first time the concept of man's stewardship of the earth has been radically secularized, or has it happened before, and with results which, if not equal to the present level of potential destructiveness, were inevitably disastrous? If this concept did arise, or was revived, in the sixth millennium teachings of Zarathuštra, the loss and recovery of its original meaning will surely have occurred more than once in the ensuing millennia. It may now be possible, through the sensitive ecological studies that are becoming an increasingly important part of archaeological research, to document these prehistoric ruptures in man's relationship to the earth.

Indeed, the growing interest in ecology in the west today may be one indication that the most recent break in the bond between man and nature has been only temporary, that this too is a cyclic phenomenon. It is not unrealistic to see the beginnings of a renewal of the concept of stewardship in contemporary efforts to restore the integrity of the natural environment. In attempting to halt the destruction of rainforests, to reclaim over-grazed or industrially depleted land, to rescue threatened species of wildlife or animals abused in confinement, to restore the purity of the earth's waters, late twentieth century men have become increasingly active—and through science increasingly effective—in nature's defense. Some have taken the next step and seek ways in which human culture might in the future enhance rather than impinge on nature's domains.

These efforts are rarely religious in the formal sense, but few of those who make them have been unaffected by the mingling of spiritual traditions that followed the breakdown of cultural barriers in our own time. The encounter of oriental religions and western ideologies once again has produced, as Cumont remarked of the results of an earlier convergence, "the most startling combinations." Ethnographers and historians have brought the multitude of primitive and ancient beliefs into western awareness as well, thereby revealing how very old and widespread is the reverence for the earth as a living organism or entity. The evident similarity of initiatory techniques among these traditional societies has also generated renewed interest in approaches to self-knowledge and self-mastery in the west, overlapping or perhaps inspiring similar trends in twentieth century psychology. And if, among the swarm of spiritual disciplines that have invaded western society, some seem less than authentic, one is reminded of both Rome and Çatal Hüyük— and encouraged to review Spengler's claim that societies which are at the same place on the cultural cycle are to be compared, regardless of their age.[376] In Spenglerian terms, we may be the "contemporary" of Çatal Hüyük as well as Rome.

see page 173

It is not an unhappy prospect. From the Çatal milieu of material opulence, converging cultures, and exhausted religions, there emerged a new (or renewed) commitment to the steward-ship of the earth in the teachings of Zarathuštra. Its interim course remains to be charted, but six thousand years later a similar idea arose amid the overturned values and merging traditions of dying antiquity, when the alchemists again conceived of man's purpose as the perfecting of nature and self.

If the present century is indeed to be compared to those earlier periods of cultural dissolution, one would expect its emerging tendencies, toward the healing of the earth and the healing of the human spirit, to unite at some point. Perhaps this time a prophet will not be needed to remind us of who we are and what needs to be done. The number of those already asking, independently, "may we be those who will renew this existence" could mean that humanity is in fact progressing, over and above — or perhaps by means of — the cycles of Time.

Appendices

Bibliography

Index

APPENDIX A

Relevant Passages from Plato's
Timaeus and *Critias**

Timaeus

HERMOCRATES: I assure you, Socrates, that, as Timaeus here said, there is no lack of willingness on our part and we don't want to excuse ourselves from our part of the bargain. Indeed we were considering it as soon as we got back yesterday to Critias's house, where we are staying, and even before that while we were on the way there. Critias then produced a story he had heard long ago. Tell it again now to Socrates, Critias, so that we can see whether it is suitable for our purpose or not.

CRITIAS: I will, if the other member of the trio, Timaeus, agrees.

TIMAEUS: I agree.

CRITIAS: Listen then, Socrates. The story is a strange one, but Solon, the wisest of the seven wise men, once vouched its truth. He was a relation and close friend of Dropides, my great-grandfather, as he often says himself in his poems, and told the story to my grandfather Critias, who in turn repeated it to us when he was an old man. It relates the many notable achievements of our city long ago, which have been lost sight of because of the lapse of time and destruction of human life. Of these the greatest is one that we could well recall now to repay our debt to you and to offer the Goddess on her festival day a just and truthful hymn of praise.

SOCRATES: Good. And what is this unrecorded yet authentic achievement of our city that Critias heard from Solon and recounted to you?

CRITIAS: I will tell you; though the story was old when I heard it and the man who told it to me was no longer young. For Critias was at the time, so he said, nearly ninety, and I was about ten. It was Children's Day in the festival of Apatouria, and there were the customary ceremonies for the boys, including prizes given by the fathers for reciting. There were recitations of many poems by different authors, but many of the competitors chose Solon's poems, which were in those days quite a novelty. And one of the clansmen, either because he thought so or out of politeness to Critias, said that he thought that Solon was not only the wisest of men but also the most outspoken of poets. And the old man — I remember it well — was extremely pleased, and said with a smile, 'I wish, Amynander,

On the previous day Socrates had described an ideal society that the three members of his audience—Timaeus, Critias, and Hermocrates —then agreed to animate on the stage of history. . . .

21

* Desmond Lee translation (Penguin Classics, 1971), copyright © H. D. P. Lee, 1965, 1971, 1977. Pages 33–40 and 129–145 from the 1977 edition are reprinted by permission of Penguin Books Ltd.

that he hadn't treated poetry as a spare-time occupation but had taken it seriously like others; if he had finished the story he brought back from Egypt, and hadn't been compelled to neglect it because of the class struggles and other evils he found here on his return, I don't think any poet, even Homer or Hesiod, would have been more famous.' 'And what was the story, Critias?' asked Amynander. 'It was about what may fairly be called the greatest and most noteworthy of all this city's achievements, but because of the lapse of time and the death of those who took part in it the story has not lasted till our day.' 'Tell us from the beginning,' came the reply; 'how and from whom did Solon hear the tale which he told you as true?'

'There is in Egypt,' said Critias, 'at the head of the delta, where the Nile divides, a district called the Saïtic. The chief city of the district, from which King Amasis came, is called Saïs. The chief goddess of the inhabitants is called in Egyptian Neïth, in Greek (according to them) Athena; and they are very friendly to the Athenians and claim some relationship to them. Solon came there on his travels and was highly honoured by them, and in the course of making inquiries from those priests who were most knowledgeable on the subject found that both he and all his countrymen were almost entirely ignorant about antiquity. And wishing to lead them on to talk about early times, he embarked on an account of the earliest events known here, telling them about Phoroneus, said to be the first man, and Niobe, and how Deucalion and Pyrrha survived the flood and who were their descendants, and trying by reckoning up the generations to calculate how long ago the events in question had taken place. And a very old priest said to him, 'Oh Solon, Solon, you Greeks are all children, and there's no such thing as an old Greek.'

'What do you mean by that?' inquired Solon.

'You are all young in mind,' came the reply: 'you have no belief rooted in old tradition and no knowledge hoary with age. And the reason is this. There have been and will be many different calamities to destroy mankind, the greatest of them by fire and water, lesser ones by countless other means. Your own story of how Phaëthon, child of the sun, harnessed his father's chariot, but was unable to guide it along his father's course and so burnt up things on the earth and was himself destroyed by a thunderbolt, is a mythical version of the truth that there is at long intervals a variation in the course of the heavenly bodies and a consequent widespread destruction by fire of things on the earth. On such occasions those who live in the mountains or in high and dry places suffer more than those living by rivers or by the sea; as for us, the Nile, our own regular saviour, is freed to preserve us in this emergency. When on the other hand the gods purge the earth with a deluge, the herdsmen and shepherds in the mountains escape, but those living in the cities in your part of the world are swept into the sea by the rivers; here water never falls on the land from above either then or at any other time, but rises up naturally from below. This is the reason why our traditions here are the oldest preserved; though it is true that in all places where excessive cold or heat does not prevent it human beings are always to be found in larger or smaller numbers. But in our temples we have preserved from earliest times a written record of any great or splendid achievement or notable event which has come to our ears whether it occurred in your part of the world or here or anywhere else; whereas with you and others, writing and the other necessities of civilization have only just been developed when the periodic scourge of the deluge descends, and spares none but the unlettered and uncultured, so that you have to begin again like children, in complete ignorance of what happened in our part of the world or in yours in early times. So these genealogies of your own people which you were just recounting are little more than children's stories. You remember only one deluge, though there have been many, and you do not know that the finest and best race of men that ever existed lived in your country; you and your fellow citizens are descended from the few survivors that remained, but you know nothing about it because so many succeeding generations left no record in writing. For before the greatest of all destructions by water, Solon, the city that is now Athens was preeminent in war and conspicuously the best governed in every way, its achievements and constitution being the finest of any in the world of which we have heard tell.'

Solon was astonished at what he heard and eagerly begged the priests to describe to him in detail the doings of these citizens of the past. 'I will gladly do so, Solon,' replied the priest, 'both for your sake and your city's, but chiefly in gratitude to the Goddess to whom it has fallen to bring up and educate both your country and ours—yours first, when she took over your seed from Earth and Hephaestos, ours a thousand years later. The age of our institutions is given in our sacred records as eight thousand years, and the citizens whose laws and whose finest achievement I will now briefly describe to you therefore lived nine thousand years ago; we will go through their history in detail later on at leisure, when we can consult the records.

'Consider their laws compared with ours; for you will find today among us many parallels to your institutions in those days. First, our priestly class is kept distinct from the others, as is also our artisan class; next, each class of craftsmen—shepherds, hunters, farmers—performs its function in isolation from others. And of course you will have noticed that our soldier class is kept separate from all others, being forbidden by the law to undertake any duties other than military: moreover their armament consists of shield and spear, which we were the first people in Asia to adopt, under the instruction of the Goddess, as you were in your part of the world. And again you see what great attention our law devotes from the beginning to learning, deriving from the divine principles of cosmology everything needed for human life down to divination and medicine for our health, and acquiring all other related branches of knowledge. The Goddess founded this whole order and system when she framed your society. She chose the place in which you were born with an eye to its temperate climate, which would produce men of high intelligence; for being herself a lover of war and wisdom she picked a place for her first foundation that would produce men most like herself in character. So you lived there under the laws I have described, and even better ones, and excelled all men in every kind of accomplishment, as one would expect of children and off-spring of the gods. And among all the wonderful achievements recorded here of your city, one great act of courage is outstanding. Our records tell how your city checked a great power which arrogantly advanced from its base in the Atlantic ocean to attack the cities

24

of Europe and Asia. For in those days the Atlantic was navigable. There was an island opposite the strait which you call (so you say) the Pillars of Heracles, an island larger than Libya and Asia combined; from it travellers could in those days reach the other islands, and from them the whole opposite continent which surrounds what can truly be called the ocean. For the sea within the strait we were talking about is like a lake with a narrow entrance; the outer ocean is the real ocean and the land which entirely surrounds it is properly termed continent. On this island of Atlantis had arisen a powerful and remarkable dynasty of kings, who ruled the whole island, and many other islands as well and parts of the continent; in addition it controlled, within the strait, Libya up to the borders of Egypt and Europe as far as Tyrrhenia. This dynasty, gathering its whole power together, attempted to enslave, at a single stroke, your country and ours and all the territory within the strait. It was then, Solon, that the power and courage and strength of your city became clear for all men to see. Her bravery and military skill were outstanding; she led an alliance of the Greeks, and then when they deserted her and she was forced to fight alone, after running into direst peril, she overcame the invaders and celebrated a victory; she rescued those not yet enslaved from the slavery threatening them, and she generously freed all others living within the Pillars of Heracles. At a later time there were earthquakes and floods of extraordinary violence, and in a single dreadful day and night all your fighting men were swallowed up by the earth, and the island of Atlantis was similarly swallowed up by the sea and vanished; this is why the sea in that area is to this day impassable to navigation, which is hindered by mud just below the surface, the remains of the sunken island.'

That is, in brief, Socrates, the story which Critias told when he was an old man, and which he had heard from Solon. When you were describing your society and its inhabitants yesterday, I was reminded of this story and noticed with astonishment how closely, by some miraculous chance, your account coincided with Solon's. I was not willing to say so at once, for after so long a time my memory was imperfect; I decided therefore that I must first rehearse the whole story to myself before telling it. That was why I was so quick to agree to your conditions yesterday, thinking that I was pretty well placed to deal with what is always the most serious difficulty in such matters, how to find a suitable story on which to base what one wants to say. And so, as Hermocrates said, as soon as we left here yesterday I started telling the story to the others as I remembered it, and when I got back I managed to recall pretty well all of it by thinking it over during the night. It is amazing, as is often said, how what we learn as children sticks in the memory. I'm not at all sure whether I could remember again all I heard yesterday; yet I should be surprised if any detail of this story I heard so long ago has escaped me. I listened to it then with a child's intense delight, and the old man was glad to answer my innumerable questions, so that the details have been indelibly branded on my memory. What is more, I have told the whole story to the others early this morning, so that they might be as well placed as I am for the day's discussion.

And now, to come to the point, I am ready to tell the story, Socrates, not only in outline but in detail, as I heard it. We will transfer the imaginary citizens and city which you described yesterday to the real world, and say that your city is the city of my story and your citizens those historical ancestors or ours whom the priest described. They will fit exactly, and there will be no disharmony if we speak as if they really were the men who lived at that time. We will divide the work between us and try to fulfil your instructions to the best of our ability. So tell us, Socrates, do you think this story will suit our purpose, or must we look for another instead?

SOCRATES: What better choice could there be, Critias? Your story is particularly well suited to the present festival of the Goddess, with whom it is connected, and it is a great point in its favour that it is not a fiction but true history. Where shall we find an alternative if we abandon it? No, you must tell it and good luck to you; and I can take it easy and listen to your reply to my narrative of yesterday.

CRITIAS: Here then, Socrates, is the plan we have made to entertain you. We thought that Timaeus, who knows more about astronomy than the rest of us and who has devoted himself particularly to studying the nature of the universe, should speak first, and starting with the origin of the cosmic system bring the story down to man. I will follow him, assuming that human beings have come into existence as he has described and that some of them have had your excellent education; these I will bring to judgement before us here by making them citizens of Athens governed as she was in the days of Solon's story — an Athens whose disappearance is accounted for in the priestly writings, and about whose citizens I shall in the rest of what I have to say assume I am speaking.

SOCRATES: I look like getting a splendid entertainment in return for mine. It falls to you then, Timaeus, it seems, to speak next, after the customary invocation to the gods. . . .

27

Critias

TIMAEUS: How glad I am, Socrates, to have brought my story safely to an end, and how pleased to get some rest after my long journey. I pray the god whose origin we have just traced in our tale, but who really existed long before, that we may safely retain all that has been truthfully said, but pay suitable penalty for any false notes we have involuntarily struck. And the suitable penalty is that we should correct our mistakes and play in tune. I pray therefore that god may grant us knowledge, the most effective and best of all medicines, so that all we say in future about the origin of the gods may be true; and with that prayer I hand over to Critias, as agreed.

CRITIAS: And I am ready, Timaeus. But I must make the same plea that you made at the beginning, and ask for indulgence because of the magnitude of my theme. Indeed I think the nature of my subject gives me an even greater claim to it. I know that what I am going to ask will seem excessive and unnecessarily embarrassing, but ask I must. No one in his senses could challenge the excellence of the account you have given: it remains for me to try to show that my subject is a more difficult one and calls for greater indulgence. For it is easier, Timaeus, to give a satisfactory impression when talking to ordinary men about the gods than when talking among ourselves about mortals. For inexperience and ignorance of a

Timaeus takes over, and describes the cosmogony and the nature of man, thus completing his part of the conversation and the dialogue bearing his name. At the opening of the Critias, he yields the floor. . . .

107

subject in your audience make it easy to handle if you are to talk about it; and we know how ignorant we are about the gods. Let me give you the following illustration to make my meaning clearer. All statements we make are inevitably pictures or images. So let us consider the relative degree of severity with which we judge the adequacy of the representation by artists of divine and of human objects. We see that we are satisfied if the artist can produce quite an elementary likeness of earth, mountains, rivers and woods, and of the sky and stars and planets; besides, because of our ignorance of the subject-matter, we don't subject his pictures to any searching criticism but are content with an imprecise and inaccurate sketch. But if anyone tries to make a portrait of the human body, we are, because of our familiarity with it, quick to notice faults and criticize severely any failure to produce a perfect likeness. We should recognize that the same is true of verbal descriptions. We are content with faint likenesses when their subjects are celestial and divine, but we criticize narrowly when they are mortal and human. So in what immediately follows, you should make allowances if my narrative is not always entirely appropriate; for you must understand that it is far from easy to give satisfactory accounts of human affairs. It is to remind you of this and to ask for a still greater degree of indulgence for what I am going to say, Socrates, that I have started with this long introduction. If you think the favour I'm asking is justified, please grant it.

108

SOCRATES: Of course we will, Critias; and Hermocrates may assume that we will grant the same indulgence to him. For when it is his turn to speak, he will obviously make the same request as you have; so let him assume the request granted and proceed without feeling any need of the same introduction, but rather produce another of his own. But I warn you, my dear Critias, that the author who preceded you has made a wonderfully favourable impression on the minds of his audience, and you will need a lot of allowance made for you if you are to take over from him.

HERMOCRATES: That warning applies to me as much as to him, Socrates. But nothing ventured nothing have, Critias; you must tackle your narrative like a man, and call on Pan and the Muses for their help in singing the praises of your fellow-citizens of old.

CRITIAS: My dear Hermocrates, you are cheerful enough because you are still in the rear rank with someone to shelter you. But you will find out soon enough what exposure is like. Meanwhile I must follow your encouraging advice and call on the gods, adding the goddess Memory in particular to those you have mentioned. For my whole narrative depends largely on her. I'm sure my audience will think I have discharged my task with reasonable credit if I can remember adequately and repeat the story which the priests told Solon and he brought home with him. To it I must now proceed without further delay.

We must first remind ourselves that in all nine thousand years have elapsed since the declaration of war between those who lived outside and all those who lived inside the Pillars of Heracles. This is the war whose course I am to trace. The leadership and conduct of the war were on the one side in the hands of our city, on the other in the hands of the kings of Atlantis. At the time, as we said, Atlantis was an island larger than Libya and Asia put together, though it was subsequently overwhelmed by earthquakes and is the source of the impenetrable mud which prevents the free passage of those who sail out of the straits into the open sea. The course of our narrative as it unfolds will give particulars about the various barbarian and Greek nations of the day; but we must begin with an account of the resources and constitutions of the Athenians and their antagonists in the war, giving precedence to the Athenians.

Once upon a time the gods divided up the Earth between them—not in the course of a quarrel; for it would be quite wrong to think that the gods do not know what is appropriate to them, or that, knowing it, they would want to annex what properly belongs to others. Each gladly received his just allocation, and settled his territories; and having done so they proceeded to look after us, their creatures and children, as shepherds look after their flocks. They did not use physical means of control, like shepherds who direct their flock with blows, but brought their influence to bear on the creature's most sensitive part, using persuasion as a steersman uses the helm to direct the mind as they saw fit and so guide the whole mortal creature. The various gods, then, administered the various regions which had been allotted to them. But Hephaestos and Athena, who shared as brother and sister a common character, and pursued the same ends in their love of knowledge and skill, were allotted this land of ours as their joint sphere and as a suitable and natural home for excellence and wisdom. They produced a native race of good men and gave them suitable political arrangements. Their names have been preserved but what they did has been forgotten because of the destruction of their successors and the long lapse of time. For as we said before, the survivors of this destruction were an unlettered mountain race who had just heard the names of the rulers of the land but knew little of their achievements. They were glad enough to give their names to their own children, but they knew nothing of the virtues and institutions of their predecessors, except for a few hazy reports; for many generations they and their children were short of bare necessities, and their minds and thoughts were occupied with providing for them, to the neglect of earlier history and tradition. For an interest in the past and historical research come only when communities have leisure and when men are already provided with the necessities of life. That is how the names but not the achievements of these early generations come to be preserved. My evidence is this, that Cecrops, Erectheus, Erichthonios, Erusichthon and most of the other names recorded before Theseus, occurred, according to Solon, in the narrative of the priests about this war; and the same is true of the women's names. What is more, as men and women in those days both took part in military exercises, so the figure and image of the goddess, following this custom, was in full armour, as a sign that whenever animals are grouped into male and female it is natural for each sex to be able to practise its appropriate excellence in the community.

In those days most classes of citizen were concerned with manufacture and agriculture. The military class lived apart, having been from the beginning separated from the others by godlike men. They were provided with what was necessary for their maintenance and training, they had no private property but regarded their possession as common to all, they did not look to the rest of the citizens for anything beyond their basic maintenance; in fact they followed in all things the regime we laid down yesterday when we were talking about our hypothetical Guardians. And indeed what we said then about our territory is true and plausible enough; for in those days its boundaries were drawn at the Isthmus, and on the mainland side at the Cithaeron and Parnes ranges coming down to the sea between Oropus on the right and the Asopus river on the left. And the soil was more fertile than that of any other country and so could maintain a large army exempt from the calls of agricultural labour. As evidence of this fertility we can point to the fact that the remnant of it still left is a match for any soil in the world for the variety of its harvests and pasture. And in those days quantity matched quality. What proof then can we offer that it is fair to call it now a mere remnant of what it once was? It runs out like a long peninsula from the mainland into the sea, and the sea basin round it is very deep. So the result of the many great floods that have taken place in the last nine thousand years (the time that has elapsed since then) is that the soil washed away from the high land in these periodical catastrophes forms no alluvial deposit of consequence as in other places, but is carried out and lost in the deeps. You are left (as with little islands) with something rather like the skeleton of a body wasted by disease; the rich, soft soil has all run away leaving the land nothing but skin and bone. But in those days the damage had not taken place, the hills had high crests, the rocky plain of Phelleus was covered with rich soil, and the mountains were covered by thick woods, of which there are some traces today. For some mountains which today will only support bees produced not so long ago trees which when cut provided roof beams for huge buildings whose roofs are still standing. And there were a lot of tall cultivated trees which bore unlimited quantities of fodder for beasts. The soil benefited from an annual rainfall which did not run to waste off the bare earth as it does today, but was absorbed in large quantities and stored in retentive layers of clay, so that what was drunk down by the higher regions flowed downwards into the valleys and appeared every-where in a multitude of rivers and springs. And the shrines which still survive at these former springs are proof of the truth of our present account of the country.

   This, then, was the general nature of the country, and it was cultivated with the skill you would expect from a class of genuine full-time agricul-turalists with good natural talents and high standards, who had an ex-cellent soil, an abundant water supply and a well-balanced climate. The lay-out of the city in those days was as follows. The Acropolis was different from what it is now. Today it is quite bare of soil which was all washed away in one appalling night of flood, by a combination of earthquakes and the third terrible deluge before that of Deucalion. Before that, in earlier days, it extended to the Eridanus and Ilisus, it included the Pnyx and was bounded on the opposite side by the Lycabettos; it was covered with soil and for the most part level. Outside, on its immediate slopes, lived the craftsmen and the agricultural workers who worked in the neighbourhood. Higher up the military class lived by itself round the temple of Athena and Hephaestos, surrounded by a single wall like the garden of a single house. On the northern side they built their common dwelling-houses and winter mess-rooms, and everything else required by their communal life in the way of buildings and temples. They had no gold or silver, and never used them for any purpose, but aimed at a balance between ex-travagance and meanness in the houses they built, in which they and their descendants grew old and which they handed on unchanged to succeeding generations who resembled themselves. In the summer they abandoned their gardens and gymnasia and mess-rooms and used the southern side of the Acropolis instead. There was a single spring in the area of the present Acropolis, which was subsequently choked by the earthquakes and survives as only a few small trickles in the vicinity; in those days there was an ample supply of good water both in winter and summer. This was how they lived; and they acted as Guardians of their own citizens, and were voluntarily recognized as leaders of the rest of Greece. They kept the number of those of military age, men and women, so far as possible, always constant at about twenty thousand.

This then was the sort of people they were and this the way in which they administered their own affairs and those of Greece; their reputation and name stood higher than any other in Europe or Asia for qualities both of body and character. I will now go on to reveal to you, as friends, if I can still remember what I was told when I was a child, the nature and origin of their antagonists in the war.

Before I begin, a brief word of explanation, in case you are surprised at   113
hearing foreigners so often referred to by Greek names. The reason is this. Solon intended to use the story in his own poem. And when, on inquiring about the significance of the names, he learned that the Egyptians had translated the originals into their own language, he went through the reverse process, and as he learned the meaning of a name wrote it down in Greek. My father had his manuscript, which is now in my possession, and I studied it often as a child. So if you hear names like those we use here, don't be surprised; I have given you the reason.

The story is a long one and it begins like this. We have already mentioned how the gods distributed the whole earth between them in larger or smaller shares and then established shrines and sacrifices for themselves. Poseidon's share was the island of Atlantis and he settled the children borne to him by a mortal woman in a particular district of it. At the centre of the island, near the sea, was a plain, said to be the most beautiful and fertile of all plains, and near the middle of this plain about fifty stades inland a hill of no great size. Here there lived one of the original earth-born inhabitants called Evenor, with his wife Leucippe. They had an only child, a daughter called Cleito. She was just of marriageable age when her father and mother died, and Poseidon was attracted by her and had intercourse with her, and fortified the hill where she lived by enclosing it with concentric rings of sea and land. There were two rings of land and three of sea, like cartwheels, with the island at their centre and equidistant from each other, making the place inaccessible to man (for there were still no ships or sailing in those days). He equipped the central island with godlike lavishness; he made two springs flow, one of hot and one of cold water, and caused the earth to grow abundant produce of every kind. He begot five pairs of male twins, brought them up, and divided the island of Atlantis into ten parts which he distributed between them. He allotted the elder of the eldest pair of twins his mother's home district and the   114
land surrounding it, the biggest and best allocation, and made him King over the others; the others he made governors, each of a populous and large territory. He gave them all names. The eldest, the King, he gave a name from which the whole island and surrounding ocean took their

designation of 'Atlantic', deriving it from Atlas the first King. His twin, to whom was allocated the furthest part of the island towards the Pillars of Heracles and facing the district now called Gadira, was called in Greek Eumelus but in his own language Gadirus, which is presumably the origin of the present name. Of the second pair he called one Ampheres and the other Euaemon. The elder of the third pair was called Mneseus, the younger Autochthon, the elder of the fourth Elasippus, the younger Mestor; the name given to the elder of the fifth pair was Azaes, to the younger Dia-prepes. They and their descendants for many generations governed their own territories and many other islands in the ocean and, as has already been said, also controlled the populations this side of the straits as far as Egypt and Tyrrhenia. Atlas had a long and distinguished line of descend-ants, eldest son succeeding eldest son and maintaining the succession unbroken for many generations; their wealth was greater than that pos-sessed by any previous dynasty of kings or likely to be accumulated by any later, and both in the city and countryside they were provided with everything they could require. Because of the extent of their power they received many imports, but for most of their needs the island itself pro-vided. It had mineral resources from which were mined both solid ma-terials and metals, including one metal which survives today only in name, but was then mined in quantities in a number of localities in the island, orichalc, in those days the most valuable metal except gold. There was a plentiful supply of timber for structural purposes, and every kind of animal domesticated and wild, among them numerous elephants. For there was plenty of grazing for this largest and most voracious of beasts, as well as for all creatures whose habitat is marsh, swamp and river, mountain or plain. Besides all this, the earth bore freely all the aromatic substances it bears today, roots, herbs, bushes and gums exuded by flowers or fruit. There were cultivated crops, cereals which provide our staple diet, and pulse (to use its generic name) which we need in addition to feed us; there were the fruits of trees, hard to store but providing the drink and food and oil which give us pleasure and relaxation and which we serve after supper as a welcome refreshment to the weary when appetite is satis-fied—all these were produced by that sacred island, then still beneath the sun, in wonderful quality and profusion.

This then was the island's natural endowment, and the inhabitants proceeded to build temples, palaces, harbours and docks, and to organize the country as a whole in the following manner. Their first work was to bridge the rings of water round their mother's original home, so forming a road to and from their palace. This palace they proceeded to build at once in a place where the gods and their ancestors had lived, and each successive king added to its beauties, doing his best to surpass his pre-decessors, until they had made a residence whose size and beauty were astonishing to see. They began by digging a canal three hundred feet wide, a hundred feet deep and fifty stades long from the sea to the out-ermost ring, thus making it accessible from the sea like a harbour; and they made the entrance to it large enough to admit the largest ships. At the bridges they made channels through the rings of land which separated those of water, large enough to admit the passage of a single trireme, and roofed over to make an underground tunnel; for the rims of the rings were of some height above sea-level. The largest of the rings, to which there was access from the sea, was three stades in breadth and the ring of land within it the same. Of the second pair the ring of water was two stades in breadth, and the ring of land again equal to it, while the ring of water running immediately round the central island was a stade across. The diameter of the island on which the palace was situated was five stades. It and the rings and the bridges (which were a hundred feet broad) were enclosed by a stone wall all round, with towers and gates guarding the bridges on either side where they crossed the water. The stone for them, which was white, black and yellow, they cut out of the central island and the outer and inner rings of land, and in the process excavated pairs of hollow docks with roofs of rock. Some of their buildings were of a single colour, in others they mixed different coloured stone to divert the eye and afford them appropriate pleasure. And they covered the whole circuit of the outermost wall with a veneer of bronze, they fused tin over the inner wall and orichalc gleaming like fire over the wall of the acropolis itself.

The construction of the palace within the acropolis was as follows. In the centre was a shrine sacred to Poseidon and Cleito, surrounded by a golden wall through which entry was forbidden, as it was the place where the family of the ten kings was conceived and begotten; and there year by year seasonal offerings were made from the ten provinces to each one of them. There was a temple of Poseidon himself, a stade in length, three hundred feet wide and proportionate in height, though somewhat out-landish in appearance. The outside of it was covered all over with silver, except for the figures on the pediment which were covered with gold. Inside, the roof was ivory picked out with gold, silver and orichalc, and all the walls, pillars, and floor were covered with orichalc. It contained gold statues of the god standing in a chariot drawn by six winged horses, so tall that his head touched the roof, and round him, riding on dolphins, a hundred Nereids (that being the accepted number of them at the time), as well as many other statues dedicated by private persons. Round the temple were statues of the original ten kings and their wives, and many others dedicated by kings and private persons belonging to the city and its dominions. There was an altar of a size and workmanship to match that of the building and a palace equally worthy of the greatness of the empire and the magnificence of its temples. The two springs, cold and hot, provided an unlimited supply of water for appropriate purposes, remarkable for its agreeable quality and excellence; and this they made available by surrounding it with suitable buildings and plantations, leading some of it into basins in the open air and some of it into covered hot baths for winter use. Here separate accommodation was provided for royalty and for commoners, and, again, for women, for horses and for other beasts of burden, appropriately equipped in each case. The outflow they led into the grove of Poseidon, which (because of the goodness of the soil) was full of trees of marvellous beauty and height, and also channelled it to the outer ring-islands by aqueducts at the bridges. On each of these ring-islands they had built many temples for different gods, and many gardens and areas for exercise, some for men and some for horses. On the middle of the larger island in particular there was a special course for horse-racing; its width was a stade and its length that of a complete circuit of the island, which was reserved for it. Round it on both sides were barracks for the main body of the king's bodyguard. A more select body of the more trustworthy were stationed on the smaller island ring nearer the citadel, and the most trustworthy of all had quarters assigned to them in the citadel and were attached to the king's person.

Finally, there were dockyards full of triremes and their equipment, all in good shape.

So much then for the arrangement of the royal residence and its environs. Beyond the three outer harbours there was a wall, beginning at the sea and running right round in a circle, at a uniform distance of fifty stades from the largest ring and harbour and returning on itself at the mouth of the canal to the sea. This wall was densely built up all round with houses and the canal and large harbour were crowded with vast numbers of merchant ships from all quarters, from which rose a constant din of shouting and noise day and night.

I have given you a pretty complete account of what was told me about the city and its original buildings; I must now try to recall the nature and organization of the rest of the country. To begin with the region as a whole was said to be high above the level of the sea, from which it rose precipitously; the city was surrounded by a uniformly flat plain, which was in turn enclosed by mountains which came right down to the sea. This plain was rectangular in shape, measuring three thousand stades in length and at its mid-point two thousand stades in breadth from the coast. This whole area of the island faced south, and was sheltered from the north winds. The mountains which surrounded it were celebrated as being more numerous, higher and more beautiful than any which exist today; and in them were numerous villages and a wealthy population, as well as rivers and lakes and meadows, which provided ample pasture for all kinds of domesticated and wild animals, and a plentiful variety of woodland to supply abundant timber for every kind of manufacture.

Over a long period of time the work of a number of kings had effected certain modifications in the natural features of the plain. It was naturally a long, regular rectangle; and any defects in its shape were corrected by means of a ditch dug round it. The depth and breadth and length of this may sound incredible for an artificial structure when compared with others of a similar kind, but I must give them as I heard them. The depth was a hundred feet, the width a stade, and the length, since it was dug right round the plain, was ten thousand stades. The rivers which flowed down from the mountains emptied into it, and it made a complete circuit of the plain, running round to the city from both directions, and there discharging into the sea. Channels about a hundred feet broad were cut from the ditch's landward limb straight across the plain, at a distance of a hundred stades from each other, till they ran into it on its seaward side. They cut cross channels between them and also to the city, and used the whole complex to float timber down from the mountains and transport seasonal produce by boat. They had two harvests a year, a winter one for which they relied on rainfall and a summer one for which the channels, fed by the rivers, provided irrigation.

The distribution of man-power was as follows: each allotment of land was under obligation to furnish one leader of a military detachment. Each allotment was ten square stades in size and there were in all 60,000 allotments; there was an unlimited supply of men in the mountains and other parts of the country and they were assigned by district and village to the leaders of the allotments. The leader was bound to provide a sixth part of the equipment of a war chariot, up to a total complement of 10,000, with two horses and riders; and in addition a pair of horses without a chariot, a charioteer to drive them and a combatant with light shield to ride with him, two hoplites, two archers and two slingers, three light-armed stone throwers and three javelin men, and four sailors as part of the complement of twelve hundred ships. Such were the military dispositions of the royal city; those of the other nine varied in detail and it would take too long to describe them.

Their arrangements for the distribution of authority and office were the following. Each of the ten kings had absolute power, in his own region and city, over persons and in general over laws, and could punish or execute at will. But the distribution of power between them and their mutual relations were governed by the injunctions of Poseidon, enshrined in the law and engraved by the first kings on an orichalc pillar in the temple of Poseidon in the middle of the island. Here they assembled alternately every fifth and sixth year (thereby showing equal respect to both odd and even numbers), consulted on matters of mutual interest and inquired into and gave judgement on any wrong committed by any of them. And before any prospective judgement they exchanged mutual pledges in the following ceremony. There were in the temple of Poseidon bulls roaming at large. The ten kings, after praying to the god that they might secure a sacrifice that would please him, entered alone and started a hunt for a bull, using clubs and nooses but no metal weapon; and when they caught him they cut his throat over the top of the pillar so that the blood flowed over the inscription. And on the pillar there was engraved, in addition to the laws, an oath invoking awful curses on those who disobeyed it. When they had finished the ritual of sacrifice and were consecrating the limbs of the bull, they mixed a bowl of wine and dropped in a clot of blood for each of them, before cleansing the pillar and burning the rest of the blood. After this they drew wine from the bowl in golden cups, poured a libation over the fire and swore an oath to give judgements in accordance with the laws written on the pillar, to punish any past offences, never knowingly in future to transgress what was written, and finally neither to give nor obey orders unless they were in accordance with the laws of their father. Each one of them swore this oath on his own behalf and that of his descendants, and after drinking dedicated his cup to the god's temple. There followed an interval for supper and necessary business, and then when darkness fell and the sacrificial fire had died down they all put on the most splendid dark blue ceremonial robes and sat on the ground by the embers of the sacrificial fire, in the dark, all glimmer of fire in the sanctuary being extinguished. And thus they gave and submitted to judgement on any complaints of wrong made against them; and afterwards, when it was light, wrote the terms of the judgement on gold plates which they dedicated together with their robes as a record. And among many other special laws governing the privileges of the kings the most important were that they should never make war on each other, but come to each other's help if any of them were threatened with a dissolution of the power of the royal house in his state; in that case, they should follow the custom of their predecessors and consult mutually about policy for war and other matters, recognizing the suzerainty of the house

120

of Atlas. But the King of that house should have no authority to put any of his fellows to death without the consent of a majority of the ten.

This was the nature and extent of the power which existed then in those parts of the world and which god brought to attack our country. His reason, so the story goes, was this. For many generations, so long as the divine element in their nature survived, they obeyed the laws and loved the divine to which they were akin. They retained a certain greatness of mind, and treated the vagaries of fortune and one another with wisdom and forbearance, as they reckoned that qualities of character were far more important than their present prosperity. So they bore the burden of their wealth and possessions lightly, and did not let their high standard of living intoxicate them or make them lose their self-control, but saw soberly and clearly that all these things flourish only on a soil of common goodwill and individual character, and if pursued too eagerly and overvalued destroy themselves and morality with them. So long as these principles and their divine nature remained unimpaired the prosperity which we have described continued to grow.

But when the divine element in them became weakened by frequent admixture with mortal stock, and their human traits became predominant, they ceased to be able to carry their prosperity with moderation. To the perceptive eye the depth of their degeneration was clear enough, but to those whose judgement of true happiness is defective they seemed, in their pursuit of unbridled ambition and power, to be at the height of their fame and fortune. And the god of gods, Zeus, who reigns by law, and whose eye can see such things, when he perceived the wretched state of this admirable stock decided to punish them and reduce them to order by discipline.

He accordingly summoned all the gods to his own most glorious abode, which stands at the centre of the universe and looks out over the whole realm of change, and when they had assembled addressed them as follows: . . .

At this point the *Critias* breaks off. Plutarch claimed that Plato died before he could complete the work; Francis Cornford believed Plato abandoned a planned trilogy *(Timaeus, Critias, Hermocrates)* midway through the *Critias* and turned to writing the *Laws* instead. See the discussion at the opening of Part III.

Calibrating Carbon-14 Dates

Radioactive carbon, "carbon-14," is present in all living things, and the moment a plant or animal dies, its supply of radiocarbon steadily begins to disintegrate. It should therefore be possible to calculate how long organic material has been dead by comparing the amount of carbon-14 it contains at the present time with the radiocarbon ratio in the same species today — provided, of course, that the level of radioactive carbon in the earth's atmosphere has remained constant throughout prehistory.

When carbon-14 dating techniques were being developed in the 1950s, one of the main assumptions upon which they were based was that there had indeed been precisely as much radiocarbon in a plant or animal living five or ten thousand years ago as there is today. But more recent work with tree rings, which reveals a difference between carbon-14 dates and the true age of events in prehistory, has shown this to be an incorrect assumption. It now appears that the amount of carbon-14 in the atmosphere increases as one goes back in time from the beginning of the Christian era. Samples of organic material from earlier periods therefore contain more radiocarbon than their present day counterparts, which were used as the standards of measurement, and consequently, the ancient samples give carbon-14 readings which are too recent, too "young" in terms of calendar time.

Radiocarbon dates in the fifth millennium B.C. are now known to be as many as six to eight hundred years too young, with carbon-14 readings of c. 4700 B.C. corrected to approximately 5300 B.C.[335] Beyond that point, however, the actual age of prehistoric events can only be estimated. Although the most ancient bristlecone pines, the main trees used in dendrochronology, are the oldest living things on earth, the matching of the rings of standing and fallen trees can presently take us no further than the early sixth millennium B.C.

The curve of corrections or "calibrations" of radiocarbon readings to that time is illustrated in the graph at figure 150, which is taken from a recent review of progress in the field.[126] Shown here as well are four different lines of extension that the curve conceivably could follow beyond this known point. Lines I and II represent the predictable paths if the deviation between carbon-14 dates and calendar time continues to increase indefinitely. Either of these possibilities would move radiocarbon dates around 8500 B.C. back at least a millennium, placing an event such as the mid-ninth-millennium eruption of tanged points very close to the c. 9600 B.C. date given in the *Critias* for the onset of war. In the opinion of the analyst, however, these are not necessarily the most likely of the alternatives he has presented.

Line III shows the path taken if the variations in the amount of radiocarbon in the atmosphere form a regular sine curve, with a period of around 15,000 years. In this case carbon-14 dates of 8500 B.C. might be only six to eight hundred years too young, still not a bad correlation between the timing of the tanged point complexes and the date given in the *Critias* for the outbreak of war. The analyst sees this third line as a more plausible path than I or II, but he considers Line IV to be a definite possibility as well. Here the variation of carbon-14 dates traces an irregular curve, requiring a step-by-step calibration. Although it would be the most difficult model with which to work, an erratic pattern such as that represented by this fourth line is particularly likely if the amount of

150 Chart showing the correction of carbon-14 dates to the sixth millennium B.C., and four possible paths taken by the calibration curve beyond that point *(after Evin, 1979)*

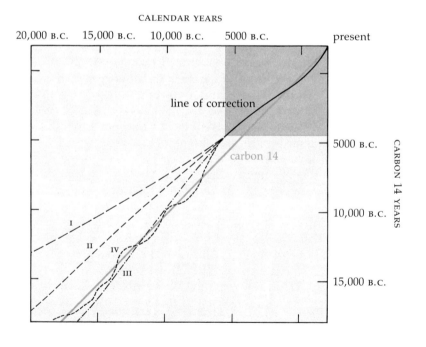

CALENDAR YEARS

20,000 B.C.   15,000 B.C.   10,000 B.C.   5000 B.C.   present

line of correction

carbon 14

5000 B.C.

10,000 B.C.

15,000 B.C.

CARBON 14 YEARS

I

II   IV

III

radiocarbon in the atmosphere is affected by climate, and especially by sudden climatic change, as several investigators suspect. If this relationship does exist, carbon-14 variability will have been particularly great during the transition from glacial to postglacial conditions, for the millennia between 10,000 and 7000 B.C. saw a series of warm-cool oscillations (fig. 151) that are unmatched for their abruptness (and for which, incidentally, no explanation has yet been found).[315, 386]

A word should also be said here about the reliability of carbon-14 dates per se. It obviously does no good to calibrate carbon-14 dates that are themselves inconsistent. Radiocarbon readings have proved unreliable often enough to give archaeologists pause unless a large series of dates shows itself to be internally consistent,[339, 328] and even the general rule that the more carbon-14 dates for an event, the greater the level of confidence, is not always applicable. Of two dates picked from the series of radiocarbon readings at Jarmo, one showed the settlement to have been founded around 6750 B.C., the other around 4750 B.C., and each had a cluster of other carbon-14 dates around it.[43] Such a disparity shows with what caution not only isolated readings but all carbon-14 dates must still be viewed.

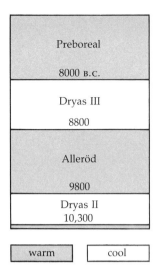

warm | cool

151 Climatic changes at end of Pleistocene era

APPENDIX C

Asiatic Art: "the nature of Nature"

The writings of Indian scholar and former Harvard lecturer Ananda Coomaraswamy are invaluable for any westerner seeking to understand oriental art. Frequently taking as his example the Ch'an or Zen art of China and Japan, Coomaraswamy notes that the art of the east is "ideally" determined, not in the popular sense of sentimental or romantic idealization, but in the mathematical sense. It reveals the operation rather than the appearance of Nature, "the operation of spirit in life-movement" (Hsieh Ho).[80] Personal feelings and passions are out of place; the oriental artist strives instead for a complete identification with his theme, a pure absorption acquired by techniques of mental discipline that are rooted in both ancient Taoism and the yoga practices of India. (That a similar approach was known, if rarely taken, in Europe is evident in Dante's *Canzone XVI:* "Who paints a figure, if he cannot be it, cannot draw it.")

Often playful and humorous, this intuitive or "mystical" Asiatic art invites the viewer as well as the creator to experience the workings of the spirit in the natural world, the artist through his subject, the observer through the painting itself:

Just as the original intuition arose from a self-identification of the artist with the appointed theme, so aesthetic experience, reproduction, arises from a self-identification of the spectator with the presented matter; criticism repeats the process of creation.[80]

Neither experience is possible, however, until the mental and affective barriers to the perception of truth are dissolved, until "all knots of the heart are undone." Oriental art is therefore a means of self-transcendence for both creator and critic, and in this sense an initiatory vehicle of great age.

If these observations have any relevance to the interpretation of Magdalenian art, so too may the Asiatic distinction between conventionalism and realism. The conventions that are evident in Magdalenian painting as early as Lascaux would not, by oriental standards, negate the possibility that the finest of these Paleolithic works were intuitively conceived. As Coomaraswamy points out, art is by definition conventional; nature can only be made comprehensible by accepted conventions. Rather than as a restriction, ascertained rules may be regarded as the form assumed by liberty.[81a] The Ch'an-Zen artist has been trained according to detailed and explicit treatises on style, yet he is said more nearly to attain a perfect spontaneity of expression than any other.

Realistic art is a different matter, however, and it is here that the term decadent would be applied in eastern traditions. To reproduce a perfectly realistic figure is to give form only to the outer shell of the species, to exclude the formative idea. Like Plato's true craftsman in the *Timaeus* (28), the accomplished oriental artist works from intelligible rather than perceptible models; and as intelligible forms are invisible—or "visible only to the intelligence which sits at the helm of the soul" (*Phaedrus* 247)—it is through contemplation and not by observation alone that the authentic work of art is achieved.[81b] (Plato's lesser artist "knows nothing of the reality but only the appearance" [*Republic* 601].) A painting that merely reproduces the sense world is both incomplete and incorrect; according to Coomaraswamy, "the more an image is 'true to nature,' the more it lies."[80]

At what point Magdalenian art became realistic rather than, or as well as, conventional must be decided by those prehistorians who are most familiar with the cave paintings. We would only note that by the end of the eleventh millennium the art of the Magdalenians had become comparable to "excellent photographs,"[237] and by the end of the tenth was clearly on the decline.

BIBLIOGRAPHY

Classical Authors Cited in the Text

Apollodorus. *The Library*
Aristotle. *Metaphysics*
—— *Meteorologica*
Callimachus. *Hymn to Zeus*
Cicero. *De Natura Deorum*
Diodorus Siculus. *The Historical Library*
Diogenes Laertius. *Lives of Eminent Philosophers* (Prologue)
Euripides. *The Cretans* (frag.)
Eusebius. *Chronica*
Herodotus. *The Histories*
Hesiod. *Theogony*
Homer. *Odyssey*
Iamblichus. *On the Mysteries*
Nonnus. *Dionysiaca*
Plato. *Critias*
—— *Laws*
—— *Phaedo*
—— *Phaedrus*
—— *Republic*
—— *Statesman*
—— *Timaeus*
Pliny. *Natural History*
Plutarch. *De Iside et Osiride*
—— *On the Ei at Delphi*
—— *The Lives of Noble Grecians and Romans* (Life of Solon)
Porphyry. *De Abstinentia*
—— *Vita Pythagorae*
Proclus. *Commentary on the Timaeus*
Strabo. *Geography*

Contemporary Authors Cited in the Text

1 AL-A'DAMI, K. A. "Excavations at Tell es-Sawwan, Second Season."
   Sumer 24 (1968): 54-94.
2 ANATI, E. *Palestine Before the Hebrews*. New York, 1963.

3 ANDERSON, J. E. "Late Paleolithic Skeletal Remains from Nubia."
The Prehistory of Nubia II, F. Wendorf, ed. Dallas, 1968. 996-1040.

4 ANGEL, J. L. "Early Neolithic Skeletons from Çatal Hüyük. Demography and Pathology." *Anatolian Studies* 21 (1971): 77-98.

5 ARKELL, A. J. *Early Khartoum.* Oxford, 1949.
6 —— *The Prehistory of the Nile Valley.* Köln, 1975.

7 ARKELL, A. J. and P. J. UCKO. "Review of Predynastic Development in the Nile Valley." *Current Anthropology* 6 (1965): 145-65.

8 AURENCHE, O., J. CAUVIN, M.-C. CAUVIN, L. COPELAND, F. HOURS, and P. SANLAVILLE. "Chronologie et organisation de l'espace dans le Proche Orient de 12,000 à 5600 AV. J.-C." *Préhistoire du Levant.* Coll. Intern. du C. N. R. S. 598 (1981): 571-78.

9 BAHN, P. G. "The 'Unacceptable Face' of the West European Upper Paleolithic." *Antiquity* 52 (1978): 183-92.

10 BAILEY, C. *Phases in the Religion of Ancient Rome.* Berkeley, 1972.

11 BAR-YOSEF, O. "Prehistory of the Levant." *Annual Review of Anthropology* 9 (1980): 101-33.
12 —— "The Epipaleolithic Complexes in the Southern Levant." *Préhistoire du Levant.* Coll. Intern. du C. N. R. S. 598 (1981): 389-408.
13 —— "The 'Pre-Pottery Neolithic' Period in the Southern Levant." *Préhistoire du Levant.* Coll. Intern. du C. N. R. S. 598 (1981): 555-69.

14 BAR-YOSEF, O., A. GOPHER, and A. N. GORING-MORRIS. "Netiv Hagdud: a 'Sultanian' Mound in the Lower Jordan Valley." *Paléorient* 6 (1980): 201-6.

15 BAR-YOSEF, O., and N. GOREN. "Natufian Remains in Hayonim Cave." *Paléorient* 1 (1973): 49-71.

16 BARICH, B. "Neue Ausgrabungen im Acacus-Gebirge." *Sahara.* Köln, 1978. 222-45.

17 BARTLETT, J. R. *Jericho.* London, 1982.

18 BENDER, B. "Gatherer-hunter to Farmer: a Social Perspective." *World Archaeology* 10 (1978): 204-22.

19 BENVENISTE, E. *The Persian Religion According to the Chief Greek Texts.* Paris, 1929.
20 —— *Les Mages dans l'ancien Iran.* Paris, 1938.
21 —— *Indo-European Language and Society.* Miami, 1973.

22 BERGHE, L. VAN DEN. "The Rich Naturalistic Influence in Iranian Painted Pottery." *Archaeologica Viva* 1 (1968): 20-33.
23 —— *Bibliographie analytique de l'archéologie de Iran ancien.* Leiden, 1979.

24 BERNOULLI, R. "Spiritual Development as Reflected in Alchemy and Related Disciplines." *Spiritual Disciplines: Papers from the Eranos Yearbooks.* New York, 1960. 305-40.

25 BIALOR, P. "The Chipped Stone Industry of Çatal Hüyük." *Anatolian Studies* 12 (1962): 67-110.

26 BIDEZ, J. and F. CUMONT. *Les Mages hellénises.* Paris, 1938.

27 BINFORD, L. R. "Post-Pleistocene Adaptations." *New Perspectives in Archaeology,* S. R. Binford and L. R. Binford, eds. Chicago, 1968. 313-36.

28 BINTLIFF, J. L. and W. VAN ZEIST, eds. *Palaeoclimates, Palaeoenvironments, and Human Communities in the Eastern Mediterranean Region in Later Prehistory.* British Archaeological Reports Int'l Series 1, 33 (i), 1982.

29 BLEEKER, C. J. "The Egyptian Goddess Neith." *Studies in Mysticism and Religion Presented to Gershom G. Scholem.* Jerusalem, 1967. 41-56.

30 —— *Egyptian Festivals.* Leiden, 1967.

31 BLINKENBERG, C. *The Thunderweapon in Religion and Folklore.* Cambridge, 1911.

32 BOER, C. *The Homeric Hymns.* Chicago, 1970.

33 BÖKÖNYI, S. "Development of Early Stock Rearing in the Near East." *Nature* 264 (1976): 19-23.

34 —— *Animal Remains from Four Sites in the Kermanshah Valley, Iran.* British Archaeological Reports Supp. Series 34, 1977.

35 BORDES, F. *The Old Stone Age.* London, 1968.

36 BOSTANCI, E. "The Mesolithic of Beldibi and Belbaşi." *Antropoloji* 3 (1965): 91-148.

37 BOYCE, M. *A History of Zoroastrianism.* Köln, 1975.

38 —— *Zoroastrians, Their Religious Beliefs and Practices.* London, 1979.

39 —— *Textual Sources for the Study of Zoroastrianism.* Totowa, New Jersey, 1984.

40 BRAIDWOOD, L. S. and R. J. BRAIDWOOD, eds. *Prehistoric Village Archaeology in Southeast Turkey.* British Archaeological Reports Int'l Series 138, 1982.

41 BRAIDWOOD, L. S., R. J. BRAIDWOOD, B. HOWE, C. A. REED, and P. J. WATSON, eds. *Prehistoric Archaeology Along the Zagros Flanks.* Chicago, 1983.

42 BRAIDWOOD, R. J. "The Background for Sumerian Civilization in the Euphrates-Tigris-Karun Drainage Basin." *The Legacy of Sumer,* D. Schmandt-Besserat, ed. Malibu, 1976. 41-49.

43 BRAIDWOOD, R. J., B. HOWE, et al. *Prehistoric Investigation in Iraqi Kurdistan*. Chicago, 1960.

44 BRAIDWOOD, R. J. et al. "New Chalcolithic Material of Samarran Type and Its Implications." *Journal of Near Eastern Studies* 3 (1944): 47-72.

45 BRAIDWOOD, R. J., H. ÇAMBEL, and W. SCHIRMER et al. "Beginnings of Village Farming Communities in Southeastern Turkey: Çayönü Tepesi, 1978 and 1979." *Journal of Field Archaeology* 3 (1981): 249-258.

46 BERNABÒ BREA, L. *Sicily Before the Greeks*. New York, 1957.

47 BREASTED, J. H. *Development of Religion and Thought in Ancient Egypt*. New York, 1912.

48 BREUIL, H. *Four Hundred Centuries of Cave Art*. New York, 1979.

49 BUDGE, E. A. W. *The Gods of the Egyptians* I. London, 1904.
50 —— *The Book of the Dead*. British Museum, 1910.
51 —— *Osiris and the Egyptian Resurrection* I. London, 1911.

52 BURKERT, W. *Orphism and Bacchic Mysteries: New Evidence and Old Problems of Interpretation*. 28th Colloquy of the Center for Hermeneutical Studies, Berkeley, 1977.
52 —— *Greek Religion*. Cambridge, Mass., 1985.

53 BURNEY, C. A. "The Excavations at Yanik Tepe, Azerbaijan, 1962; Third Preliminary Report." *Iraq* 26 (1964): 54-61.
54 —— *From Village to Empire*. Oxford, 1977.

55 BURNEY, C. A. and D. M. LANG. *The Peoples of the Hills: Ancient Ararat and Caucasus*. London, 1971.

56 BURNHAM, H. B. "Çatal Hüyük—The Textiles and Twined Fabrics." *Anatolian Studies* 15 (1965): 169-174.

57 BUTTERFIELD, H. *The Origins of Modern Science 1300-1800*. New York, 1961.

58 BUTZER, K. W. in ARKELL and UCKO, "Review of Predynastic Development in the Nile Valley." *Current Anthropology* 6 (1965): 157.

59 ÇAMBEL, H. and R. J. BRAIDWOOD. *The Joint Istanbul-Chicago Universities' Prehistoric Research in Southeastern Anatolia* I. Istanbul, 1980.

60 CAMPS, G. *Les civilisations préhistoriques de l'Afrique du Nord et du Sahara*. Paris, 1974.
61 —— "Nouvelles remarques sur le Néolithique du Sahara central et méridional." *Libyca* 23 (1975): 123-32.
62 —— "Beginnings of Pastoralism and Cultivation in North Africa and the Sahara." *The Cambridge History of Africa* I, J. D. Clark, ed. Cambridge, 1982. 548-623.

63 CAMPS-FABRER, H. *Matière et art mobilier dans la préhistoire nord-africaine et saharienne.* Paris, 1966.

64 CASKEY, J. L. and M. ELIOT. "A Neolithic Figurine from Lerna." *Hesperia* 25 (1956): 175-77.

65 CAUVIN, J. *Religions néolithiques de Syro-Palestine.* Paris, 1972.
66 —— "Les débuts de la céramique sur le Moyen-Euphrate: nouveaux documents." *Paléorient* 2/1 (1974): 199-205.
67 —— *Les premiers villages de Syrie-Palestine du IXème au VIIème millénaire avant J.C.* Paris, 1978.
68 —— "Les fouilles de Mureybet (1971-1974) et leur signification pour les origines de la sedentarisation au Proche-Orient." *Archaeological Reports from the Tabqa Dam Project—Euphrates Valley, Syria,* 1979. 19-48.

69 CAUVIN, M.-C. "Flèches à encoches de Syria—essai de classification et d'interprétation culturelle." *Paléorient* 2/2 (1974): 311-22.
70 —— "Outillage lithique et chronologie à Tell Aswad." *Paléorient* 2/2 (1974): 429-36.

71 CHILDE, V. G. *Man Makes Himself.* London, 1936.

72 CHRISTENSEN, A. *Les types du premier Homme et du premier Roi dans l'histoire legendaire des Iraniens* II. Uppsala, 1934.

73 CLARK, J. D. "Prehistoric Cultural Continuity and Economic Change in the Central Sudan in the Early Holocene." *From Hunters to Farmers,* J. D. Clark and S. A. Brandt, eds. Berkeley, 1984. 113-126.

74 CLUTTON-BROCK, J. "The Mammalian Remains from the Jericho Tell." *Proceedings of the Prehistoric Society* 45 (1979): 135-57.

75 COLES, J. M. and E. S. HIGGS. *The Archaeology of Early Man.* New York, 1969.

76 COLLINS, DESMOND. *The Origins of Europe.* New York, 1976.

77 CONTENSEN, H. DE. "New Correlations Between Ras Shamra and Al-Amuq." *Bulletin of the American Schools of Oriental Research* 172 (1963): 35-40.
78 —— "Tell Aswad (Damascène)." *Paléorient* 5 (1979): 153-56.

79 COOK, A.B. *Zeus* I-III. Cambridge, 1914–40.

80 COOMARASWAMY, A. K. *The Transformation of Nature in Art.* Cambridge, Mass., 1934.
81 —— "Symplegades." *Coomaraswamy* I, R. Lipsey, ed. Princeton, 1977. 521-44.
81[a] —— "Introduction to the Art of Eastern Asia." *Coomaraswamy* I, R. Lipsey, ed. Princeton, 1977. 101-127.
81[b] —— "A Figure of Speech or a Figure of Thought?" *Coomaraswamy* I, R. Lipsey, ed. Princeton, 1977. 13-42.

82 CORBIN, H. "Le récit d'initiation et l'hermetisme en Iran." *Eranos Jahrbuch* 17 (1949): 121-87.

83 —— "Terre céleste et corps de résurrection d'après quelques traditions Iraniennes." *Eranos Jahrbuch* 22 (1953): 97-194.

84 —— "Cyclical Time in Mazdaism and Ismailism." *Man and Time: Papers from the Eranos Yearbooks*. London, 1958. 115-72.

85 CORNFORD, F. *From Religion to Philosophy*. London, 1912.

86 —— *Plato's Cosmology*. London, 1937.

87 —— *Principium Sapientiae: The Origins of Greek Philosophical Thought*. Cambridge, 1952.

88 —— "Mystery Religions and Pre-Socratic Philosophy." *Cambridge Ancient History* IV (1953): 522-78.

89 CROWFOOT-PAYNE, J. "The Terminology of the Aceramic Neolithic Period in the Levant." *9th Int'l Congress of Prehistoric and Protohistoric Sciences, Nice* 3 (1976): 131-37.

90 —— "The Flint Industries of Jericho." *Excavations at Jericho* V, K. M. Kenyon and T. A. Holland, eds. London, 1983. 622-758.

91 CUMONT, F. *The Mysteries of Mithra*. London, 1903.

92 DARMESTETER, J. *The Zend-Avesta*. Oxford, 1895.

93 DASTUGUE, J, and M.-A. DE LUMLEY. "Les maladies des hommes préhistoriques du Paléolithique et du Mésolithique." *La préhistoire française*. Paris, 1976. 612-22.

94 DAVIS, G. M. N. *The Asiatic Dionysos*. London, 1914.

95 DECHEND, H. VON. "Bemerkungen zum Donnerkeil." *Prismata: Festschrift für Willi Hartner*. Weisbaden, 1977.

96 DELOUGAZ, P. and H. J. KANTOR. "New Evidence for the Prehistoric and Protoliterate Culture Development of Khuzistan." *Fifth Int'l Congress of Iranian Art and Archaeology, Tehran, 1968* 1 (1972): 14-25.

97 DIETRICH, B. C. *The Origins of Greek Religion*. New York, 1974.

98 DIMBLEBY, G. W. in D. WILSON, *The New Archaeology*. New York, 1975.

99 DOLUKHANOV, P. M. *Ecology and Economy in Neolithic Eastern Europe*. London, 1979.

100 DONNELLY, IGNATIUS. *Atlantis: The Antediluvian World*. New York, 1949 (1882).

101 DORRELL, P. G. "Stone Vessels, Tools, and Objects." *Excavations at Jericho* V, K. M. Kenyon and T. A. Holland, eds. London, 1983. 485-515.

102 DUCHESNE-GUILLEMIN, J. *The Hymns of Zarathustra*. London, 1952.

103 —— *The Western Response to Zoroaster*. Oxford, 1958.

104 —— *Symbols and Values in Zoroastrianism*. New York, 1966.

105 DUCOS, P. "A New Find of an Equid Metatarsal Bone from Tell Mureybet in Syria and its Relevance to the Identification of Equids from the Early Holocene of the Levant." *Journal of Archaeological Science* 2 (1975): 71-73.

106 DUMEZIL, G. *The Destiny of the Warrior*. Chicago, 1970.

107 DUNAND, M. "Rapport préliminaire sur les fouilles de Byblos." *Bulletin au Musée de Beyrouth* 12 (1955): 7-23.

108 DYSON, R. H. "Problems in the Relative Chronology of Iran, 6000-2000 B.C." *Chronologies in Old World Archaeology*, R. W. Ehrlich, ed. Chicago, 1965. 215-56.
109 —— "Annotations and Corrections of the Relative Chronology of Iran, 1968." *American Journal of Archaeology* 72/4 (1968): 308-12.
110 —— "A Decade in Iran." *Expedition* 11 (1969): 42-3.

111 EISLER, R. *Orpheus the Fisher*. London, 1921.
112 —— "L'origine babylonienne de l'alchimie." *Revue de Synthèse Historique* 25 (1926): 5-25.

113 ELIADE, M. *The Myth of the Eternal Return*. Princeton, 1954.
114 —— *Images and Symbols*. London, 1961.
115 —— *Myth and Reality*. New York, 1963.
116 —— *Shamanism: Archaic Techniques of Ecstasy*. New York, 1964.
117 —— *The Forge and the Crucible: The Origins and Structures of Alchemy*. New York, 1971.
118 —— *Rites and Symbols of Initiation*. New York, 1975.
119 —— *A History of Religious Ideas* I. Chicago, 1978.
120 —— *A History of Religious Ideas* II. Chicago, 1982.

121 EMERY, W. B. *Archaic Egypt*. Baltimore, 1961.

122 ESCALON DE FONTON, M. "From the End of the Ice Age to the First Agriculturalists: 10,000–4000 B.C." *France Before the Romans*, S. Piggot, ed. London, 1973. 61-101.

123 EVANS, J. D. "Excavations in the Neolithic Settlement of Knossos, 1957–1960. Part I." *Annual of the British School at Athens* 59 (1964): 132-240.
124 —— "Neolithic Knossos—the Growth of a Settlement." *Proceedings of the Prehistoric Society* 37/2 (1971): 95-117.

125 EVANS, J. *The Ancient Stone Implements, Weapons, and Armaments of Great Britain*. New York, 1872.

126 EVIN, J. "Réflexions générales et données nouvelles sur la chronologie absolue 14C des industries de la fin du Paléolithique Supérieur et du début du Mésolithique." *La fin des temps glaciaires en Europe*. Coll. Intern. du C. N. R. S. 271/1 (1979): 5-13.

127 FAIRSERVIS, W. A. *The Threshold of Civilization*. New York, 1975.

128 FARNELL, L. R. *The Cults of the Greek States* I–IV. Oxford, 1896-1909.

129 FEREMBACH, D. "Les Cro-Magnoides de l'Afrique du Nord." *L'Homme de Cro-Magnon*, G. Camps, ed. Paris, 1970, 81-92.

130 —— "L'évolution humaine au Proche-Orient." *Paléorient* 1/2 (1973): 213-20.

131 FILLIOZAT, J. *The Classical Doctrine of Indian Medicine: Its Origins and Its Greek Parallels*. Delhi, 1964.

132 FONTENROSE, J. *Python: A Study of Delphic Myth and Origin*. Berkeley, 1980.

133 FORBES, A., JR. and T. R. CROWDER. "The Problem of Franco-Cantabrian Abstract Signs: Agenda for a New Approach." *World Archaeology* 10 (1979): 350-66.

134 FORBES, R. J. "The Origin of Alchemy." *Studies in Ancient Technology* I. Leiden, 1955. 121-44.

135 FORMOZOV, A. A. "The Petroglyphs of Kobystan and Their Chronology." *Rivista di scienze preistorichi* XVIII (1963): 91-114.

136 —— "Ocherki pervobitnomy iskusstvy." *Materialy i Issledovanija po Arkheologii SSSR* 165 (1969): 24-59. (in Russian)

137 FORSYTH, P. Y. *Atlantis: The Making of a Myth*. Montreal, 1980.

138 FRANKFORT, H. *Kingship and the Gods*. Chicago, 1948.

139 FRAZER, J. G. *Pausanias and Other Greek Sketches*. London, 1900.

140 —— translator, *Apollodorus Atheniensis. The Library*. New York, 1921.

141 FREDERICKS, S. C. "Plato's Atlantis: A Mythologist Looks at Myth." *Atlantis: Fact or Fiction?* E. S. Ramage, ed. Bloomington, 1978. 82-99.

142 FRENCH, D. H. "Excavations at Can Hasan." *Anatolian Studies* 12 (1962): 27-40.

143 FRENCH, D. H., G. C. HILLMAN, S. PAYNE, and R. J. PAYNE. "Excavations at Can Hasan III, 1969–1970." *Papers in Economic Prehistory*, E. S. Higgs, ed. Cambridge, 1972, 180-90.

144 FRIEDLANDER, P. *Plato*. Princeton, 1958.

145 FRYE, R. N. *The Heritage of Persia*. Cleveland, 1963.

145ª FURTWÄNGLER, A. and K. REICHHOLD. *Griechische Vasenmalerei*. Munich, 1904-1932.

146 GALANOPOULAS, A. G. and E. BACON. *Atlantis: The Truth Behind the Legend*. London, 1969.

147 GARAŠANIN, M. "The Stone Age in the Central Balkan Area." *Cambridge Ancient History* III/I (1982): 75-135.

148 GARRARD, A. N. "The Environmental Implications of a Re-Analysis of the Large Mammal Fauna from the Wadi El-Mughara Caves, Palestine." *Palaeoclimates, Palaeoenvironments*

and Human Communities in the Eastern Mediterranean Region in Later Prehistory. J. L. Bintliff and W. Van Zeist, eds. British Archaeological Reports Int'l Series I, 33 (1), 1982. 165-87.

149 GARROD, D. A. E. *The Stone Age of Mount Carmel*. Oxford, 1937.
150 —— *The Natufian Culture*. London, 1957.

151 GARSTANG, J. *Prehistoric Mersin*. Oxford, 1953.

152 GASTER, T. H. *Thespis: Ritual, Myth and Drama in the Ancient Near East*. New York, 1950.

153 GEIGER, W. *Civilization of the Eastern Iranians in Ancient Times*. London, 1885.
154 —— *The Age of the Avesta and Zoroaster*. London, 1886.
155 —— *Zarathustra in the Gathas*. Bombay, 1899.

156 GERSHEVITCH, I. *The Avestan Hymn to Mithra*. Cambridge, 1959.

157 GHIRSHMAN, R. *Fouilles de Tepe Sialk* I. Paris, 1938.

158 GIMBUTAS, M. "Proto-Indo-European Culture: The Kurgan Culture During the Fifth, Fourth and Third Millennia B.C." *Indo-European and Indo-Europeans*, G. Cordona et al, eds. Philadelphia, 1970. 155-97.
159 —— "Old Europe c. 7000–3500 B.C.: The Earliest European Civilization Before the Infiltration of the Indo-European Peoples." *Journal of Indo-European Studies* 1/1 (1973): 1-20.
160 —— *The Gods and Goddesses of Old Europe*. London, 1974.
161 —— "The Temples of Old Europe." *Archaeology* 33 (1980): 41-50.
162 —— "The 'Monstrous Venus' of Prehistory or Goddess Creatrix." *The Comparative Civilizations Review No. 7*, Bulletin 10/3 (1981): 1-26.

163 GOFF, B. L. *Symbols of Prehistoric Mesopotamia*. New Haven, 1963.

164 GRAVES, R. *The Greek Myths* I. London, 1955.

165 GREEN, P. *Ancient Greece*. London, 1973.

166 GUTHRIE, W. K. C. *Orpheus and the Greek Religion*. New York, 1934.
167 —— *The Greeks and Their Gods*. Boston, 1950.
168 —— "Early Greek Religion in the Light of the Decipherment of Linear B." *Bulletin of the Institute of Classical Studies* 6 (1959): 35-46.

169 HADINGHAM, E. *Secrets of the Ice Age: the World of the Cave Artists*. New York, 1979.

170 HANSEN, J. and J. M. RENFREW. "Paleolithic-Neolithic Seed Remains at Franchthi Cave, Greece." *Nature* 271 (1978): 350-52.

171 HARRIS, D. R. "New Light on Plant Domestication and the Origins of Agriculture: A Review." *The Geographical Review* 57 (1967): 90-107.

172 HARRISON, J. *Prologomena to the Study of Greek Religion*. London, 1961 (1903).

173 —— *Themis: A Study of the Social Origins of Greek Religion*. Cambridge, 1912.

174 HAUG, M. *The Origin of the Parsee Religion*. Bombay, 1861.

175 HAWKES, J. *The History of Mankind: Prehistory* I. New York, 1963.

176 HAYDEN, B. "Research and Development in the Stone Age: Technological Transitions Among Hunter-Gatherers." *Current Anthropology* 22 (1981): 519-31.

177 HEIRTZLER, J. R. and W. B. BRYAN. "The Floor of the Mid-Atlantic Rift." *Continents Adrift and Continents Aground*, J. T. Wilson, ed. San Francisco, 1975. 159-70.

178 HELBAEK, H. "The Plant Husbandry of Hacılar." *Excavations at Hacılar*, J. Mellaart, ed. Edinburgh, 1970. 189-244.

179 HEMINGWAY, M. F. *The Initial Magdalenian in France*. British Archaeological Reports, Int'l Series 90, 1980.

180 HENRY, D. O. *The Natufian of Palestine: Its Material Culture and Ecology*. Unpublished doctoral dissertation, Southern Methodist University, 1973.

181 HENRY, D. O. and A. F. SERVELLO. "Compendium of Carbon-14 Determinations Derived from Near Eastern Prehistoric Deposits." *Paléorient* 2 (1974): 19-44.

182 HERZFELD, E. E. *Zoroaster and His World*. Princeton, 1947.

183 HIGGS, E. S. and M. R. JARMAN. "The Origins of Animal and Plant Husbandry." *Papers in Economic Prehistory*, E. S. Higgs, ed. Cambridge, 1972. 3-13.

184 HIJARA, I. et al. "Arpachiyah 1976." *Iraq* 42 (1980): 131-54.

185 HINNELLS, J. R. *Persian Mythology*. London, 1973.

186 —— "Reflections on the Bull-Slaying Scene." *Mithraic Studies* II, J. R. Hinnells, ed. Manchester, 1975. 290-312.

187 HOFFMAN, M. A. *Egypt Before the Pharoahs*. New York, 1979.

188 HOLE, F. and K. V. FLANNERY. "The Prehistory of Southwestern Iran." *Proceedings of the Prehistoric Society* 33 (1967): 147-206.

189 HOLE, F., K. V. FLANNERY, J. A. NEELY, and H. HELBAEK. *Prehistory and Human Ecology of the Deh Luran Plain*. Ann Arbor, 1969.

190 HOLM, E. "The Rock Art of South Africa." *The Art of the Stone Age: Forty Thousand Years of Rock Art*, H. G. Bandi et al, eds. London, 1961. 153-203.

191 HOPF, M. "Plant Remains and Early Farming in Jericho." *The Domestication and Exploitation of Plants and Animals*, P. J. Ucko and G. W. Dimbleby, eds. Chicago, 1969. 355-59.

192 HUXLEY, A. *The Perennial Philosophy*. New York, 1945.

193 IPPOLITONI, F. "The Pottery of Tell es-Sawwan—First Season." *Mesopotamia* 5-6 (1970-71): 105-79.

194 JACKSON, A. V. W. *Zoroaster: The Prophet of Ancient Iran*. London, 1899.

195 —— *Zoroastrian Studies*. New York, 1928.

196 JACOBSEN, T. W. "Excavations at Porto Cheli and Vicinity. Preliminary Report II: The Franchthi Cave, 1967-8." *Hesperia* 38 (1969): 241-61.

197 —— "Excavations in the Franchthi Cave, 1969-1971, Parts I and II." *Hesperia* 42 (1973): 45-88, 253-83.

198 —— "17,000 Years of Greek Prehistory." *Scientific American* 234 (1976): 76-87.

199 —— "Franchthi Cave and the Beginning of Settled Village Life in Greece." *Hesperia* 50 (1981): 303-19.

200 JARMAN, M. R. "Early Animal Husbandry." *The Early History of Agriculture*. Oxford, 1977. 85-97.

201 JARMAN, M. R. and P. F. WILKINSON. "Criteria of Animal Domestication." *Papers in Economic Prehistory*, E. S. Higgs, ed. Cambridge, 1972. 83-96.

202 JARMAN, M. R., G. N. BAILEY, and H. N. JARMAN, eds. *Early European Agriculture*. Cambridge, 1982.

203 JOWETT, B. *The Dialogues of Plato*. New York, 1892.

204 JUDE, P. E. *La Grotte de Rochereil*. Archives de l'Institut de Paléontologie Humaine, Mémoire 30, 1960.

205 JULIEN, M. "Harpons unilatéraux et bilatéraux: évolution morphologique ou adaptation différenciée?" *Coll. Intern. du C. N. R. S.* 568 (1977): 177-89.

206 —— *Les harpons Magdaléniens*. Paris, 1982.

207 KAMMINGA, J. Response to Hayden in *Current Anthropology* 22 (1981): 535-36.

208 KENYON, K. M. "Excavations at Jericho—1956." *Palestine Exploration Quarterly* (1956): 67-82.

209 —— *Digging Up Jericho*. London, 1957.

210 —— "Excavations at Jericho, 1957-58." *Palestine Excavation Quarterly* (1960): 1-21.

211 KENYON, K. M. and T. A. HOLLAND. *Excavations at Jericho V*. London, 1983.

212 KIRK, G. S. *Myth: Its Meaning and Functions in Ancient and Other Cultures*. Cambridge, 1970.

213 KIRKBRIDE, D. "Beidha: Early Neolithic Village Life South of the Dead Sea." *Antiquity* 42 (1968): 263-74.

214 —— "Early Byblos and the Beqa'a." *Mélanges de l'Université St. Joseph* 45 (1969): 45-59.

215 —— "Umm Dabaghiyah: A Trading Outpost?" *Iraq* 36 (1974): 85-92.

216 —— "Umm Dabaghiyah, 1974: A Fourth Preliminary Report." *Iraq* 37 (1975): 3-10.

217 —— "Umm Dabaghiyah." *Fifty Years of Mesopotamian Discovery.* London, 1982. 11-21.

218 KLEIN, R. G. *Man and Culture in the Late Pleistocene.* San Francisco, 1969.

219 —— *Ice Age Hunters of the Ukraine.* Chicago, 1973.

220 KLIMA, B. "The First Ground-Plan of an Upper Paleolithic Loess Settlement in Middle Europe and Its Meaning." *Courses Toward Urban Life*, R. J. Braidwood and G. R. Willey, eds. New York, 1962. 193-210.

221 KOZLOWSKI, J. K. "The Problem of the So-Called Danubian Mesolithic." *The Mesolithic in Europe*, S. K. Kozlowski, ed. Warsaw, 1973. 315-30.

222 KOZLOWSKI, J. K. and S. K. KOZLOWSKI. *Upper Paleolithic and Mesolithic in Europe.* Warsaw, 1979.

223 KOZLOWSKI, S. K. "Introduction to the History of Europe in Early Holocene." *The Mesolithic in Europe*, S. K. Kozlowski, ed. Warsaw, 1973. 331-66.

224 —— *Cultural Differentiation of Europe from the 10th to 5th Millennium B.C.* Warsaw, 1975.

225 KUHN, H. "Herkunft und Heimat der Indo-germanen." *First International Congress of Prehistoric and Protohistoric Sciences, 1932.* London, 1934. 237-42.

226 KUHN, T. S. *The Structure of Scientific Revolutions.* Chicago, 1962.

227 KUPER, R. "Vom Jäger zum Hirten—Was ist das Sahara Neolithikum?" *Sahara.* Köln, 1978. 60-69.

228 LAJOUX, J-D. *The Rock Paintings of Tassili.* London, 1963.

229 LAMING-EMPERAIRE, A. *Lascaux.* Harmondsworth, 1959.

230 —— *La signification de l'art rupestre paléolithique.* Paris, 1962.

231 LEBLANC, S. A. and P. J. WATSON. "A Comparative Statistical Analysis of Painted Pottery from Seven Halafian Sites." *Paléorient* I (1973): 117-33.

232 LEE, H. D. P., translator. *Plato: Timaeus and Critias.* Harmondsworth, 1977.

233 LEE, R. B. "What Hunters Do For a Living, or, How to Make Out on Scarce Resources." *Man the Hunter*, R. B. Lee and I. Devore, eds. Chicago, 1968. 30-48.

234 LEGGE, A. J. Prehistoric Exploitation of the Gazelle in Palestine."
Papers in Economic Prehistory, E. S. Higgs, ed. Cambridge, 1972.
119-24.

235 LENORMANT, C. *Élite des monuments céramographiques* I. Paris,
1844.

236 LEROI-GOURHAN, A. *Les religions de la préhistoire*. Paris, 1964.
237 —— *The Art of Prehistoric Man in Western Europe*. London, 1968.
238 —— *The Dawn of European Art*. Cambridge, 1982.

239 LEROI-GOURHAN, ARL. "Analyse pollinique à Tell Aswad."
Paléorient 5 (1979): 170-76.

240 LEROI-GOURHAN, ARL., J. ALLAIN et al. *Lascaux inconnu*. Paris,
1979.

241 LEVINE, L. D. and M. M. A. MCDONALD. "The Neolithic and
Chalcolithic Periods in the Mahidasht." *Iran* 15 (1977): 39-50.

242 LHOTE, H. *The Search for the Tassili Frescoes*. New York, 1959.

243 LINCOLN, B. "The Indo-European Myth of Creation." *History of
Religions* 15 (1975): 121-45.
244 —— *Priests, Warriors, and Cattle*. Berkeley, 1981.

245 LLOYD, S. and F. SAFAR. "Tell Hassuna." *Journal of Near Eastern
Studies* 4 (1945): 255-89.

246 LOON, M. VAN. "The Oriental Institute Excavations at Mureybet,
Syria." *Journal of Near Eastern Studies* 27 (1968): 265-90.

247 LUCE J. V. *The End of Atlantis*. London, 1969.
248 —— "The Sources and Literary Form of Plato's Atlantis Narrative." *Atlantis: Fact or Fiction?* E. S. Ramage, ed., Bloomington,
1978. 50-75.

249 LUPACCIOLU, M. "The Absolute Dating of the Earliest Saharan
Rock Art." *Paideuma* 24 (1978): 43-51.

250 MAJIDZADEH, Y. "An Early Prehistoric Coppersmith Workshop
at Tepe Ghabristan." *Archaeologische Mitteilungen aus Iran*,
Ergänzungsband 6 (1979): 82-92.
251 —— "Sialk III and the Pottery Sequence at Tepe Ghabristan."
Iran 19 (1981): 141-46.

252 MALANDRA, W. W. *An Introduction to Ancient Iranian Religion*.
Minneapolis, 1983.

253 MALEKI, Y. "Abstract Art and Animal Motifs Among the Ceramics of the Region of Tehran." *Archaeologica Viva* 1 (1968): 42-50.

254 MALLORY, J. F. "A Short History of the Indo-European
Problem." *Journal of Indo-European Studies* 1/1 (1973): 21-65.
255 —— "The Chronology of the Early Kurgan Tradition, II."
Journal of Indo-European Studies 5 (1977): 339-68.

256 MALLOWAN, M. E. L. "The Excavations at Tell Chagar Bazar 1934-5." *Iraq* 3 (1936): 1-86.

257 —— "The Development of Cities from Al-'Ubaid to the End of Uruk 5." *Cambridge Ancient History* I. Cambridge, 1970. 327-462.

258 MALLOWAN, M. E. L. and J. C. ROSE. "Excavations at Tell Arpachiyah 1933." *Iraq* 2 (1935): 1-178.

259 MARINATOS, S. "Ethnic Problems Raised by Recent Discoveries on Thera." *Bronze Age Migrations in the Aegean*, R. A. Crossland and A. Birchall, eds. New Jersey, 1974. 199-202.

260 MARINGER, J. *The Gods of Prehistoric Man*. New York, 1960.
261 —— "Adorants in Prehistoric Art." *Numen* 26/2 (1979): 215-30.

262 MARINGER, J. and H. G. BANDI. *Art in the Ice Age — Spanish Levant Art — Arctic Art*. New York, 1953.

263 MARKS, A. E. "The Harif Point: A New Tool Type from the Terminal Epipaleolithic of the Central Negev, Israel." *Paléorient* 1 (1973): 97-99.

264 —— "An Outline of Prehistoric Occurrences and Chronology in the Central Negev, Israel." *Problems in Prehistory: North Africa and the Levant*, F. Wendorf and A. E. Marks, eds. Dallas, 1975. 351-61.

265 MARSHACK, A. *The Roots of Civilization*. New York, 1972.

266 MASSON, V. M. "The First Farmers in Turkmenia." *Antiquity* 35 (1961): 203-13.

267 —— "Prehistoric Settlement Patterns in Soviet Central Asia." *Man, Settlement, and Urbanism*, P. Ucko, R. Tringham, and G. W. Dimbleby, eds. London, 1972. 263-77.

268 MASSON, V. M. and V. I. SARIANDI. *Central Asia: Turkmenia Before the Achaemenids*. New York, 1972.

269 MASUDA, S. "Excavations in Iran During 1972-73: Tepe Sang-e Čaxamaq." *Iran* 12 (1974): 222-23.

270 MAYER, M. *Die Giganten und Titanen*. Berlin, 1887.

271 MCBURNEY, C. B. M. *The Haua Fteah (Cyrenaica) and the Stone Age of the South-east Mediterranean*. Cambridge, 1967.
272 —— "The Cave of Ali Tappeh and the Epi-Paleolithic in North-east Iran." *Proceedings of the Prehistoric Society* 34 (1968): 385-413.

273 MCCOWN, D. E. "The Material Culture of Early Iran." *Journal of Near Eastern Studies* 1 (1942): 424-49.

274 MELLAART, J. "Excavations at Çatal Hüyük: First Preliminary Report." *Anatolian Studies* 12 (1962): 41-65.
275 —— "Excavations at Çatal Hüyük: Second Preliminary Report." *Anatolian Studies* 13 (1963): 43-103.
276 —— "Excavations at Çatal Hüyük: Third Preliminary Report." *Anatolian Studies* 14 (1964): 39-119.

277 —— "Excavations at Çatal Hüyük: Fourth Preliminary Report." *Anatolian Studies* 16 (1966): 165-91.

278 —— *Çatal Hüyük, A Neolithic Town in Anatolia.* London, 1967.

279 —— *Excavations at Hacılar.* Edinburgh, 1970.

280 —— *The Neolithic of the Near East.* London, 1975.

281 —— *The Archaeology of Ancient Turkey.* London, 1978.

282 —— "Early Urban Communities in the Near East c. 9000-3400 B.C." *The Origins of Civilization,* P. R. S. Moorey, ed. Oxford, 1979. 22-33.

283 MERPERT, N. Y. and R. M. MUNCHAEV. "Early Agricultural Settlements in the Sinjar Plain, Northern Iraq." *Iraq* 35 (1973): 93-114.

284 MESSINA, G. *Der Ursprung der Magier und die Zarathuštrische Religion.* Rome, 1930.

285 MILLS, L. H. *The Zend-Avesta.* Part III. *Sacred Books of the East,* M. Mueller, ed. Oxford, 1887.

286 MOLE, M. "Rituel et eschatologie dans le Mazdeisme." *Numen* 7 (1960): 148-71.

287 —— *Culte, mythe et cosmologie dans l'Iran ancien.* Paris, 1963.

288 MOORE, A. M. T. "The Excavation of Tell Abu Hureyra in Syria: A Preliminary Report." *Proceedings of the Prehistoric Society* 41 (1975): 50-77.

289 —— "North Syria in Neolithic 2." *Préhistoire du Levant,* O. Aurenche et al, eds. Coll. Intern. du C. N. R. S. 598 (1981): 445-56.

290 —— "A Four-Stage Sequence for the Levantine Neolithic, ca. 8500-3750 B.C." *Bulletin of the American School of Oriental Research* 246 (1982): 1-34.

291 MORI, F. *Tadrart Acacus: arte rupestre des Sahara preistorico:* Turin, 1965.

292 —— "Brief Remarks on Cultural Evolution." *Paideuma* 24 (1978): 35-41.

293 MORTENSEN, P. "Excavations at Tepe Guran, Luristan. Early Village Farming Occupation." *Acta Archaeologica* 34 (1963): 110-21.

294 —— "Seasonal Camps and Early Villages in the Zagros." *Man, Settlement and Urbanism,* P. Ucko, R. Tringham, and G. W. Dimbleby, eds. London, 1972. 293-97.

295 MOULTON, J. H. *Early Zoroastrianism.* London, 1913.

296 MÜLLER-KARPE, H. *Handbuch des Vorgeschichte* II. Munich, 1968.

297 NEGAHBAN, E. O. "Survey of Excavations in Iran During 1972-73: Sagzabad." *Iran* 12 (1974): 216.

298 —— "A Brief Report on the Painted Building at Zaghe." *Paléorient* 5 (1979): 239-50.

299 —— Personal communication. Fall, 1984.

300 NEUNINGER, H., R. PITTIONI, and W. SIEGL. "Frühkeramik-zeitliche Kupfergewinnung in Anatolien." *Archaeologia Austriaca* 35 (1964): 98-110.

301 NICHOLĂESCU-PLOPSOR, C. S., A. PĂUNESCU, and F. MOGOŞANU. "Le paléolithique de Ceahlău." *Dacia* 10 (1966): 5-116.

302 NIETZSCHE, F. *Thus Spoke Zarathustra*. W. Kaufmann, translator. New York, 1966.

303 —— *Ecce Homo*. W. Kaufman, translator. New York, 1969.

304 NILSSON, M. P. *The Minoan-Mycenaean Religion and Its Survival in Greek Religion*. Lund, 1927.

305 NOY, T., A. J. LEGGE, and E. S. HIGGS. "Excavations at Nahal Oren, Israel." *Proceedings of the Prehistoric Society* 39 (1973): 75-99.

306 NOY, T., J. SCHULDENREIN, and E. TCHERNOV. "Gilgal, A Pre-Pottery Neolithic A Site in the Lower Jordan Valley." *Israel Exploration Journal* 30 (1980): 63-82.

307 NYBERG, H. S. "Questions de cosmogonie et de cosmologie mazdéennes." *Journal asiatique* 229 (1931): 1-134.

308 —— *Die Religionen des Alten Iran*. Leipzig, 1938.

309 OATES, D. and J. *The Rise of Civilization*. Oxford, 1976.

310 OATES, J. "Ur and Eridu, the Prehistory." *Iraq* 22 (1960): 32-50.

311 —— "The Baked Clay Figurines from Tell es-Sawwan." *Iraq* 27 (1966): 146-53.

312 —— "Choga Mami, 1967-68: A Preliminary Report." *Iraq* 31 (1969): 115-52.

313 —— "Prehistoric Settlement Patterns in Mesopotamia." *Man, Settlement and Urbanism*, P. Ucko, R. Tringham, and G. W. Dimbleby, eds. London, 1972. 299-310.

314 —— "The Background and the Development of Early Farming Communities in Mesopotamia and the Zagros." *Proceedings of the Prehistoric Society* 39 (1973): 147-81.

315 OESCHEGER, H. et al. "C-14 and Other Parameters During the Younger Dryas Cold Phase." *Radiocarbon* 22/2 (1980): 299-310.

316 OTTO, W. F. *Dionysos: Myth and Cult*. Bloomington, 1965.

317 PALES, L. and M-T. DE SAINT PEREUSE. "Un cheval-prétexte. Retour du chevêtre." *Objets et mondes* 6/3 (1966): 187-206.

318 PAYNE, S. "Can Hasan III, the Anatolian Aceramic, and the Greek Neolithic." *Papers in Economic Prehistory*, E. S. Higgs, ed. Cambridge, 1972. 191-254.

319 PERICOT GARCIA, L. "The Social Life of Spanish Paleolithic Hunters as Shown by Levantine Art." *Social Life of Early Man*, S. L. Washburn, ed. Chicago, 1961. 194-213.

320 PERKINS, A. *The Comparative Archaeology of Early Mesopotamia.* Studies in Ancient Oriental Civilization 25. Chicago, 1949.

321 PERKINS, A. and S. S. WEINBERG. "Connections of the Greek Neolithic and the Near East." *American Journal of Archaeology* 62 (1958): 225.

322 PERLES, C. "Des navigateurs méditerranéens il y a 10,000 ans." *La Recherche* 10 (1979): 82-83.

323 PERROT, J. "Têtes de flèches du Natoufien et du Tahounien (Palestine)." *Bulletin de la société préhistorique française* 49 (1952): 439-49.

324 —— "Le gisement natoufien de Mallaha (Eynan), Israel," *L'Anthropologie* 70 (1966): 437-84.

325 —— *La préhistoire palestinienne.* Supplément au dictionare de la Bible. Paris, 1968.

326 —— "Twelve Thousand Years Ago in the Jordan Valley." *CNRS Research* 8 (1978): 2-8.

327 PHILLIPS, P. *Early Farmers of West Mediterranean Europe.* London, 1975.

328 —— *The Prehistory of Europe.* London, 1980.

329 PHILLIPSON, D. W. *African Archaeology.* Cambridge, 1985.

330 PIETTE, E. "Les galets coloriés du Mas d'Azil." *L'Anthropologie* 7 (1896): 385-427.

331 —— "Le chevêtre et la semi-domestication des animaux aux temps pléistocènes." *L'Anthropologie* 17 (1906): 27-53.

332 PITTIONI, R. "Southern Middle Europe and Southeastern Europe." *Courses Toward Urban Life,* R. J. Braidwood and G. R. Willey, eds. New York, 1962. 211-26.

333 PLEINIER, A. *L'Art de la Grotte de Marsoulas.* Toulouse, 1971.

334 PRAUSNITZ, M. W. *From Hunter to Farmer and Trader.* Jerusalem, 1970.

335 RALPH, E. K., H. N. MICHAEL, and M. C. HAN. "Radiocarbon Dates and Reality." *MASCA Newsletter* 9 (1973): 1-19.

336 RAMAGE, E. S. "Perspectives Ancient and Modern." *Atlantis: Fact or Fiction?* E. S. Ramage, ed. Bloomington, 1978. 3-45.

337 REDMAN, C. L. *The Rise of Civilization.* San Francisco, 1978.

338 —— "The Çayönü Chipped Stone Industry." *Prehistoric Village Archaeology in South-eastern Turkey,* L. S. and R. J. Braidwood, eds. British Archaeological Reports Int'l. Series 138 (1982): 17-71.

339 RENFREW, C. *Before Civilization: The Radiocarbon Revolution and Prehistoric Europe.* New York, 1973.

340 —— "Problems in the General Correlation of Archaeological and Linguistic Strata in Prehistoric Greece: the Model of Autochthonous Origin." *Bronze Age Migrations in the Aegean*, R. A. Crossland and A. Birchall, eds. New Jersey, 1974. 263-80.

341 RENFREW, C. and J. DIXON. "Obsidian in Western Asia: A Review." *Problems in Economic and Social Archaeology*, G. de G. Sieveking, I. H. Longworth, and K. E. Wilson, eds. Boulder, 1976. 137-150.

342 RENFREW, C., J. E. DIXON, and J. R. CANN. "Obsidian and Early Cultural Contact in the Near East." *Proceedings of the Prehistoric Society* 32 (1966): 30-72.

343 RENFREW, J. "The First Farmers in Southeast Europe." *Archaeo-Physika* 8 (1979): 243-65.

344 REY, A. *La science orientale avant les Grecs*. Paris, 1930.

345 ROBERT, C. "Der Streit der Götter um Athen." *Hermes* 16 (1881): 60-87.

346 RODDEN, R. J. "Excavations at Nea Nikomedeia." *Proceedings of the Prehistoric Society* 27 (1962): 267-88.

347 —— "A European Link with Çatal Hüyük: Nea Nikomedeia." *Illustrated London News* 244 (April 11, 1964): 564-67, (April 18, 1964): 604-7.

348 ROHDE, E. *Psyche: The Cult of Souls and Belief in Immortality Among the Greeks*. London, 1925.

349 ROSE, H. J. *A Handbook of Greek Mythology*. New York, 1959.

350 ROSENMAYER, T. C. "Plato's Atlantis Myth: Timaeus or Critias?" *Phoenix* 10 (1956): 163-72.

351 ROUX, G. *Ancient Iraq*. Baltimore, 1976.

352 ROZOY, J. G. "The Franco-Belgian Epipaleolithic: Current Problems." *The Mesolithic in Europe*, S. K. Kozlowski, ed. Warsaw, 1973. 501-30.

353 RYDER, M. L. "Report of Textiles from Çatal Hüyük." *Anatolian Studies* 15 (1965): 175-76.

354 SANDARS, N. K. *Prehistoric Art in Europe*. Baltimore, 1968.

355 SANTILLANA, G. DE, and H. VON DECHEND. *Hamlet's Mill: An Essay Investigating the Origins of Human Knowledge and Its Transmission Through Myth*. Boston, 1977.

356 SARDARIAN, S. A. *Primitive Society in Armenia*. Erevan, Mitk, 1967.

357 SAXON, E. C. et al. "Results of Recent Investigations at Tamar Hat." *Libyca* 22 (1974): 49-92.

358 SCHEFOLD, K. *Myth and Legend in Early Greek Art*. London, 1966.

359 SCHILD, R. "Chronostratigraphie et environnement du Paléo-lithique final en Pologne." *La fin des temps glaciaires en Europe*, Coll. Intern. du C. N. R. S. 271 (1979): 799-818.

360 SCHMANDT-BESSERAT, D. "The Use of Clay Before Pottery in the Zagros." *Expedition* 16 (1974): 11-17.

361 SCHMIDT, E. F. "The Persian Expedition." *Bulletin of the Museum of the University of Pennsylvania* 5/5 (1935): 41-49.

362 SHACKELTON, J. C. and T. H. VAN ANDEL. "Prehistoric Shell Assemblages from Franchthi Cave and Evolution of the Adjacent Coastal Zone." *Nature* 288 (1980): 357-59.

363 SIEVEKING, A. *The Cave Artists*. London, 1979.

364 —— "Style and Regional Grouping in Magdalenian Cave Art." *Bulletin of the Institute of Archaeology, London* 16 (1979): 95-109.

365 SMITH, A. B. "Origins of the Neolithic in the Sahara." *From Hunters to Farmers*, J. D. Clark and S. A. Brandt, eds. Berkeley, 1984. 84-92.

366 SMITH, M. W. *Studies in the Syntax of the Gathas*. Linguistic Society of America IV, 1929.

367 SMITH, P. E. L. "Survey of Excavations (Ganj Dareh)." *Iran* 10 (1972): 165-68.

368 —— "Ganj Dareh Tepe." *Paléorient* 2 (1974): 207-8.

369 —— "An Interim Report on Ganj Dareh Tepe, Iran." *American Journal of Archaeology* 82 (1978): 538-40.

370 —— "The Late Paleolithic and Epi-Paleolithic of Northern Africa." *The Cambridge History of Africa* I, J. D. Clark, ed. Cambridge, 1982. 342-409.

371 SÖDERBLOM, N. "Ages of the World: Zoroastrian." *Encyclopaedia of Religion and Ethics*, J. Hastings, ed. New York, n. d.

372 SOLECKI, R. L. and T. H. MCGOVERN. "Predatory Birds and Prehistoric Man." *Theory and Practice*, S. Diamond, ed. The Hague, 1980. 79-95.

373 SOLECKI, R. S. "Prehistory in Shanidar Valley, Northern Iraq." *Science* 139 (1963): 179-93.

374 —— "Art Motifs and Prehistory in the Middle East." *Theory and Practice*, S. Diamond, ed. The Hague, 1980. 59-71.

375 SONNEVILLE-BORDES, D. DE. "The Upper Paleolithic: 33,000-10,000 B.C." *France Before the Romans*, S. Piggott, ed. London, 1973. 30-60.

376 SPENGLER, O. *The Decline of the West*. New York, 1926.

377 SPRAGUE DE CAMP, L. *Lost Continents: The Atlantis Theme in History and Literature*. New York, 1954.

378 STEKELIS, M. and O. BAR-YOSEF. "Un habitat du Paléolithique supérieur à Ein Guev (Israël)." *L'Anthropologie* 69 (1965): 176-83.

379 STERN, P. VAN D. *Prehistoric Europe*. New York, 1969.

380 STEWART, J. A. *The Myths of Plato*. London, 1905.

381 STROUHAL, E. "Five Plastered Skulls from Pre-Pottery Neolithic B Jericho." *Paléorient* 1/2 (1973): 231-46.

382 SULIMIRSKI, T. *Prehistoric Russia*. London, 1970.

383 SULLIVAN, W. *Continents in Motion*. New York, 1974.

384 SUTTON, J. E. G. "The Aquatic Civilization of Middle Africa." *Journal of African History* 15 (1974): 527-46.

385 TARAPOREWALA, I. J. S. *The Gathas of Zarathushtra*. Bombay, 1947.

386 TAUBER, H. "The Scandinavian Varve Chronology and C-14 Dating." *Radiocarbon Variations and Absolute Chronology*, I. U. Olsson, ed. Stockholm, 1970. 173-96.

387 TAUTE, W. *Die Stielspitzen-Gruppen im Nördlichen Mitteleuropa*. Köln, 1968.

388 TAYLOR, A. E. *Platonism and Its Influence*. New York, 1927.
389 —— *A Commentary on Plato's Timaeus*. Oxford, 1928.

390 TAYLOR, F. S. "The Origins of Greek Alchemy." *Ambix* 1/1 (1937): 30-47.

391 TELEHIN, D. IA. "New Information on the Stone-Age Population of the Ukraine." *Visnyk Akademii Nauk Ukr. R. S. R.* 4 (1957): 51-54. (in Russian)
392 —— "The Vasylivka 3 Necropolis in Nadporizhahia." *Arkheolochia XIII, Akademii Nauk Ukr. R. S. R. Kiev* (1961): 3-17. (in Russian)

393 TE VELDE, H. *Seth, God of Confusion*. Leiden, 1977.

394 THEOCHARIS, D. R. "Nea Makri. Eine grosse neolithische Siedlung in der Nähe von Marathon." *Athenische Mitteilungen des Deutschen Archaeologischen Instituts* 71 (1956): 1-29.
395 —— *Neolithic Greece*. Athens, 1973.

396 THIBAULT, CL. "L'évolution géologique de l'Aquitaine méridionale à la fin des temps glaciaires." *La fin des temps glaciaires en Europe*, Coll. Intern. du C. N. R. S. 271 (1979): 143-50.

397 THORNE, A. "The Arrival of Man in Australia." *Cambridge Encyclopaedia of Archaeology*, A. Sherrat, ed. Cambridge, 1980. 96-100.

398 TODD, I. "Aşıklı Hüyük, a Protoneolithic Site in Anatolia." *Anatolian Studies* 16 (1966): 139-63.
399 —— *Çatal Hüyük in Perspective*. Menlo Park, 1976.

400 TOSI, M. "The Northeastern Frontier of the Ancient Near East." *Mesopotamia* 8-9 (1973-1974): 21-76.

401 TRIGGER, B. G. "The Rise of Civilization in Egypt." *The Cambridge History of Africa* I, J. D. Clark, ed. Cambridge, 1982. 478-547.

402 TRINGHAM, R. *Hunters, Fishers, and Farmers of Eastern Europe: 6000-3000* B.C. London, 1971.

403 —— "The Mesolithic of Southeastern Europe." *The Mesolithic in Europe*, S. K. Kozlowski, ed. Warsaw, 1973. 551-73.

404 TURVILLE-PETRE, F. "Excavations in the Mugharet el-Kebarah." *Journal of the Royal Anthropological Institute* 62 (1932): 271-76.

405 UCKO, P. J. and A. ROSENFELD. *Paleolithic Cave Art*. New York, 1967.

406 VALLOIS, H. V. "Les ossements natoufiens d'Erq el-Ahmar, Palestine." *L'Anthropologie* 46 (1936): 529-39.

407 VAN ANDEL, T. H. and J. C. SHACKELTON. "Late Paleolithic and Mesolithic Coastlines of Greece and the Aegean." *Journal of Field Archaeology* 9 (1982): 445-54.

408 VERMASEREN, M. J. *Corpus Inscriptionum et Monumentorum Religionis Mithriacae*. The Hague, 1956.

409 —— "A Magical Time God." *Mithraic Studies* II, J. R. Hinnells, ed. Manchester, 1975. 446-56.

410 VITA-FINZI, C. "Supply of Pluvial Sediment to the Mediterranean During the Last 20,000 Years." *The Mediterranean Sea*, D. J. Stanley, ed. Stroudsburg, Penn., 1972. 43-46.

411 VITA-FINZI, C. and E. S. HIGGS. "Prehistoric Economy in the Mt. Carmel Area of Palestine." *Proceedings of the Prehistoric Society* 36 (1970): 1-37.

412 VOIGHT, M. M. *Hajii Firuz Tepe, Iran: The Neolithic Settlement*. Philadelphia, 1983.

413 WAAGE, F. O. *Prehistoric Art*. Dubuque, Iowa, 1967.

414 WADDELL, W. G., translator. *Manetho*. Cambridge, Mass., 1940.

415 WEINBERG, S. S. "Halafian and Ubaidian Influence in Neolithic Greece." *5th Intern. Congress of Prehistoric and Protohistoric Sciences, Hamburg, 1958*. Berlin, 1961. 858.

416 —— "The Relative Chronology of the Aegean in the Stone and Early Bronze Ages." *Chronologies in Old World Archaeology*, R. W. Ehrlich, ed. Chicago, 1965. 285-320.

417 —— "The Stone Age in the Aegean." *Cambridge Ancient History* I (1970): 557-618.

418 WEINSTEIN, J. M. "Radiocarbon Dating in the Southern Levant." *Radiocarbon* 26 (1984): 297-366.

419 WELLIVER, W. *Character, Plot and Thought in Plato's Timaeus-Critias*. Leiden, 1977.

420 WENDORF, F. "Site 117: A Nubian Final Paleolithic Graveyard Near Djebel Sahaba, Sudan." *The Prehistory of Nubia* II, F. Wendorf, ed. Dallas, 1968. 954-95.

421 WENDORF, F. and F. A. HASSAN. "Holocene Ecology and Prehistory in the Egyptian Sahara." *The Sahara and the Nile*, M. A. J. Williams and H. Faure, eds. Rotterdam, 1980. 407-19.

422 WENDORF, F. and R. SCHILD. "The Use of Ground Grain During the Late Paleolithic of the Lower Nile Valley, Egypt." *Origins of African Plant Domestication*, J. C. Harlan et al, eds. Chicago, 1976. 269-88.

423 WERTIME, T. A. "The Beginnings of Metallurgy: A New Look." *Science* 182 (1973): 875-87.

424 WEST, M. L. *Hesiod: Theogony*. Oxford, 1966.

425 —— *Early Greek Philosophy and the Orient*. Oxford, 1971.

426 WHEELER, M. "Greenstone Amulets." *Excavations at Jericho* V. K. M. Kenyon and T. A. Holland, eds. London, 1983. 781-87.

427 WIDENGREN, G. "Stand und Aufgaben der Iranischen Religionsgeschichte." *Numen* 1/1-2/1 (1954-1955): 16-83.

428 —— *Die Religionen Irans*. Stuttgart, 1965.

429 —— "The Mithraic Mysteries in the Greco-Roman World with Special Regard to their Iranian Background." *La Persia e il mondo greco-romano*. Accad. Naz. dei Lincei 76 (1966): 433-56.

430 WIJNEN, M. H. J. M. N. "The Early Neolithic I Settlement at Sesklo: An Early Farming Community in Thessaly, Greece." *Analecta Praehistorica Leidensia* 14 (1981): 1-146.

431 WILHELM, R. *LaoTse und der Taoismus*. Stuttgart, 1925.

432 WILI, W. "The Orphic Mysteries and the Greek Spirit." *The Mysteries: Papers from the Eranos Yearbooks*. New York, 1955. 64-92.

433 WILLETTS, R. F. *Cretan Cults and Festivals*. London, 1962.

433ᵃ —— *The Civilization of Ancient Crete*. London, 1977.

434 WILSON, D. *The New Archaeology*. New York, 1975.

435 WITT, R. E. "Some Thoughts on Isis in Relation to Mithras." *Mithraic Studies* II, J. R. Hinnells, ed. Manchester, 1975. 479-93.

436 WRIGHT, G. A. and A. A. GORDUS. "Distribution and Utilization of Obsidian from Lake Van Sources Between 7500 and 3500 B.C." *American Journal of Archaeology* 73 (1969): 75-77.

437 WYMER, J. *The Paleolithic Age*. London, 1982.

438 YALOURIS, N. in "Myth Proves a Factual Guide to Archaeology." *New York Times* (December 12, 1976): IV, 8.

439 YOUNG, T. C., JR. "Taking the History of the Hasanlu Area Back Another Five Thousand Years." *The Illustrated London News* (November 3, 1962): 707-8.

440 ZAEHNER, R. C. *Zurvān, A Zoroastrian Dilemma*. Oxford, 1955.

441 —— *The Teachings of the Magi*. London, 1956.

442 —— *The Dawn and Twilight of Zoroastrianism*. London, 1961.

443 ZEIST, W. VAN. "Paleobotanical Results of the 1970 Season at Çayönü." *Helinium* 3 (1972): 3-19.
444 —— "On Macroscopic Traces of Food Plants in Southwestern Asia." *The Early History of Agriculture.* Oxford, 1977. 27-41.

445 ZEIST, W. VAN and J. A. H. BAKKER-HEERES. "Some Economic and Ecological Aspects of the Plant Husbandry of Tell Aswad." *Paléorient* 5 (1979): 161-69.

446 ZUNTZ, G. *Persephone: Three Essays in Religion and Thought in Magna Graecia.* Oxford, 1971.

INDEX

Bold numerals refer to illustrations. Sub-headings are arranged chronologically or in the order in which they appear in the text.

K

Kabeiroi, 185
Kapovaia Cave (Urals), 30, 113
Karatepe (Iran), 229, **122**, **123**, **130**, **148**
Kebaran culture, 42, 51–52, 53
kešvar, 212, 212n
Khartoum (Sudan), 154, 156, **85**
    harpoons at, 90, 154, **52**
Khshathra, 221
kilim, 169n, 190
Kirkbride, Diana, 159, 253
Knossos (Crete), 186–87, 195
    kouros figurine from Neolithic, **109**
Kobystan (Transcaucasia), 59–61, 103, **36**, **37**, **62**
    and proto-Mithraic traditions, 113–14, 115, 250
kore figurine
    in Middle Neolithic Greece, 256–57, **146**
    at Mureybet III, 64, 256, **41**
Korybantes, 185–86
Koshar-wa-Hasis, 83
Kouretes, 79, 144, 145, 147–48, 186, 187
    prototypes of, at Çatal Hüyük, 183–85, 203, 250
kouros, 184, 187, 195, **109**
Kronos, 79
Kuhn, Herbert, 107
Kultepe (Transcaucasia), 248, **122**
Kurgan culture, 90, 107, 115
Kybele, 167, 170, 173, 185–86, 254

L

La Gravette (France), 21
La Madeleine (France), 23, **8**
La Marche (France), 27, **9**
Laming-Emperaire, Annette, 109
Large Wild Fauna phase in Saharan art, 97
Lascaux (France), 1, 24, 25, 58, **2**, **4**, **6**, **7**
    Shaft painting, 107–110, 115, **63**
Laugerie-Basse points, 30, **11**
Laws, 119–20, 138
Leaf points, 56, 136, **74**
Lee, Desmond, 277n
Leopard. *See also under* Çatal Hüyük
    in Zagros village remains, 143, 146, 168, 186
    associated with Dionysos, 85, 146, 181–82, **49**
    associated with Osiris, 181
    on Halaf pottery, 245, 261, **139**
    on Sialk III ceramics, 261, **149**
Lerna (Greece), 256, **141**, **146**
Leroi-Gourhan, André, 23, 26, 108
Les Eyzies (France), 110, **64**
Lespugue (France), **3**
Levanzo Cave (Sicily), 102–3, **60**
Lhote, Henri, 97, 98, 100, 101

Linear B, 87
Literacy, Paleolithic, 28–29, 70
Luce, John, 20
Lyngby tanged point culture, 55, **29**
    points in, **28**

M

maat, 218, 259
Mace
    at Çatal Hüyük, 168, 175, 178–79, 192
    Mithraic, 178–79, 236
    at Sialk I, 227, 236
    cast copper, at Can Hasan, 179, 237, 253
Magdalenian culture, 1, 19, 23–31, 35, 69, **2**, **4**
    artistic cycle in, 23, **5**
    purposes of art, 24–26, 294–95
    initiatory practices in, 26, 113
    horses in, 1, 26–27, 90, 115, **1b**, **6**, **9**
    harpoons in, 28, 90–91, 107, **8**
    and Paleolithic signs, 28–29, **10**
    uniformity of art in, 29, 72
    expansion of, across Europe, 30, 70, 113, 115,
        251
    population increase in, 30, 70
    Late, arrowheads, 30–31, **11**
    decline of, 23–24, 30–31, 70, 71, 295
    parallels to, in Kurgan culture, 90, 115
    as proto-Indo-European, 90, 107, 115–16
    as Golden Age, 24, 106–11, 115
    parallels to, in Iranian myth, 106–115, **63**, **64**
Magi, 201–5, 218, 250–51. *See also* Zervanism.
    strongholds of, 179, 215, 238–39
    and Mithra, 179, 250
    exposure of dead to vultures by, 179, 216
    relationship of, to Zarathuštra, 215–16, 266–67,
        271–72
    and the alchemical tradition, 268–72, 270n
Manetho, 94n
Master of the Animals, 178, 178n, 186, 203, **101**
Mechta-Afalou physical type (Iberomaurusian), 35, 39
Medusa, 91
megaron, 134
Mellaart, James, 128, 146, 147, 164, 169, 170, 171,
        176, 178, 182, 183, 184, 185, 188, 189, 190,
        192, 194, 196, 205, 248, 249, 254
Melos (Aegean), 47, **24**
Menes, 94n
Menok-i-Xrat, 201
Merimde (Egypt), 96, **55**
Mersin (Anatolia), **68**, **75**
    and Byblos Early Neolithic culture, 152
    Dark-faced Burnished ware at, 152, 156, **83**
    and the spread of Halaf, 253, 255, **141**, **142**, **148**

Pottery (*cont.*)
    at Anau IA, 233, **128**, **148**
    in Hajii Firuz culture, 233, 238, **129**
    Samarran, 233, 240–43, 246–47, 257, 261, **133**,
        135, **139**, **148**
    Halafian, 244–48, 250, 253, 255–57, 261–62, **121**,
        137, **138**, **139**, **142**, **143**, **148**
    at Hacılar, 254–55, **144**, **148**
    in Neolithic Greece, 123–24, 255–57, **145**, **147**,
        148
    higher firing temperatures for, 228, 231, 236,
        245, 271
Precession of the Equinoxes, 189, 204, 223
Pre-Greek, 87–88, 144, 186, 251
Pre-Pottery Neolithic A (PPNA), 45–46, 62–64,
    126n, 138, **39**. *See also* Jericho, walled town
    phase
    domestic grain in, 45, 136
    arrowheads in, 62, 64, **38**, **40**
Pre-Pottery Neolithic B (PPNB), 126n. *See also under*
    Red plaster, use of
    weaponry in, 126, 135–37, **73**, **74**
    ancestor worship in, 126, 135, **66**
    links to Mureybet III, 137, 257
    origins of, 137–38, 257
    decline of, 151, 173
Pressure-flaking, 135, 136, 163
Proclus, 190
Progress, 3, 265, 272, 274
    in Zoroastrian world view, 222, 266, 266n
    in Neolithic Iran, 234, 236–37
Proto-Mediterranean physical type, 40, 41, 53, 65,
    173
Ptah, 92
Purusa, 109
Pythagoras, 84, 167, 198, 200, 201, 203

Q

Qadan culture. *See* Djebel Sahaba
Queen of the Underworld, 190, 193, 200, 203. *See
    also* Persephone

R

Ragha. *See* Rayy
Ram. *See also* Sheep, herding of
    at Ganj Dareh D, 134, 168
    at Çatal Hüyük, 166, 168, 192, 193, 196, **92**, **116**
    identified with the sun, 196n
    in Halaf culture, 195, 244, 245
Ras Shamra (Syria), 83–84, 151, 253, **68**, **75**, **141**
    and Ugaritic mythology, 83
Raymonden (France), 111, **64**

Rayy (Iran), 213, 215, 237–38
Rectangular architecture. *See under* Mureybet; *names
    of individual sites*
Red plaster, use of
    at Ain Mallaha, 44, 138
    in PPNB sites, 134, 135–36, 138
    in Zagros (Tepe Guran), 142, 150
    at Zaghe, 150, 227
    at Çatal Hüyük, 137, 164–65, 175, 207
    in mid-to-late sixth millennium Iran, 228, 232,
        233
Reincarnation, 200–201, 203, 266–67
Reindeer, 25, 27, 57
Renfrew, Jane, 123
Rhea, 79, 185–86
Rig Veda, 109, 217, 218, 220
Rochereil (France), 27–28, 31, **8**, **12**
Rockall Bank, 72
Rocker-stamping, on ceramics, 152, 153, 154, **83**, **84**
Romanelli curved-back point culture, 31–33, **14**
Round Head art (Sahara), 97–102, 103, 166, **56**, **57**,
    59, **62**. See also *Period of Egyptian Influence*
    sequence of, 100, **58**
    parallels to *Decadent Phase* of, in Levanzo Cave,
        102, **60**
    and Sahara-Sudanese pottery, 153, 156
Round-house architecture
    Gravettian, 44, 63
    at Ain Mallaha, 44, 51, 138, 248
    at Jericho PPNA, 46, 63, 138, 248
    at Mureybet, 64
    Halafian, 244, 248, **140**
    Transcaucasian, 248
rta, 218, 259

S

Sabazios, 178
Sabz phase, 230–31, **127**. *See also* Tepe Sabz
    "bracelets" in, 231, 236, **131**
    links to Iranian plateau, 232
    links to Samarra-Halaf, 232, 243
Sahara, 97. *See also* Round Head art; Sahara-
    Sudanese Neolithic ware; Harpoons, exten-
    sion across Middle Africa
    drought in, 157
Sahara-Sudanese Neolithic ware, 96, 153–56, 180,
    84, **85**
St. Michel d' Arudy (France), **9**
St. Pereuse, Marie Tassin de, 27
Sais, 15, 94–95, 190, **55**
Sakçagözü (Anatolia), 253, **141**
Saltadora Cave (Spain), 58, **35**
Samarra (Iraq), **148**

Index   331